Psyche and Symbol

C. G. JUNG was born in Kasswyl, Switzerland, in 1875. He took his medical degree at the University of Basel in 1902, after deserting his original plans to be an archeologist. He studied under Pierre Janet in Paris and joined the Psychiatric Clinic at the University of Zurich in 1900. By the time he came to America for his first series of lectures in 1909 he was in private practice in Zurich and had made his famous association with Freud. He was president of the International Psychoanalytic Society before he rejected Freudian theory in 1913 and advanced his own views of human psychology. From 1938 until his death in 1961, he was professor of psychiatry at the Federal Polytechnical University in Zurich. Among his published books are *Modern Man in Search of a Soul, Psychological Types, Psychology and Religion, Symbols of Transformation, Undiscovered Self,* and his last work, *Man and His Symbols,* which is a popular presentation of Jungian psychology.

Psyche and Symbol

A Selection from the Writings of

C. G. JUNG

EDITED BY

Violet S. de Laszlo

Anchor Original

DOUBLEDAY ANCHOR BOOKS
DOUBLEDAY & COMPANY, INC.
GARDEN CITY, NEW YORK

COVER BY LEONARD BASKIN

TYPOGRAPHY BY EDWARD GOREY

The Anchor Books edition is the first publication of *Psyche and Symbol*.

Anchor Books edition: 1958

"Aion" from Part II, Volume 9, *Collected Works of C. G. Jung* to be published by Bollingen Foundation probably in 1958.
"The Phenomenology of the Spirit in Fairy Tales" from *Spirit and Nature*, Volume I, Papers from the Eranos Yearbooks. Copyright 1954 by Bollingen Foundation, Inc., New York, New York.
"The Psychology of the Child Archetype" from *Essays on a Science of Mythology*. Copyright 1949 by Bollingen Foundation, Inc., New York, New York.
"Transformation Symbolism in the Mass" from *The Mysteries*, Volume II, Papers from the Eranos Yearbooks. Copyright © 1955 by Bollingen Foundation, Inc., New York, New York.
Foreword to the *I Ching* or *Book of Changes*. Copyright 1950 by Bollingen Foundation, Inc., New York, New York.
"Forerunners of the Idea of Synchronicity" and Conclusion from "The Interpretation of Nature and the Psyche." Copyright 1955 by Bollingen Foundation, Inc., New York, New York.
Commentary on the *Secret of the Golden Flower*. Harcourt Brace & Co., Inc., copyright 1931. Rights granted to Bollingen Foundation, Inc., 1948.

Library of Congress Catalog Card Number 58-6627
Copyright © 1958 by Bollingen Foundation, Inc., New York, New York.
Printed in the United States of America

The editor wishes to express her gratitude to Professor C. G. Jung and to the Bollingen Foundation for their interest in this volume. She also acknowledges gratefully the friendly cooperation of the translators, Cary Baynes and F. C. R. Hull, respectively.

CONTENTS

Preface by C. G. Jung	xi
Editor's Introduction	xix

PART I

Five Chapters from: *Aion: Contributions to the Symbolism of the Self*

I.	The Ego	1
II.	The Shadow	6
III.	The Syzygy: Anima and Animus	9
IV.	The Self	22
V.	Christ, a Symbol of the Self	35

[Chapters 1–5, Bollingen Series XX, Collected Works of C. G. Jung, Volume 9, Part II. R. F. C. Hull, Translator. In preparation]

The Phenomenology of the Spirit in Fairy Tales — 61

[pp. 3–45, Papers from the Eranos Yearbooks, Volume I, Bollingen Series XXX, 1954. R. F. C. Hull, Translator]

The Psychology of the Child Archetype — 113
The Special Phenomenology of the Child Archetype — 132

[C. G. Jung and C. Kerényi: Essays on a Science of Mythology, Bollingen Series XXII, 1949. R. F. C. Hull, Translator]

Transformation Symbolism in the Mass — 148

I.	Introduction	149
II.	The Sequence of the Rite of Transformation	153
III.	A Parallel from Pagan Antiquity	168
IV.	The Psychology of the Mass	196

[pp. 274–336, Papers from the Eranos Yearbooks, Volume II, Bollingen Series XXX, 1955. R. F. C. Hull, Translator]

PART II

Foreword to the *I Ching* or *Book of Changes*   225
    [pp. 1–20, Bollingen Series XIX, 1950. Cary Baynes, Translator]

Two Chapters from: *The Interpretation of Nature and the Psyche*
   III. Forerunners of the Idea of Synchronicity   245
   IV. Conclusion   266
    [pp. 95–143, Bollingen Series LI, 1955. R. F. C. Hull, Translator]

Psychological Commentary on *The Tibetan Book of the Dead*   283
    [Oxford University Press, in preparation. Also Bollingen Series XX, Collected Works, Volume 11. R. F. C. Hull, Translator. In preparation]

Commentary on *The Secret of the Golden Flower*   302
    [Kegan Paul, Trench, Trubner and Co., Ltd., London, 1931. Also in *Alchemical Studies*, Bollingen Series XX, Collected Works, Volume 13. Cary Baynes, Translator. In preparation]

Bibliographical note: For the sake of greater clarity it should be pointed out that the studies included in this volume have originally appeared in the Swiss publications of Jung's works. Prior to their inclusion in the Collected Works, a number of them have appeared in English as parts of other publications, to which reference is made by the Editor in the footnotes appended to each of the sections. The full Bibliography of the Collected Works appears at the end of this volume.

Preface

Dr. de Laszlo has risked shocking the American reader by including some of my most difficult essays in her selection from my writings. In sympathy with the reader I acknowledge the fact that it is most tempting if not unavoidable to fall into the trap of appearances which catch the eye that wanders over the pages in a vain attempt to get at the gist of the matter in the shortest possible time. I know of so many who, opening one of my books and, stumbling upon a number of Latin quotations, shut it with a bang, because Latin suggests history and therefore death and unreality. I am afraid my works demand some patience and some thinking. I know: it is very hard on the reader who expects to be fed by informative headlines. It is not the conscientious scientist's way to bluff the public with impressive résumés and bold assertions. He tries to explain, to produce the necessary evidence and thus to create the foundation of understanding. The understanding in my case, moreover, does not refer to generally known facts, but rather to events little known or even new. It was therefore incumbent upon me to make known such facts. In so far as such unexpected novelties demand equally unexpected means of explanation I found myself confronted with the task of representing and explaining the very nature of my evidential material.

The facts are experiences gained through a careful and

painstaking analysis of certain psychic processes observed in the course of psychic treatments. In as much as those facts refused to be satisfactorily explained through themselves, it became necessary to search for possible comparisons. If, for instance, one comes across a patient who produces symbolic *mandālas*[1] in his dreams or his waking imagination and proceeds to explain these circular images in terms of certain sexual or other phantasies, then this explanation carries no conviction, in so far as another patient develops wholly different motivations. It is also not permissible to assume that a sexual phantasy is a more likely motivation than, for instance, a power drive, since we know by experience that the individual's disposition will of necessity lead him to prefer the one over against the other. Both patients on the other hand may have one fact in common; namely, a state of mental and moral confusion and upset. We do decidedly better to follow up this clue and to try to discover whether the circular images are not connected with such states of mind. Our third case producing mandālas is perhaps a schizophrenic in such a disturbed frame of mind that he cannot even be asked for his accompanying phantasies. This patient is obviously already completely dissolved in a chaotic condition. Our fourth case is a little boy of seven who has decorated the corner where his bed stands with numerous mandālas which he has drawn and without which he cannot go to sleep. He only feels safe when they are around him. His phantasy tells him that they protect him against nameless fears assailing him in the night. What is his confusion? His parents are contemplating divorce. And what shall we say in the case of a hard-boiled scientific rationalist who produced mandālas in his dreams and in his wakeful phantasies? He had to consult an alienist, as he was about to lose his reason because he suddenly had become assailed by the most amazing dreams and visions. What was his confusion? The clash between two equally *real* worlds, one external the other internal: a fact he could no longer deny.

[1] See: Editor's introduction, and the "Commentary on the Secret of the Golden Flower" in this volume.—Ed.

There is no need to prolong this series since, quite apart from all theoretical prejudices, the underlying reason for a mandāla seems to be a certain definable mental state. But have we got any evidence which might explain why such a state should produce a mandāla? Or is this sequence merely chance?

Consequently we must ask whether our experiences are the only ones on record and, if not, where we can find comparable events. There is no difficulty in finding them; plenty of parallels exist, for instance, in the Far East and the Far West, or right here in Europe, several hundred years ago. The books of reference can be found in our university libraries, but within the last two hundred years nobody has read them, and they are—oh horror—written in Latin and some even in Greek. But are they dead? Are those books not the distant echo of life once lived, of minds and hearts quick with passions, hopes and visions, as keen as our own? Does it matter so much whether the sheets before us tell the story of a patient still alive, or dead for fifty years? Does it really matter whether their confessions, their anguish, their strivings speak the English of today or Latin or Greek? No matter how much we are of today, there has been a yesterday, which was just as real, just as human and warm as the moment we call Now, which—hélas—in a few hours will be a Yesterday as dead as the first of January anno Domini 1300. A good half of the reasons why things now are what they are is buried in Yesterday. Science in its attempt to establish causal chains has to refer to the past. We teach comparative anatomy, why not comparative psychology? The psyche is not only of today. It reaches right back to prehistoric ages. Has man really changed in ten thousand years? Have stags changed their antlers in this short lapse of time? Of course the hairy man of the Ice Ages has become unrecognizable when you try to discover him among the persons whom you meet on Fifth Avenue. But you will be amazed when you have talked to such moderns for a hundred hours about their intimate life. You will then read the mouldy parchments as if they were the most recent thrillers. You will find the secrets of the modern consulting room curiously expressed in abbreviated mediaeval Latin or by an intricate Byzantine hand.

What the doctor can hear, when he attentively listens, of phantasies, dreams and intimate experiences is not mentioned in the Encyclopaedia Britannica nor in the textbooks and scientific journals. These secrets are jealously guarded, anxiously concealed and highly feared and esteemed. They are very private possessions, never divulged and talked about, because they are feared as ridiculous and revered as revelations. They are numinous, a dubious treasure, perhaps comical, perhaps miraculous, at all events a painfully vulnerable spot, yet presiding over all the crossroads of one's individual life. They are officially and by general consent just as unknown and despised as the old parchments with their undecipherable and unaesthetic hieroglyphics, evidence of old obscurantisms and foolishness. As we are unaware of their contexts, we are equally ignorant of what is going on in the deeper layers of our unconscious, because "who knows does not talk, and who talks does not know". In the same proportion as the amount of such inner experience increases, the social nexus between humans decreases. The individual becomes isolated for no apparent reason. Finally this will become unbearable and he has to confide in someone. Much will then depend upon whether he is essentially understood or not. It would be fatal were he to be misinterpreted. Fortunately enough, such people are instinctively careful and as a rule do not talk more than necessary.

When one hears such a confession, and the patient wants to understand himself better, some comparative knowledge will be most helpful. When the hard-boiled rationalist mentioned above came to consult me for the first time, he was in such a state of panic that not only he himself but I also felt the wind coming over from the side of the lunatic asylum! As he told me of his experiences in detail he mentioned a particularly impressive dream. I got up and fetched an ancient volume from my bookshelf and showed it to him, asking: "You see the date? Just about four hundred years old. Now watch!" I opened the book at the place where there was a curious woodcut, representing his dream almost literally. "You see," I said, "your dream is no secret. You are not shocked by a pathological insult and separated from mankind by an inexplicable psychosis. You are merely ignorant of certain experiences well within human knowledge and understanding." It was worth seeing the relief which came over him. He had seen with his own eyes the documentary evidence for his own sanity.

This can illustrate the reason why historical comparison is not a mere learned hobby but of very practical and concrete usefulness. It opens the door to life and humanity again, which had seemed to close inexorably for him. It is of no ultimate advantage to deny or reason away or ridicule such seemingly abnormal or out-of-the-way experiences. They should not get lost, because they contain an intrinsic value of the individuality, the loss of which entails a definite damage to one's personality. One should be aware of the high esteem which in past centuries was felt for such experiences, because it explains the extraordinary importance that our ignorant moderns are forced to attribute to them in spite of themselves.

Understanding does not cure evil, but it is a definite help, inasmuch as one can cope with a comprehensible difficulty far more easily than with an incomprehensible darkness. Even if in the end a rational explanation cannot be reached, one knows at least that one is not the only one confronted by a "merely imaginary" wall, but rather one of the many that have hitherto vainly tried to climb it. One still shares the common human fate and one is not excluded from humanity by a subjective defect. Thus one has not undergone the irreparable loss of a personality-value and one is not forced to continue one's way upon the crutches of a dry and lifeless rationalism. On the contrary, one gains a new courage to accept and integrate the irrationality of one's own life and of life in general.

Instincts are the most conservative determinants of any kind of life. Mind is not born as a *tabula rasa*. Like the body, it has its pre-established individual definiteness; namely, forms of behaviour. They become manifest in the ever-recurring patterns of psychic functioning. As the weaver bird will build its nest infallibly in its accustomed form, so man despite his freedom and superficial changeability will function psychologically according to his original patterns—up to a certain point; that is, until for some reason he collides with his still living and ever-present instinctual roots. The instincts will then protest and engender peculiarly shaped thoughts and emotions, which will be all the more alien and incomprehensible the more man's consciousness has deviated from its original conformity to these instincts. As nowadays we are threatened by the self-destruction of mankind through radioactivity, we are experiencing a fundamental reassertion of our instincts in many forms. The psychological manifestations of the latter I have termed "archetypes".

The archetypes are by no means useless archaic survivals or relics. They are living entities, which cause the praeformation of numinous ideas or dominant representations. Insufficient understanding, however, accepts these praeformations in their archaic form, because they have a numinous appeal to the underdeveloped mind. Thus Communism is an archaic, primitive and therefore highly insidious pattern which characterizes primitive social groups. It implies lawless chieftainship as a vitally necessary compensation, a fact which can only be overlooked by means of a rationalistic one-sidedness, the prerogative of the barbarous mind.

It is important to bear in mind that my concept of the "archetypes" has been frequently misunderstood as denoting inherited patterns of thought or as a kind of philosophical speculation. In reality they belong to the realm of the activities of the instincts and in that sense they represent inherited forms of psychic behaviour. As such they are invested with certain dynamic qualities which, psychologically speaking, are designated as "autonomy" and "numinosity".

I do not know of any more reliable way back to the instinctual basis than through the understanding of these psychological patterns, which enable us to recognize the nature of an instinctive attitude. The instinct to survive is aroused as a reaction against the tendency to mass-suicide represented by the H-bomb and the underlying political schism of the world. The latter is clearly man-made and due to rationalistic distortions. Conversely, if understood by a mature mind, the archetypal praeformations can yield numinous ideas ahead of our actual intellectual level. That is just what our time is in need of. Herein, it seems to me, lies an additional motivation to pay attention to the unconscious processes which in many persons today anticipate future developments.

I warn the reader: this book will not be an easy pastime. Once in a while he will meet with thoughts which demand the effort of concentration and careful reflection—a condition unfortunately rare in modern times. On the other hand, the times of today seem to be serious enough to cause at least uneasy dreams if nothing else.

C. G. Jung

August 1957

Introduction

The edifice of C. G. Jung's work is reminiscent of a cathedral that has been built in the course of many centuries. Those who are willing to undertake the effort of contemplating it in a spirit of genuine inquiry and with only the inevitable minimum of preconceived notions are bound to find themselves astonishingly well rewarded. They will make countless discoveries in regard to the grandeur of his original conceptions and the unanticipated richness of detail which, in the phrase of the Quakers, "speak to their condition"—the human condition of doubt and distress, of the search for meaning, of the joyful recognition of universal human sentiment and of the contemporaneous formulation of abiding truths.

Like the cathedral with its altar, its cross and its rose window, this edifice has been erected *ad majorem Dei Gloriam*—to the greater glory of God—as is true of all valid creative efforts, even those which appear to be agnostically motivated. Materially speaking, its foundations rest upon the objective approach of empirical observation. Spiritually, they are informed by the omnipresent need of mankind to relate itself to that which is dimly perceived to be greater than any individual and to transcend even the total group—under whatever name the transcendent power may be invoked.

As in the case of the cathedral, the structural foundations are not discernible to the beholder or intelligible to the untrained eye, but this does not disprove their existence or their vital function. The architect's skill serves only as the carrier of the emotional, intellectual and esthetic message and achievement which in their turn culminate in the spiritual and ultimately religious experience which validates the structure as a whole. Just as the architect is influenced by and needs to take into consideration the techniques and knowledge of past generations, his conception—provided he be not a mere imitator or a juggler clever at devising striking effects—will be unique within the confines of a given style: so must C. G. Jung's work be viewed in order to arrive at a significant appraisal of it. Its numerous aspects and perspectives confront the editor with many difficult choices comparable perhaps to the dilemmas experienced by the photographer attempting to convey an adequate impression of so vast an edifice.

The chief question to be asked must concern itself with the object of Jung's interest. The answer is: the human psyche in its totality; meaning consciousness plus the unconscious. Indeed it is the latter which has received his main attention during more than half a century of passionate and painstaking research, in the course of which the concept itself grew and became transformed until it finally included the subsoil of life itself—and not the subsoil alone at the level of its instinctive sources, but also its spiritual ferment and essence. In other words, it came to comprise the totality of existence outside of consciousness, surrounding and carrying the conscious ego. The growth of the concept took place by means of observation and deduction guided by the intuitive vision characteristic of all pioneering research and creative endeavor. The elements under observation were, to begin with, the spontaneous manifestations of the unconscious which every person experiences so frequently as to take them for granted, that is, the dreams occurring during sleep, as well as various fantasy activities which take place in the waking state. From these everyday occurrences in their normal individual expression one path of observation leads in the direction of their pathological forms culminating in insanity. Another path leads towards the common denominators which can be recognized as the dominant themes in the creative phantasy activity not only on the part of individuals but of entire groups and civilizations, in the form of fairy tales, legends, myths and rituals. The deeper psyche is thus understood to express itself through its imaginative activity, either individually or collectively, and it is in this sense that Jung conceives of its symbolic language.

The psychological definition of the symbol can be said to represent the focal point of Jung's entire research. It is therefore necessary to become acquainted with this definition.[1] The living symbol expresses an essential unconscious factor. The more widely this factor operates, the more generally valid is the symbol, for in every soul it evokes a resonance. (For examples of specifically religious symbols the reader is referred to the table of contents of the present volume, viz., the symbol of the Heavenly Child, Christ as a symbol of the Self, symbols of Transformation in the Ritual of the Mass, the Eastern symbol of the Golden Flower, the Taoist symbols from the Book of Changes, as well as the Buddhist Wheel of Life, the Tibetan Thunderbolt. For impressive reproductions see also *The World's Great Religions*, Time, Inc., N.Y., 1957.) Since the symbol is the most complete expression of that which in any given epoch is as yet unknown—and cannot be replaced by any other statement at that time—it must proceed from the most complex and subtle strata of the contemporary psychological atmosphere. Conversely, the effective, living symbol must also contain something which is shared by considerable numbers of men: it embraces that which is common to a larger group. Consequently, it must include those primitive elements, emotional and otherwise, whose omnipresence stands beyond all doubt. Only when the symbol comprehends all those and conveys them with ultimate force can it evoke a universal response. Therein resides the powerful and redeeming effect of the living social symbol.

[1] C. G. Jung, *Psychological Types*, trans. by H. G. Baynes (London and New York, 1923), pp. 601–10.

The same holds true, says Jung, for the individual symbol. There exist individual psychic products whose manifestly symbolic character invites a symbolic approach and understanding. He is referring here to elements in dreams and phantasy sequences which are woven into the context with a clearly non-concrete, symbolic intent. For instance, the dream figure of a child who is personally known to the dreamer, while drawing his attention to his relationship with this particular child, may and does nevertheless carry a symbolical message referring to the significance of the child image as the dreamer's potential for the inner growth of his own personality. Hence also it is both rational and irrational: while the data of rationally deducible character appeal to reason, the prospective meaning and pregnant significance of the symbol speak as strongly to our feeling as to our thinking. The singularly plastic imagery of the symbol when shaped into sensuous form stimulates both our sensation and our intuition. Only the passionate yearning of a highly developed mind, for which the conventional symbol no longer expresses in one image the ultimate reconciliation of painfully conflicting elements, can create a new symbol. Yet, inasmuch as the symbol not only proceeds from man's most complex mental achievement, but has at least an equal source in the lowest and most primitive motions of his psyche, this polarity needs to stand fully revealed. Such a condition necessarily entails a violent disunion with oneself, even to the point where the conflicting elements mutually deny each other, while the ego nevertheless is forced to acknowledge their existence and its own participation in the conflict. The energy engendered by the tension of the opposites flows into the creation of the symbol, since through the activity of the unconscious a content is brought to life in which thesis and antithesis participate in equal measure—in other words, the birth of the symbol portends a reconciliation into a more fully inclusive and comprehending plane of experience, which is tantamount to the attainment of greater meaning.

This process of the integration of the personality achieved by means of the mutual participation of consciousness and the unconscious, and made manifest through the spontaneous creation of the living symbol, Jung has named the *transcendent function*. He wishes it to be understood that the word "function" in this context denotes not a simple function, but a function-complex involving every area of the psyche, while the word "transcendent" denotes not a metaphysical quality, but rather the fact that through this function a transition is created from the previous attitude to a more fully integrated one.

It is evident that this conception postulates and acknowledges the essential participation of the unconscious in the creative process. Therein is expressed a fundamental contribution on the part of Jung regarding the totality of the psyche, according to which consciousness and the unconscious are related to each other in a reciprocity where each conscious element has its unconscious counterpart of an opposite yet compensating character. Their constant interplay engenders the kaleidoscopic dynamics which in the course of any individual existence create the individual biography. In this conception the conscious ego fulfills the function of a recipient of the crude ore brought to the surface out of varying depths of the unconscious, in addition to pursuing its own goals in terms of volition, learning and judgment, and of the multiple facets of its relationships both personal and impersonal. Clearly this conception in its turn is based upon the understanding of a relative functional autonomy of the component areas of the psyche.

If the psyche is thus conceived as an organism in its own right in which no element is fortuitous, there begins to emerge the image of an inner man whose nature and functioning is the proper field of investigation of the science of psychology. Evidently psychology has yet to find and to co-ordinate a terminology designed to describe the healthy normal psyche and its experience of itself and of its environment in a language no longer borrowed from psychopathology. This is especially important at the level of the higher functions (e.g., those not shared by the animal) which when described in terms appropriate to the lower must needs lose their specific value and become reduced to a "nothing-but." It is one of the outstanding merits of C. G. Jung to have outlined for our era and in contemporary language a portrait of spiritual man: one is tempted to say of the anatomy and physiology of spiritual man. This is clearly illustrated in the chapters from his publication *Aion* which are included in the present volume. The chapters "The Ego," "Anima and Animus," and "The Self" represent an outline of his approach and a résumé of his far-reaching conclusions. (The meaning of "Aion" or "Aeon" is perhaps best rendered according to the Oxford Dictionary as it relates itself to Platonic philosophy as a "Power existing from eternity.") If it be true that the search for self-knowledge in the widest sense has from time immemorial been one of the most urgent passions of mankind, then it can be said that this archetypal quest itself, culminating in the manifold varieties of spiritual experience, has formed the core of Jung's research and observation. Instead of attempting to establish premature correlations or naïve concretizations, he has for several decades sought out the most meaningful representations of man's spiritual self-portraits in which by their very nature man transcends himself. These portraits have an intrinsic common factor: they are expressed symbolically and not conceptually. It would seem that the psyche speaks to the psyche in its own language, and that this language is no other than the symbol itself.

The pioneer work of C. G. Jung has moved far into hitherto unexplored regions. It is as yet very little understood since the general understanding of the unconscious is still in its infancy. The comparative newness and consequent alien-ness of his conceptions places great demands upon the reader, particularly upon those who are still consciously or unconsciously committed to a positivist-rationalist viewpoint. The difficulties are further increased by his dramatically intuitive approach which sweeps across the neatly established and carefully guarded confines of many disciplines. This is irksome to the specialist and admittedly dangerous. But it is not only justified but truly life-giving when rigid barriers begin to fall as the result of a logically sustained creative effort towards a wider understanding and a more complete synthesis.

In speaking of Jung's intuitive approach I have in mind the specific sense in which he himself refers to the function of intuition in his work on the *Psychological Types*.[2] It is characteristic of the introverted intuitive personality that the inner image constitutes the most convincing aspect of the totality of his life experience. This inner image, the symbol, carries for the intuitive introvert more than for any other personality type the essential meaning of existence. This is basic to an understanding of Jung's lifelong dedication to the experience of and research into symbolic expression, to which he has sacrificed to a considerable extent his clinical research in the more limited sense of the word. In a wider sense however there is manifest in his work if not exactly a clinical then definitely an empirical attitude—a fact which he has repeatedly emphasized. It would be altogether more nearly accurate to say that the wealth of his clinical observations collected during a lifetime of psychotherapeutic practice has been absorbed into the wider presentation of those common denominators of psychic existence, the archetypes. He is as yet one of the few who, like William James, have dared to assert that the features of spiritual experience can be investigated scientifically with due reverence. This is bound to be misunderstood by considerable sectors of the public, partly for reasons of superficiality and partly because the vested interests of various branches of religious and secular science prevent them from realizing that it can never be anything but the psyche itself which is the carrier of any and all experience. And it is indeed the basic types of experience—the archetypes of experience—which have formed the center of Jung's scientific preoccupation through more than half a century. The archetypes of experience can be said to extend from the instinctual-organic to the spiritual realm. The Christian antithesis of nature and the spirit becomes, in the wider view, the polarity which among all the pairs of opposites has received his most passionate attention. No doubt in obedience to his ancestral endowment, part medical and part ecclesiastical, and faithful to his own creative-spiritual caliber, he has laid a cornerstone towards the foundation of a modern understanding of the healing functions and

[2] C. G. Jung, *Psychological Types*, trans. by H. G. Baynes (London and New York, 1923), pp. 567–69.

processes in the psyche, and of the role of the healer. Psychology and religion—the cure of souls through the care of the therapist and by the grace of redemption, as well as by the self-healing and recreative faculties inherent in the psyche: these themes form the therapeutic aspect of Jung's research. Small wonder therefore that the experiential, symbolic and ideational content of many religions have furnished the substance for his investigations.

Small wonder also that he has been particularly attracted by the figure of Paracelsus, the sixteenth-century physician whose insights into psycho-physical relations reached far beyond his contemporaries, and who was at the same time an original expounder of alchemical theory in which he invested his unremitting thought and labor. Much of Jung's interest, like that of Paracelsus, has been devoted to the teachings of the medieval European alchemists. From the vantage point of modern psychiatric and psychological observation, the core of their endeavor has come to reveal itself as a search for the wholeness of the personality and for the indestructible essence of the soul which they expressed in countless images and symbols ranging from the elixir of life and the philosopher's stone to the image of the hermaphrodite. Even the transmutation of base metals into gold, which is commonly assumed to have been the object of their practical labors, had its transcendent counterpart, for the gold itself became a symbol of the pure indestructible essence whose sun-like color reflected the immortal quality of the psyche. The stages of transformation which the alchemist believed to have observed in the vessels of his laboratory were transposed in his imagination into the animated personification of the various elements and substances which he was trying to synthesize into a new wholeness. According to Jung's conclusions the medieval alchemical symbolism represents a powerful upsurge on the part of the unconscious in the spiritual history of Western Europe. If one were to write a history not of the conscious manifestations, but of the unconscious formative elements and forces in the Western European *Geistesgeschichte* or cultural evolution, it would probably reveal certain important parallels to the symbol content of Jung's successive phases of interest in primitive religion, in the ancient Mediterranean and the Far Eastern religions, in Gnosticism, in the profound visionary and meditational experiences of such Christian saints as Ignatius Loyola and the Swiss Nicolaus vonder Flue, and in the intermingling of their scientific-psychological-religious thinking of the alchemists and of Paracelsus, and finally in the dynamics of the symbolical message of Christianity itself.

The search for wholeness, for an integration of the personality, has been designated by Jung as the process of *individuation*. This process is twofold in that it comprises the spontaneously arising symbol to which he refers as the *unifying symbol*,[3] and also an assimilation of its value and message into consciousness in terms of an understanding and of a responsible participation. This in its turn signifies the birth of a new attitude on the part of the experiencing subject towards himself and towards his life. The birth and growth of the new attitude are discussed by Jung in reference to the symbol of the child in his "Psychology of the Child Archetype" included in the present volume. There is a striking similarity between Jung's concept of the principle of individuation and S. T. Coleridge's definition of life as "the principle of Individuation, or the power that unites a given all into a whole which is presupposed by all its parts."

Jung defines the term "individuation" as the psychological process that makes of a human being an "individual"—a unique, indivisible unit or "whole man."[4] His frequent and extensive references to medieval alchemical literature are the result of over twenty years of study which led him to the conclusion that the profuse and variegated symbolism contained in these texts are spontaneous products of a more or less un-

---

[3] "Unifying" is the expression used in the translation of the Collected Works; the earlier translators used the word "reconciling."—Ed.

[4] *The Integration of the Personality* (Farrar and Rinehart, 1939), p. 3. (to appear in *Archetypes and the Collective Unconscious*, The Collected Works of C. G. Jung, Bollingen Series XX Vol. 9, Part II).

interrupted imaginative activity on the part of these authors. His interpretation of the symbol content of their treatises stems from his conviction that *the conscious mind is based upon, and results from, an unconscious psyche which is prior to consciousness and continues to function together with, or despite, consciousness.*[5] In the case of dream activity during sleep consciousness is at its lowest ebb and the unconscious has relatively free play. Similarly, unconscious activity can take precedence over conscious intent within the waking state, in which case symbolic expression displaces the rational processes. In Jung's view all symbolic expression or activity has an inner purpose. This purpose is precisely that of "individuation," of the birth and growth of the indivisible inner "whole man." This, then, is an urge which operates with or without the cooperation of consciousness, but the degree of achievement is nevertheless dependent upon the realization and understanding of which the conscious ego is capable.

The practical incentive for his research into alchemy came to Jung through certain significant series of the dreams of several patients. The images occurring in these dreams refused to fit themselves into the then known categories of interpretation and it was only when the striking similarities with many illustrations contained in alchemical texts came to his attention that the clues presented themselves, thus leading to ever more extensive studies in this particular field.

It was as a result of the ensuing reflections that Jung came to speak of "symbols of individuation," thereby designating in effect all symbols whose impact and meaning transcend the sphere of the fleetingly secular preoccupations. The empirical material and psychological-philosophical conclusions are presented in his work on *Psychology and Alchemy*[6] with its careful investigation of individual dream symbolism in relation to alchemical symbolism on the one hand, and of religious ideas in alchemy on the other hand. Although no part of *Psychology and Alchemy* is reproduced in the present volume, it is nonetheless necessary to refer to it since all of Jung's publications

[5] *Ibid.*, p. 13.
[6] Coll. Works, Vol. 12.

of the past two decades have been impregnated by his contact with alchemical literature. Strange though it appears to the twentieth-century mind this literature has served as the crystallizing agent for his conception and presentation of the individuation process, the process of becoming the independent personality who is (relatively!) free from the domination of the parental archetypes and independent of the supportive structures of the social environment. He can therefore establish his own individual values and relationships which are valid because they are based on the reality of his self-knowledge and not on a system of illusions and rationalizations. Seen in this perspective, individuation is its own goal, its own meaning and fulfillment and is at the same time a religious experience and, one might say, a religious way of life, because it means to live one's own existence creatively in the awareness of its participation in the stream of an eternal becoming.

Returning once more to the subject of alchemy, some further comment appears indicated at this point. This is in further reference to its symbol content which previous to Jung's research had received little attention. Briefly, the writings of the leading alchemists prove that they regarded their efforts as a lifelong "opus," a labor demanding the adept's total dedication. This opus proceeded as a series of well-defined stages in the course of which the events observed in the chemist's retort were accompanied by a vast amount of theoretical and imaginative speculation and of philosophical reflection. Each of the substances entering into the process appeared to be animated by a character and a destiny of its own, frequently conceived of in terms of mythological persons (Mercury, Saturn, the King and Queen, Sol and Luna). The adept was taught in what manner these bodies were to be treated and how they were going to effect each other when brought into mutual contact. Adverse processes of disintegration were described as alternating with beneficent combinations and were interpreted as taking place in accordance with certain inner laws which it was the alchemist's endeavor to discover and interpret. The goal itself was the transformation of the crude *prima materia* into the symbolical indestructible quint-essence, the *quinta es-*

sentia or *lapis philosophorum*, the philosopher's stone, also known under a multitude of other names each of which denotes its character of ultimate timeless value. Jung has demonstrated the psychic aspects of the alchemical work in the pursuit of which the alchemist's inner life processes, the contents of the unconscious became projected into the opus which was itself regarded as a process of redemption, of a freeing of the spirit imprisoned in matter, the successful conclusion of which therefore brought about a renewal of life. Thus it becomes clear that over and above the obvious implications of a scientific discipline the alchemical speculations expressed a religious search which in its turn culminated in a concept of the timeless inner man, the "anthropos," brought about through the integration of its constituent elements.

All this would appear to be far removed from the practice of modern depth psychology. However the contrary is true. It has become evident to the alert observer that many of the symbolic images described in alchemical writings reoccur in the dream sequences of modern men and women, inviting interpretations akin to those offered by the alchemists. This in itself would seem to justify the conclusion that the unconscious has at its disposal a language of its own. Remembering the ever-recurring themes in the religious mythologies, the motifs of initiation, of death and rebirth, of expiation and redemption and of the superhuman labors and sufferings of the redeemer-hero, one is led to the conviction that these mythologies express the ultimate concerns of the psyche in its search for spiritual fulfillment. It is C. G. Jung's specific contribution to have demonstrated the role of the transpersonal unconscious psyche as the matrix and active carrier of this search. The designation which he chose for it, the *collective unconscious,* is intended to stress its quality of omnipresence. The quest itself is thus understood as the manifestation of a primordial or archetypal urge or drive. Seen in this light all religious as well as cultural expressions become an authentic part of psychic existence and cannot be regarded as derivative. Hence the concept of sublimation becomes void. In its place we find the concept of *transformation* as evidenced by the manifold symbols which bear witness to man's deepest desire.

Indeed, Jung's first major work, published in 1912, bore the German title: *Wandlungen und Symbole der Libido* meaning "Transformation and Symbols of the Libido."[7] For Jung the concept of *libido* has a different or rather a wider meaning than it had for Freud. It comprehends the sum total of the energic life processes, of all the vital forces of which sexuality represents only one area. Jung speaks of libido as an energy value which is able to communicate itself to any field of activity whatsoever, be it power, hunger, hatred, sexuality or religion, without ever being itself a specific instinct.[8] In other words, the psychic functioning is understood as taking place within a number of relatively autonomous areas each of which is invested with a certain amount of energy. The specific energy quantum cannot be transferred from one area to another through an effort of the conscious will, but a *transformation* can take place which can be conceived of in analogy to the transformation of energy in the physical realm. The transformer itself is the symbol. The study of the symbols of transformation centers upon the basic demand which is imposed upon every individual, that is, the urge as well as the necessity to become conscious of himself, to develop that human awareness which distinguishes the mature personality from the infantile one. For Jung, the path towards this awareness is identical with the process of individuation. Insofar as the transformation results in a new and deeper awareness, it is experienced as a rebirth, and all rebirth rituals are intended to bring this about. Specifically, the basic dynamism consists in a profound reorientation from an ego-centered subjective attitude to an objective awareness of the limitations of the ego and of the existence of that greater psyche which Jung designates as the *self*. Thus the transformation of the libido implies

---

[7] Recently revised and republished under the title *Symbols of Transformation*, subtitled: "An Analysis of the Prelude to a Case of Schizophrenia" (Coll. Works, Vol. 5).

[8] *Ibid.*, p. 137.

a liberation of creative forces and the possibility to put them to the service of the greater-than-personal objectives.

Jacques Maritain[9] speaks of the poet's creative intuition as "an obscure grasping of his own self and of things in a knowledge through a union or through connaturality which is born in the spiritual unconscious, and which fructifies only in the work. . . . To attain, through the Void, an intuitive experience of the existence of the Self, of the Atman, in its pure and full actuality, is the specific aim of natural mysticism." In these two passages the word *self* carries implications which are akin to the content given to it in Jung's psychological use and definition. For Jung, the *self* connotes the totality of the psyche, embracing both consciousness and the unconscious and including the individual's rootedness in the matrix of the collective unconscious. He speaks of the *soul* as the function of relationship between consciousness and the *self*,[10] and emphasizes the necessity to realize the spiritual experience not only intellectually but also fully through feeling, and finally through the imaginative activity of intuition, without which no realization is complete. "This rounds off the work into an experience of the totality of the individual. . . . Such an experience is completely foreign to our age although no previous epoch has ever needed wholeness so much. It is abundantly clear that this is the prime problem confronting the art of psychic healing in our day."[11] Since the present volume includes Jung's discussion of the *self* in Chapters IV and V of his work *AION* under the headings of "The Self" and "Christ: a Symbol of the Self," it is hoped that despite their brevity these remarks may serve as an adequate introduction.

As is evident in the essay on the Child Archetype (see this volume), the image of the child is a symbol par excellence of the reborn psyche. In its highest incarnation, as it were, it is also a symbol of the *self*. Jung defines the *self* as the

---

[9] Jacques Maritain, *Creative Intuition in Art and Poetry*, Bollingen Series XXXV (Pantheon, 1953), p. 115.
[10] *The Practice of Psychotherapy* (Coll. Works, Vol. 16), p. 265 and pp. 277-79.
[11] *Ibid.*

complete personality comprising the ego as the center of the conscious functioning, plus the infinitely vaster areas of the unconscious. Of these areas, the one situated closest to the ego he designates as the personal unconscious. Beyond this, the reaches of the psyche extending into the subhuman on the one part and the supra-human on the other part are what he describes as the collective unconscious. In and through the *self*, the human personality is therefore related (paradoxical though this appears from the viewpoint of the ego) to what we might call its innermost center as well as the universe of which it forms a particle. (Compare also the attribute of the Tibetan Dalai Lama as the "Inmost One.")

What, then, are the symbols which the psyche itself has produced that it might give expression to the tremendous experience of its own potential wholeness? I can mention here only that symbol which more than any other has preoccupied Jung throughout his therapeutic and scientific endeavors, and which we find shaped into the rose window of the medieval cathedral as well as into the religious ritualistic paintings of Buddhism in the form of the *mandāla*. He has adopted the Sanskrit term *mandāla* as the general designation for all those symbolic representations of the circle motif, more specifically in its manifold combinations with the square. He regards the general pattern of these images as the "archetype of wholeness." The completeness or totality expressed in the Fourfoldness of the One therefore represents the "innermost godlike essence of man," characterized by symbols which can stand for the deity as well as for the *self*, since they reflect the image of the godhead in the unfolded creation in nature and in man.[12] According to Dr. Jung, this archetypal "leitmotif" has the vital function of giving expression to the dynamics of the self-healing process through which the psyche maintains its sanity and nurtures its own growth. The reader of this volume will find in the "Commentary on the Secret of the Golden Flower" Dr. Jung's discussion of the nature of the mandāla, and in the chapter "Christ as a Symbol of the Self" from his

[12] C. G. Jung: "Mandālas". Swiss periodical *Du* (April 1955).

book *Aion*, his presentation of the psychological significance of the quaternity associated with the circle. These interpretations also provide the master key to the psychological understanding of countless symbolic representations in the fields of the visual arts, architecture and the dance. Seen in this perspective, these representations can be said to give form to the experience of the self, not only on behalf of their creators, but also through their resonance in the mind of the beholder.

As the editor of the present volume it has been my intention to present a selection from the writings of C. G. Jung which would illustrate in convincing fashion the objects of his symbol research and the manner of his approach, as well as a synopsis of the conclusions to which he was led by exposing himself with great courage and thoroughness to the creative manifestations of the unconscious of many epochs and cultures.

Violet Staub de Laszlo

Danbury, Connecticut
May 1957

Aion[1]

I. The Ego

Investigation of the psychology of the unconscious confronted me with facts which required the formulation of new concepts. One of these concepts is the *self*. The entity so denoted is not meant to take the place of the one that has always been known as the *ego*, but includes it in a superordinate concept. We understand the ego as the complex factor to which all conscious contents are related. It forms, as it were, the center of the field

[1] *Aion* is one of Dr. C. G. Jung's recent works, having been published in Switzerland in 1951, with the subtitle "Contributions to the Symbolism of the Self." The parts here included represent the first five of its fifteen chapters. The remaining major portion of the work, as can be seen from the appended bibliography of the Collected Works, is devoted to a research study concerned mainly with the symbolism of the fish in the contexts of Christianity and of alchemy.

In this, as in several other sections of this volume, many weighty footnotes have had to be omitted for reasons of space. Certain slight cuts in the text have been made for similar reasons, and a small number of changes in rendering have been introduced for the sake of greater clarity in presenting the body of Jung's original and intricate thought to a reading public which has as yet had all too little opportunity to become familiar with his writings.—Ed.

of consciousness, and, insofar as this comprises the empirical personality, the ego is the subject of all personal acts of consciousness. The relation of a psychic content to the ego forms the criterion of its consciousness, for no content can be conscious unless it is represented to a subject.

With this definition we have described and delimited the scope of the subject. Theoretically, no limits can be set to the field of consciousness, since it is capable of indefinite extension. Empirically, however, it always finds its limit when it comes up against the unknown. This consists of everything we do not know—which, therefore, is not related to the ego as the center of the field of consciousness. The unknown falls into two groups of objects: those which are outside and can be experienced by the senses, and those which are inside and are experienced immediately. The first group comprises the unknown in the outer world; the second the unknown in the inner world. We call this latter territory the *unconscious*.

The ego, as a specific content of consciousness, is not a simple or elementary factor but a complex one which, as such, cannot be described exhaustively. Experience shows that it rests on two seemingly different bases: the *somatic* and the *psychic*. The somatic basis is inferred from the totality of endosomatic perceptions, which for their part are already of a psychic nature and are associated with the ego, and are therefore conscious. They are produced by endosomatic stimuli, only some of which cross the threshold of consciousness. A considerable proportion of these stimuli occur unconsciously, that is, subliminally. The fact that they are subliminal does not necessarily mean that their status is merely physiological, any more than this would be true of a psychic content. Sometimes they are capable of crossing the threshold, that is, of becoming perceptions. But there is no doubt that a large proportion of these endosomatic stimuli are simply incapable of consciousness and are so elementary that there is no reason to assign them a psychic nature—unless of course one favors the philosophical view that all life processes are psychic anyway. The chief objection to this hardly demonstrable hypothesis is that it enlarges the concept of the psyche beyond all bounds and interprets the life process in a way not absolutely warranted by the facts. Concepts that are too broad usually prove to be unsuitable instruments because they are too vague and nebulous. I have therefore suggested that the term "psychic" be used only where there is evidence of a will capable of modifying reflex or instinctual processes.[2]

The somatic basis of the ego consists, then, of conscious and unconscious factors. The same is true of the psychic basis: on the one hand the ego rests on the *total field of consciousness*, and, on the other, on the *sum total of unconscious contents*. These fall into three groups: first, temporarily subliminal contents that can be reproduced voluntarily (memory); second, unconscious contents that cannot be reproduced voluntarily; third, contents that are not capable of becoming conscious at all. Group two can be inferred from the spontaneous irruption of subliminal contents into consciousness. Group three is hypothetical; it is a logical inference from the facts underlying group two. This contains contents which have not yet irrupted into consciousness, or which never will.

When I said that the ego *rests* on the total field of consciousness, I do not mean that it *consists* of this. Were that so, it would be indistinguishable from the field of consciousness as a whole. The ego is only the latter's point of reference, grounded on and limited by the somatic factor described above.

Although its bases are in themselves relatively unknown and unconscious, the ego is a conscious factor par excellence. It is even acquired, empirically speaking, during the individual's lifetime. It seems to arise in the first place from the collision between the somatic factor and the environment, and, once established as a subject, it goes on developing from further collisions with the outer world and the inner.

Despite the unlimited extent of its bases, the ego is never more and never less than consciousness as a whole. As a conscious factor the ego could, theoretically at least, be described completely. But this would never amount to more than a pic-

---

[2] For a discussion of the definition of the "psychic" see "The Phenomenology of the Spirit in Fairy Tales" in this volume.—Ed.

ture of the *conscious personality*, in which all those features which are unknown or unconscious to the subject would be missing. A total picture would have to include these. But a total description of the personality is, even in theory, absolutely impossible, because the unconscious portion of it cannot be grasped cognitively. This unconscious portion, as experience has abundantly shown, is by no means unimportant. On the contrary, the most decisive qualities in a person are often unconscious and can be perceived only by others, or have to be laboriously discovered with outside help.

Clearly, then, the personality as a total phenomenon does not coincide with the ego, that is, with the conscious personality, but forms an entity that has to be distinguished from the ego. Naturally the need to do this is incumbent only on a psychology that reckons with the fact of the unconscious, but for such a psychology the distinction is of paramount importance. Even for jurisprudence it should be of some importance whether certain psychic facts are conscious or not —for instance, in adjudging the question of responsibility.

I have therefore suggested calling the total personality which, though present, cannot be fully known, the *self*. The *ego* is, by definition, subordinate to the *self* and is related to it like a part to the whole. Inside the field of consciousness it has, as we say, free will. By this I do not mean anything philosophical, only the well-known psychological fact of "free choice", or rather the subjective feeling of freedom. But just as our free will clashes with necessity in the outside world, so also it finds its limits outside the field of consciousness in the subjective inner world, where it comes into conflict with the facts of the self. And just as circumstances or outside events happen to us and limit our freedom, so the self acts upon the ego like an objective occurrence which free will can do very little to alter. It is, indeed, well known that the ego not only can do nothing against the self, but is sometimes actually assimilated by unconscious components of the personality that are in the process of development and is greatly altered by them.

It is, in the nature of the case, impossible to give any general description of the ego except a formal one. Any other mode of observation would have to take account of the *individuality* which attaches to the ego as one of its main characteristics. Although the numerous elements composing this complex factor are, in themselves, everywhere the same, they are infinitely varied as regards clarity, emotional coloring, and scope. The result of their combination—the ego—is therefore, so far as one can judge, individual and unique, and retains its identity up to a certain point. Its stability is relative, because far-reaching changes of personality can sometimes occur. Alterations of this kind need not always be pathological; they can also be developmental and hence fall within the scope of the normal.

Since it is the point of reference for the field of consciousness, the ego is the subject of all successful attempts at adaptation so far as these are achieved by the will. The ego therefore has a significant part to play in the psychic economy. Its position there is so important that there are good grounds for the prejudice that the ego is the center of the personality, and that the field of consciousness is the psyche per se. If we discount certain suggestive ideas in Leibniz, Kant, Schelling, and Schopenhauer, and the philosophical excursions of Carus and Von Hartmann, it is only since the end of the nineteenth century that modern psychology, with its inductive methods, has discovered the foundations of consciousness and proved empirically the existence of a psyche outside consciousness. With this discovery the position of the ego, till then absolute, became relativized; that is to say, though it retains its quality as the center of the field of consciousness, it has become questionable whether it is the center of the personality. It is part of the personality but not the whole of it. As I have said, it is simply impossible to estimate how large or how small its share is; how free or how dependent it is on the qualities of this "extra-conscious" psyche. We can only say that its freedom is limited and its dependence proved in ways that are often decisive. In my experience one would do well not to underestimate its dependence on the unconscious. Naturally there is no need to say this to persons who already overestimate the latter's importance. Some criterion for the right measure is afforded by the psychic consequences of a wrong estimate, a point to which we shall return later on.

We have seen that, from the standpoint of the psychology of consciousness, the unconscious can be divided into three groups of contents. But from the standpoint of the psychology of the personality a two-fold division ensues: an "extra-conscious" psyche whose contents are personal, and an "extra-conscious" psyche whose contents are impersonal and collective. The first group comprises contents which are integral components of the individual personality and could therefore just as well be conscious; the second group forms, as it were, an omnipresent, unchanging, and everywhere identical *condition or substrate of the psyche per se*. This is, of course, no more than a hypothesis. But we are driven to it by the peculiar nature of the empirical material, not to mention the high probability that the general similarity of psychic processes in all individuals must be based on an equally general and impersonal principle that conforms to law, just as the instinct manifesting itself in the individual is only the partial manifestation of an instinctual substrate common to all men.

II. *The Shadow*

Whereas the contents of the *personal unconscious* are acquired during the individual's lifetime, the contents of the *collective unconscious* are invariably archetypes that were present from the beginning. Their relation to the instincts has been discussed elsewhere.[1] The archetypes most clearly characterized from the empirical point of view are those which have the most frequent and the most disturbing influence on the ego. These are the *shadow*, the *anima*, and the *animus*. The most accessible of these, and the easiest to experience, is the

[1] See "Instinct and the Unconscious", *Contributions to Analytical Psychology* (London: Routledge and Kegan Paul, 1928) and "The Phenomenology of the Spirit in Fairy Tales" in this volume. —Ed.

shadow, for its nature can in large measure be inferred from the contents of the personal unconscious. The only exceptions to this rule are those rather rare cases where the positive qualities of the personality are repressed, and the ego in consequence plays an essentially negative or unfavorable role.

The shadow is a moral problem that challenges the whole ego personality, for no one can become conscious of the shadow without considerable moral effort. To become conscious of it involves recognizing the dark aspects of the personality as present and real. This act is the essential condition for any kind of self-knowledge, and it therefore, as a rule, meets with considerable resistance. Indeed, self-knowledge as a psychotherapeutic measure frequently requires much painstaking work extending over a long period.

Closer examination of the dark characteristics—that is, the inferiorities constituting the shadow—reveals that they have an *emotional* nature, a kind of *autonomy*, and accordingly an *obsessive* or, better, *possessive* quality. Emotion, incidentally, is not an activity of the individual but something that happens to him. Affects occur usually where adaptation is weakest, and at the same time they reveal the reason for its weakness, namely, a certain degree of inferiority and the existence of a lower level of personality. On this lower level with its uncontrolled or scarcely controlled emotions one behaves more or less like a primitive, who is not only the passive victim of his affects but also singularly incapable of moral judgment.

Although, with insight and good will, the shadow can to some extent be assimilated into the conscious personality, experience shows that there are certain features which offer the most obstinate resistance to moral control and prove almost impossible to influence. These resistances are usually bound up with *projections,* which are not recognized as such, and their recognition is a moral achievement beyond the ordinary. While some traits peculiar to the shadow can be recognized without too much difficulty as one's own personal qualities, in this case both insight and good will are unavailing because the cause of the emotion appears to lie, beyond all possibility of doubt, in the *other person*. No matter how obvious it may be to the neutral observer that it is a matter of projections, there is little hope that the subject will perceive this himself. He must be convinced that he throws a very long shadow before he is willing to withdraw his emotionally toned projections from their object.

Let us suppose that a certain individual shows no inclination whatever to recognize his projections. The projection-making factor then has a free hand and can realize its object —if it has one—or bring about some other situation characteristic of its potency. As we know, it is not the conscious subject but the unconscious which does the projecting. *Hence one encounters projections, one does not make them.* The effect of projection is to *isolate the subject* from his environment, since instead of a real relation to it there is now only an illusory one. Projections change the world into the replica of one's own unknown face. In the last analysis, therefore, they lead to an autoerotic or autistic condition in which one dreams a world whose reality remains forever unattainable. The resultant *sentiment d'incomplétude* and the still worse feeling of sterility are in their turn explained by projection as the malevolence of the environment, and by means of this vicious circle the isolation is intensified. The more projections interpose themselves between the subject and the environment, the harder it becomes for the ego to see through its illusions. A forty-five-year-old patient who had suffered from a compulsion neurosis since he was twenty and had become completely cut off from the world once said to me: "But I can never admit to myself that I've wasted the best twenty-five years of my life!"

It is often tragic to see how blatantly a man bungles his own life and the lives of others yet remains totally incapable of seeing how much the whole tragedy originates in himself, and how he continually feeds it and keeps it going. Not *consciously*, of course—for consciously he is engaged in bewailing and cursing a faithless world that recedes further and further into the distance. Rather, it is an unconscious factor which spins the illusions that veil his world. And what is being spun is a cocoon, which in the end will completely envelop him.

One might assume that projections like these, which are so very difficult if not impossible to dissolve, would belong to the realm of the shadow—that is, to the negative side of the personality. This assumption however becomes untenable after a certain point, because the symbols that then appear no longer refer to the same but to the opposite sex, in a man's case to a woman and vice versa. The source of projections is no longer the shadow—which is always of the same sex as the subject—but a contrasexual figure. Here we meet the *animus* of a woman and the *anima* of a man, two corresponding archetypes whose autonomy and unconsciousness explain the stubbornness of their projections. Though the shadow is a motif as well known to mythology as anima and animus, it represents first and foremost the personal unconscious, and its content can therefore be made conscious without too much difficulty. In this it differs from anima and animus, for whereas the shadow can be seen through and recognized fairly easily, the anima and animus are much further away from consciousness and in normal circumstances are seldom if ever realized. With a little self-criticism one can see through the shadow—so far as its nature is personal. But when it appears as an archetype, one encounters the same difficulties as with anima and animus. In other words, it is quite within the bounds of possibility for a man to recognize the relative evil of his nature, but it is a rare and shattering experience for him to gaze into the face of absolute evil.

III. The Syzygy:[1] Anima[2] and Animus

What, then, is this projection-making factor? The East calls it the "Spinning Woman"—Maya, who creates illusion by her dancing. Had we not long since known it from the symbolism of dreams, this hint from the Orient would put us on the

[1] Syzygy; syzygia: a joining together, conjunction (from the Merriam-Webster International Dictionary).—Ed.
[2] Jung has "also defined the anima as a personification of the unconscious.—Ed.

right track: the enveloping, embracing, and devouring element points unmistakably to the mother,[3] that is, to the son's relation to the real mother, to her imago, and to the woman who is to become a mother for him. His Eros is passive like a child's; he hopes to be caught, sucked in, enveloped, and devoured. He seeks, as it were, the protecting, nourishing, charmed circle of the mother, the condition of the infant released from every care, in which the outside world bends over him and even forces happiness upon him. No wonder the real world vanishes from sight!

If this situation is dramatized, as the unconscious usually dramatizes it, then there appears before you on the psychological stage a man living regressively, seeking his childhood and his mother, fleeing from a cold cruel world which denies him understanding. Not infrequently a mother appears beside him who apparently shows not the slightest concern that her little son should become a man, but who, with tireless and self-immolating effort, neglects nothing that might hinder him from growing up and marrying. You behold the secret conspiracy between mother and son, and how each helps the other to betray life.

Where does the guilt lie? With the mother, or with the son? Probably with both. The unsatisfied longing of the son for life and the world ought to be taken seriously. There is in him a desire to touch reality, to embrace the earth and fructify the field of the world. But he makes no more than a series of impatient beginnings, for his initiative as well as his staying power are crippled by the secret memory that the world and happiness may be had as a gift—from the mother. It makes demands on the masculinity of a man, on his ardor, above all on his courage and resolution, when it comes to throwing his whole being into the scales. For this he would need a faithless Eros, one capable of forgetting the mother and of hurting himself by deserting the first love of his life. The mother, foreseeing this danger, has carefully inculcated

[3] Here and in what follows, the word "mother" is not meant in the literal sense but as a symbol of everything that functions as a mother.

into him the virtues of faithfulness, devotion, loyalty, so as to protect him from the moral disruption which is the risk of every life adventure. He has learned these lessons only too well, and remains true to his mother, perhaps causing her the deepest anxiety (when, in her honor, he turns out to be a homosexual, for example) and at the same time affords her an unconscious satisfaction of a mythological nature, for in the relationship now reigning between them, there is consummated the immemorial and most sacred archetype of the marriage of mother and son.

At this level of the myth, which probably illustrates the nature of the collective unconscious better than any other, the mother is both old and young, Demeter and Persephone, and the son is spouse and sleeping infant all in one. The imperfections of real life, with its laborious adaptations and manifold disappointments, naturally cannot compete with such a state of indescribable fulfillment.

In the case of the son, the projection-making factor is identical with the *mother imago*, and this is consequently taken to be the real mother. The projection can only be dissolved when he comes to realize that in the realm of his psyche there exists an image of the mother and not only of the mother, but also of the daughter, the sister, the beloved, the heavenly goddess, and the earth spirit Baubo. Every mother and every beloved is forced to become the carrier and embodiment of this omnipresent and ageless image which corresponds to the deepest reality in a man. It is his own, this perilous image of Woman; she stands for the loyalty which in the interests of life he cannot always maintain; she is the vital compensation for the risks, struggles, sacrifices which all end in disappointment; she is the solace for all the bitterness of life. Simultaneously, she is the great illusionist, the seductress who draws him into life—not only into its reasonable and useful aspects but into its frightful paradoxes and ambivalences where good and evil, success and ruin, hope and despair counterbalance one another.

This image is "My Lady Soul", as Spitteler has called her. I have suggested the term "anima" as indicating something specific, for which the expression "soul" is too general and too vague. The empirical reality summed up under the concept of the anima forms an extremely dramatic content of the unconscious. It is possible to describe this content in rational, scientific language, but in this way one entirely fails to express its living character. Therefore, in describing the living processes of the psyche, I deliberately and consciously give preference to a dramatic, mythological way of thinking and speaking, because this is not only more expressive but also more exact than an abstract scientific terminology, which is wont to flirt with the notion that its theoretic formulations may one fine day be resolved into algebraic equations.

The projection-making factor is the anima, or rather the unconscious as represented by the anima. Whenever she appears, in dreams, visions, and fantasies, she takes on personified form, thus demonstrating that the factor she embodies possesses all the outstanding characteristics of a feminine being. She is not an invention of the conscious mind, but a spontaneous production of the unconscious. Nor is she a substitute figure for the mother. On the contrary, there is every likelihood that the numinous qualities which make the mother imago so dangerously powerful stem from the collective archetype of the anima, which is incarnated anew in every male child.

Since the anima is an archetype that is manifest in men, it is reasonable to suppose that an equivalent archetype must be present in women; for just as the man is compensated by a feminine element, so woman is compensated by a masculine one. I do not, however, wish this argument to give the impression that these compensatory relationships were arrived at by deduction. On the contrary, long and varied experience was needed in order to grasp the nature of anima and animus empirically. Whatever we have to say about these archetypes, therefore, is either directly verifiable or at least rendered probable by the facts. At the same time, I am fully aware that we are discussing pioneer work which by its very nature can only be provisional.

Just as the mother seems to be the first carrier of the

projection-making factor for the son, so is the father for the daughter. Practical experience of these relationships is made up of many individual cases presenting all kinds of variations on the same basic theme. A concise description of them can, therefore, be no more than schematic.

Woman is compensated by a masculine element and therefore her unconscious has, so to speak, a masculine imprint. This results in a considerable psychological difference between men and women, and accordingly I have called the projection-making factor in women the animus, which means reason or spirit. The animus corresponds to the paternal Logos just as the anima corresponds to the maternal Eros. It is far from my intention to give these two intuitive concepts too specific a definition. I use Eros and Logos merely as conceptual aids to describe the fact that woman's consciousness is characterized more by the connective quality of Eros than by the discrimination and cognition associated with Logos. In men, Eros, the function of relationship, is usually less developed than Logos. In women, on the other hand, Eros is an expression of their true nature, while their Logos is often only a regrettable accident. It gives rise to misunderstandings and annoying interpretations in the family circle and among friends. This is because it consists of *opinions* instead of reflections, and by opinions I mean a priori assumptions which lay claim, as it were, to absolute truth. Such assumptions, as everyone knows, can be extremely irritating. As the animus is partial to argument, he can best be seen at work in disputes where both parties know they are right. Men can argue in a very womanish way, too, when they are anima-possessed and have thus been transformed into the animus of their own anima. With them the question becomes one of personal *vanity* and *touchiness* (as if they were females); with women it is a question of *power*, whether of truth or justice or some kind of "ism"—for the dressmaker and hairdresser have already taken care of their vanity. The "Father" (i.e., the sum of conventional opinions) always plays a great role in female argumentation. No matter how friendly and obliging a woman's Eros may be, no logic on earth can shake her if she is ridden by the animus. Often the man has the feeling—and he is not altogether wrong—that only seduction or a beating or rape would have the necessary power of "persuasion". He is unaware that this highly dramatic situation would instantly come to a banal and unexciting end if he were to quit the field of battle. This sound idea seldom or never occurs to him, because no man can converse with an animus for even the shortest time without becoming the victim of his own anima. Anyone with sufficient sense of humor to listen objectively to the ensuing dialogue would be staggered by the vast number of commonplaces, misapplied truisms, clichés from newspapers and novels, shop-soiled platitudes of every description interspersed with vulgar abuse and a vastly dismaying absence of logic. It is a dialogue which, irrespective of its participants, is repeated millions of times in all the languages of the world and always remains essentially the same.

This apparently singular fact is due to the following circumstance: When animus and anima meet, the animus draws the sword of his power and the anima ejects the poison of her illusion and seduction. The outcome need not always be negative, since the two are equally likely to fall in love (a special instance of love at first sight!). The language of love is of astonishing uniformity, using the popular forms with the greatest devotion and fidelity, so that once again the two partners find themselves in a banal collective situation. Yet they live in the illusion that they are related to one another in a most individual way.

In both its positive and its negative aspects the anima-animus relationship is always full of "animosity," i.e., it is emotional, and hence collective. Affects lower the level of the relationship and bring it closer to the common instinctual basis, which no longer has anything individual about it. Very often the relationship runs its course heedless of its human performers, who afterwards do not know what happened to them.

Whereas the cloud of "animosity" surrounding the man is composed chiefly of sentimentality and resentment, in woman it expresses itself in the form of opinionated views, interpretations, insinuations, and misconstructions, which all have the purpose (sometimes attained) of severing the relation between two human beings.

Like the anima, the animus too has a positive aspect. Through the figure of the father he expresses not only conventional opinion but—equally—what we call "spirit", philosophical or religious ideas in particular, or rather the attitude resulting from them. Thus the animus is a psychopomp, a mediator between the conscious and the unconscious and a personification of the latter. Just as the anima becomes, through integration, the Eros of consciousness, so the animus becomes a Logos; and in the same way that the anima gives relationship and relatedness to a man's consciousness, the animus gives woman's consciousness a capacity for reflection, deliberation, and self-knowledge.

The effect of anima and animus on the ego is in principle the same. This effect is extremely difficult to eliminate because, in the first place, it is uncommonly strong and immediately fills the ego personality with an unshakable feeling of rightness and righteousness. In the second place, the cause of the effect is projected and appears to lie in objects and objective situations. Both characteristics can, I believe, be traced back to the peculiarities of the archetype. For the archetype, of course, exists a priori. This may possibly explain the often totally irrational yet undisputed and indisputable existence of certain moods and opinions. Perhaps these are so notoriously difficult to influence because of the powerfully suggestive effect emanating from the archetype. Consciousness is fascinated by it, held captive, as if hypnotized. Very often the ego experiences a vague feeling of moral defeat and then behaves all the more defensively, defiantly, and self-righteously, thus setting up a vicious circle which only increases its feeling of inferiority. The bottom is then knocked out of the human relationship, for, like megalomania, a feeling of inferiority makes mutual recognition impossible, and without this there is no relationship.

As I said, it is easier to gain insight into the shadow than into the anima or animus. With the shadow, we have the advantage of being prepared in some sort by our education, which has always endeavored to convince people that they are not one hundred per cent pure gold. Hence everyone immediately understands what is meant by "shadow", "inferior personality", etc. And if he should have forgotten this, his memory could easily be refreshed by a Sunday sermon, his wife, or the tax collector. With the anima and animus, however, things are by no means so simple. Firstly, there is no moral education in this respect, and secondly, most people are content to be self-righteous and prefer mutual vilification (if nothing worse!) to the recognition of their projections. Indeed, it seems a very natural state of affairs for men to have irrational moods and women irrational opinions. Presumably this situation is grounded on instinct and must remain as it is to ensure that the Empedoclean game of the hate (*neikos*) and love (*philia*) of the elements shall continue for all eternity. Nature is conservative and does not easily allow her courses to be altered, she defends in the most stubborn way the inviolability of the preserves where anima and animus roam. Hence it is much more difficult to become conscious of one's anima-animus projections than to acknowledge one's shadow side. One has, of course, to overcome certain moral obstacles, such as vanity, ambition, conceit, resentment, etc., but in the case of projections all sorts of purely intellectual difficulties are added, quite apart from the contents of the projection, which one simply doesn't know how to cope with. And in addition to all this there arises a profound doubt as to whether one is not meddling too much with nature's business by prodding into consciousness things which it would have been better to leave asleep.

Although there are, in my experience, a fair number of people who can understand without special intellectual or moral difficulties what is meant by anima and animus, one finds very many more who have the greatest trouble in understanding these concepts and visualizing them as anything concrete. This shows that these concepts fall a little outside the usual range of experience. They are unpopular precisely because they seem unfamiliar. The consequence is that they mobilize prejudice and become taboo, as has always been the case with the unexpected.

So if we set it up as a kind of requirement that projections should be dissolved, because it is more wholesome that way and in every respect more advantageous, we are entering upon new ground. Up till now everybody has been convinced that the idea "my father", "my mother", etc., is nothing but a faithful reflection of the real parent, corresponding in every detail to the original, so that when someone says "my father" he means no more and no less than what his father is in reality. This is actually what he does mean, but a supposition of identity by no means brings about that identity. This is where the fallacy of the *enkekalymnenos* ("the veiled one") operates.[4] If one includes in the psychological equation X's picture of his father, which he takes for the real father, the equation will not work out, because the unknown quantity he has introduced does not tally with reality. X has overlooked the fact that his idea of a person consists, in the first place, of the possibly very incomplete picture he has received of the real person and, in the second place, of the subjective modifications he has imposed upon this picture. X's idea of his father is a complex quantity for which the real father is only in part responsible, an indefinitely large share falling to the son. So true is this that every time he criticizes or praises his father he is unconsciously hitting back at himself, thereby bringing about those psychic consequences that overtake people who habitually disparage or overpraise themselves. If, however, X carefully compares his reactions with reality, he stands a chance of noticing that he has miscalculated somewhere by not realizing long ago from his father's behavior that the picture he has of him is a false one. But as a rule X is convinced that he is right, and if anybody is wrong it must be the other fellow. Should X have a poorly developed Eros, he will be either indifferent to the inadequate relationship he has with his

---

[4] The fallacy stems from Eubulides the Megarian and runs: "Can you recognize your father? Yes. Can you recognize this veiled one? No. This veiled one is your father. Hence you can recognize your father and yet not recognize him."

father or else annoyed by the inconsistency and general incomprehensibility of a father whose behavior never really corresponds to the picture X has of him. Therefore X thinks he has every right to feel hurt, misunderstood, and even betrayed.

One can imagine how desirable it would be in such cases to dissolve the projection. And there are always optimists who believe that the golden age can be ushered in simply by telling people the right way to go. But just let them try to explain to these people that they are acting like a dog chasing its own tail. To make a person see the shortcomings of his attitude, considerably more than mere "telling" is needed, for more is involved than ordinary common sense can allow. What one is up against here is the kind of fateful misunderstanding which, under ordinary conditions, remains forever inaccessible to insight. It is rather like expecting the average respectable citizen to recognize himself as a criminal.

I mention all this just to illustrate the order of magnitude to which the anima-animus projections belong, and the moral and intellectual exertions that are needed to dissolve them. Not all the contents of the anima and animus are projected, however. Many of them appear spontaneously in dreams and so on, and many more can be made conscious through active imagination. In this way we find that thoughts, feelings, and affects are alive in us which we would never have believed possible. Naturally, possibilities of this sort seem utterly fantastic to anyone who has not experienced them himself, for a normal person "knows what he thinks." Such a childish attitude on the part of the "normal person" is simply the rule, so that no one without experience in this field can be expected to understand the real nature of anima and animus. With these reflections one gets into an entirely new world of psychological experience, provided of course that one succeeds in realizing them in practice. Those who do succeed can hardly fail to be impressed by all that the ego does not know and never has known. This increase in self-knowledge is still very rare nowadays and is usually paid for in advance with a neurosis, if not with something worse.

The autonomy of the collective unconscious expresses itself

in the figures of anima and animus. They personify those of its contents which, when withdrawn from projection, can be integrated into consciousness. To this extent, both figures represent *functions* which filter the contents of the collective unconscious through to the conscious mind. They appear or behave as such, however, only so long as the tendencies of the conscious and unconscious do not diverge too greatly. Should any tension arise, these functions, harmless till then, confront the conscious mind in personified form and behave rather like systems split off from the personality, or like part souls. This comparison is inadequate insofar as nothing previously belonging to the ego personality has split off from it; on the contrary, the two figures represent a disturbing accretion. The reason for their behaving in this way is that though the *contents* of anima and animus can be integrated, they themselves cannot, since they are archetypes. As such they are the foundation stones of the psychic structure, which in its totality exceeds the limits of consciousness and therefore can never become the object of direct cognition. The effects of anima and animus can indeed be made conscious, but they themselves are factors transcending consciousness and beyond the reach of perception and volition. Hence they remain autonomous despite the integration of their contents, and for this reason they should be kept constantly in mind. This is extremely important from the therapeutic standpoint, because constant observation pays the unconscious a tribute that more or less guarantees its cooperation. The unconscious, as we know, can never be "done with" once and for all. It is, in fact, one of the most important tasks of psychic hygiene to pay continual attention to the symptomatology of unconscious contents and processes, for the good reason that the conscious mind is always in danger of becoming one-sided, of keeping to well-worn paths and getting stuck in blind alleys. The complementary and compensating function of the unconscious ensures that these dangers, which are especially great in neurosis, can in some measure be avoided. It is only under ideal conditions, when life is still simple and unconscious enough to follow the serpentine path of instinct without hesitation or misgiving, that the compensation works with entire success. The more civilized, the more unconscious and complicated a man is, the less he is able to follow his instincts. His complicated living conditions and the influence of his environment are so strong that they drown the quiet voice of nature. Opinions, beliefs, theories, and collective tendencies appear in its stead and back up all the aberrations of the conscious mind. Deliberate attention should then be given to the unconscious so that the compensation can set to work. Hence it is especially important to picture the archetypes of the unconscious not as a rushing phantasmagoria of fugitive images, but as constant, autonomous factors, which indeed they are.

Both these archetypes, as practical experience shows, possess a fatality that can on occasion produce tragic results. They are quite literally the father and mother of all the disastrous entanglements of fate and have long been recognized as such by the whole world. Together they form a divine pair,[5] one of whom, in accordance with his Logos nature, is characterized by *pneuma* and *nous*, rather like Hermes with his ever-shifting hues, while the other, in accordance with her Eros nature, wears the features of Aphrodite, Helen (Selene), Persephone, and Hecate. Both of them are unconscious powers, "gods" in fact, as the ancient world quite rightly conceived them to be. To call them by this name is to give them that central position in the scale of psychological values which has always been theirs whether consciously acknowledged or not, for their power grows in proportion to the degree that they remain unconscious. Those who do not see them are in their hands, just as a typhus epidemic flourishes best when its source

[5] Naturally this is not meant as a psychological definition, let alone a metaphysical one. As I pointed out in "The Relations between the Ego and the Unconscious" (*Two Essays on Analytical Psychology*, 1954, pp. 124–239), the syzygy consists of three elements apiece: the femininity pertaining to the man and the masculinity pertaining to the woman, the experience which man has of woman and vice versa, and finally the masculine and feminine archetypal image. The first two elements can be integrated into the personality by the process of conscious realization, but the last one cannot.

is undiscovered. Even in Christianity the divine syzygy has not become obsolete, but occupies the highest place as Christ and his bride the Church.[6] Parallels like these prove extremely helpful in our attempts to find the right yardstick for gauging the significance of these two archetypes. What we can discover about them from the conscious side is so slight as to be almost imperceptible. It is only when we throw light into the dark depths of the psyche and explore the strange and tortuous paths of human fate that it gradually becomes clear to us how immense is the influence wielded by these two factors that complement our conscious life.

Recapitulating, I should like to emphasize that the integration of the shadow, or the realization of the personal unconscious, marks the first stage in the analytic process, and that without it a recognition of anima and animus is impossible. The shadow can be realized only through a relation to a partner, and anima and animus only through a relation to the opposite sex, because only in such a relation do their projections become operative. The recognition of anima or animus gives rise, in a man, to a triad, one third of which is transcendent: the masculine subject, the opposing feminine subject, and the transcendent anima. With a woman the situation is reversed. The missing fourth element that would make the triad a quaternity is, in a man, the archetype of the Wise Old Man, which I have not discussed here, and in a woman the chthonic Mother. These four constitute a half-immanent and half-transcendent quaternity, an archetype which I have called the marriage *quaternio*.[7] The marriage quaternio provides the pattern not only for the self but also for the structure of primitive society with its cross-cousin marriage, marriage classes, and division of settlements into quarters. The self, on the other

[6] "For the Scripture says, 'God made man male and female'; the male is Christ, the female is the Church." (Second Epistle of Clement to the Corinthians, XIV, 2, *The Apostolic Fathers*, I, 1912, p. 151.) In pictorial representations Mary often takes the place of the Church.

[7] "Psychology of the Transference," *The Practice of Psychotherapy* (Coll. Works, Vol. 16), pp. 211ff.

hand, is a God-image, or at least cannot be distinguished from one. Of this the early Christian spirit was not ignorant, otherwise Clement of Alexandria could never have said that he who knows himself knows God.

IV. *The Self*

We shall now turn to the question of whether the increase in self-knowledge resulting from the withdrawal of impersonal projections—in other words, the integration of the contents of the collective unconscious—exerts a specific influence on the ego personality. To the extent that the integrated contents are *parts of the self,* we can expect this influence to be considerable. Their assimilation augments not only the area of the field of consciousness but also the importance of the ego, especially when, as usually happens, the ego lacks any critical approach to the unconscious. In that case it is easily overpowered and becomes identical with the contents that have been assimilated. In this way, for instance, a masculine consciousness comes under the influence of the anima and can even be possessed by her.

I have discussed the wider effects of the integration of unconscious contents elsewhere[1] and can therefore omit going into details here. I should only like to mention that the more numerous and the more significant the unconscious contents which are assimilated to the ego, the closer the approximation of the ego to the self, even though this approximation must be a never-ending process. This inevitably produces an inflation of the *ego,* unless a critical line of demarcation is drawn between it and the unconscious figures. But this act of discrimination yields practical results only if it succeeds in fixing reasonable boundaries to the ego and in granting the figures of the unconscious—the self, anima, animus, and shadow— relative autonomy and reality (of a psychic nature). To psy-

[1] "The Relations between the Ego and the Unconscious", *Two Essays on Analytical Psychology* (Coll. Works, Vol. 7), also reprinted as a Meridian Book, New York, 1956.—Ed.

chologize this reality out of existence either is ineffectual or else merely increases the inflation of the ego. One cannot dispose of facts by declaring them unreal. The projection-making factor, for instance, has undeniable reality. Anyone who insists on denying it becomes identical with it, which is not only dubious in itself but a positive danger to the well-being of the individual. Everyone who has dealings with such cases knows how perilous an inflation can be. No more than a flight of steps or a smooth floor is needed to precipitate a fatal fall. Besides the "pride goeth before a fall" motif, there are other factors of a no less disagreeable psychosomatic and psychic nature which serve to reduce inflation. This condition should not be interpreted as one of conscious self-aggrandizement. Such is far from being the rule. In general we are not directly conscious of this condition at all, but can at best infer its existence indirectly from the symptoms. These include the reactions of our immediate environment. Inflation magnifies the blind spot in the eye, and the more we are assimilated by the projection-making factor, the greater becomes the tendency to identify with it. A clear symptom of this is our growing disinclination to take note of the reactions of the environment and pay heed to them.

It must be reckoned a psychic catastrophe when the *ego is assimilated by the self*. The image of wholeness then remains in the unconscious, so that on the one hand it shares the archaic nature of the unconscious and on the other finds itself in the psychically relative space-time continuum that is characteristic of the unconscious as such.[2] Both these qualities are numinous and hence have an unlimited determining effect on ego consciousness, which is differentiated, i.e., separated, from the unconscious and moreover exists in an absolute space and an absolute time. It is a vital necessity that this should be so. If, therefore, the ego falls for any length of time under the control of an unconscious factor, its adaptation is disturbed and the way opened for all sorts of possible accidents.

Hence it is of the greatest importance that the ego should

[2] See "The Phenomenology of the Spirit in Fairy Tales" in this volume.—Ed.

be anchored in the world of consciousness and that consciousness should be reinforced by a very precise adaptation. For this, certain virtues like attention, conscientiousness, patience, etc., are of great value on the moral side, just as accurate observation of the symptomatology of the unconscious is valuable on the intellectual side.

However, accentuation of the ego personality and the world of consciousness may easily assume such proportions that the figures of the unconscious are psychologized and the *self consequently becomes assimilated to the ego*. Although this is the exact opposite of the process we have just described, it is followed by the same result: inflation. The world of consciousness must now be levelled down in favor of the reality of the unconscious. In the first case, reality had to be protected against an archaic, "eternal", and "ubiquitous" dream state; in the second, room must be made for the dream at the expense of the world of consciousness. In the first case, mobilization of all the virtues is indicated; in the second, the presumption of the ego can only be damped down by moral defeat. This is necessary, because otherwise one will never attain that median degree of modesty which is essential for the maintenance of a balanced state. It is not a question, as one might think, of relaxing morality itself, but of making a moral effort in a different direction. For instance, a man who is not conscientious enough has to make a moral effort in order to come up to the mark; while for one who is sufficiently rooted in the world through his own efforts it is no small moral achievement to inflict defeat on his virtues by loosening his ties with the world and reducing his adaptive performance. (One thinks in this connection of Brother Klaus, now canonized, who for the salvation of his soul left his wife to her own devices, along with numerous progeny.)

Since real moral problems all begin where the penal code leaves off, their solution can seldom or never depend on precedent, much less on precepts and commandments. The real moral problems spring from *conflicts of duty*. Anyone who is sufficiently humble, or easy-going, can always reach a decision with the help of some outside authority. But one who trusts others as little as himself can never reach a decision at all, unless it is brought about in the manner which Common Law calls an "Act of God." The Oxford Dictionary defines this concept as the "action of uncontrollable natural forces". In all such cases there is an unconscious authority which puts an end to doubt by creating a *fait accompli*. (In the last analysis this is true also of those who get their decision from a higher authority, only in more veiled form.) One can describe this authority either as the "will of God" or as an "action of uncontrollable natural forces", though psychologically it makes a good deal of difference how one thinks of it. The rationalistic interpretation of this inner authority as "natural forces" or the instincts satisfies the modern intellect but has the great disadvantage that the apparent victory of instinct offends our moral self-esteem; hence we like to persuade ourselves that the matter has been decided solely by the rational motions of the will. Civilized man has such a fear of the *crimen laesae maiestatis humanae* that whenever possible he indulges in a retrospective coloration of the facts in order to cover up the feeling of having suffered a moral defeat. He prides himself on what he believes to be his self-control and the omnipotence of his will, and despises the man who lets himself be outwitted by mere nature.

If, on the other hand, the inner authority is conceived as the "will of God" (which implies that "natural forces" are divine forces), our self-esteem is benefited because the decision then appears to be an act of obedience and the result a divine intention. This way of looking at it can, with some show of justice, be accused not only of being very convenient but of cloaking moral laxity in the mantle of virtue. The accusation, however, is justified only when one is in fact *knowingly* hiding one's own egoistic opinion behind a hypocritical façade of words. But this is by no means the rule, for in most cases instinctive tendencies assert themselves for or against one's subjective interests no matter whether an outside authority approves or not. The inner authority does not need to be consulted first, as it is present at the outset in the intensity of the tendencies struggling for decision. In this struggle the individual is never a spectator only; he takes part in it more or less "voluntarily" and tries to throw the weight of his feeling of moral freedom onto the scales. Nevertheless, it remains a matter of doubt how much his seemingly free decision has a causal, and possibly unconscious, motivation. This may be quite as much an "act of God" as any natural cataclysm. The problem seems to me unanswerable, because we do not know where the roots of the feeling of moral freedom lie and yet they exist no less surely than the instincts, which are felt as compelling forces.

All in all, it is not only more advantageous but more "correct" psychologically to explain as the "will of God" the natural forces that appear in us as impulses. In this way we find ourselves living in harmony with the *habitus* of our ancestral psychic life; that is, we function as man has functioned at all times and in all places. The existence of this *habitus* proves its viability, for, if it were not viable, all those who obeyed it would long since have perished of maladaptation. On the other hand, by conforming to it one has a reasonable life expectancy. When an habitual conception guarantees as much as this there is not only no ground for declaring it incorrect but, on the contrary, every reason to take it as "true" or "correct" in the psychological sense. Psychological truths are not metaphysical insights; they are habitual modes of thinking, feeling and behaving which experience has proved appropriate and useful.

So when I say that the impulses which we find in ourselves should be understood as the "will of God", I wish to emphasize that they ought not to be regarded as an arbitrary wishing and willing, but as absolutes which one must learn how to handle correctly. The will can control them only in part. It may be able to suppress them, but it cannot alter their nature, and what is suppressed comes up again in another place in altered form, but this time loaded with a resentment that makes the otherwise harmless natural impulse our enemy. I should also like the term "God" in the phrase "the will of God" to be understood not so much in the Christian sense as in the sense intended by Diotima, when she said: "Eros, dear Socrates, is a mighty daemon." The Greek words *daimon* and *daimonion* express a determining power which comes upon man from outside, like providence or fate, though the ethical decision is left to man. He must know, however, what he is deciding about and what he is doing. Then, if he obeys, he is following not just his own opinion, and if he rejects, he is destroying not just his own invention.

The purely biological or scientific standpoint falls short in psychology because it is, in the main, intellectual only. That this should be so is not a disadvantage, since the methods of natural science have proved of great heuristic value in psychological research. But the psychic phenomenon cannot be grasped in its totality by the intellect, for it consists not only of *meaning* but of *value,* and this depends on the intensity of the accompanying feeling-tones. Hence at least the two "rational" functions[3] are needed in order to map out anything like a complete diagram of a given psychic content.

If, therefore, in dealing with psychic contents one makes allowance not only for intellectual judgments but for value judgments as well, not only is the result a more complete picture of the content in question, but also one gets a better idea of the particular position it holds in the hierarchy of psychic contents in general. The feeling value is a very important criterion which psychology cannot do without, because it determines in large measure the role which the content will play in the psychic economy. That is to say, the affective value gives the measure of the intensity of an idea, and the intensity in its turn expresses that idea's energic tension, its effective potential. The shadow, for instance, usually has a decidedly negative feeling value, while the anima, like the animus, has more of a positive one. Whereas the shadow is accompanied by more or less definite and describable feeling tones, the anima and animus exhibit feeling qualities that are harder to define. Mostly they are felt to be fascinating or numinous. Often they are surrounded by an atmosphere of sensitivity, touchy reserve, secretiveness, painful intimacy, and even absoluteness. The relative autonomy of the anima and animus

[3] See definitions 36 and 44 in Jung, *Psychological Types* (London: Routledge and Kegan Paul, 1923, 1946).

figures expresses itself in these qualities. In order of affective rank they stand to the shadow very much as the shadow stands in relation to ego consciousness. The main affective emphasis seems to lie on the latter; at any rate it is able, by means of a considerable expenditure of energy, to repress the shadow, at least temporarily. But if for any reason the unconscious gains the upper hand, then the valency of the shadow and of the other figures increases proportionately, so that the scale of values is reversed. What lay furthest away from waking consciousness and seemed unconscious, assumes, as it were, a threatening shape, and the affective value increases the higher up the scale you go: ego consciousness, shadow, anima, self. This reversal of the conscious waking state occurs regularly during the transition from waking to sleeping, and what then emerge most vividly are the very things that were unconscious by day. Every *abaissement du niveau mental* brings about a relative reversal of values.

I am speaking here of the *subjective* feeling tone, which is subject to the more or less periodic changes described above. But there are also *objective* values which are founded on a *consensus omnium*—moral, aesthetic, and religious values, for instance—and these are universally recognized ideals or feeling-toned collective ideas (Lévy-Bruhl's *représentations collectives*).[4] The subjective feeling-tones or "value quanta" are easily recognized by the kind and number of constellations, or symptoms of disturbance, they produce. Collective ideals often have no subjective feeling-tone, but nevertheless retain their feeling-value. This value, therefore, cannot be demonstrated by subjective symptoms, though it may be by the attributes attaching to these collective ideas and by their characteristic symbolism, quite apart from their suggestive effect.

The problem has a practical aspect, since it may easily happen that a collective idea, though significant in itself, is—because of its lack of subjective feeling-tone—represented in a dream only by a subordinate attribute, as when a god is rep-

[4] Lévy-Bruhl, *Les Fonctions Mentales dans les Sociétés Inférieures* (Paris, 1910).

resented by his theriomorphic[5] attribute, etc. Conversely, the idea may appear in consciousness lacking the affective emphasis that properly belongs to it, and must then be transposed back into its archetypal context—a task that is usually discharged by poets and prophets.

The first case we mentioned, where the collective idea is represented in a dream by a lowly aspect of itself, is certainly the more frequent: the "goddess" appears as a black cat, and the Deity as the *lapis exilis* (stone of no worth). Interpretation then demands a knowledge of certain things which have less to do with zoology and mineralogy than with the existence of an historical *consensus omnium* in regard to the object in question. These "mythological" aspects are always present, even though in a given case they may be unconscious. If for instance one doesn't happen to recall, when considering whether to paint the garden gate green or white, that green is the color of life and hope, the symbolic aspect of "green" is nevertheless present as an unconscious *sous-entendu*. So we find something which has the highest significance for the life of the unconscious standing lowest on the scale of conscious values, and vice versa. The figure of the shadow already belongs to the realm of bodiless phantoms—not to speak of anima and animus, which do not seem to appear at all except as projections upon our fellow human beings. As for the self, it is completely outside the personal sphere, and appears, if at all, only as a religious mythologem, and its symbols range from the highest to the lowest. Anyone who identifies with the daylight half of his psychic life will therefore declare the dreams of the night to be null and void, notwithstanding that the night is as long as the day and that all consciousness is manifestly founded on unconsciousness, is rooted in it, and every night is extinguished in it. What is more, psychopathology knows with tolerable certainty what the unconscious can do to the conscious, and for this reason devotes to the unconscious an attention that often seems incomprehensible to the layman.

This knowledge is an essential prerequisite for any integra-

[5] In animal shape.—Ed.

tion—that is to say, a content can only be integrated when its double aspect has become conscious and when it is grasped not merely intellectually but understood according to its feeling value. Intellect and feeling, however, are difficult to put into one harness—they conflict with one another by definition. Whoever identifies with an intellectual standpoint will occasionally find his feeling confronting him like an enemy in the guise of the anima; conversely, an intellectual animus will make violent attacks on the feeling standpoint. Therefore, if one wants to bring off the trick not only intellectually but realize the feeling value as well, one must for better or worse come to grips with the anima-animus problem in order to open the way for a higher union, a *coniunctio oppositorum*. This is an indispensable prerequisite for wholeness.

Although "wholeness" seems at first sight to be nothing but an abstract idea (like anima and animus), it is nevertheless empirical in so far as it is anticipated by the psyche in the form of spontaneous or autonomous symbols. These are the quaternity or *mandāla* symbols, which occur not only in the dreams of moderns who have never heard of them, but are widely disseminated in the historical records of many peoples and many epochs. Their significance as *symbols of unity and totality* is amply confirmed by history as well as by empirical psychology. What at first looks like an abstract idea stands in reality for something that exists and can be experienced, that demonstrates its a priori presence spontaneously. Wholeness is thus an objective factor that confronts the subject independently of him, like anima or animus; and just as the latter have a higher position in the hierarchy than the shadow, so wholeness lays claim to a position and a value superior to those of the syzygy. The syzygy seems to be at least an essential part of it, or like the two halves of the totality represented by the royal brother-sister pair, and hence the tension of opposites from which the divine child[6] is born as the symbol of unity.

Unity and totality stand at the highest point on the scale of objective values because their symbols can no longer be dis-

[6] See "The Psychology of the Child Archetype" in this volume. —Ed.

tinguished from the *imago Dei*. Hence all statements about the God-image apply also to the empirical symbols of totality. Experience shows that individual *mandālas* are symbols of *order*, and that they occur in patients chiefly during times of psychic disorientation or reorientation. As magic circles they bind and subdue the lawless powers belonging to the world of darkness, and depict or create an order that transforms the chaos into a cosmos.[7] To the conscious mind the *mandāla* appears at first as an unimpressive point or dot,[8] and a great deal of hard and painstaking work as well as the integration of many projections are generally required before the full range of the symbol can be anything like completely understood. If this insight were purely intellectual it could be achieved without much difficulty, for the all-embracing pronouncements about the God within us and above us, about Christ and the *corpus mysticum*, the personal and suprapersonal *atman*, etc., are all formulations that can easily be mastered by the philosophic intellect. This is the common source of the illusion that one is then in possession of the thing itself. But actually one has acquired nothing more than its name, despite the age-old prejudice that the name magically represents the thing, and that it is sufficient to pronounce the name in order to posit the thing's existence. In the course of the millennia the reasoning mind has been given every opportunity to see through the futility of this conceit, though that has done nothing to prevent the intellectual mastery of a thing from being accepted at its face value. It is precisely our experiences in psychology which demonstrate as plainly as could be wished that the intellectual "grasp" of a psychological fact produces no more than a concept of it, and that a concept is no more than a name, a *flatus vocis*. These intellectual counters can be bandied about easily enough. They pass lightly from hand to hand, for they have no weight or substance. They sound full but are hollow; and though purporting to designate

[7] *Psychology and Alchemy* (Coll. Works, Vol. 12, Part II. Ch. 3).—Ed.

[8] See Prof. Jung's Preface and Editor's Introduction to this volume.

a heavy task and obligation, they commit us to nothing. The intellect is undeniably useful in its own field, but is a great cheat and illusionist outside of it whenever it tries to manipulate values.

It would seem that one can pursue any science with the intellect alone except psychology, whose subject—the psyche—has more than the two aspects mediated by sense perception and thinking. The function of value—feeling—is an integral part of our conscious orientation and ought not to be missing in a psychological judgment of any scope; otherwise the model we are trying to build of the real process will be incomplete. Every psychic process has a value quality attached to it, namely, its feeling-tone. This indicates the degree to which the subject is *affected* by the process, or how much it means to him (in so far as the process reaches consciousness at all). It is through the "affect" that the subject becomes involved and so comes to feel the whole weight of reality. The difference amounts roughly to that between a severe illness which one reads about in a textbook and the real illness which one has. In psychology one possesses nothing unless one has experienced it in reality. Hence a purely intellectual insight is not enough, because one knows only the words and not the substance of the thing from inside.

There are far more people who are afraid of the unconscious than one would expect. They are even afraid of their own shadow. And when it comes to the anima and animus, this fear turns to panic. For the syzygy does indeed represent the psychic contents that irrupt into consciousness in a psychosis (most clearly of all in the paranoid forms of schizophrenia).[9] The overcoming of this fear is often a moral achievement of unusual magnitude, and yet it is not the only condition that must be fulfilled on the way to a real experience of the self.

The shadow, the syzygy, and the self are psychic factors of which an adequate picture can be formed only on the basis

[9] A classic case is the one published by Nelken, *Jahrbuch für Psychoanalytische und Psychopathologische Forschungen*, 1912, IV. Another is Schreber's *Memoirs of My Nervous Illness* (London, 1955).

of a fairly thorough experience of them. Just as these concepts arose out of an experience of reality, so they can be elucidated only by further experience. Philosophical criticism will find everything to object to in them unless it begins by recognizing that they are concerned with *facts*, and that the "concept" is simply an abbreviated description or definition of these facts. Such criticism has as little effect on the object as zoological criticism on a duckbill platypus. It is not the concept that matters; the concept is only a word, a counter, and it has meaning and use only because it stands for a certain sum of experience. Unfortunately I cannot pass on this experience to my public. I have tried in a number of publications, with the help of case material, to present the nature of these experiences and also the method of obtaining them. Wherever my methods were really applied the facts I give have been confirmed. One could see the moons of Jupiter even in Galileo's day if one took the trouble to use his telescope.

Outside the narrower field of professional psychology these figures meet with understanding from all who have any knowledge of comparative mythology. They have no difficulty in recognizing the shadow as the adverse representative of the dark chthonic world, a figure whose characteristics are universal. The syzygy is immediately comprehensible as the psychic prototype of all divine couples. Finally the self, on account of its empirical peculiarities, proves to be the *eidos* behind the supreme ideas of unity and totality that are inherent in all monotheistic and monistic systems.

I regard these parallels as important because it is possible, through them, to relate so-called *metaphysical* concepts, which have lost their root connection with natural experience, to living, universal psychic processes, so that they can recover their true and original meaning. In this way the connection is reestablished between the ego and projected contents now formulated as "metaphysical" ideas. Unfortunately, as already said, the fact that metaphysical ideas exist and are believed in does nothing to prove the actual existence of their content or of the object they refer to, although the coincidence of idea and reality in the form of a special psychic state, a state of grace, should not be deemed impossible, even if the subject cannot bring it about by an act of will. Once metaphysical ideas have lost their capacity to recall and evoke the original experience, they have not only become useless but prove to be actual impediments on the road to wider development. One clings to possessions that have once meant wealth; and the more ineffective, incomprehensible, and lifeless they become the more obstinately people cling to them. (Naturally it is only sterile ideas that they cling to; living ideas have content and riches enough, so there is no need to cling to them.) Thus in the course of time the meaningful turns into the meaningless. This is unfortunately the fate of metaphysical ideas.

Today it is a real problem what on earth such ideas can mean. The world—so far as it has not completely turned its back on tradition—has long ago stopped wanting to hear a "message"; it would rather be told what the message means. The words that resound from the pulpit are incomprehensible and cry for an explanation. How has the death of Christ brought us redemption when no one feels redeemed? In what way is Jesus a God-man and what is such a being? What is the Trinity about, and the parthenogenesis, the eating of the body and the drinking of the blood, and all the rest of it? How hopeless is a relationship between the world of such concepts and the everyday world, whose material reality is the concern of natural science on the widest possible scale? At least sixteen hours out of twenty-four we live exclusively in this everyday world, and the remaining eight we spend preferably in an unconscious condition. Where and when does anything take place to remind us even remotely of phenomena like angels, miraculous feedings, benedictions, the resurrection of the dead, etc.? It was therefore something of a discovery to find that during the unconscious state of sleep intervals occur, called "dreams", which occasionally contain scenes having a not inconsiderable resemblance to the motifs of mythology. For myths are miracle tales and treat of all those things which, very often, are also objects of belief.

In the everyday world of consciousness such things hardly exist; that is to say, until 1933 only lunatics would have been found in possession of living fragments of mythology. After this date the world of heroes and monsters spread like a devastating fire over whole nations, proving that the strange world of myth had suffered no loss of vitality during the centuries of reason and enlightenment. If metaphysical ideas no longer have such a fascinating effect as before, this is certainly not due to any lack of primitivity in the European psyche, but simply and solely to the fact that the erstwhile symbols no longer express what is now welling up from the unconscious as the end result of the development of Christian consciousness through the centuries. This end result is a true *antimimon pneuma,* a false spirit of arrogance, hysteria, woolly-mindedness, criminal amorality, and doctrinaire fanaticism, a purveyor of shoddy spiritual goods, spurious art, philosophical stutterings, and Utopian humbug, fit only to be fed wholesale to the mass man of today. That is what the post-Christian spirit looks like.

V. *Christ, a Symbol of the Self*

The de-Christianization of our world, the Luciferian development of science and technology, and the frightful material and moral destruction left behind by the Second World War have been compared more than once with the *eschatological* events foretold in the New Testament. These, as we know, are concerned with the coming of the Antichrist: "This is Antichrist, who denieth the Father and the Son."[1] The Apocalypse is full of expectations of terrible things that will take place at the end of time, before the marriage of the Lamb. This shows plainly that the *anima christiana* has a sure knowledge not only of the existence of an adversary but also of his future usurpation of power.

Why—my reader will ask—do I discourse here upon Christ and his adversary, the Antichrist? Our discourse necessarily brings us to Christ, because he is the still living myth of our

[1] Epistles of St. John I: 2:22 (D.V.).

culture. He is our culture hero, who, regardless of his historical existence, embodies the myth of the divine Primordial Man, the mystic Adam. It is he who occupies the center of the Christian *mandāla*, who is the Lord of the Tetramorph, i.e., the four symbols of the evangelists, which are like the four columns of his throne. He is in us and we in him. His kingdom is the pearl of great price, the treasure buried in the field, the grain of mustard seed which will become a great tree, and the heavenly city.[2] As Christ is in us, so also is his heavenly kingdom.

These few familiar references should be sufficient to make the psychological position of the Christ symbol quite clear. *Christ exemplifies the archetype of the self.*[3] He represents a totality of a divine or heavenly kind, a glorified man, a son of God *sine macula peccati*, unspotted by sin. As Adam *secundus* he corresponds to the first Adam before the Fall, when the latter was still a pure image of God, of which Tertullian says: "And this therefore is to be considered as the image of God in man, that the human spirit has the same motions and senses as God has, though not in the same way as God has them." Origen is very much more explicit: The *imago Dei* imprinted on the soul, not on the body, is an image of an image, "for my soul is not directly the image of God, but is made after the likeness of the former image. Christ, on the other hand, is the true image of God, after whose likeness our inner man is made, invisible, incorporeal, incorrupt, and immortal. The God-image in us reveals itself through *"prudentia, iustitia, moderatio, virtus, sapientia et disciplina."*

St. Augustine distinguishes between the God-image which is Christ and the image which is implanted in man as a means or possibility of becoming like God. The God-image is not in the corporeal man, but in the *anima rationalis*, the possession of which distinguishes man from animals. "The God-image is

[2] For "city" cf. *Psychology and Alchemy* (Coll. Works, Vol. 12), pp. 104ff.

[3] Cf. my observations on Christ as archetype in "A Psychological Approach to the Dogma of the Trinity," in *Psychology and Religion* (Coll. Works, Vol. 11).

within, not in the body. . . . Where the understanding is, where the mind is, where the power of investigating truth is, there God has his image." Therefore we should remind ourselves, says Augustine, that we are fashioned after the image of God nowhere save in the understanding. "But where man knows himself to be made after the image of God, there he knows there is something more in him than is given to the beasts." From this it is clear that the God-image is, so to speak, identical with the *anima rationalis*. The latter is the higher spiritual man, the *homo coelestis* of St. Paul.[4] Like Adam before the Fall, Christ is an embodiment of the God-image, whose totality is specially emphasized by St. Augustine. "The Word," he says, "took on complete manhood, as it were in its fullness: the soul and body of a man. And if you would have me put it more exactly—since even a beast of the field has a "soul" and a body—when I say a human soul and human flesh, I mean he took upon him a complete human soul."

The God-image in man was not destroyed by the Fall but was only damaged and corrupted ("deformed"), and can be restored through God's grace. The scope of the integration is suggested by the *descensus ad inferos*, the descent of Christ's soul to hell, its work of redemption embracing even the dead. The psychological equivalent of this is the integration of the collective unconscious which forms an essential part of the individuation process. St. Augustine says: "Therefore our end must be our perfection, but our perfection is Christ," since he is the perfect God-image. For this reason he is also called "King". His bride (*sponsa*) is the human soul, which "in an inwardly hidden spiritual mystery is joined to the Word, that two may be one in flesh," to correspond with the mystic marriage of Christ and the Church. Apart from the continued existence of this *hieros gamos* in the dogma and rites of the Church, the symbolism developed in the course of the Middle Ages into the alchemical conjunction of opposites, or "chymical wedding", thus giving rise on the one hand to the concept of

[4] I Cor. 15:47.

the *lapis philosophorum,* signifying totality, and on the other hand to the concept of chemical combination.

The God-image in man that was damaged by the first sin can be "reformed"[5] with the help of God, in accordance with Rom. 12:2: "And be not conformed to this world, but be transformed by the renewal of your mind, that you may prove what is . . . the will of God" (R.S.V.). The totality images which the unconscious produces in the course of an individuation process are similar "reformations" of an a priori archetype (the *mandāla*).[6] As I have already emphasized, the spontaneous symbols of the self, or of wholeness, cannot in practice be distinguished from a God-image. Despite the word *metamorphousthe* ("be transformed") in the Greek text of the above quotation, the "renewal" (*anakainosis, reformatio*) of the mind is not meant as an actual alteration of consciousness, but rather as the restoration of an original condition, an apocatastasis. This is in exact agreement with the empirical findings of psychology, that there is an ever-present archetype of wholeness[7] which may easily disappear from the purview of consciousness or may never be perceived at all until a consciousness illuminated by conversion recognizes it in the figure of Christ. As a result of this *anamnesis* the original state of oneness with the God-image is restored. It brings about an integration, a bridging of the split in the personality caused by the instincts striving apart in different and mutually contradictory directions. The only time the split does not occur is when a person is still as legitimately unconscious of his instinctual life as an animal. But it proves harmful and impossible to endure when an artificial unconsciousness—a repression—no longer reflects the life of the instincts.

There can be no doubt that the original Christian conception of the *imago Dei* embodied in Christ meant an all-embracing totality that even includes the animal side of man. Nevertheless the Christ symbol lacks wholeness in the modern

[5] Augustine, *De Trinitate,* XIV, 22.
[6] Cf. "Concerning Mandāla Symbolism" in *Archetypes and the Collective Unconscious* (Coll. Works, Vol. 9, Part I).
[7] *Psychology and Alchemy* (Coll. Works, Vol. 12), pp. 207ff.

psychological sense, since it does not include the dark side of things but specifically excludes it in the form of a Luciferian opponent. Although the exclusion of the power of evil was something the Christian consciousness was well aware of, all it lost in effect was an insubstantial shadow, for, through the doctrine of the *privatio boni* first propounded by Origen, evil was characterized as a mere diminution of good and thus deprived of substance. According to the teachings of the Church, evil is simply "the accidental lack of perfection". This assumption resulted in the proposition *omne bonum a Deo, omne malum ab homine*. Another logical consequence was the subsequent elimination of the devil in certain Protestant sects.

Thanks to the doctrine of the *privatio boni,* wholeness seemed guaranteed in the figure of Christ. One must, however, take evil rather more substantially when one meets it on the plane of empirical psychology. There it is simply the opposite of good. In the ancient world the Gnostics, whose arguments were very much influenced by psychic experience, tackled the problem of evil on a broader basis than the Church Fathers. For instance, one of the things they taught was that Christ "cast off his shadow from himself". If we give this view the weight it deserves, we can easily recognize the cut-off counterpart in the figure of Antichrist. The Antichrist develops in legend as a perverse imitator of Christ's life. He is a true *antimimon pneuma*, an imitating spirit of evil who follows in Christ's footsteps like a shadow following the body. This complementing of the bright but one-sided figure of the Redeemer —we even find traces of it in the New Testament—must be of especial significance. And indeed, considerable attention was paid to it quite early.

If we see the traditional figure of Christ as a parallel to the psychic manifestation of the self, then the Antichrist would correspond to the shadow of the self, namely, the dark half of the human totality, which ought not to be judged too optimistically. So far as we can judge from experience, light and shadow are so evenly distributed in man's nature that his psychic totality appears, to say the least of it, in a somewhat murky light. The psychological concept of the self, in part derived from our knowledge of the whole man, but for the rest depicting itself spontaneously in the products of the unconscious as an archetypal quaternity bound together by inner antinomies, cannot omit the shadow that belongs to the light figure, for without it this figure lacks body and humanity. In the empirical self, light and shadow form a paradoxical unity. In the Christian concept, on the other hand, the archetype is hopelessly split into two irreconcilable halves, leading ultimately to a metaphysical dualism—the final separation of the kingdom of heaven from the fiery world of the damned.

For anyone who has a positive attitude towards Christianity the problem of the Antichrist is a hard nut to crack. It is nothing less than the counterstroke of the devil, provoked by God's Incarnation; for the devil attains his true stature as the adversary of Christ, and hence of God, only after the rise of Christianity, while as late as the Book of Job he was still one of God's sons and on familiar terms with Yahweh. Psychologically the case is clear, since the dogmatic figure of Christ is so sublime and spotless that everything else turns dark beside it. It is, in fact, so one-sidedly perfect that it demands a psychic complement to restore the balance. This inevitable opposition led very early to the doctrine of the two sons of God, of whom the elder was called Satanaël. The coming of the Antichrist is not just a prophetic prediction—it is an inexorable psychological law whose existence, though unknown to the author of the Johannine Epistles, brought him a sure knowledge of the impending enantiodromia. Consequently he wrote as if he were conscious of the inner necessity for this transformation, though we may be sure that the idea seemed to him like a divine revelation. In reality every intensified differentiation of the Christ-image brings about a corresponding accentuation of its unconscious complement, thereby increasing the tension between above and below.

In making these statements we are keeping entirely within the sphere of Christian psychology and symbolism. A factor that no one has reckoned with, however, is the fatality inherent in the Christian disposition itself which leads inevitably to a reversal of its spirit—not through the obscure workings of chance but in accordance with psychological law. The ideal of spirituality striving for the heights was doomed to clash with the materialistic earth-bound passion to conquer matter and master the world. This change became visible at the time of the Renaissance. The word means "rebirth", and it referred to the renewal of the antique spirit. We know today that this spirit was chiefly a mask; it was not the spirit of antiquity that was reborn but the spirit of medieval Christianity, which underwent strange pagan transformations, exchanging the heavenly goal for an earthly one, and the vertical of the Gothic style for the horizontal of world exploration and the investigation of nature (voyages of discovery, etc.). The subsequent developments that led to the Enlightenment and the French Revolution have produced a world-wide situation today which can only be called "Antichristian" in a sense that confirms the early Christian anticipation of the "end of time." It is as if, with the coming of Christ, opposites that were latent till then had become manifest, or as if a pendulum had swung violently to one side and were now carrying out the complementary movement in the opposite direction. No tree, it is said, can grow to heaven unless its roots reach down to hell. The double meaning of this movement lies in the nature of the pendulum. Christ is without spot, but right at the beginning of his career there occurs the encounter with Satan, the Adversary, who represents the counterpole of that tremendous tension in the world psyche which Christ's advent signified. He is the *mysterium iniquitatis* that accompanies the *sol iustitiae* as inseparably as the shadow belongs to the light, in exactly the same way, so the Ebionites[8] and Euchites[9] thought, that one brother cleaves to the other. Both strive for a kingdom: one for the kingdom of heaven, the other for the *principatus huius mundi*. We hear of a reign of a "thousand years" and of a "coming of the Antichrist" just as if a partition of worlds and

[8] Jewish Christians who formed a Gnostic-syncretistic party.
[9] A Gnostic sect mentioned in Epiphanius, *Panarium adversus octoginta Haereses*, LXXX, 1–3, and in Michael Psellus, *De Daemonibus* (Iamblichus de Mysteriis Aegyptiorum). Cf. Marsilius Ficinus, *Auctores Platonici* (Venice, 1497).

epochs had taken place between two royal brothers. The meeting with Satan was therefore more than mere chance; it was a link in the chain.

Just as we have to remember the gods of antiquity in order to appreciate the psychological value of the anima-animus archetype, so Christ is our nearest analogy of the self and its meaning. It is naturally not a question of a collective value artificially manufactured or arbitrarily awarded, but of one that is effective and present per se, and that makes its effectiveness felt whether the subject is conscious of it or not. Yet, although the attributes of Christ (consubstantiality with the Father, co-eternity, filiation, parthenogenesis, crucifixion, Lamb sacrificed between opposites, One divided into Many, etc.) undoubtedly mark him out as an embodiment of the self, looked at from the psychological angle he corresponds to only one half of the archetype. The other half appears in the Antichrist. The latter is equally a manifestation of the self, representing however its dark aspect. Both are Christian symbols, and they have the same meaning as the image of the Saviour crucified between two thieves. This great symbol tells us that the progressive development and differentiation of consciousness leads to an ever more menacing awareness of the conflict and involves nothing less than a crucifixion of the ego, its agonizing suspension between irreconcilable opposites.[10] Naturally there can be no question of a total extinction of the ego, for then the focus of consciousness would be destroyed, and the result would be complete unconsciousness. The relative abolition of the ego affects only those supreme and ultimate decisions which confront us in situations where there are insoluble conflicts of duty. This means, in other words, that in such cases the ego is a suffering bystander who decides nothing but must submit to a decision and surrender unconditionally. The "genius" of man, the higher and more spacious part

---

[10] ("But it is fitting that one of these two extremes, and that the best, should be called the Son of God because of his excellence, and the other, *diametrically opposed* to him, the son of the evil demon, of Satan and the devil.") Origen, *Contra Celsum*, VI, 45 (P. G. Migne, Vol. 11, col. 1367).

of him whose extent no one knows, has the final word. It is therefore well to examine carefully the psychological aspects of the individuation process in the light of Christian tradition, which can describe it for us with an exactness and impressiveness far surpassing our feeble attempts, even though the Christian image of the self—Christ—lacks the shadow that properly belongs to it.

The reason for this, as already indicated, is the doctrine of the Summum Bonum. Irenaeus says very rightly, in refuting the Gnostics, that exception must be taken to the "light of their Father" because it "could not illuminate and fill even those things which were within it,"[11] namely, the shadow and the void. It seemed to him scandalous and reprehensible to suppose that within the pleroma of light there could be a "dark and formless void." For the Christian neither God nor Christ could be a paradox; they had to have a single meaning, and this holds true to the present day. No one knew, and apparently (with a few honorable exceptions) no one knows even now, that the hybris of the speculative intellect had already emboldened the ancients to propound a philosophical definition of God that more or less obliged him to be the Summum Bonum. A Protestant theologian has even had the audacity to assert that "God *can* only be good"! Yahweh could certainly have taught him a thing or two in this respect, if he himself is unable to see his intellectual trespass against God's freedom and omnipotence. This forcible usurpation of the Summum Bonum naturally has its reasons, the origins of which lie far back in the past (though I cannot enter into this here). Nevertheless, it is the effective source of the concept of the *privatio boni* which nullifies the reality of evil and which can be found as early as Basil the Great (330–379) and Dionysius the Areopagite (second half of the fourth century), and is fully developed in Augustine.

The earliest authority of all for the later axiom *Omne bonum a Deo, omne malum ab homine* is Tatian (second century), who says: "Nothing evil was created by God; we ourselves

[11] *Adv. Haer.*, II, 4, 3.

have produced all wickedness."[12] Basil says: "You must not look upon God as the author of the existence of evil, nor consider that evil has any subsistence in itself (*idian hypostasin tou kakou einai*). For evil does not subsist as a living being does, nor can we set before our eyes any substantial essence (*usian enhypostaton*) thereof. For evil is the privation (*steresis*) of good. . . . And thus evil does not inhere in its own substance (*en idia hyparxei*), but arises from the mutilation (*peromasin*) of the soul. Neither is it uncreated, as the wicked say who set up evil for the equal of good . . . nor is it created. For if all things are of God, how can evil arise from good?" Another passage sheds light on the logic of this statement. In the second homily of the *Hexaemeron*, Basil says: "It is equally impious to say that evil has its origin from God, because the contrary cannot proceed from the contrary. Life does not engender death, darkness is not the origin of light, sickness is not the maker of health. . . . Now if evil is neither uncreated nor created by God, whence comes its nature? That evil exists no one living in the world will deny. What shall we say, then? That evil is not a living and animated entity, but a condition (*diathesis*) of the soul opposed to virtue, proceeding from light-minded persons on account of their falling away from good. . . . Each of us should acknowledge that he is the first author of the wickedness in him."[13]

The perfectly natural fact that when you say "high" you immediately postulate "low" is here twisted into a causal relationship and reduced to absurdity, since it is sufficiently obvious that darkness produces no light and light produces no darkness. The idea of good and evil, however, is the premise for any moral judgment. They are a logically equivalent pair of opposites and, as such, the sine qua non of all acts of cognition. From the empirical standpoint we cannot say more than this. And from this standpoint we would have to assert that

[12] *Oratio ad Graecos*, P. G. Migne, *Patr. Graec.* I. IV, col. 829.
[13] *De Spiritu Sancto* (P. G. Migne, Vol. 29, col. 37). Cf. *Nine Homilies of the Hexaemeron* (Select Library of Nicene and Post-Nicene Fathers of the Christian Church, 2nd Series, Vol. VIII, 1895, pp. 61f.), trans. Blomfield Jackson.

good and evil, being coexistent halves of a moral judgment, do not derive from one another but are always there together. Evil, like good, belongs to the category of human values, and we are the authors of moral value judgments, but only to a limited degree are we authors of the facts submitted to our moral judgment. These facts are called by one person good and by another evil. Only in capital cases is there anything like a consensus generalis. If we hold with Basil that man is the author of evil, we are saying in the same breath that he is also the author of good. But man is first and foremost the author merely of judgments; in relation to the facts judged his responsibility is not so easy to determine. In order to do this, we would have to give a clear definition of the extent of his free will. The psychiatrist knows what a desperately difficult task this is.

For these reasons the psychologist shrinks from metaphysical assertions but must criticize the admittedly human foundations of the *privatio boni*. When therefore Basil asserts on the one hand that evil has no substance of its own but arises from a "mutilation of the soul," and if on the other hand he is convinced that evil really exists, then the relative reality of evil is grounded on a real "mutilation" of the soul which must have an equally real cause. If the soul was originally created good, then it has really been corrupted and by something that is real, even if this is nothing more than carelessness, indifference, and frivolity, which are the meaning of the word *rhathymia*. When something—I must stress this with all possible emphasis—is traced back to a psychic condition or fact, it is very definitely not reduced to nothing and thereby nullified, but is shifted on to the plane of *psychic reality*, which is very much easier to establish empirically than, say, the reality of the devil in dogma, who, according to the authentic sources, was not invented by man at all but existed long before he did. If the devil fell away from God of his own free will, this proves firstly that evil was in the world before man, and therefore that man cannot be the sole author of it, and secondly that the devil already had a "mutilated" soul for which we must hold a real cause responsible. The basic flaw in Basil's argument is the *petitio principii* that lands him in insoluble contradictions: it is laid down from the start that the independent existence of evil must be denied even in face of the eternity of the devil as asserted by dogma. The historical reason for this was the threat presented by Manichaean dualism. This is especially clear in the treatise of Titus of Bostra (*circa* 370), entitled *Adversus Manichaeos,* where he states in refutation of the Manichaeans that, so far as substance is concerned, there is no such thing as evil.

John Chrysostom (*circa* 344–407) uses, instead of steresis (*privatio*), the expression *ektrope tou kalou* (deviation, or turning away, from good). He says: "Evil is nothing other than a turning away from good, and therefore evil is secondary in relation to good."

Dionysius the Areopagite gives a detailed explanation of evil in the fourth chapter of *De Divinis Nominibus*. Evil, he says, cannot come from good, because if it came from good it would not be evil. But since everything that exists comes from good, everything is in some way good: "evil does not exist at all. . . . Evil in its nature is neither a thing nor does it bring anything forth. . . . Evil does not exist at all and is neither good nor productive of good. . . . All things which are, by the very fact that they are, are good and come from good; but in so far as they are deprived of good, they are neither good nor do they exist. . . . That which has no existence is not altogether evil, for the absolutely nonexistent will be nothing, unless it be thought of as subsisting in the good superessentially. Good, then, as absolutely existing and as absolutely nonexisting, will stand in the foremost and highest place, while evil is neither in that which exists nor in that which does not exist."[14]

These quotations show with what emphasis the reality of evil was denied by the Church Fathers. As already mentioned, this hangs together with the Church's attitude to Manichaean dualism, as can plainly be seen in St. Augustine. In his polemic against the Manichaeans and Marcionites he makes the fol-

[14] Cf. the *Works of Dionysius the Areopagite,* trans. John Parker (London, 1897–99), Vol. I, pp. 53ff.

lowing declaration: "For this reason all things are good, since some things are better than others and the goodness of the less good adds to the glory of the better.... Those things we call evil, then, are defects in good things, and quite incapable of existing in their own right outside good things.... But those very defects testify to the natural goodness of things. For what is evil by reason of a defect must obviously be good of its own nature. For a defect is something contrary to nature, something which damages the nature of a thing—and it can do so only by diminishing that thing's goodness. *Evil therefore is nothing but the privation of good.* And thus it can have no existence anywhere except in some good thing.... So there can be things which are good without any evil in them, such as God himself, and the higher celestial beings; but there can be no evil things without good. For if evils cause no damage to anything, they are not evils; if they do damage something, they diminish its goodness; and if they damage it still more, it is because it still has some goodness which they diminish; and if they swallow it up altogether, nothing of its nature is left to be damaged. And so there will be no evil by which it can be damaged, since there is then no nature left whose goodness any damage can diminish."[15]

These quotations clearly exemplify the standpoint of Dionysius and Augustine: evil has no substance or existence in itself, since it is merely a diminution of good, which alone has substance. Evil is a *vitium*, a bad use of things as a result of erroneous decisions of the will (blindness due to evil desire, etc.). Thomas Aquinas, the great theoretician of the Church, says with reference to the above quotation from Dionysius: "One opposite is known through the other, as darkness is known through light. Hence also what evil is must be known from the nature of good. Now we have said above that good is everything appetible; and thus, since every nature desires its own being and its own perfection, it must necessarily be said that the being and perfection of every created thing is essentially good. Hence it cannot be that evil signifies a being,

[15] *Contra adversarium legis et prophetarum*, I, 6f., P. G. Migne, Vol. 42, cols. 606–7.

or any form or nature. Therefore it must be that by the name of evil is signified the absence of good. . . .[16] Evil is not a being, whereas good is a being. . . .[17] That every agent works for an end clearly follows from the fact that every agent tends to something definite. Now that to which an agent tends definitely must needs be befitting to that agent, since the latter would not tend to it save on account of some fittingness thereto. But that which is befitting to a thing is good for it. Therefore every agent works for a good."[18]

St. Thomas himself recalls the saying of Aristotle that "the thing is the whiter, the less it is mixed with black,"[19] without mentioning, however, that the reverse proposition: "The thing is the blacker, the less it is mixed with white" not only has the same validity as the first but is also its logical equivalent. He might also have mentioned that not only darkness is known through light, but that, conversely, light is known through darkness.

As only that which works is real, so, according to St. Thomas, only good is real in the sense of "existing." His argument, however, introduces a good that is tantamount to "convenient, sufficient, appropriate, suitable." One ought therefore to translate *Omne agens agit propter bonum* as "Every agent works for the sake of what suits it." That's what the devil does too, as we all know. He too has an "appetite" and strives after perfection—not in good but in evil. Even so, one could hardly conclude from this that his striving is "essentially good."

Obviously evil can be represented as a diminution of good, but with this kind of logic one could just as well say: The temperature of the Arctic winter, which freezes our noses and ears, is relatively speaking only a little below the heat prevailing at the Equator. For the Arctic temperature seldom falls much lower than 230 degrees Centigrade above absolute zero.

---

[16] *Summa Theologica*, translated by the Fathers of the English Dominican Province, 1911–22, Vol. 2, p. 264.

[17] *Ibid.*, p. 268.

[18] ". . . Quod autem conveniens est alicui est illi bonum. Ergo omne agens agit propter bonum." *Summa Contra Gentiles*, trans. by the English Dominican Fathers, 1924–29, Vol. 3, p. 7.

[19] *Summa Theologica*, Vol. 2, p. 266, citing Aristotle's *Topic*, iii, 4.

All things on earth are "warm" in the sense that nowhere is absolute zero even approximately reached. Similarly, all things are more or less "good," and just as cold is nothing but a diminution of warmth, so evil is nothing but a diminution of good. The *privatio boni* argument remains a euphemistic *petitio principii* no matter whether evil is regarded as a lesser good or as an effect of the finiteness and limitedness of created things. The false conclusion necessarily follows from the premise "Deus=Summum Bonum," since it is unthinkable that the perfect good could ever have created evil.

Psychology does not know what good and evil are in themselves; it knows them only as judgments about relationships. "Good" is what seems suitable, acceptable, or valuable from a certain point of view; evil is its opposite. If the things we call good are "really" good, then there must be evil things that are "real" too. It is evident that psychology is concerned with a more or less subjective judgment, i.e., with a psychic antithesis that cannot be avoided in naming value relationships: "good" denotes something that is not bad, and "bad" something that is not good. There are things which from a certain point of view are extremely evil, that is to say, dangerous. There are also things in human nature which are very dangerous and which therefore seem proportionately evil to anyone standing in their line of fire. It is pointless to gloss over these evil things, because that only lulls one into a sense of false security. Human nature is capable of an infinite amount of evil, and the evil deeds are as real as the good ones so far as human experience goes and so far as the psyche judges and differentiates between them. Only unconsciousness makes no difference between good and evil. Inside the psychological realm one honestly does not know which of them predominates in the world. We hope merely that good prevails—i.e., what seems fitting to us. No one could possibly say what the general good might be. No amount of insight into the relativity and fallibility of our moral judgment can deliver us from them, and those who deem themselves beyond good and evil are usually the worst tormentors of mankind, because they are twisted with the pain and fear of their own sickness.

Today as never before it is important that human beings

should not overlook the danger of the evil lurking within them. It is unfortunately only too real, which is why psychology must insist on the reality of evil and must reject any definition that regards it as insignificant or actually nonexistent. Psychology is an empirical science and has to do with realities. As a psychologist, therefore, I have neither the inclination nor the competence to mix myself up with metaphysics. However I must start getting polemical when metaphysics encroaches on experience and interprets it in a way that is not justified empirically. My criticism of the *privatio boni* holds only so far as psychological experience goes. From the scientific point of view the *privatio boni*, as must be apparent to everyone, is founded on a *petitio principii*, where what invariably comes out at the end is what you put in at the beginning. Arguments of this kind have no power of conviction. But the fact that such arguments are not only used but are undoubtedly believed is something that cannot be disposed of so easily. It proves that there is a tendency, existing right from the start, to give priority to "good," and to do so with all the means in our power, whether suitable or unsuitable. So if Christian metaphysics clings to the *privatio boni*, it is giving expression to the tendency always to increase the good and diminish the bad. The *privatio boni* may therefore be a psychological truth. I presume to no judgment in this respect. I must only insist that in our field of experience white and black, light and dark, good and bad are equivalent opposites which always predicate one another.

This elementary fact was correctly appreciated in the so-called Clementine Homilies, a collection of Gnostic-Christian writings dating from about A.D. 150. The unknown author understands good and evil as the right and left hand of God, and views the whole of creation in terms of syzygies, or pairs of opposites.

Since psychology is not metaphysics, no metaphysical dualism can be derived from, or imputed to, its statements concerning the equivalence of opposites. It knows that equivalent opposites are necessary conditions inherent in the act of cognition, and that without them no discrimination would be possible. Even so, it is not exactly probable that anything so intrinsically bound up with the act of cognition should be at the same time a property of the object. It is far easier to suppose that it is primarily our consciousness which names and evaluates the differences between things, and perhaps even creates distinctions where no differences are discernible.

I have gone into the doctrine of the *privatio boni* at such length because it is in a sense responsible for a too optimistic conception of the evil in human nature and for a too pessimistic view of the human soul. To offset this, early Christianity, with unerring logic, balanced Christ against an Antichrist. For how can you speak of "high" if there is no "low," or "right" if there is no "left," of "good" if there is no "bad," and the one is as real as the other? Only with Christ did a devil enter the world as the real counterpart of God, and in early Jewish-Christian circles Satan, as already mentioned, was regarded as Christ's elder brother.

But there is still another reason why I must lay such critical stress on the *privatio boni*. As early as Basilius we meet with the tendency to attribute evil to the disposition (*diathesis*) of the soul, and at the same time to give it a "nonexistent" character. Since, according to this author, evil originates simply in human frivolity and therefore owes its existence to mere negligence, it exists, so to speak, only as a by-product of psychological oversight, and this is such a *quantité négligeable* that evil vanishes altogether in smoke. Frivolity as a cause of evil is certainly a factor to be taken seriously, but it is a factor that can be got rid of by a change of attitude. We *can* act differently, if we want to. Psychological causation is something so elusive and seemingly unreal that everything which is reduced to it inevitably takes on the character of futility or of a purely accidental mistake and is thereby minimized to the utmost. It is an open question how much of our modern undervaluation of the psyche stems from this prejudice. This prejudice is all the more serious in that it causes the psyche to be suspected of being the birthplace of all evil. The Church Fathers can hardly have considered what a fatal power they were ascribing to the soul. One must be positively blind not to see the colossal role that evil plays in the world. Indeed, it took the intervention of God himself to deliver humanity from the curse of evil, for without his intervention man would have been lost. If this paramount power of evil is imputed to the soul, the result can only be a negative inflation, i.e., a daemonic claim to power on the part of the unconscious which only reinforces the latter and makes it all the more formidable. This inevitable consequence is anticipated in the figure of the Antichrist and is reflected in the course of contemporary events, whose nature corresponds to the Christian aeon of the Fishes, now running to its end.

In the world of Christian ideas Christ undoubtedly represents the self.[20] As the apotheosis of individuality, the self has the attributes of uniqueness and of occurring only once in time. But since the psychological self is a transcendental concept, expressing the totality of conscious and unconscious contents, it can be described only in antinomial terms;[21] that is, the above attributes must be supplemented by their opposites if the transcendental situation is to be characterized correctly. We can do this most simply in the form of a quaternio of opposites:

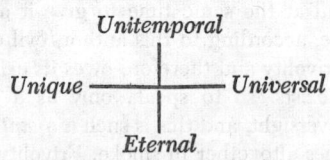

$$\begin{array}{c} \textit{Unitemporal} \\ | \\ \textit{Unique} \longrightarrow \textit{Universal} \\ | \\ \textit{Eternal} \end{array}$$

This formula expresses not only the psychological self but

[20] It has been objected that Christ cannot have been a valid symbol of the self, or was only an illusory substitute for it. I can agree with this view only if it refers strictly to the present time, when psychological criticism has become possible, but not if it pretends to judge the pre-psychological age. Christ did not merely *symbolize* wholeness, but, as a psychic phenomenon, he *was* wholeness. This is proved by the symbolism as well as by the phenomenology of the past, for which—be it noted—evil was a *privatio boni*. The idea of totality is, at any given time, as total as one is oneself. Who can guarantee that our conception of totality is not equally in need of completion? The mere *concept* of totality does not by any means posit totality. (Italics mine, Ed.)

[21] Just as the transcendental nature of light can only be expressed through the image of waves *and* particles.

also the dogmatic figure of Christ. As an historical personage Christ is unitemporal and unique; as God, universal and eternal. Likewise the self: as an individual thing it is unitemporal and unique; as an archetypal symbol it is a God-image and therefore universal and eternal.[22] Now if theology describes Christ as simply "good" and "spiritual," something "evil" and "material"—or "chthonic"—is bound to arise on the other side, to represent the Antichrist. The resultant quaternio of opposites is united on the psychological plane by the fact that the self is not deemed exclusively "good" and "spiritual"; consequently its shadow turns out to be much less black. A further result is that the opposites of "good" and "spiritual" need no longer be separated from the whole:

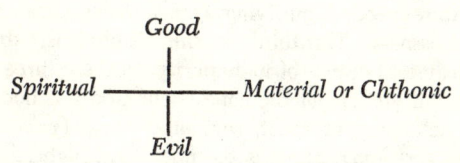

$$\begin{array}{c} Good \\ | \\ Spiritual \text{———|———} Material \text{ or } Chthonic \\ | \\ Evil \end{array}$$

This *quaternio* characterizes the psychological self. Being a totality, it must by definition include the light and dark aspects, in the same way that the self embraces both masculine and feminine and is therefore symbolized by the marriage quaternio.[23] This last is by no means a new discovery, since according to Hippolytus it was known to the Naassenes. Hence individuation is a *mysterium coniunctionis*, the self being experienced as a nuptial union of opposite halves[24] and depicted as a composite whole in *mandālas* that are drawn spontaneously by patients.

It was known, and stated, very early that the man Jesus, the son of Mary, was the *principium individuationis*. Thus Basilides is reported by Hippolytus[25] as saying: "Now Jesus

[22] See also *Psychology and Alchemy* (Coll. Works, Vol. 12) and *Two Essays on Analytical Psychology* (Coll. Works, Vol. 7).
[23] See also *The Practice of Psychotherapy* (Coll. Works, Vol. 16).
[24] See also *Psychology and Alchemy* (Coll. Works, Vol. 12) and *The Practice of Psychotherapy* (Coll. Works, Vol. 16).
[25] *Elenchos*, VII, 27, 12.

became the first sacrifice in the separation of categories (*phylokrinesis*), and the Passion came to pass for no other reason than the separation of composite things. For in this manner, he says, the sonship that had been left behind in a formless state (*amorphia*) . . . needed separating into its components (*phylokrinethenai*), in the same way that Jesus was separated." According to the rather complicated teachings of Basilides, the "nonexistent" God begot a threefold sonship (*hyotes*). The first "son," whose nature was the finest and most subtle, remained up above with the Father. The second son, having a grosser (*pachymerestera*) nature, descended a bit lower, but received "some such wing as that with which Plato . . . equips the soul in his *Phaedrus*."[26] The third son, as his nature needed purifying (*apokatharsis*), fell deepest into "formlessness." This third "sonship" is obviously the grossest and heaviest because of its impurity. In these three emanations or manifestations of the nonexistent God it is not hard to see the trichotomy of spirit, soul, and body (*pneumatikon, psychikon, sarkikon*). Spirit is the finest and highest; soul, as the *ligamentum spiritus et corporis,* is grosser than spirit, but has "the wings of an eagle,"[27] so that it may lift its heaviness up to the higher regions. Both are of a "subtle" nature and dwell, like the aether and the eagle, in or near the region of light, whereas the body, being heavy, dark, and impure, is deprived of the light but nevertheless contains the divine seed of the third sonship, though still *unconscious and formless.* This seed is as it were awakened by Jesus, purified and made capable of ascension (*anadrome*),[28] by virtue of the fact that the opposites were separated in Jesus through the Passion (i.e., through his division into four).[29] Jesus is thus the prototype

[26] *Ibid.*, VII, 22, 10.
[27] *Ibid.*, VII, 22, 15. The eagle has the same significance in alchemy.
[28] This word also occurs in the well-known passage about the *krater* in Zosimos. (Berthelot, *Alch. Grecs,* III, li, 8.)
[29] I must say a word here about the *horos* doctrine of the Valentinians in Irenaeus (*Adv. Haer.*, I, 2, 2ff.). *Horos* (boundary) is a "power" or numen identical with Christ, or at least proceeding from him. It has the following synonyms: boundary-fixer, he who

for the awakening of the third sonship slumbering in the darkness of humanity. He is the "spiritual inner man." He is also a complete trichotomy in himself, for Jesus the son of Mary represents the incarnate man, but his immediate predecessor is the second Christ, the son of the highest archon of the hebdomad, and his first prefiguration is Christ the son of the highest archon of the ogdoad, the demiurge Yahweh.[30] This trichotomy of Anthropos figures corresponds exactly to the three sonships of the nonexistent God and to the division of human nature into three parts. We have therefore three trichotomies:

I	II	III
First sonship	*Christ of the Ogdoad*	*Spirit*
Second sonship	*Christ of the Hebdomad*	*Soul*
Third sonship	*Jesus the son of Mary*	*Body*

It is in the sphere of the dark, heavy body that we must look for the *amorphia*, the "formlessness" wherein the third sonship lies hidden. As suggested above, this formlessness seems to be practically the equivalent of "unconsciousness." Quispel has drawn attention to the concept of *agnosia* (unconsciousness) in Epiphanius: "When in the beginning the Autopator himself contained all things, which are in him in a state of unconsciousness . . .";[31] likewise to *anoeton* in Hippolytus,[32] which is best translated by "unconscious." *Amorphia*,

---

leads across, emancipator, redeemer, cross. In this capacity he is the regulator and mainstay of the universe, like Jesus. When Sophia was "formless and shapeless as an embryo, Christ took pity on her, stretched her out through his Cross and gave her form through his power," so that at least she acquired substance. (*Adv. Haer.*, I, 4.) He also left behind for her an "intimation of immortality." The identity of the Cross with Horos, or with Christ, is clear from the text, an image that we find also in Paulinus of Nola: "Christ reigns over all things as God, who, on the outstretched cross, reaches out through the four extremities of the wood to the four parts of the wide world, that he may draw unto life the peoples from all lands."

[30] *Elenchos*, VII, 26, 5.
[31] *Panarium* XXXI, 5.
[32] *Elenchos*, VII, 22, 16.

agnosia, and *anoeton* all refer to the initial state of things, to the potentiality of unconscious contents, aptly formulated by Basilides as "the nonexistent, many-formed, and all-empowering seed of the world."

This picture of the third sonship has certain analogies with the medieval *filius philosophorum* and the *filius Macrocosmi*, who also symbolize the world-soul slumbering in matter. Even with Basilides the body acquires a special and unexpected significance, since in it and its materiality is lodged a third of the revealed Godhead. This means nothing less than that matter is predicated as having considerable numinosity in itself, and I see this as an anticipation of the "mystic" significance which matter subsequently assumed in alchemy and—later on —in natural science. From a psychological point of view it is particularly important that Jesus corresponds to the third sonship and is the prototype of the "awakener" because the opposites were separated in him through the Passion and so became conscious, whereas in the third sonship itself they remain unconscious so long as the latter is formless and undifferentiated. This amounts to saying that in unconscious humanity there is a latent seed that corresponds to the prototype Jesus. Just as the man Jesus became conscious only through the light that emanated from the higher Christ and separated the natures in him, so the seed in unconscious humanity is awakened by the light emanating from Jesus, and is thereby impelled to a similar discrimination of opposites. This view is entirely in accord with the psychological fact that the archetypal image of the self has been shown to occur in dreams even when no such conceptions exist in the conscious mind of the dreamer.[33]

I would not like to end this chapter without a few final remarks that are forced on me by the importance of the material we have been discussing. The standpoint of a psychology whose subject is the phenomenology of the psyche is evidently

[33] For full presentation see "Individual Dream Symbolism in Relation to Alchemy," *Psychology and Alchemy* (Coll. Works, Vol. 12, Part II).

something that is not easy to grasp and is very often misunderstood. If, therefore, at the risk of repeating myself, I come back to fundamentals, I do so only in order to forestall certain wrong impressions which might be occasioned by what I have said, and to spare my reader unnecessary difficulties.

The parallel I have drawn here between Christ and the *self* is not to be taken as anything more than a psychological one, just as the parallel with the fish is mythological. There is no question of any intrusion into the sphere of metaphysics, i.e., of faith. The images of God and Christ which man's religious fantasy projects cannot avoid being anthropomorphic and are admitted to be so; hence they are capable of psychological elucidation like any other symbol. Just as the ancients believed that they had said something important about Christ with their fish symbol, so it seemed to the alchemists that their parallel with the stone served to illuminate and deepen the meaning of the Christ image. In the course of time the fish symbolism disappeared completely, and so likewise did the *lapis philosophorum*. Concerning this latter symbol, however, there are plenty of statements to be found which show it in a special light—views and ideas which attach such importance to the stone that one begins to wonder whether, in the end, it was Christ who was taken as a symbol of the stone, rather than the other way round. This marks a development which —with the help of certain ideas in the epistles of John and Paul—includes Christ in the realm of immediate inner experience and makes him appear as the figure of the total man. It also links up directly with the psychological evidence for the existence of an archetypal content possessing all those qualities which are characteristic of the Christ image in its archaic and medieval forms. Modern psychology is therefore confronted with a question very like the one that faced the alchemists: Is the *self* a symbol of Christ, or is Christ a symbol of the *self*?

In the present study I have affirmed the latter alternative. I have tried to show how the traditional Christ-image concentrates upon itself the characteristics of an archetype—the archetype of the self. My aim and method do not purport to be anything more in principle than, shall we say, the efforts of an art historian to trace the various influences which have contributed towards the formation of a particular Christ-image. Thus we find the concept of the archetype in the history of art as well as in philology and textual criticism. The psychological archetype differs from its parallels in other fields only in one respect: it refers to a living and ubiquitous psychic fact, and this naturally shows the whole situation in a rather different light. One is then tempted to attach greater importance to the immediate and living presence of the archetype than to the idea of the historical Christ. As I have said, there is among certain of the alchemists, too, a tendency to give the *lapis* priority over Christ. Since I am far from cherishing any missionary intentions, I must expressly emphasize that I am not concerned here with confessions of faith but with proved scientific facts. If one inclines to regard the archetype of the self as the real agent and hence takes Christ as a symbol of the self, one must bear in mind that there is a considerable difference between *perfection* and *completeness*. The Christ-image is as good as perfect (at least it is meant to be so), while the archetype (so far as known) denotes completeness but is far from being perfect. It is a paradox, a statement about something indescribable and transcendental. Accordingly, the realization of the self, which would logically follow from a recognition of its supremacy, leads to a fundamental conflict, to a real suspension between opposites (reminiscent of the crucified Christ hanging between two thieves), and to an approximate state of wholeness that lacks perfection. To strive after *teleiosis*—completion—in this sense is not only legitimate but is inborn in man as a peculiarity which provides civilization with one of its strongest roots. This striving is so powerful, even, that it can turn into a passion that draws everything into its service. Natural as it is to seek perfection in one way or another, the archetype fulfills itself in completeness, and this is a *teleiosis* of quite another kind. Where the archetype predominates, completeness is *forced* upon us against all our conscious strivings, in accordance with the archaic nature of the archetype. The individual may strive after perfection ("Be you therefore perfect [*teleioi*] as also your heavenly Father is perfect"),[34] but must suffer from the opposite of his intentions for the sake of his completeness. "I find then a law, that, when I would do good, evil is present with me."[35]

The Christ-image fully corresponds to this situation: Christ is the perfect man who is crucified. One could hardly think of a truer picture of the goal of ethical endeavor. At any rate the transcendental idea of the self that serves psychology as a working hypothesis can never match that image because, although it is a symbol, it lacks the character of a revelatory historical event. Like the related ideas of *atman* and *tao* in the East, the idea of the self is at least in part a product of cognition, grounded neither on faith nor on metaphysical speculation but on the experience that under certain conditions the unconscious spontaneously brings forth an archetypal symbol of wholeness. From this we must conclude that some such archetype occurs universally and is endowed with a certain numinosity. And there is in fact any amount of historical evidence as well as modern case material to prove this.[36] These naïve and completely uninfluenced pictorial representations of the symbol show that it is given central and supreme importance precisely because it stands for the conjunction of opposites. Naturally the conjunction can only be understood as a paradox, since a union of opposites can be thought of only as their annihilation. This paradox is characteristic of all transcendental situations because it gives adequate expression to their indescribable nature.

Whenever the archetype of the self predominates, the inevitable psychological consequence is a state of conflict vividly exemplified by the Christian symbol of crucifixion—that acute state of unredeemedness which comes to an end only with the words *consummatum est*. Recognition of the archetype, therefore, does not in any way circumvent the Christian mystery; rather, it creates the psychological preconditions without

[34] Matt. 5:48 (D.V.).
[35] Rom. 7:21 (A.V.).
[36] See *Archetypes and the Collective Unconscious* (Coll. Works, Vol. 9, Part I).—Ed.

which "redemption" would appear meaningless. "Redemption" does not mean that a burden is taken from one's shoulders which one was never meant to bear. Only the "complete" person knows how unbearable man is to himself. So far as I can see, no relevant objection could be raised from the Christian point of view against anyone's accepting the task of individuation imposed on us by nature and also the recognition of our wholeness or completeness as a binding personal commitment. If he does this consciously and intentionally, he avoids all the unhappy consequences of repressed individuation. In other words, if he voluntarily takes the burden of completeness on himself, he need not find it "happening" to him against his will in a negative form. This is as much as to say that anyone who is destined to descend into a deep pit had better set about it with all the necessary precautions rather than risk falling into the hole backwards.

The irreconcilable nature of the opposites in Christian psychology is due to their moral accentuation. This accentuation seems natural to us, although, looked at historically, it is a legacy from the Old Testament with its emphasis on righteousness in the eyes of the law. Such an influence is notably lacking in the East, in the philosophical religions of India and China. Without stopping to discuss the question of whether this exacerbation of the opposites, much as it increases suffering, may not after all correspond to a higher degree of truth, I should like merely to express the hope that the present world situation may be looked upon in the light of the psychological rule alluded to above. Today humanity, as never before, is split into two apparently irreconcilable halves. The psychological rule says that when an inner situation is not made conscious, it happens outside, as fate. That is to say, when the individual remains undivided and does not become conscious of his inner contradictions, the world must perforce act out the conflict and be torn into opposite halves.

The Phenomenology of the Spirit in Fairy Tales[1]

Foreword

One of the unbreakable rules in scientific research is to take an object as known only so far as the inquirer is in a position to make scientifically valid statements about it. "Valid" in this sense simply means what can be verified by facts. The object of inquiry is the natural phenomenon. To inquire into the substance of what has been observed is possible in natural science only where there is an Archimedean point outside. For the psyche no such outside standpoint exists, since only the psyche can observe the psyche. Consequently, knowledge of the psychic substance is impossible for us, at least with the means

[1] This essay is the expanded version of a lecture which Dr. Jung delivered in 1945 under the title *Zur Psychologie des Geistes* ("On the Psychology of the Spirit"). The present version, translated by R. F. C. Hull, is taken from *Spirit and Nature*, Papers from the Eranos Yearbooks, edited by Joseph Campbell, Bollingen Series XXX, (Pantheon Books, 1954), Vol. I. In addition, later changes made by the translator for inclusion in the Collected Works have been incorporated.—Ed.

at present available. This does not rule out the possibility that the atomic physics of the future may supply us with the said Archimedean point. For the time being, however, our subtlest lucubrations can establish no more than is contained in the statement: this is how the psyche behaves. The honest investigator will piously refrain from meddling with questions of substance. I do not think it superfluous to acquaint my reader with the necessary limitations that psychology voluntarily imposes on itself, for he will then be in a position to appreciate the phenomenological standpoint of modern psychology, which is not always understood. This standpoint does not exclude the existence of faith, conviction, and experienced certainties of whatever description, nor does it contest their possible validity. Great as is their importance for the individual and for collective life, psychology completely lacks the means to prove their validity in the scientific sense. One may lament this incapacity on the part of science, but that does not enable it to jump over its own shadow.

1. Concerning the Word "Spirit"

The word "spirit" possesses such a wide range of application that it requires considerable effort to make clear to oneself all the things it can mean. Spirit, we say, is the principle that stands in opposition to matter. By this we understand an immaterial substance or form of existence which on the highest and most universal level is called "God." We imagine this immaterial substance also as the vehicle of psychic phenomena or even of life itself. In contradiction to this view there stands the opposition: spirit and nature. Here the concept of spirit is restricted to the supernatural or antinatural, and has lost its substantial connection with psyche and life. A similar restriction is implied in Spinoza's view that spirit is an attribute of the One Substance. Hylozoism[2] goes even further, taking spirit to be a quality of matter.

[2] The theory that matter has life, or that life is a property of matter (Oxford Universal Dictionary).—Ed.

A very widespread view conceives spirit as a higher and psyche as a lower principle of activity, and conversely the alchemists thought of spirit as the *ligamentum animae et corporis,* obviously regarding it as a *spiritus vegetativus* (the later life spirit or nerve spirit). Equally common is the view that spirit and psyche are essentially the same and can be separated only arbitrarily. Wundt takes spirit as "the inner being, regardless of any connection with an outer being." Others restrict spirit to certain psychic capacities or functions or qualities, such as the capacity to think and reason in contradistinction to the more "psychic" sentiments. Here spirit means the sum total of all the phenomena of rational thought, or of the intellect, including the will, memory, imagination, creative power, and aspirations motivated by ideals. Spirit has the further connotation of *sprightliness,* as when we say that a person is "spirited," meaning that he is versatile and full of ideas, with a brilliant, witty, and surprising turn of mind. Again, spirit denotes a certain attitude or the principle underlying it; for instance, one is "educated in the spirit of Pestalozzi," or one says that the "spirit of Weimar is the immortal German heritage." A special instance is the time spirit, or spirit of the age, which stands for the principle and motive force behind certain views, judgments, and actions of a collective nature. Then there is the "objective spirit,"[3] by which is meant the whole stock of man's cultural possessions with particular regard to his intellectual and religious achievements.

As linguistic usage shows, spirit in the sense of an attitude has unmistakable leanings towards personification: the spirit of Pestalozzi can also be taken concretistically as his ghost or imago, just as the spirits of Weimar are the personal specters of Goethe and Schiller; for spirit still has the spookish meaning of the soul of one departed. The "cold breath of the spirits" points on the one hand to the ancient affinity of *psyche* with *psychros* and *psychos,* which both mean "cold," and on the other hand to the original meaning of *pneuma,* which simply denoted "air in motion"; and in the same way animus and

[3] [An Hegelian term, roughly equivalent to our "spirit of man." —TRANS.]

anima were connected with *animos,* "wind." The German word *Geist* probably has more to do with something frothing, effervescing, or fermenting; hence affinities with *Gischt* (foam), *Gäscht* (yeast), "ghost," "gas," and also with the emotional "ghastly" and "aghast," are not to be rejected. From time immemorial emotion has been regarded as possession, which is why we still say today, of a hot-tempered person, that he is possessed of a devil or that an evil spirit has entered into him.[4]

Just as, according to the old view, the spirits or souls of the dead are of a subtle disposition like a vapor or a smoke, so to the alchemist *spiritus* was a subtle, volatile, active, and vivifying essence, such as alcohol was understood to be, and all the arcane substances. On this level, spirit includes spirits of salts, spirits of ammonia, formic spirit, etc.

This score or so of meanings and shades of meaning attributable to the word "spirit" makes it difficult for the psychologist to delimit his subject conceptually, but on the other hand they lighten the task of describing it, since the many different aspects go to form a vivid and concrete picture of the phenomenon in question. We are concerned with a functional complex which originally, on the primitive level, was apprehended as an invisible, breathlike "presence." William James has given us a lively account of this primordial phenomenon in his *Varieties of Religious Experience.* Another well-known example is the wind of the Pentecostal miracle. The primitive mentality finds it quite natural to personify the invisible presence as a ghost or demon. The souls or spirits of the dead are identical with the psychic activity of the living; they merely continue it. The view that the psyche is a spirit is implicit in this. When therefore something psychic happens in the individual which he feels as belonging to himself, that something is his own spirit. But if anything psychic happens which seems to him strange, then it is somebody else's spirit, and it may be causing a possession. The spirit in the first case corresponds to the subjective attitude, in the latter case to public opinion, to

[4] See my "Spirit and Life" in *Contributions to Analytical Psychology,* tr. H. G. and Cary F. Baynes (New York and London, 1928).

the time spirit, or to the original, not yet human, anthropoid disposition which we also call the *unconscious*.

In keeping with its original wind-nature, spirit is always an active, winged, swift-moving being as well as that which vivifies, stimulates, incites, fires, and inspires. To put it in modern language, spirit is the dynamic principle, forming for that very reason the classical antithesis of matter—the antithesis, that is, of its stasis and inertia. Basically it is the contrast between life and death. The subsequent differentiation of this contrast leads to the actually very remarkable opposition of spirit and nature. Even though spirit is regarded as essentially alive and enlivening, one cannot really feel nature as unspiritual and dead. We must therefore be dealing here with the (Christian) postulate of a spirit whose life is so vastly superior to the life of nature that in comparison with it the latter is no better than death.

This special development in man's idea of spirit rests on the recognition that its invisible presence is a psychic phenomenon, i.e., one's own spirit, and that this consists not only in uprushes of life but in formal contents too. Among the first, the most prominent are the images and shadowy presentations that occupy our inner field of vision; among the second, thinking and reason, which organize the world of images. In this way a transcendent spirit superimposed itself upon the original, natural life-spirit and even swung over to the opposite position, as though the latter were merely naturalistic. The transcendent spirit became the supranatural and transmundane cosmic principle of order and as such was given the name of "God," or at least it became an attribute of the One Substance (as in Spinoza) or one Person in the Godhead (as in Christianity).

The corresponding development of spirit in the reverse, hylozoistic direction—*a maiori ad minus*—took place under anti-Christian auspices in materialism. The premise underlying this reaction is the exclusive certainty of the spirit's identity with psychic functions, whose dependence upon brain and metabolism became increasingly clear. One had only to give the One Substance another name and call it "matter," to produce the idea of a spirit which was entirely dependent on nutrition and environment, and whose highest form was the intellect or reason. This meant that the original pneumatic presence had taken up its abode in man's physiology, and a writer like Klages could arraign the spirit as the "adversary of the soul."[5] For it was into this latter concept that the original spontaneity of the spirit withdrew after it had been degraded to an unfree attribute of matter. Somewhere or other the *deus ex machina* quality of spirit had to be preserved—if not in the spirit itself, then in its synonym the soul, that glancing, Aeolian[6] thing, elusive as a butterfly (anima, psyche).

Even though the materialistic conception of the spirit did not prevail everywhere, it still persisted outside the sphere of religion in the realm of conscious phenomena. Spirit as "subjective spirit" came to mean a purely endopsychic phenomenon, while "objective spirit" did not mean the universal spirit, or God, but merely the sum-total of intellectual and cultural possessions which make up our human institutions and the content of our libraries. Spirit had forfeited its original nature, its autonomy and spontaneity over a very wide area, with the solitary exception of the religious field, where, at least in principle, its pristine character remained unimpaired.

In this résumé we have described an entity which presents itself to us as an immediate psychic phenomenon distinguished from other psychisms whose existence is naïvely believed to be causally dependent upon physical influences. A connection between spirit and physical conditions is not immediately apparent, and for this reason it was credited with immateriality to a much higher degree than was the case with psychic phenomena in the narrower sense. Not only is a certain physical dependence attributed to the latter, but they are themselves thought of as possessing a certain materiality, as the idea of

[5] Ludwig Klages, *Der Geist als Widersacher der Seele* (Leipzig, 1929–32; 3 vols.).
[6] "Soul," from the Old German *saiwalô*, may be cognate with *eiolos*, "quick-moving, changeful of hue, shifting." It also has the meaning of "wily" or "shifty"; hence an air of probability attaches to the alchemical definition of *anima* as Mercurius.

the subtle body and the Chinese *kuei*-soul clearly show. In view of the intimate connection that exists between certain psychic processes and their physical parallels we cannot very well accept the total immateriality of the psyche. As against this, the *consensus omnium* insists on the immateriality of spirit, though not everyone would agree that it also has a reality of its own. It is, however, not easy to see why our hypothetical "matter," which looks quite different from what it did even thirty years ago, alone should be real, and spirit not. Although the idea of immateriality does not in itself exclude that of reality, popular opinion invariably associates reality with materiality. Spirit and matter may well be forms of one and the same transcendental being. For instance the Tantrists, with as much right, say that matter is nothing other than the concreteness of God's thoughts. The sole immediate reality is the psychic reality of conscious contents, which are as it were labeled with a spiritual or material origin as the case may be.

The hallmarks of spirit are, firstly, the principle of spontaneous movement and activity; secondly, the spontaneous capacity to produce images independently of sense perception; and thirdly, the autonomous and sovereign manipulation of these images. This spiritual entity approaches primitive man from outside; but with increasing development it gets lodged in man's consciousness and becomes a subordinate function, thus apparently forfeiting its original character of autonomy. That character is now retained only in the most conservative views, namely in the religions. The descent of spirit into the sphere of human consciousness is expressed in the myth of the divine *nous* caught in the embrace of *phusis*. This process, continuing over the ages, is probably an unavoidable necessity, and the religions would find themselves in a very forlorn situation if they believed in the attempt to hold up evolution. Their task, if they are well advised, is not to impede the ineluctable march of events, but to guide it in such a way that it can proceed without fatal injury to the soul. The religions should therefore constantly recall to us the origin and original character of the spirit, lest man should forget what he is drawing into himself and with what he is filling his consciousness. He himself did not create the spirit, rather the spirit makes *him* creative, always spurring him on, giving him happy ideas, staying power, "enthusiasm" and "inspiration." So much, indeed, does it permeate his whole being that he is in gravest danger of thinking that he actually created the spirit and that he "has" it. In reality however, the primordial phenomenon of the spirit takes possession of *him*, and, while appearing to be the willing object of human intentions, it binds his freedom, just as the physical world does, with a thousand chains and becomes an obsessive idée-force. Spirit threatens the naïve-minded man with inflation, of which our own times have given us the most horribly instructive examples. The danger becomes all the greater the more our interest fastens upon external objects and the more we forget that the differentiation of our relations to nature should go hand in hand with a correspondingly differentiated relation to the spirit, so as to establish the necessary balance. If the outer object is not offset by an inner, unbridled materialism results, coupled with maniacal arrogance or else the extinction of the autonomous personality, which is in any case the ideal of the totalitarian mass state.

As can readily be seen, the common modern idea of spirit ill accords with the Christian view, which regards it as the *summum bonum*, as God himself. To be sure, there is also the idea of an evil spirit. But the modern idea cannot be equated with that either, since for us spirit is not necessarily evil; we would have to call it morally indifferent or neutral. When the Bible says "God is a spirit," it sounds more like the definition of a substance, or like a qualification. But the devil too, it seems, is endowed with the same peculiar spiritual substance, albeit an evil and corrupt one. The original identity of substance is still expressed in the idea of the fallen angel, as well as in the close connection between Jehovah and Satan in the Old Testament. There may be an echo of this primitive connection in the Lord's Prayer, where we say "Lead us not into temptation"—for is not this really the business of the *tempter*, the devil himself?

This brings us to a point we have not considered at all in the course of our observations so far. We have availed ourselves of cultural and everyday conceptions which are the product of human consciousness and its reflections, in order to form a picture of the psychic modes of manifestation of the factor "spirit." But we have yet to consider that because of its original autonomy,[7] about which there can be no doubt in the psychological sense, the spirit is quite capable of staging its own manifestations spontaneously.

2. *Self-Representation of the Spirit in Dreams*

The psychic manifestations of the spirit at once indicate that they are of an archetypal nature—in other words, the phenomenon we call spirit depends on the existence of an autonomous primordial image which is universally present in the preconscious makeup of the human psyche. As usual, I first came up against this problem when investigating the dreams of my patients. It struck me that a certain kind of father complex has a "spiritual" character, so to speak, in the sense that the father image gives rise to statements, actions, tendencies, impulses, opinions, etc., to which one could hardly deny the attribute "spiritual." In men a positive father complex very often produces a certain credulity with regard to authority and a distinct willingness to bow down before all spiritual dogmas and values; while in women it induces the liveliest spiritual aspirations and interests. In dreams it is always the father figure from whom the decisive beliefs, prohibitions, and wise counsels emanate. The invisibility of this source is frequently emphasized by the fact that it consists simply of an authoritative voice which passes final judgments.[8] Mostly, therefore, it is the figure of a "wise old man" who symbolizes the spiritual factor. Sometimes the part is played by a "real" spirit, namely,

---

[7] Even if one accepts the view that a self-revelation of spirit—an apparition for instance—is nothing but an hallucination, the fact remains that this is a spontaneous psychic event not subject to our control. At any rate it is an autonomous complex, and that is quite sufficient for our purpose.

[8] Cf. *Psychology and Alchemy* (Coll. Works, Vol. 12), pp. 49ff.

the ghost of one dead, or, more rarely, by grotesque gnomelike figures or talking animals. The dwarf forms are found, at least in my experience, mainly in women; hence it seems to me logical that in Ernst Barlach's play *Der tote Tag* (1912), the gnomelike figure of Steissbart ("Rump-beard") is associated with the mother, just as Bes is associated with the mother-goddess at Karnak. In both sexes the spirit can also take the form of a boy or a youth. In women he corresponds to the so-called "positive" animus who indicates the possibility of conscious spiritual effort. In men his meaning is not so simple. He can be positive, in which case he signifies the "higher" personality, the self or *filius regius* as conceived by the alchemists.[9] But he can also be negative, and then he signifies the infantile shadow. In both cases the boy means some form of spirit.[10] Graybeard and boy belong together. The pair of them play a considerable role in alchemy as symbols of Mercurius.

It can never be established with one-hundred-per-cent certainty whether the spirit figures in dreams are morally good. Very often they show all the signs of duplicity, if not of outright malice. I must emphasize, however, that the grand plan on which the unconscious life of the psyche is constructed is so inaccessible to our understanding that we can never know what evil may not be necessary in order to produce good by enantiodromia, and what good may very possibly lead to evil. Sometimes the *probate spiritus* recommended by John cannot, with the best will in the world, be anything other than a cautious and patient waiting to see how things will finally turn out.

The figure of the Wise Old Man can appear so plastically, not only in dreams but also in visionary meditation (or what we call "active imagination"), that, as is sometimes apparently the case in India, it takes over the role of a guru.[11] The Wise

---

[9] Cf. the vision of the "naked boy" in Meister Eckhart.

[10] Cf. the "divine child" in *The Psychology of the Child Archetype* in this volume.

[11] Hence the many miraculous stories about rishis and mahatmas. A cultured Indian with whom I once conversed on the subject of gurus told me, when I asked him who his guru had been, that it

Old Man appears in dreams in the guise of a magician, doctor, priest, teacher, professor, grandfather, or any other person possessing authority. The archetype of spirit in the shape of a man, hobgoblin, or animal always appears in a situation where insight, understanding, good advice, determination, planning, etc., are needed but cannot be mustered on one's own resources. The archetype compensates this state of spiritual deficiency by contents designed to fill the gap. An excellent example of this is the dream about the white and black magicians, which tried to compensate the spiritual difficulties of a young theological student. I did not know the dreamer myself, so the question of my personal influence is ruled out. He dreamed he was standing in the presence of a sublime hieratic figure called the "white magician," who was nevertheless clothed in a long black robe. This magician had just ended a lengthy discourse with the words "And for that we require the help of the black magician." Then the door suddenly opened and another old man came in, the "black magician," who however was dressed in a white robe. He too looked noble and sublime. The black magician evidently wanted to speak with the white, but hesitated to do so in the presence of the dreamer. At that the white magician, pointing to the dreamer, said, "Speak, he is an innocent." So the black magician began to relate a strange story of how he had found the lost keys of Paradise and did not know how to use them. He had, he said, come to the white magician for an explanation of the secret of the keys. He told him that the king of the country in which he lived was seeking a suitable tomb for himself. His subjects had chanced to dig up an old sarcophagus containing the mortal remains of a virgin. The king opened the sarcophagus, threw away the bones, and had the empty sarcophagus buried again for later use. But no sooner had the bones seen the light of day than the being to whom they once had belonged—the virgin—changed into a

---

was Shankaracharya (who lived in the 8th and 9th centuries). "But that's the celebrated commentator," I remarked in amazement. Whereupon he replied, "Yes, so he was; but naturally it was his spirit," not in the least perturbed by my Western bewilderment.

black horse that galloped off into the desert. The black magician pursued it across the sandy wastes and beyond, and there after many vicissitudes and difficulties he found the lost keys of Paradise. That was the end of his story, and also, unfortunately, of the dream.

Here the compensation certainly did not fall out as the dreamer would wish, by handing him a solution on a plate; rather it confronted him with a problem to which I have already alluded, and one which life is always bringing us up against: namely, the uncertainty of all moral valuation, the bewildering interplay of good and evil, and the remorseless concatenation of guilt, suffering, and redemption. This path to the primordial religious experience is the right one, but how many can recognize it? It is like a still small voice, and it sounds from afar. It is ambiguous, questionable, dark, presaging danger and hazardous adventure; a razor-edged path, to be trodden for God's sake only, without assurance and without sanction.

3. *The Spirit in Fairy Tales*

I would gladly present the reader with some more modern dream material, but I fear that the individualism of dreams would make too high a demand upon our exposition and would claim more space than is here at our disposal. We shall therefore turn to folklore, where we need not get involved in the grim confrontations and entanglements of individual case histories and can observe the variations of the spirit motif without having to consider conditions that are more or less unique. In myths and fairy tales, as in dreams, the psyche tells its own story, and the interplay of the archetypes is revealed in its natural setting as "formation, transformation / the eternal Mind's eternal recreation."

The frequency with which the spirit type appears as an old man is about the same in fairy tales as in dreams. The old man always appears when the hero is in a hopeless and desperate situation from which only profound reflection or a lucky idea

—in other words, a spiritual function or an endopsychic automatism of some kind—can extricate him. But since, for internal and external reasons, the hero cannot accomplish this himself, the knowledge needed to compensate the deficiency comes in the form of a personified thought, i.e., in the shape of this sagacious and helpful old man. An Esthonian fairy tale,[12] for instance, tells how an ill-treated little orphan boy who had let a cow escape was afraid to return home again for fear of more punishment. So he ran away, chancing to luck. He naturally got himself into a hopeless situation, with no visible way out. Exhausted, he fell into a deep sleep. When he awoke, "it seemed to him that he had something liquid in his mouth, and he saw a little old man with a long gray beard standing before him, who was in the act of replacing the stopper in his little milk flask. 'Give me some more to drink,' begged the boy. 'You have had enough for today,' replied the old man. 'If my path had not chanced to lead me to you, that would assuredly have been your last sleep, for when I found you, you were half dead.' Then the old man asked the boy who he was and where he wanted to go. The boy recounted everything he could remember happening to him up to the beating he had received the previous evening. 'My dear child,' said the old man, 'you are no better and no worse off than many others whose dear protectors and comforters rest in their coffins under the earth. You can no longer turn back. Now that you have run away, you must seek a new fortune in the world. As I have neither house nor home, nor wife nor child, I cannot go on looking after you, but I will give you some good advice for nothing.'"

So far the old man has been expressing no more than what the boy, the hero of the tale, could have thought out for himself. Having given way to the stress of emotion and simply run off like that into the blue, he would at least have had to

[12] *Finnische und estnische Volksmärchen* (Die Märchen der Weltliteratur, ed. Friedrich von der Leyen and Paul Zaunert; Jena, 1922), No. 68, p. 208 ["How an Orphan Boy Unexpectedly Found His Luck"]. [All of the German collections of tales here cited are in this series. English titles of tales are given in brackets, though no attempt has been made to locate published translations.—Ed.]

reflect that he needed food. It would also have been necessary, at such a moment, to consider his position. The whole story of his life up to the recent past would then have passed before his mind, as is usual in such cases. An anamnesis of this kind is a purposeful process whose aim is to gather the assets of the whole personality together at the critical moment, when all one's spiritual and physical forces are challenged, and with this united strength to fling open the door of the future. No one can help the boy to do this; he has to rely entirely on himself. There is no going back. This realization will give the necessary resolution to his actions. By forcing him to face the issue, the old man spares him the trouble of making up his mind. Indeed the old man is himself this purposeful reflection and concentration of moral and physical forces that comes about spontaneously in the psychic space outside consciousness when conscious thought is not yet—or is no longer —possible. The concentration and tension of psychic forces have something about them that always looks like magic: they develop an unexpected power of endurance which is often superior to the conscious effort of will. One can observe this experimentally in the artificial concentration induced by hypnosis: in my demonstrations I used regularly to put an hysteric, of weak bodily build, into a deep hypnotic sleep and then get her to lie with the back of her head on one chair and her heels resting on another, stiff as a board, and leave her there for about a minute. Her pulse would gradually go up to 90. A husky young athlete among the students tried in vain to imitate this feat with a conscious effort of will. He collapsed in the middle with his pulse racing at 120.

When the clever old man had brought the boy to this point he could begin his good advice, i.e., the situation no longer looked hopeless. He advised him to continue his wanderings, always to the eastward, where after seven years he would reach the great mountain that betokened his good fortune. The bigness and tallness of the mountain are allusions to his adult personality.[13] Concentration of his powers brings assurance

[13] The mountain stands for the goal of the pilgrimage and ascent, hence it often has the psychological meaning of the self. The *I*

and is therefore the best guarantee of success.[14] From now on he will lack for nothing. "Take my scrip and my flask," says the old man, "and each day you will find in them all the food and drink you need." At the same time he gave him a burdock leaf that could change into a boat whenever the boy had to cross water.

<u>Often the old man in fairy tales asks questions like who? why? whence? and whither?[15] for the purpose of inducing self-reflection and mobilizing the moral forces</u>, and more often still he gives the necessary magical talisman,[16] the un-

---

Ching describes the goal thus: "The king introduces him / To the Western Mountain" (tr. Richard Wilhelm–Cary F. Baynes, Bollingen Series XIX; New York, 1950: Vol. I, p. 78—Hexagram 17, *Sui*, "Following"). Cf. Honorius of Autun (*Speculum de mysteriis ecclesiae*, in J. P. Migne, *Patrologiae cursus completus*, Latin Series, Vol. CLXXII, p. 345): "The mountains are patriarchs and prophets." Richard of St. Victor says: *"Vis videre Christum transfiguratum? Ascende in montem istum, disce cognoscere te ipsum"* (Do you wish to see the transfigured Christ? Ascend that mountain and learn to know yourself). (*Benjamin minor*, in Migne, *Patr., Lat.,* Vol. CXCVI, coll. 53–56.)

[14] In this respect we would call attention to the phenomenology of yoga.

[15] There are numerous examples of this: *Spanische und portugiesische Volksmärchen* (1940), pp. 158, 199 ["The White Parrot" and "Queen Rose, or Little Tom"]; *Russische Volksmärchen* (1914), p. 149 ["The Girl with No Hands"]; *Balkanmärchen* (1915), p. 64 ["The Shepherd and the Three Samovilas (Nymphs)"]; *Märchen aus Iran* (1939), pp. 150ff. ["The Secret of the Bath of Windburg"]; *Nordische Volksmärchen*, Vol. I (1915), p. 231 ["The Werewolf"].

[16] To the girl looking for her brothers he gives a ball of thread that rolls towards them (*Finnische und estnische Volksmärchen*, p. 260 ["The Contending Brothers"]). The prince who is searching for the kingdom of heaven is given a boat that goes by itself (*Deutsche Märchen seit Grimm*, 1912, pp. 381f. ["The Iron Boots"]). Other gifts are a flute that sets everybody dancing (*Balkanmärchen*, p. 173 ["The Twelve Crumbs"]), or the path-finding ball that points the way, the staff of invisibility (*Nordische Volksmärchen*, Vol. I, p. 97 ["The Princess with Twelve Pairs of Golden Shoes"]), miraculous dogs (*ibid.*, p. 287 ["The Three Dogs"]), or a book of secret wisdom (*Chinesische Volksmärchen*, 1913, p. 258 ["Jang Liang"]).

expected and improbable power to succeed, which is one of the peculiarities of the unified personality in good or bad alike. But the intervention of the old man—the spontaneous objectivation of the archetype—would seem to be equally indispensable, since the conscious will by itself is hardly ever capable of uniting the personality to the point where it acquires this extraordinary power to succeed. For that, not only in fairy tales but in life generally, the objective intervention of the archetype is needed, which checks the purely affective reactions with a chain of inner confrontations and realizations. These cause the who? where? how? why? to emerge clearly and in this wise bring knowledge of the immediate situation as well as of the goal. The resultant enlightenment and untying of the fatal tangle often has something positively magical about it—an experience not unknown to the psychotherapist.

The old man's fondness for prompting reflection also takes the form of urging people to "sleep on it." Thus he says to the girl who is searching for her lost brothers: "Lie down: morning is cleverer than evening."[17] He also sees through the gloomy situation of the hero who has got himself into trouble, or at least can give him such information as will help him on his journey. To this end he makes ready use of animals, particularly birds. To the prince who has gone in search of the kingdom of heaven the old hermit says: "I have lived here for three hundred years, but never yet has anybody asked me about the kingdom of heaven. I cannot tell you myself; but up there, on another floor of the house, live all kinds of birds, and they at any rate can tell you."[18] The old man knows what roads lead to the goal and points them out to the hero.[19] He warns of dangers to come and supplies the means of meeting them effectively. For instance, he tells the boy who has gone

[17] *Finnische und estnische Volksmärchen*, loc. cit.

[18] *Deutsche Märchen seit Grimm*, p. 382 [*op. cit.*]. In one Balkan tale (*Balkanmärchen*, p. 65 ["The Sheperd and the Three Samovilas"]) the old man is called the "Czar of all the birds." Here the magpie knows all the answers. Cf. the mysterious "master of the dovecot" in Gustav Meyrink's novel *Der weisse Dominikaner* (Vienna, 1921).

[19] *Märchen aus Iran*, p. 152 [*op. cit.*].

to fetch the silver water that the well is guarded by a lion who has the deceptive trick of sleeping with his eyes open and watching with his eyes shut; or he counsels the youth who is riding to a magic fountain in order to fetch the healing draught for the king, only to draw the water at a trot because of the lurking witches who lasso everybody that comes to the fountain. He charges the princess whose lover has been changed into a werewolf to make a fire and put a cauldron of tar over it. Then she must plunge her beloved white lily into the boiling tar, and when the werewolf comes, she must empty the cauldron over its head, which will release her lover from the spell. Occasionally the old man is a very critical old man, as in the Caucasian tale of the youngest prince who wanted to build a flawless church for his father, so as to inherit the kingdom. This he does, and nobody can discover a single flaw, but then an old man comes along and says, "That's a fine church you've built, to be sure! What a pity the main wall is a bit crooked!" The prince has the church pulled down again and builds a new one, but here too the old man discovers a flaw, and so on for the third time.

The old man thus represents knowledge, reflection, insight, wisdom, cleverness, and intuition on the one hand, and on the other, moral qualities such as good will and readiness to help, which make his "spiritual" character sufficiently plain. Since the archetype is an autonomous content of the unconscious, the fairy tale, which usually concretizes the archetypes, can cause the old man to appear in a dream in much the same way as happens in modern dreams. In a Balkan tale the old man appears to the hard-pressed hero in a dream and gives him good advice about accomplishing the impossible tasks that have been imposed upon him. His relation to the unconscious is clearly expressed in one Russian fairy tale, where he is called the "King of the Forest." As the peasant sat down wearily on a tree stump, a little old man crept out: "all wrinkled he was and a green beard hung down to his knees." "Who are you?" asked the peasant. "I am Och, King of the Forest," said the manikin. The peasant hired out his profligate son to him, "and the King of the Forest departed with the young man, and conducted him to that other world under the earth and brought him to a green hut. . . . In the hut everything was green: the walls were green and the benches, Och's wife was green and the children were green . . . and the little water-women who waited on him were as green as rue." Even the food was green. The King of the Forest is here a vegetation or tree numen who reigns in the woods and, through the nixies, also has connections with water, which clearly shows his relation to the unconscious since the latter is frequently expressed through wood and water symbols.

There is equally a connection with the unconscious when the old man appears as a dwarf. The fairy tale about the princess who was searching for her lover says: "Night came and the darkness, and still the princess sat in the same place and wept. As she sat there lost in thought she heard a voice greeting her: 'Good evening, pretty maid! why are you sitting here so lonely and sad?' She sprang up hastily and felt very confused, and that was no wonder. But when she looked round there was only a tiny little old man standing before her, who nodded his head at her and looked so kind and simple." In a Swiss fairy tale the peasant's son who wants to bring the king's daughter a basket of apples encounters *"es chlis isigs Männdli, das frogt-ne, was er do i dem Chratte häig?"* (a little iron man who asked what he had there in the basket). In another passage the *"Männdli"* has *"es isigs Chlaidli a"* (iron clothes on). By *"isig"* presumably *"eisern"* (iron) is meant, which is more probable than *"eisig"* (icy). In the latter case it would have to be *"es Chlaidli vo Is"* (clothes of ice).[20] There are indeed little ice men, and little metal men too; in fact in a modern dream I have even come across a little black iron man who appeared at a critical juncture, like the one in this fairy tale of the country bumpkin who wanted to marry the princess.

[20] This occurs in the tale of the griffin, No. 84 in the volume of children's fairy tales collected by the brothers Grimm (Diederichs, 1912), Vol. II, pp. 84ff. The text swarms with phonetic mistakes. [The English text (tr. by Margaret Hunt, revised by James Stern, ed. by Joseph Campbell, New York, 1944, tale No. 165) has "hoary."—TRANS.]

In a modern series of visions in which the figure of the wise old man occurred several times, he was on one occasion of normal size and appeared at the very bottom of a crater surrounded by high rocky walls; on another occasion he was a tiny figure on the top of a mountain set inside a low, stony enclosure. We find the same motif in Goethe's tale of the dwarf princess who lived in a casket.[21] In this connection we might also mention the Anthroparion, the little leaden man of the Zosimos vision,[22] as well as the metallic men who dwell in the mines, the crafty dactyls of antiquity, the homunculi of the alchemists, and the gnomic throng of hobgoblins, brownies, gremlins, etc. How "real" such conceptions are became clear to me on the occasion of a serious mountaineering accident: after the catastrophe two of the climbers had the collective vision, in broad daylight, of a little hooded man who scrambled out of an inaccessible crevasse in the ice face and passed across the glacier, creating a regular panic in the two beholders. I have often encountered motifs which made me think that the unconscious must be the world of the infinitesimally small. Such an idea could be derived rationalistically from the obscure feeling that in all these visions we are dealing with something endopsychic, the inference being that a thing must be exceedingly small in order to fit inside the head. I am no friend of any such "rational" conjectures, though I would not say that they are all beside the mark. It seems to me more probable that this liking for diminutives on the one hand and for superlatives—giants, etc.—on the other is connected with the queer uncertainty of spatial and temporal relations in the unconscious.[23] Man's sense of proportion, his rational conception of big and small, is distinctly anthropomorphic, and it loses its validity not only in the realm of physical phenomena but also in those parts of the collective unconscious beyond the range

[21] Goethe, "Die neue Melusine."
[22] Cf. "Einige Bemerkungen zu den Visionen des Zosimos," *Eranos-Jahrbuch 1937.*
[23] In one Siberian fairy tale (*Märchen aus Sibirien*, 2nd ed., 1940, No. 13 ["The Man Turned to Stone"]) the old man is a white shape towering up to heaven.

of the specifically human. The atman is "smaller than small and bigger than big," he is "the size of a thumb" yet he "encompasses the earth on every side and rules over the ten-finger space." And of the Cabiri, Goethe says: "little in length / mighty in strength." In the same way, the archetype of the wise old man is quite tiny, almost imperceptible, and yet it possesses a fateful potency, as anyone can see when he gets down to fundamentals. The archetypes have this peculiarity in common with the atomic world, which is demonstrating before our eyes that the more deeply the investigator penetrates into the universe of microphysics, the more devastating are the explosive forces he finds enchained there. That the greatest effects come from the smallest causes has become patently clear not only in physics but in the field of psychological research as well. How often in the critical moments of life everything hangs on what appears to be a mere nothing!

In certain primitive fairy tales the illuminating quality of our archetype is expressed by the fact that the old man is identified with the sun. He brings a firebrand with him which he uses for roasting a pumpkin. After he has eaten, he takes the fire away again, which causes mankind to steal it from him.[24] In a North American tale the old man is a witch doctor who owns the fire.[25] Spirit too has a fiery aspect, as we know from the language of the Old Testament and from the story of the Pentecostal miracle.

Apart from his cleverness, wisdom, and insight, the old man, as we have already mentioned, is also notable for his moral qualities; what is more, he even tests the moral qualities of others and makes his gifts dependent on this test. There is a particularly instructive example of this in the Esthonian fairy tale of the stepdaughter and the real daughter. The former is an orphan distinguished for her obedience and good behavior. The story begins with her distaff falling into a well. She jumps in after it, but does not drown, and comes to a magic country

[24] *Indianermärchen aus Südamerika* (1920), p. 285 ["The End of the World and the Theft of Fire"—Bolivian].
[25] *Indianermärchen aus Nordamerika* (1924), p. 74 [Tales of Manabos: "The Theft of Fire"].

where, continuing her quest, she meets a cow, a ram, and an apple tree whose wishes she fulfills. She now comes to a wash house where a dirty old man is sitting who wants her to wash him. The following dialogue develops: "Pretty maid, pretty maid, wash me, do, it is hard for me to be so dirty!" "What shall I heat the stove with?" "Collect wooden pegs and crows' dung and make a fire with that." But she fetches sticks, and asks, "Where shall I get the bath water?" "Under the barn there stands a white mare. Get her to piss into the tub!" But she takes clean water, and asks, "Where shall I get a bath switch?" "Cut off the white mare's tail and make a bath switch of that!" But she makes one out of birch twigs, and asks, "Where shall I get soap?" "Take a pumice stone and scrub me with that!" But she fetches soap from the village and with that she washes the old man.

As a reward he gives her a bag full of gold and precious stones. The daughter of the house naturally becomes jealous, throws her distaff into the well, where she finds it again instantly. Nevertheless she goes on and does everything wrong that the stepdaughter had done right, and is rewarded accordingly. The frequency of this motif makes further examples superfluous.

The figure of the superior and helpful old man tempts one to connect him somehow or other with God. In the German tale of the soldier and the black princess it is related how the princess, on whom a curse has been laid, creeps out of her iron coffin every night and devours the soldier standing guard over the tomb. One soldier, when his turn came, tried to escape. "That evening he stole away, fled over the fields and mountains, and came to a beautiful meadow. Suddenly a little man stood before him with a long gray beard, but it was none other than the Lord God himself, who could no longer go on looking at all the mischief the devil wrought every night. 'Whither away?' said the little gray man. 'May I come with you?' And because the little old man looked so friendly the soldier told him that he had run away and why he had done so." Good advice follows, as always. In this story the old man is taken for God in the same naïve way that the English alchemist, Sir

George Ripley,[26] describes the "old king" as *"antiquus dierum"* —"the Ancient of Days."

Just as all archetypes have a positive, favorable, bright side that points upwards, so also they have one that points downwards, partly negative and unfavorable, partly chthonic, but for the rest merely neutral. To this the spirit archetype is no exception. Even his dwarf form implies a kind of limitation and suggests a naturalistic vegetation numen sprung from the underworld. In one Balkan tale the old man is handicapped by the loss of an eye. It has been gouged out by the Vili, a species of winged demon, and the hero is charged with the task of getting them to restore it to him. The old man has therefore lost part of his eyesight—that is, his insight and enlightenment —to the daemonic world of darkness; this handicap is reminiscent of the fate of Osiris, who lost an eye at the sight of a black pig (his wicked brother Set), or again of Wotan, who sacrificed his eye at the spring of Mimir. Characteristically enough the animal ridden by the old man in our fairy tale is a goat, a sign that he himself has a dark side. In a Siberian tale he appears as a one-legged, one-handed, and one-eyed graybeard who wakens a dead man with an iron staff. In the course of the story the latter, after being brought back to life several times, kills the old man by a mistake, and thus throws away his good fortune. The story is entitled "The One-sided Old Man," and in truth his handicap shows that he consists of one half only. The other half is invisible, but appears in the shape of a murderer who seeks the hero's life. Eventually the hero succeeds in killing his persistent murderer, but in the struggle he also kills the one-sided old man, so that the identity of the two victims is clearly revealed. It is thus possible that the old man is his own opposite, a life-bringer as well as a death-dealer —*"ad utrumque peritus"* (skilled in both), as is said of Hermes.[27]

[26] In his "Cantilena" (17th cen.).
[27] Prudentius, *Contra Symmachum*, I, 94 (tr. H. J. Thompson, Loeb Classical Library, Cambridge, Mass., 1949, Vol. I, p. 356). See Hugo Rahner, "Die seelenheilende Blume," *Eranos-Jahrbuch 1944.*

THE PHENOMENOLOGY OF THE SPIRIT IN FAIRY TALES 83

In these circumstances, whenever the "simple" and "kindly" old man appears, it is advisable for heuristic and other reasons to scrutinize the context with some care. For instance in the Esthonian tale we first mentioned, about the hired boy who lost the cow, there is a suspicion that the helpful old man who happened to be on the spot so opportunely had surreptitiously made away with the cow beforehand in order to give his protégé an excellent reason for taking to flight. This may very well be, for everyday experience shows that it is quite possible for a superior though subliminal foreknowledge of fate to contrive some annoying incident for the sole purpose of bullying our Simple Simon of an ego consciousness into the way he should go, which for sheer stupidity he would never have found by himself. Had our orphan guessed that it was the old man who had whisked off his cow as if by magic, he would have seemed like a spiteful troll or a devil. And indeed the old man has a wicked aspect too, just as the primitive medicine man is a healer and helper and also the dreaded concocter of poisons. The very word *pharmakon* means "poison" as well as "antidote," and poison can in fact be both.

The old man, then, has an ambiguous elfin character—witness the extremely instructive figure of Merlin—seeming, in certain of his forms, to be good incarnate and in others an aspect of evil. Then again, he is the wicked magician who, from sheer egoism, does evil for evil's sake. In a Siberian fairy tale he is an evil spirit "on whose head were two lakes with two ducks swimming in them." He feeds on human flesh. The story relates how the hero and his companions go to a feast in the next village, leaving their dogs at home. These, acting on the principle "when the cat's away the mice do play," also arrange a feast at the climax of which they all hurl themselves on the stores of meat. The men return home and chase out the dogs, who dash off into the wilderness. "Then the Creator spoke to Ememqut [the hero of the tale]: 'Go and look for the dogs with your wife.'" But he gets caught in a terrible snowstorm and has to seek shelter in the hut of the evil spirit. There now follows the well-known motif of the biter bit. The "Creator" is Ememqut's father, but the father of the Creator is called the

"Self-created" because he created himself. Although we are nowhere told that the old man with the two lakes on his head lured the hero and his wife into the hut in order to satisfy his hunger, it may be conjectured that a very peculiar spirit must have got into the dogs to cause them to celebrate a feast like the men and afterwards—contrary to their nature—to run away, so that Ememqut had to go out and look for them; and that the hero was then caught in a snowstorm in order to drive him into the arms of the wicked old man. The fact that the Creator, son of the Self-created, was a party to the advice raises a knotty problem whose solution we had best leave to the Siberian theologians.

In a Balkan fairy tale the old man gives the childless Czarina a magic apple to eat, from which she becomes pregnant and bears a son, it being stipulated that the old man shall be his godfather. The boy, however, grows up into a horrid little tough who bullies all the children and slaughters the cattle. For ten years he is given no name. Then the old man appears, sticks a knife in his leg, and calls him the "Knife Prince." The boy now wants to set forth on his adventures, which his father, after long hesitation, finally allows him to do. The knife in his leg is of vital importance: if he draws it out himself, he will live; if anybody else does so, he will die. In the end the knife becomes his doom, for an old witch pulls it out when he is asleep. He dies, but is restored to life by the friends he has won. Here the old man is a helper, but also the contriver of a dangerous fate which might just as easily have turned out for the bad. The evil showed itself early and plainly in the boy's villainous character.

In another Balkan tale there is a variant of our motif that is worth mentioning: a king is looking for his sister who has been abducted by a stranger. His wanderings bring him to the hut of an old woman who warns him against continuing the search. But a tree laden with fruit, ever receding before him, lures him away from the hut. When at last the tree comes to a halt, an old man climbs down from the branches. He regales the king and takes him to the castle where the sister is living with the old man as his wife. She tells her brother that the old man is a wicked spirit who will kill him. And sure enough, three days afterwards the king vanishes without trace. His younger brother now takes up the search and kills the wicked spirit in the form of a dragon. A handsome young man is thereby released from the spell and forthwith marries the sister. The old man, appearing at first as a tree numen, is obviously connected with the sister. He is a murderer. In an interpolated episode he is accused of enchanting a whole city by turning it to iron, i.e., making it immovable, rigid, and locked up. He also holds the king's sister a captive and will not let her return to her relatives. This amounts to saying that the sister is animus-possessed. The old man is therefore to be regarded as her animus. But the manner in which the king is drawn into this possession, and the way he seeks for his sister, make us think that she has an anima significance for her brother. The fateful archetype (of the old man) has accordingly first taken possession of the king's anima—in other words, robbed him of the archetype of life which the anima personifies —and forced him to go in search of the lost charm, the "treasure hard to attain," thus making him the mythical hero, the higher personality who is an expression of the self. Meanwhile the old man acts the part of the villain and has to be forcibly removed, only to appear at the end as the husband of the sister anima, or more properly as the bridegroom of the soul, who celebrates the sacred incest that symbolizes the union of opposites and equals. This bold enantiodromia, a very common occurrence, not only signifies the rejuvenation and transformation of the old man, but hints at a secret inner relation of evil to good and vice versa.

So in this story we see the archetype of the old man in the guise of an evildoer, caught up in all the twists and turns of an individuation process that ends suggestively with the *hieros gamos*. Conversely, in the Russian tale of the Forest King, he starts by being helpful and benevolent, but then refuses to let his hired boy go, so that the main episodes in the story deal with the boy's repeated attempts to escape from the clutches of the magician. Instead of the quest we have flight, which nonetheless appears to win the same reward as adventures valiantly sought, for in the end the hero marries the king's daughter. The magician, however, must rest content with the role of the biter bit.

4. *Theriomorphic Spirit Symbolism in Fairy Tales*

The description of our archetype would not be complete if we omitted to consider one special form of its manifestation, namely, its animal form. This belongs essentially to the theriomorphism of gods and demons and has the same psychological significance. The animal form shows that the contents and functions in question are still in the extrahuman sphere, i.e., on a plane beyond human consciousness, and consequently have a share on the one hand in the daemonically superhuman and on the other in the bestially subhuman. It must be remembered, however, that this division is only true within the sphere of consciousness, where it is a necessary condition of thought. Logic says *tertium non datur*, meaning that we cannot envisage the opposites in their oneness. In other words, while the abolition of an obstinate antinomy can be no more than a postulate for us, this is by no means so for the unconscious, whose contents are without exception paradoxical or antinomial by nature, not excluding the category of being. If anyone unacquainted with the psychology of the unconscious wants to get a working knowledge of these matters, I would recommend a study of Christian mysticism and Indian philosophy, where he will find the clearest elaboration of the antinomies of the unconscious.

Although the old man has, up to now, looked and behaved more or less like a human being, his magical powers and his spiritual superiority suggest that, in good and bad alike, he is outside, or above, or below the human level. Neither for the primitive nor for the unconscious does his animal aspect imply any devaluation, for in certain respects the animal is superior to man. It has not yet blundered into consciousness nor pitted a self-willed ego against the power from which it lives; on the contrary, it fulfills the will that actuates it in a well-nigh perfect manner. Were it conscious, it would be morally better than man. There is deep doctrine in the legend of the Fall: it is the expression of a dim presentiment that the emancipation of ego consciousness was a Luciferian deed. Man's whole history consists from the very beginning in a conflict between his feeling of inferiority and his arrogance. Wisdom seeks the middle path and pays for this audacity by a dubious affinition with demon and beast, and so is open to moral misinterpretation.

Again and again in fairy tales we encounter the motif of helpful animals. These act like humans, speak a human language, and display a sagacity and a knowledge superior to man's. In these circumstances we can say with some justification that the archetype of the spirit is being expressed through an animal form. A German fairy tale[28] relates how a young man, while searching for his lost princess, meets a wolf, who says, "Do not be afraid! But tell me, where is your way leading you?" The young man recounts his story, whereupon the wolf gives him as a magic gift a few of his hairs, with which the young man can summon his help at any time. This intermezzo proceeds exactly like the meeting with the helpful old man. In the same story the archetype also displays its other, wicked side. In order to make this clear I shall give a summary of the story:

While the young man is watching his pigs in the woods he discovers a large tree whose branches lose themselves in the clouds. "How would it be," says he to himself, "if you were to look at the world from the top of that great tree?" So he climbs up, all day long he climbs, without even reaching the branches. Evening comes and he has to pass the night in a fork of the tree. Next day he goes on climbing and by noon has reached the foliage. Only towards evening does he come to a village nestling in the branches. The peasants who live there give him food and shelter for the night. In the morning he climbs still further. Towards noon he reaches a castle in which a young girl lives. Here he finds that the tree goes no higher.

[28] *Deutsche Märchen seit Grimm*, pp. 1ff. ["The Princess in the Tree"].

She is a king's daughter, held prisoner by a wicked magician. So the young man stays with the princess, and she allows him to go into all the rooms of the castle: one room alone she forbids him to enter. But curiosity is too strong. He unlocks the door, and there in the room he finds a raven fixed to the wall with three nails. One nail goes through his throat, the two others through the wings. The raven complains of thirst and the young man, moved by pity, gives him water to drink. At each sip a nail falls out, and at the third sip the raven is free and flies out of the window. When the princess hears of it she is very frightened and says, "That was the devil who enchanted me! It won't be long now before he fetches me again." And one fine morning she has indeed vanished.

The young man now sets out in search of her and, as we have described above, meets the wolf. In the same way he meets a bear and a lion, who also give him some hairs. In addition the lion informs him that the princess is imprisoned nearby in a hunting lodge. The young man finds the house and the princess, but is told that flight is impossible, because the hunter possesses a three-legged white horse that knows everything and would infallibly warn its master. Despite that the young man tries to flee away with her, but in vain. The hunter overtakes him but, because he had saved his life as a raven, lets him go, and rides off again with the princess. When the hunter has disappeared into the wood, the young man creeps back to the house and persuades the princess to wheedle from the hunter the secret of how he obtained his clever white horse. This she successfully does in the night, and the young man, who has hidden himself under the bed, learns that about an hour's journey from the hunting lodge there dwells a witch who breeds magic horses. Whoever was able to guard the foals for three days might choose a horse as a reward. In former times, said the hunter, she used to make a gift of twelve lambs into the bargain, in order to satisfy the hunger of the twelve wolves who lived in the woods near the farmstead, and prevent them from attacking; but to him she gave no lambs. So the wolves followed him as he rode away, and while crossing the borders of her domain they succeeded in tearing off one of his horse's hoofs. That was why it had only three legs.

Then the young man made haste to seek out the witch and agreed to serve her on condition that she give him not only a horse of his own choosing but twelve lambs as well. To this she consented. Instantly she commanded the foals to run away, and, to make him sleepy, she gave him brandy. He drinks, falls asleep, and the foals escape. On the first day he catches them with the help of the wolf, on the second day the bear helps him, and on the third the lion. He can now go and choose his reward. The witch's little daughter tells him which horse her mother rides. This is naturally the best horse, and it too is white. Hardly has he got it out of the stall when the witch pierces the four hoofs and sucks the marrow out of the bones. From this she bakes a cake and gives it to the young man for his journey. The horse grows deathly weak, but the young man feeds it on the cake, whereupon the horse recovers its former strength. He gets out of the woods unscathed after quieting the twelve wolves with the twelve lambs. He then fetches the princess and rides away with her. But the three-legged horse calls out to the hunter, who sets off in pursuit and quickly catches up with them, because the four-legged horse refuses to gallop. As the hunter approaches, the four-legged horse cries out to the three-legged, "Sister, throw him off!" The magician is thrown and trampled to pieces by the two horses. The young man sets the princess on the three-legged horse, and the pair of them ride away to her father's kingdom, where they get married. The four-legged horse begs him to cut off both their heads, for otherwise they would bring disaster upon him. This he does, and the horses are transformed into a handsome prince and a wonderfully beautiful princess, who after a while repair "to their own kingdom." They had been changed into horses by the hunter long ago.

Apart from the theriomorphic spirit symbolism in this tale, it is especially interesting to note that the function of knowing and intuition is represented by a riding-animal. This is as much as to say that the spirit can be somebody's property. The three-legged white horse is thus the property of the daemonic hunter, and the four-legged one the property of the witch. Spirit is here partly a function, which like any other object (horse), can change its owner and partly an autonomous subject (magician as owner of the horse). By obtaining the four-legged horse from the witch, the young man frees a spirit or a thought of some special kind from the grip of the unconscious. Here as elsewhere, the witch stands for a *mater natura* or the original "matriarchal" state of the unconscious indicating a psychic constitution in which the unconscious is offset only by a feeble and still dependent consciousness. The four-legged horse shows itself superior to the three-legged, since it can command the latter. And since the quaternity is a symbol of wholeness and wholeness plays a considerable role in the picture world of the unconscious,[29] the victory of four-leggedness over three-leggedness is not altogether unexpected. But what is the meaning of the opposition between threeness and fourness, or rather, what does threeness mean as compared with wholeness? In alchemy this problem is known as the axiom of Maria and runs all through alchemical philosophy for more than a thousand years, finally to be taken up again in the Cabiri scene in *Faust*. The earliest literary version of it is to be found in the opening words of Plato's *Timaeus*,[30] of which Goethe gives us a reminder. Among the alchemists we can see clearly how the divine Trinity has its counterpart in a lower, chthonic triad (similar to Dante's three-headed devil). This represents a principle which, by reason of its symbolism, betrays affinities with evil, though it is by no means certain that it expresses nothing but evil. Everything points rather to the fact that evil, or its familiar sym-

[29] With reference to the quaternity I would call attention to my earlier writings, and in particular to *Psychology and Alchemy* (Coll. Works, Vol. 12), and *Psychology and Religion* (Yale University Press, 1938).

[30] The oldest representation I know of this problem is that of the four sons of Horus, three of whom are occasionally depicted with the heads of animals, and the other with the head of a man. Chronologically this links up with Ezekiel's vision of the four figures, which then reappear in the attributes of the four evangelists. Three have animal heads and one a human head (the angel).

bolism, belongs to the family of figures which describe the dark, nocturnal, lower, chthonic element. In this symbolism the lower stands to the higher as a correspondence[31] in reverse; that is to say, it is conceived, like the upper, as a triad.

Three, being a masculine number, is logically correlated with the wicked hunter, who can be thought of alchemically as the lower triad. Four, a feminine number, is assigned to the old woman. The two horses are miraculous animals that talk and know and thus represent the unconscious spirit, which in one case is subordinated to the wicked magician and in the other to the old witch.

Between the three and the four there exists the primary opposition of male and female, but whereas fourness is a symbol of wholeness, threeness is not. The latter, according to alchemy, denotes polarity, since one triad always presupposes another, just as high presupposes low, lightness darkness, good evil. In terms of energy polarity means a potential, and wherever a potential exists there is the possibility of a current, a flow of events, for the tension of opposites strives for balance. If one imagines the quaternity as a square divided into two halves by a diagonal, one gets two triangles whose apices point in opposite directions. One could therefore say metaphorically that if the wholeness symbolized by the quaternity is divided into equal halves, it produces two opposing triads. This simple reflection shows how three can be derived from four, and in the same way the hunter of the captured princess explains how his horse, from being four-legged, became three-legged, through having one hoof torn off by the twelve wolves. The three-leggedness is due to an accident, therefore, which occurred at the very moment when the horse was leaving the territory of the dark mother. In psychological language we should say that when the unconscious wholeness becomes manifest, i.e., leaves the unconscious and crosses over into the sphere of consciousness, one of the four remains behind, held fast by the *horror vacui* of the unconscious. There thus arises

---

[31] According to the dictum in the "Tabula smaragdina," "Quod est inferius, est sicut quod est superius" (That which is below is like that which is above).

a triad, which as we know—not from the fairy tale but from the history of symbolism—constellates a triad in opposition to it[32]—in other words, a conflict ensues. Here too we could ask Socrates, "One, two, three—but, my dear Timaeus, of those who yesterday were the banqueters and today are the banquet-givers, where is the fourth?"[33] He has remained in the realm of the dark mother, caught by the wolfish greed of the unconscious, which is unwilling to let anything escape from its magic circle save at the cost of a corresponding sacrifice.

The hunter or old magician and the witch correspond to the negative parental imagos in the magic world of the unconscious. The hunter first appears in the story as a black raven. He has stolen away the princess and holds her a prisoner. She describes him as "the devil." But it is exceedingly odd that he himself is locked up in the one forbidden room of the castle and fixed to the wall with three nails, as though *crucified*. He is imprisoned, like all jailers, in his own prison, and bound like all who curse. The prison of both is a magic castle at the top of a gigantic tree, presumably the world tree. The princess belongs to the upper region of light near the sun. Sitting there in captivity on the world tree, she is a kind of *anima mundi* who has got herself into the power of darkness. But this catch does not seem to have done the latter much good either, seeing that the captor is crucified and moreover with three nails. The crucifixion evidently betokens a state of agonizing bondage suspension, fit punishment for one foolhardy enough to venture like a Prometheus into the orbit of the opposing principle. This was what the raven, who is identical with the hunter, did when he ravished a precious soul from the upper world of light; and so, as a punishment, he is nailed to the wall in that upper world. That this is an inverted reflection of the primordial Christian image should be obvious enough. The Saviour who freed the soul of humanity from

[32] Cf. *Psychology and Alchemy*, fig. 54 and par. 539; and, for a more detailed account, "Der Geist Mercurius," *Eranos-Jahrbuch 1942*, p. 215.

[33] This unexplained passage has been put down to Plato's "drollery."

the dominion of the prince of this world was nailed to a cross down below on earth, just as the thieving raven is nailed to the wall in the celestial branches of the world tree for his presumptuous meddling. In our fairy tale the peculiar instrument of the magic spell is the triad of nails. Who it was that made the raven captive is not told in the tale, but it sounds as if a spell had been laid upon him in the triune name.[34]

Having climbed up the world tree and penetrated into the magic castle where he is to rescue the princess, our young hero is permitted to enter all the rooms but one, the very room in which the raven is imprisoned. Just as in Paradise there was one tree of which it was forbidden to eat, so here there is one room that is not to be opened, with the natural result that it is entered at once. Nothing excites our interest more than a prohibition. It is the surest way of provoking disobedience.

Obviously there is some secret scheme afoot to free not so much the princess as the raven. As soon as the hero catches sight of him, the raven begins to cry piteously and to complain of thirst,[35] and the young man, moved by the virtue of compassion, slakes it, not with hyssop and gall, but with

[34] In *Deutsche Märchen seit Grimm* (Vol. I, p. 256 ["The Mary-Child"]) it is said that the "Three-in-One" is the forbidden room, which seems to me a fact worth noting.

[35] Aelian (*De natura animalium,* I, 47) relates that Apollo condemned the ravens to perpetual thirst because a raven sent to fetch water took too long over it. In German folklore the raven has to suffer thirst in June or August, the reason given being that he alone was not troubled at the death of Christ, or that he failed to return when Noah sent him forth from the ark. (Friedrich Panzer in *Zeitschrift für deutsche Mythologie,* II (1855), 171; and Reinhold Köhler, *Kleinere Schriften zur Märchenforschung* (Weimar, 1898, p. 3). For the raven as an allegory of evil, see the exhaustive account by Hugo Rahner, "Earth Spirit and Divine Spirit in Patristic Theology," in the present (Eranos) volume. On the other hand, the raven is closely connected with Apollo as his sacred animal, and in the Bible too he has a positive significance. See Psalm 147:9: "He giveth to the beast his food, and to the young ravens which cry"; Job 38:41: "Who provideth for the raven his food? when his young ones cry unto God, they wander for lack of meat." Cf. also Luke 12:24. Ravens appear as true "ministering spirits" in I Kings 17:6, where they bring Elijah the Tishbite his daily fare.

quickening water, whereupon the three nails fall out and the raven escapes through the open window. Thus the evil spirit regains his freedom, changes into the hunter, steals the princess for the second time, but this time locks her up in his hunting lodge on earth. The secret scheme is partially unveiled: the princess must be brought down from the upper world to the world of men, which was evidently not possible without the help of the evil spirit and man's disobedience.

But since in the human world too the hunter of souls is the princess's master, the hero has to intervene anew, to which end, as we have seen, he filches the four-legged horse from the witch and breaks the three-legged spell of the magician. It was the triad that first transfixed the raven, and the triad also represents the power of the evil spirit. These are the two triads that point in opposite directions.

Turning now to quite another field, the realm of psychological experience, we know that three of the four functions of consciousness can become differentiated, i.e., conscious, while the other remains connected with the matrix, the unconscious, and is known as the "inferior" function. It is the Achilles heel of even the most heroic consciousness: somewhere the strong man is weak, the clever man foolish, the good man bad, and the reverse is also true. In our fairy tale the triad appears as a mutilated quaternity. If only one leg could be added to the other three, it would make a whole. The enigmatic axiom of Maria runs: ". . . from the third comes the one as the fourth" (*ek ton triton to hen tetarkon*) —which presumably means, when the third produces the fourth it at once produces unity. The lost component which is in the possession of the wolves belonging to the Great Mother is indeed only a quarter, but, together with the three, it makes a whole which does away with division and conflict.

But how is it that a quarter, on the evidence of symbolism, is at the same time a triad? Here the symbolism of our fairy tale leaves us in the lurch, and we are obliged to have recourse to the facts of psychology. I have said previously that three functions can become differentiated, and only one remains under the spell of the unconscious. This statement must be defined more closely. It is an empirical fact that only *one* function becomes more or less successfully differentiated, which on that account is known as the superior or main function, and together with extraversion or introversion constitutes the type of conscious attitude. This function has associated with it one or two partially differentiated auxiliary functions which hardly ever attain the same degree of differentiation as the main function, that is, the same degree of applicability by the will. Accordingly they possess a higher degree of spontaneity than the main function, which displays a large measure of reliability and is amenable to our intentions. The fourth, inferior function proves on the other hand to be inaccessible to our will. It appears now as a teasing and distracting imp, now as a *deus ex machina*. But always it comes and goes of its own volition. From this it is clear that even the differentiated functions have only partially freed themselves from the unconscious; for the rest they are still rooted in it and to that extent they operate under its rule. Hence the three "differentiated" functions at the disposal of the ego have three corresponding unconscious components that have not yet broken loose from the unconscious.[36] And just as the three conscious and differentiated parts of these functions are confronted by a fourth, undifferentiated function which acts as a painfully disturbing factor, so also the superior function seems to have its worst enemy in the unconscious. Nor should we omit to mention one final turn of the screw: like the devil who delights in disguising himself as an angel of light, the inferior function secretly and mischievously influences the superior function most of all, just as the latter represses the former most strongly.[37]

These unfortunately somewhat abstract formulations are necessary in order to throw some light on the tricky and allusive associations in our—save the mark!—"childishly simple" fairy tale. The two antithetical triads, the one banning and

---

[36] Pictured as three princesses, buried neck deep, in *Nordische Volksmärchen*, Vol. II (1922), pp. 126ff. ["The Three Princesses in the White Land"].

[37] For the function theory see *Psychological Types* (London and New York, 1923).

the other representing the power of evil, tally to a hair's breadth with the functional structure of the conscious and unconscious psyche. Being a spontaneous, naïve, and uncontrived product of the psyche, the fairy tale cannot very well express anything except what the psyche actually is. It is not only *our* fairy tale that depicts these structural psychic relations, but countless other fairy tales do the same.[38]

Our fairy tale reveals with unusual clarity the essentially antithetical nature of the spirit archetype, while on the other hand it shows the bewildering play of antinomies all aiming at the great goal of higher consciousness. The young swineherd who climbs from the animal level up to the top of the giant world tree and there, in the upper world of light, discovers his captive anima, the high-born princess, symbolizes the ascent of consciousness, rising from almost bestial regions to a lofty perch with a broad outlook, which is a singularly appropriate image for the enlargement of the conscious horizon.[39] Once the masculine consciousness has attained this height, it comes face to face with its feminine counterpart, the anima.[40] She is a personification of the unconscious. The meeting shows how inept it is to designate the latter as the "subconscious": it is not merely "below" consciousness but also above it, so far above it indeed that the hero has to climb up to it with considerable effort. This "upper" unconscious, however, is far from being a "superconscious" in the sense that anyone who reaches it, like our hero, would stand as high above the "subconscious" as above the earth's surface. On the contrary,

[38] I would like to add, for the layman's benefit, that the theory of the psyche's structure was not derived from fairy tales and myths, but is grounded on empirical observations made in the field of medicopsychological research and was corroborated only secondarily through the study of comparative symbology, in spheres very far removed from ordinary medical practice.

[39] A typical enantiodromia is played out here: as one cannot go any higher along this road, one must now realize the other side of one's being, and climb down again.

[40] The young man asks himself, on catching sight of the tree, "How would it be if you were to look at the world from the top of that great tree?"

he makes the disagreeable discovery that his high and mighty anima, the Princess Soul, is bewitched up there and no freer than a bird in a golden cage. He may pat himself on the back for having soared up from the flatlands and from almost bestial stupidity, but his soul is in the power of an evil spirit, a sinister father imago of sub-terrestrial nature in the guise of a raven, the celebrated theriomorphic figure of the devil. What use now is his lofty perch and his wide horizon, when his own dear soul is languishing in prison? Worse, she plays the game of the underworld and ostensibly tries to stop the young man from discovering the secret of her imprisonment, by forbidding him to enter that one room. But secretly she leads him to it by the very fact of her veto. It is as though the unconscious had two hands of which one always does the opposite of the other. The princess wants and does not want to be rescued. But the evil spirit too has got himself into a fix, by all accounts: he wanted to filch a fine soul from the shining upper world—which he could easily do as a winged being—but had not bargained on being shut up there himself. Black spirit though he is, he longs for the light. That is his secret justification, just as his being spellbound is a punishment for his transgression. But so long as the evil spirit is caught in the upper world, the princess cannot get down to earth either, and the hero remains lost in paradise. So now he commits the sin of disobedience and thereby enables the robber to escape, thus causing the abduction of the princess for the second time—a whole chain of calamities. In the result, however, the princess comes down to earth and the devilish raven assumes the human shape of the hunter. The otherworldly anima and the evil principle both descend to the human sphere, that is, they dwindle to human proportions and thus become approachable. The three-legged, all-knowing horse represents the hunter's own power: it corresponds to the unconscious components of the differentiated functions.[41] The hunter himself personifies the inferior

---

[41] The "omniscience" of the unconscious components is naturally an exaggeration. Nevertheless they do have at their disposal—or are influenced by—subliminal perceptions and memories of the unconscious, as well as by its instinctive archetypal contents. It is

function, which also manifests itself in the hero as his inquisitiveness and love of adventure. As the story unfolds he becomes more and more like the hunter: he too obtains his horse from the witch. But, unlike him, the hunter omitted to obtain the twelve lambs in order to feed the wolves, who then injured his horse. He forgot to pay tribute to the chthonic powers because he was nothing but a robber. Through this omission the hero learns that the unconscious lets its creatures go only at the cost of sacrifice.[42] The number 12 is presumably a time symbol, with the subsidiary meaning of the twelve labors (*athla*)[43] that have to be performed for the unconscious before one can get free.[44] The hunter looks like a previous unsuccessful attempt of the hero to gain possession of his soul through robbery and violence. But the conquest of the soul is in reality a work of patience, self-sacrifice, and devotion. By gaining possession of the four-legged horse the hero steps right into the shoes of the hunter and carries off the princess as well. The quaternity in our tale proves to be the greater power, for it integrates into its totality that which it still needed in order to become whole.

The archetype of the spirit in this, be it said, by no means primitive fairy tale is expressed theriomorphically as a system of three functions which is subordinated to a unity, the evil spirit, in the same way that some unnamed authority has crucified the raven with a triad of three nails. The two supraordinate unities correspond in the first case to the inferior function which is the archenemy of the main function, namely, to the hunter; and in the second case to the main function,

---

these that give unconscious activities their unexpectedly accurate information.

[42] The hunter has reckoned without his host, as generally happens. Seldom or never do we think of the price exacted by the spirit's activity.

[43] Cf. the Herakles cycle.

[44] The alchemists stress the long duration of the work and speak of the *"longissima via," "diuturnitas immensae meditationis,"* etc. The number 12 may be connected with the ecclesiastical year, when the redemptive work of Christ is fulfilled. The lamb sacrifice probably comes from this source too.

namely, to the hero. Hunter and hero are ultimately equated with one another, so that the hunter's function is resolved in the hero. As a matter of fact, the hero lies dormant in the hunter from the very beginning, egging him on, with all the unmoral means at his disposal, to carry out the rape of the soul, and then causing him to play her into the hero's hands against the hunter's will. On the surface a furious conflict rages between them, but down below the one goes about the other's business. The knot is unraveled directly the hero succeeds in capturing the quaternity—or in psychological language, when he assimilates the inferior function into the ternary system. That puts an end to the conflict at one blow, and the figure of the hunter melts into thin air. After this victory the hero sets his princess upon the three-legged steed and together they ride away to her father's kingdom. From now on she rules and personifies the realm of spirit that formerly served the wicked hunter. Thus the anima is and remains the representative of that part of the unconscious which can never be assimilated into a humanly attainable whole.

Postscript. Only after the completion of my manuscript was my attention drawn by a friend to a Russian variant of our story. It bears the title "Maria Morevna."[45] The hero of the story is no swineherd, but Czarevitch Ivan. There is an interesting explanation of the three helpful animals: correspond to Ivan's three sisters and their husbands, who are really birds. The three sisters represent an unconscious triad of functions related to both the animal and spiritual realms. The bird men are a species of angel and emphasize the auxiliary nature of the unconscious functions. In the story they intervene at the critical moment when the hero—unlike his German counterpart—gets into the power of the evil spirit and is killed and dismembered (the typical fate of the God-man!).[46] The evil

---

[45] "Daughter of the sea."—*Russian Fairy Tales* (New York, 1945), pp. 553ff.

[46] The old man puts the dismembered body into a barrel which he throws into the sea. This is reminiscent of the fate of Osiris (head and phallus).

spirit is an old man who is often shown naked and is called Koschei[47] the Deathless. The corresponding witch is the well-known Baba Yaga. The three helpful animals of the German variant are doubled here, appearing first as the bird men and then as the lion, the strange bird, and the bees. The princess is Queen Maria Morevna, a redoubtable martial leader—Mary the queen of heaven is lauded in the Russian Orthodox hymnal as "leader of hosts"!—who has chained up the evil spirit with twelve chains in the forbidden room in her castle. When Ivan slakes the old devil's thirst he makes off with the queen. The magic riding animals do not in the end turn into human beings. This Russian story has a distinctly more primitive character.

5. Supplement

The following remarks lay no claim to general interest, being in the main technical. I wanted at first to delete them from this revised version of my essay, but then I changed my mind and appended them in a Supplement. The reader who is not specifically interested in psychology can safely skip this section. For, in what follows, I have dealt with the abstruse-looking problem of the three- and four-leggedness of the magic horses, and presented my reflections in such a way as to demonstrate the method I have employed. This piece of psychological reasoning rests firstly on the irrational data of the material, that is, of the fairy tale, myth, or dream, and secondly on the conscious realization of the "latent" rational connections which these data have with one another. That such connections exist at all is something of an hypothesis, like that which asserts that dreams have a meaning. The truth of this assumption is not established a priori: its usefulness can only be proved by application. It therefore remains to be seen whether its methodical application to irrational material enables one to interpret the latter in a meaningful way. Its application consists in approaching the material as if it had a coherent inner

[47] From *kost*, "bone," and *pakost, kapost*, "disgusting, dirty."

meaning. For this purpose most of the data require a certain amplification, that is, they need to be clarified, generalized, and approximated to a more or less general concept in accordance with Cardan's rule of interpretation. For instance, the three-leggedness, in order to be recognized for what it is, has first to be separated from the horse and then approximated to its specific principle—the principle of threeness. Likewise the four-leggedness in the fairy tale, when raised to the level of a general concept, enters into relationship with the threeness and as a result we have the enigma mentioned in the *Timaeus*, the problem of three and four. Triads and tetrads represent archetypal structures that play a significant part in all symbolism and are equally important for the investigation of myths and dreams. By raising the irrational datum (three-leggedness and four-leggedness) to the level of a general concept we elicit the universal meaning of this motif and encourage the inquiring mind to tackle the problem seriously. This task involves a series of reflections and deductions of a technical nature which I would not wish to withhold from the psychologically interested reader and especially from the professional, the less so as this labor of the intellect represents a typical unraveling of symbols and is indispensable for an adequate understanding of the products of the unconscious. Only in this way can the nexus of unconscious relationships be made to yield their own meaning, in contrast to those deductive interpretations derived from a preconceived theory, e.g., interpretations based on astronomy, meteorology, mythology, and —last but not least—the sexual theory.

The three-legged and four-legged horses are in truth a recondite matter worthy of closer examination. The three and the four remind us not only of the dilemma we have already met in the theory of psychological functions, but also of the axiom of Maria Prophetissa, which plays a considerable role in alchemy. It may therefore be rewarding to examine more closely the meaning of the miraculous horses.

The first thing that seems to me worthy of note is that the three-legged horse which is assigned to the princess as her mount is a mare, and is moreover herself a bewitched princess. Threeness is unmistakably connected here with femininity, whereas from the dominating religious standpoint of consciousness it is an exclusively masculine affair, quite apart from the fact that 3, as an uneven number, is masculine in the first place. One could therefore translate threeness as "masculinity" outright, this being all the more significant when one remembers the ancient Egyptian triunity of God, Ka-mutef,[48] and Pharaoh.

Three-leggedness, as the attribute of some animal, denotes the unconscious masculinity immanent in a female creature. In a real woman it would correspond to the animus who, like the magic horse, represents "spirit." In the case of the anima, however, threeness does not coincide with any Christian idea of the Trinity but with the "lower triangle," the inferior function triad that constitutes the "shadow." The inferior half of the personality is for the greater part unconscious. It does not denote the whole of the unconscious, but only the personal segment of it. The anima, on the other hand, so far as she is distinguished from the shadow, personifies the collective unconscious. If threeness is assigned to her as a riding-animal, it means that she "rides" the shadow, is related to it as "Mara."[49] In that case she possesses the shadow. But if she herself is the horse, then she has lost her dominating position as a personification of the collective unconscious and is "ridden"—possessed—by Princess A, spouse of the hero. As the fairy tale rightly says, she has been changed by witchcraft into the three-legged horse (Princess B).

We can sort out this imbroglio more or less as follows:

1. Princess A is the anima[50] of the hero. She rides—that is,

---

[48] Ka-mutef means "bull of his mother." See Helmuth Jacobsohn, "Die dogmatische Stellung des Königs in der Theologie der alten Aegypter," *Aegyptologische Forschungen* (Glückstadt), No. 8 (1939), pp. 17, 35, 41ff.

[49] In *Symbols of Transformation* (Coll. Works, Vol. 5), p. 249, Jung speaks of Mara as "ogress, incubus, demon" and, by extension, "nightmare".—Ed.

[50] The fact that she is no ordinary girl, but is of royal descent and moreover the *electa* of the evil spirit, proves her nonhuman,

possesses—the three-legged horse, who is the shadow, the inferior function triad of her later spouse. To put it more simply: she has taken possession of the inferior half of the hero's personality. She has caught him on his weak side, as so often happens in ordinary life, for where one is weak one needs support and completion. In fact, a woman's place is on the weak side of a man. This is how we would have to formulate the situation if we regarded the hero and Princess A as two ordinary people. But since it is a fairy story played out mainly in the world of magic, we are probably more correct in interpreting Princess A as the hero's anima. In that case the hero has been wafted out of the profane world through his encounter with the anima, like Merlin by his fairy: as an ordinary man he is like one caught in a marvelous dream, viewing the world through a veil of mist.

2. The matter is now considerably complicated by the unexpected fact that the three-legged horse is a mare, an equivalent of Princess A. She (the mare) is Princess B, who in the shape of a horse corresponds to Princess A's shadow (i.e., her inferior function triad). Princess B, however, differs from Princess A in that, unlike her, she does not ride the horse but is contained in it: she is bewitched and has thus come under the spell of a masculine triad. Therefore, she is possessed by a shadow.

3. The question now is, *whose* shadow? It cannot be the shadow of the hero, for this is already taken up by the latter's anima. The fairy tale gives us the answer: it is the hunter or magician who has bewitched her. As we have seen, the hunter is somehow connected with the hero, since the latter gradually puts himself in his shoes. Hence one could easily arrive at the conjecture that the hunter is at bottom none other than the shadow of the hero. But this supposition is contradicted by the fact that the hunter stands for a formidable power which extends not only to the hero's anima but much further, namely, to the royal brother-sister pair of whose existence the hero and

---

mythological nature. I must assume that the reader is acquainted with the idea of the anima (see Editor's Introduction).

his anima have no notion, and who appear very much out of the blue in the story itself. The power that extends beyond the orbit of the individual has a more than individual character and cannot therefore be identified with the shadow, if we conceive and define this as the dark half of the personality. As a supra-individual factor the numen of the hunter is a dominant of the collective unconscious whose characteristic features —hunter, magician, raven, miraculous horse, crucifixion or suspension high up in the boughs of the world tree[51]—touch the Germanic psyche very closely. Hence the Christian *Weltanschauung*, when reflected in the ocean of the (Germanic) unconscious, logically takes on the features of Wotan.[52] In the figure of the hunter we meet an *imago Dei*, a God-image, for Wotan is also a god of winds and spirits, on which account the Romans fittingly interpreted him as Mercury.

4. The Prince and his sister, Princess B, have therefore been seized by a pagan god and changed into horses, i.e., thrust down to the animal level, into the realm of the unconscious. The inference is that in their proper human shape the pair of them once belonged to the sphere of collective consciousness. But who are they?

In order to answer this question we must proceed from the fact that these two are an undoubted counterpart of the hero and Princess A. They are connected with the latter also be-

[51] "I ween that I hung / on the windy tree,
  Hung there for nights full nine;
With the spear I was wounded, / and offered I was
  To Othin, myself to myself,
On the tree that none / may ever know
  What root beneath it runs."
          (*The Poetic Edda*, New York, 1923, p. 60, trans. Henry Adams Bellows.)

[52] Cf. the experience of God as described by Nietzsche in "Ariadne's Lament":
      "I am but thy quarry,
      Cruellest of hunters!
      Thy proudest captive,
      Thou brigand back of the clouds!"
          Gedichte und Spüche von Friedrich Nietzsche (Leipzig, 1898), pp. 155ff.

cause they serve as their mounts, and in consequence they appear as their lower, animal halves. Because of its almost total unconsciousness the animal has always symbolized the psychic sphere in man which lies hidden in the darkness of the body's instinctual life. The hero rides the stallion, characterized by the even (feminine) number 4; Princess A rides the mare who has only three legs (3: a masculine number). These numbers make it clear that the transformation into animals has brought with it a modification of sex character: the stallion has a feminine attribute, the mare a masculine one. Psychology can confirm this development as follows: to the degree that a man is overpowered by the (collective) unconscious there is not only a more unbridled intrusion of the instinctual sphere, but a certain feminine character also makes its appearance, which I have suggested should be called "anima." If, on the other hand, a woman comes under the domination of the unconscious, the darker side of her feminine nature emerges all the more strongly, coupled with markedly masculine traits. These latter are comprised under the term "animus."

5. According to the fairy tale, however, the animal form of the brother-sister pair is "unreal" and due simply to the magic influence of the pagan hunter god. If they were nothing but animals, we could rest content with this interpretation. But that would be to pass over in unmerited silence the singular allusion to a modification of sex character. The white horses are no ordinary horses: they are miraculous beasts with supernatural powers. Therefore the human figures out of which the horses were magically conjured must likewise have had something supernatural about them. The fairy tale makes no comment here, but if our assumption is correct that the two animal forms correspond to the subhuman components of hero and princess, then it follows that the human forms—Prince and Princess B—must correspond to their superhuman components. The superhuman quality of the original swineherd is shown by the fact that he becomes a hero, practically a half-god, since he does not stay with his swine but climbs the world tree, where he is very nearly made its prisoner, like Wotan. Similarly, he could not have become like the hunter if he did

not have a certain resemblance to him in the first place. In the same way the imprisonment of Princess A on the top of the world tree proves her electness, and in so far as she shares the hunter's bed, as stated by the tale, she is actually the bride of God.

It is these extraordinary forces of heroism and election, bordering on the superhuman, which involve two quite ordinary humans in a superhuman fate. Accordingly, in the profane world a swineherd becomes a king, and a princess gets an agreeable husband. But since, for fairy tales, there is not only a profane but also a magical world, human fate does not have the final word. The fairy tale therefore does not omit to point out what happens in the world of magic. There too a prince and princess have got into the power of the evil spirit, who is himself in a tight corner from which he cannot extricate himself without extraneous help. So the human fate that befalls the swineherd and Princess A is paralleled in the world of magic. But in so far as the hunter is a pagan god image and thus exalted above the world of heroes and paramours of the gods, the parallelism goes beyond the merely magical into a divine and spiritual sphere, where the evil spirit, the Devil himself—or at least *a* devil—is bound by the spell of an equally mighty or even mightier counter principle indicated by the three nails. This supreme tension of opposites, the mainspring of the whole drama, is obviously the conflict between the upper and lower triads, or, to put it in theological terms, between the Christian God and the devil who has assumed the features of Wotan.[53]

6. We must, it seems, start from this supreme authority if we want to understand the story correctly, for the drama takes its rise from the initial transgression of the evil spirit. The immediate consequence of this is his crucifixion. In that distressing situation he needs outside help, and as it is not forthcoming from above, it can only be summoned from below. A young swineherd, possessed with the boyish spirit of adventure, is

[53] As regards the triadic nature of Wotan cf. Martin Ninck, *Wotan und germanischer Schicksalsglaube* (Jena, 1935), p. 142. His horse is also described as, among other things, three-legged.

reckless and inquisitive enough to climb the world tree. Had he fallen and broken his neck, no doubt everybody would have said, "What evil spirit could have given him the crazy idea of climbing up an enormous tree like that!" Nor would they have been altogether wrong, for that is precisely what the evil spirit was after. The capture of Princess A was a transgression in the profane world, and the bewitching of the—as we may suppose—semidivine brother-sister pair was just such an enormity in the magical world. We do not know, but it is possible, that this heinous crime was committed before the bewitching of Princess A. At any rate both episodes point to a transgression of the evil spirit in the magical world as well as in the profane.

It is assuredly not without a deeper meaning that the rescuer or redeemer should be a swineherd, like the Prodigal Son. He is of lowly origin and has this much in common with the curious conception of the redeemer in alchemy. His first liberating act is to deliver the evil spirit from the divine punishment meted out to him. It is from this act, representing the first stage of lysis, that the whole dramatic tangle develops.

7. The moral of this story is in truth exceedingly odd. The finale satisfies in so far as the swineherd and Princess A are married and become the royal pair. Prince and Princess B likewise celebrate their wedding, but this—in accordance with the archaic prerogative of kings—takes the form of incest, which, though somewhat repellent, must be regarded as more or less habitual in semidivine circles.[54] But what, we may ask, happens to the evil spirit, whose rescue from condign punishment sets the whole thing in motion? The wicked hunter is trampled to pieces by the horses, which presumably does no lasting damage to a spirit. Apparently he vanishes without trace, but only apparently, for he does after all leave a trace

[54] The assumption that they are a brother-sister pair is supported by the fact that the stallion addresses the mare as "sister." This may be just a figure of speech; on the other hand, sister means sister, whether we take it figuratively or nonfiguratively. Apart from this incest plays a significant part in mythology as well as in alchemy.

behind him, namely a hard-won happiness in both the profane and the magical world. Two halves of the quaternity, represented on one side by the swineherd and Princess A and on the other by Prince and Princess B, have each come together and united: two marriage-pairs now confront one another, parallel but otherwise divided, inasmuch as the one pair belongs to the profane and the other to the magical world. But in spite of this indubitable division, secret psychological connections, as we have seen, exist between them which allow us to derive the one pair from the other.

Speaking in the spirit of the fairy tale, which unfolds its drama from the highest point, one would have to say that the world of half-gods is anterior to the profane world and produces it out of itself, just as the former must be thought of as proceeding from the world of gods. Conceived in this way, the swineherd and Princess A are nothing less than earthly simulacra of Prince and Princess B, who in their turn would be the descendants of heavenly prototypes. Nor should we forget that the horse-breeding witch belongs to the hunter as his female counterpart, rather like an ancient Epona (the Celtic goddess of horses). Unfortunately we are not told how the magical conjuration into horses happened. But it is evident that the witch had a hand in the game because both horses were raised from her stock and are thus, in a sense, her productions. Hunter and witch form a pair—the reflection, in the nocturnal-chthonic part of the magical world, of a divine parental pair. The latter is easily recognized in the central Christian idea of *sponsus et sponsa,* Christ and his bride, the Church.

If we wanted to explain the fairy tale personalistically the attempt would founder on the fact that the archetypes are not whimsical inventions, but autonomous elements of the unconscious psyche which were there before any invention was thought of. They represent the unalterable structure of a psychic world whose "reality" is attested by the determining effects it has upon the conscious mind. Thus, it is a significant psychic reality that the human pair[55] is matched by another

[55] Human in so far as the anima is replaced by a human person.

pair in the unconscious, the latter pair being only in appearance a reflection of the first. In reality the royal pair invariably comes first, as an a priori, so that the human pair has far more the significance of an individual concretization, in space and time, of an eternal and primordial image—at least in so far as its spiritual structure is imprinted upon the biological continuum.

We could say, then, that the swineherd stands for the "animal" man who has a soul mate somewhere in the upper world. By her royal birth she betrays her connection with the pre-existent, semidivine pair. Looked at from this angle, the latter stands for everything a man can become if only he climbs high enough up the world tree.[56] For to the degree that the young swineherd gains possession of the patrician, feminine half of himself, he approximates to the pair of half-gods and lifts himself into the sphere of kingship, that is, of universal validity. We come across the same theme in Christian Rosencreutz's *Chymical Wedding*, where the king's son must first free his bride from the power of a Moor, to whom she has *voluntarily* given herself as a concubine. The Moor represents the alchemical *nigredo* in which the arcane substance lies hidden, an idea that forms yet another parallel to our mythologem, or, as we would say in psychological language, another variant of this archetype.

As in alchemy, our fairy tale depicts those unconscious processes that compensate the Christian, conscious situation. It describes the workings of a spirit who plies away at our Christian ideas, carrying them beyond the fixed confines of ecclesiasticism, to seek an answer to those questions which neither the Middle Ages nor the present day could answer. It is not difficult to see in the image of the second royal pair a correspondence to the ecclesiastical conception of bridegroom and bride, and in that of the hunter and witch a distortion of

[56] The great tree corresponds to the *arbor philosophica* of the alchemists. The meeting between an earthly human being and the anima, swimming down in the shape of a mermaid, is to be found in the so-called "Ripley Scrowle." Cf. *Psychology and Alchemy*, fig. 257.

it, veering towards an atavistic, unconscious Wotanism. The fact that it is a *German* fairy tale makes the position particularly interesting, since the same Wotanism stood psychological godfather to National Socialism, which carried the distortion to the lowest pitch before the eyes of the world.[57] On the other hand the fairy tale makes it clear that it is possible for a man to reach wholeness, to become the total man, only with the co-operation of the spirit of darkness, indeed that the latter is actually a *causa instrumentalis* of redemption and individuation. In utter perversion of this goal of spiritual development, to which all nature aspires and which is also prefigured in Christian doctrine, National Socialism destroyed man's moral autonomy and set up the nonsensical totalitarianism of the State. The fairy tale tells us how to proceed if we want to overcome the power of darkness: we must turn his own weapons against him, which naturally cannot be done if the magical underworld of the hunter remains unconscious, and if the best men in the nation would rather preach dogmatisms and platitudes than take the human soul seriously.

6. Conclusion

When we consider the spirit in its archetypal form as it appears to us in fairy tales and dreams, it presents a picture that differs strangely from the conscious idea of spirit, which is split up into so many meanings. Spirit was originally a spirit in human or animal form, a *daimonion* that came upon man from without. But our material already shows traces of an expansion of consciousness which has gradually begun to occupy that originally unconscious territory and to transform those *daimonia*, at least partially, into voluntary acts. Man conquers not only nature, but spirit also, without realizing what he is doing. To the man of enlightened intellect it seems like the correction of a fallacy when he recognizes that what he took to be spirits is simply the human spirit and ultimately his own spirit. All the superhuman things, whether good or bad, that

---

[57] Cf. *Essays on Contemporary Events* (London, 1947).

former ages predicated of the *daimonia*, are reduced to "reasonable" proportions as though they were pure exaggeration, and everything seems to be in the best possible order. But were the unanimous convictions of the past really and truly only exaggerations? If they were not, then the integration of the spirit means nothing less than its daemonization, since the superhuman spiritual agencies that were formerly tied up in nature are introjected into human nature, thus endowing it with a power which extends the bounds of the personality ad infinitum, in the most perilous way. I put it to the enlightened rationalist: has his rational reduction led to the beneficial control of matter and spirit? He will point proudly to the advances in physics and medicine, to the freeing of the mind from medieval stupidity and—as a well-meaning Christian—to our deliverance from the fear of demons. But we continue to ask: what have all our other cultural achievements led to? The fearful answer is there before our eyes: man has been delivered from no fear, a hideous nightmare lies upon the world. So far reason has failed lamentably, and the very thing that everybody wanted to avoid rolls on in ghastly progression. Man has achieved a wealth of useful gadgets, but, to offset that, he has torn open the abyss, and what will become of him now—where can he make a halt? After the last World War we hoped for reason: we go on hoping. But already we are fascinated by the possibilities of atomic fission and promise ourselves a Golden Age—the surest guarantee that the abomination of desolation will grow to limitless dimensions. And who or what is it that causes all this? It is none other than that harmless (!), ingenious, inventive, and sweetly reasonable human spirit who unfortunately is abysmally unconscious of the daemonism that still clings to him. Worse, this spirit does everything to avoid looking himself in the face, and we all help him like mad. Only, heaven preserve us from psychology—*that* depravity might lead to self-knowledge! Rather let us have wars, for which somebody else is always to blame, nobody seeing that all the world is driven to do just what all the world flees from in terror.

It seems to me, frankly, that former ages did not exaggerate, that the spirit has not sloughed off its daemonisms, and that mankind, because of its scientific and technological development, has in increasing measure delivered itself over to the danger of possession. True, the archetype of the spirit is capable of working for good as well as for evil, but it depends upon man's free—i.e., conscious—decision whether the good also will be perverted into something satanic. Man's worst sin is unconsciousness, but it is indulged in with the greatest piety even by those who should serve mankind as teachers and examples. When will the time come when we shall not simply take man for granted in this barbarous manner, but shall in all seriousness seek for ways and means to exorcise him, to rescue him from possession and unconsciousness, and make this the most vital task of civilization? Can we not understand that all the outward tinkerings and improvements do not touch man's inner nature, and that everything ultimately depends upon whether the man who wields the science and the technics is capable of responsibility or not? Christianity has shown us the way, but, as the facts bear witness, it has not penetrated deeply enough below the surface. What depths of despair are still needed to open the eyes of the world's responsible leaders, so that at least they can refrain from leading themselves into temptation?

The Psychology of the Child Archetype[1]

Introduction

The author of the companion essay[2] on the mythology of the "child" or the child-god has asked me for a psychological commentary on the subject of his investigations. I am glad to accede to his request, although the undertaking seems to me no small venture in view of the great significance of the child-motif in mythology. Kerényi himself has enlarged upon the occurrence of this motif in Greece and Rome, with parallels drawn from Indian, Finnish, and other sources, thus indicating that the presentation of the theme would allow of yet further extensions. Though a comprehensive description would contribute nothing decisive in principle, it would nevertheless produce an overwhelming impression of the world-wide inci-

[1] This chapter was published in *Essays on a Science of Mythology* by C. G. Jung and the Greek scholar C. Kerényi, translated by R. F. C. Hull, Bollingen Series XXII (Pantheon Books, 1949). —Ed.

[2] C. Kerényi, whose essay is entitled "The Primordial Child in Primordial Times."—Ed.

dence and frequency of the motif. The customary treatment of mythological motifs so far in separate departments of science, such as philology, ethnology, history of civilization, and comparative religion, was not exactly a help to the recognition of their universality; and the psychological problems raised by this universality could easily be shelved by hypotheses of migration. Consequently Adolf Bastian's ideas met with little success in their day. Even then there was sufficient empirical evidence available to permit far-reaching psychological conclusions, but the necessary premises were lacking. Although the psychological knowledge of that time included myth formation in its province—witness W. Wundt's *Völkerpsychologie*—it was not in a position to demonstrate this same process as a living function actually present in the psyche of civilized man, any more than it could understand mythological motifs as structural elements of the psyche. True to its history, where psychology was first of all metaphysics, then the study of the senses and their functions, then of the conscious mind and *its* functions, psychology identified its proper subject with the conscious psyche and its contents and thus completely overlooked the existence of an unconscious psyche. Although various philosophers, among them Leibniz, Kant, and Schelling, had already pointed very clearly to the problem of the dark side of the psyche, it was a physician who felt impelled, from his scientific and medical experience, to point to the *unconscious* as the essential basis of the psyche. This was C. G. Carus, the authority whom Eduard von Hartmann followed. In recent times it was, once again, medical psychology that approached the problem of the unconscious without philosophical preconceptions. It became clear from many separate investigations that the psychopathology of the neuroses and of many psychoses cannot dispense with the hypothesis of a dark side of the psyche, i.e., the unconscious. It is the same with the psychology of dreams, which is really the *terra intermedia* between normal and pathological psychology. In the dream, as in the products of psychoses, there are numberless interconnections to which one can find parallels only in mythological associations of ideas (or perhaps in certain poetic creations which are often characterized by a borrowing, not always conscious, from myths). Had thorough investigation shown that in the majority of such cases it was simply a matter of forgotten knowledge, the physician would not have gone to the trouble of making extensive researches into individual and collective parallels. But, in point of fact, typical mythologems were observed among individuals to whom all knowledge of this kind was absolutely out of the question, and where indirect derivation from religious ideas that might have been known to them, or from popular figures of speech, was impossible. Such conclusions forced us to assume that we must be dealing with "autochthonous" revivals independent of all tradition, and, consequently, that "myth-forming" structural elements must be present in the unconscious psyche.[3]

These products are never (or at least very seldom) myths with a definite form, but rather mythological components which, because of their typical nature, we can call "motifs," "primordial images," types or—as I have named them—*archetypes*. The child archetype is an excellent example. Today we can hazard the formula that *the archetypes appear in myths and fairy tales just as they do in dreams and in the products of psychotic fantasy*. The medium in which they are embedded is, in the former case, an ordered and for the most part immediately understandable context, but in the latter case a generally unintelligible, irrational, not to say delirious sequence of images which nonetheless does not lack a certain hidden coherence. In the individual, the archetypes occur as involuntary manifestations of unconscious processes whose existence and meaning can only be inferred, whereas the myth deals with traditional forms of incalculable age. They hark back to a prehistoric world whose spiritual preconceptions and

[3] Freud, in his *Interpretation of Dreams,* paralleled certain aspects of infantile psychology with the Oedipus legend and observed that its "universal validity" was to be explained in terms of a similar infantile preconception. In the *Psychology of the Unconscious* (1911), revised and expanded as *Symbols of Transformation* (1956), I presented a somewhat more comprehensive examination of psychic and mythological parallels. Cf. also my essay "Ueber den Archetypus," *Zentralblatt für Psychotherapie,* IX (1936).

general conditions we can still observe today among existing primitives. Myths on this level are as a rule *tribal history* handed down from generation to generation by word of mouth. Primitive mentality differs from the civilized chiefly in that the conscious mind is far less developed in scope and intensity. Functions such as thinking, willing, etc., are not yet differentiated; they are pre-conscious, a fact which in the case of thinking, for instance, shows itself in the circumstance that the primitive does not think *consciously,* but that thoughts *appear*. The primitive cannot assert that he thinks; it is rather that "something thinks in him." The spontaneity of the act of thinking does not lie, causally, in his conscious mind, but in his unconscious. Moreover, he is incapable of any conscious effort of will; he must put himself beforehand into the "mood of willing," or let himself be put—hence his *rites d'entrée et de sortie*. His consciousness is menaced by an almighty unconscious: hence his fear of magical influences which may cross his path at any moment; and for this reason, too, he is surrounded by unknown forces and must adjust himself to them as best he can. Owing to the chronic twilight state of his consciousness, it is often next to impossible to find out whether he merely dreamed something or whether he really experienced it. The spontaneous manifestation of the unconscious and its archetypes intrudes everywhere into his conscious mind, and the mythical world of his ancestors—for instance, the *aljira* or *bugari* of the Australian aborigines—is a reality equal if not superior to the material world.[4] It is not the world as we know it that speaks out of his unconscious, but the unknown world of the psyche, of which we know that it mirrors our empirical world only in part, and that, for the other part, it molds this empirical world in accordance with its own psychic assumptions. The archetype does not proceed from physical facts; it describes how the psyche experiences the physical fact, and in so doing the psyche often behaves so autocratically that it denies tangible reality or makes statements that fly in the face of it.

[4] This fact is well known, and the relevant ethnological literature is too great to be mentioned here.

The primitive mentality does not invent *myths*, it *experiences* them. Myths are original revelations of the pre-conscious psyche, involuntary statements about unconscious psychic happenings, and anything but allegories of physical processes. Such allegories would be an idle amusement for an unscientific intellect. Myths, on the contrary, have a vital meaning. Not merely do they represent, they *are* the psychic life of the primitive tribe, which immediately falls to pieces and decays when it loses its mythological heritage, like a man who has lost his soul. A tribe's mythology is its living religion, whose loss is always and everywhere, even among the civilized, a moral catastrophe. But religion is a vital link with psychic processes independent of and beyond consciousness, in the dark hinterland of the psyche. Many of these unconscious processes may be indirectly occasioned by consciousness, but never by conscious choice. Others appear to arise spontaneously, that is to say, from no discernible or demonstrable conscious cause.

Modern psychology treats the products of unconscious phantasy-activity as self-portraits of what is going on in the unconscious, or as statements of the unconscious psyche about itself. They fall into two categories. First, fantasies (including dreams) of a personal character, which go back unquestionably to personal experiences, things forgotten or repressed, and can thus be completely explained by individual anamnesis. Second, fantasies (including dreams) of an impersonal character, which cannot be reduced to experiences in the individual's past, and thus cannot be explained as something individually acquired. These fantasy-images undoubtedly have their closest analogues in mythological types. We must therefore assume that they correspond to certain *collective* (and not personal) structural elements of the human psyche in general, and, like the morphological elements of the human body, are *inherited*. Although tradition and transmission by migration certainly play a part there are, as we have said, very many cases that cannot be accounted for in this way and drive us to the hypothesis of "autochthonous revival." These cases are so numerous that we cannot but assume the existence of a collective psychic substratum. I have called this the *collective unconscious*.

The products of this second category resemble the types of structures to be met with in myth and fairy tale so much that we must regard them as related. It is therefore wholly within the realm of possibility that both, the mythological types as well as the individual types, arise under quite similar conditions. As already mentioned, the fantasy-products of the second category (as also those of the first) arise in a state of reduced intensity of consciousness (in dreams, delirium, reveries, visions, etc.). In all these states the check put upon unconscious contents by the concentration of the conscious mind ceases, so that the hitherto unconscious material streams, as though from opened side-sluices, into the field of consciousness. This mode of origination is the general rule.[5]

Reduced intensity of consciousness and absence of concentration and attention, Janet's *abaissement du niveau mental*, correspond pretty exactly to the primitive state of consciousness in which, we must suppose, myths were originally formed. It is therefore exceedingly probable that the mythological archetypes, too, made their appearance in much the same manner as the manifestations of archetypal structures among individuals today.

The methodological principle in accordance with which psychology treats the products of the unconscious is this: *Contents of an archetypal character are manifestations of processes in the collective unconscious*. Hence they do not refer to anything that is or has been conscious, but to something *essentially unconscious*. In the last analysis, therefore, *it is impossible to say what they refer to*. Every interpretation necessarily remains an "as-if." The ultimate core of meaning may be circumscribed, but not described. Even so, the bare circumscription denotes an essential step forward in our knowledge of the preconscious structure of the psyche, which was already in existence when there was as yet no unity of personality (even

[5] Except for certain cases of spontaneous vision, *automatismes téléologiques* (Flournoy), and the processes in the method of "active imagination," which I have described elsewhere.

today the primitive is not securely possessed of it) and no consciousness at all. We can also observe this pre-conscious state in early childhood, and as a matter of fact it is the dreams of this early period that not infrequently bring extremely remarkable archetypal contents to light.[6]

If, then, we proceed in accordance with the above principle, there is no longer any question of whether a myth refers to the sun or the moon, the father or the mother, sexuality or fire or water; all we can do is to circumscribe and give an approximate description of an *unconscious core of meaning*. The ultimate meaning of this nucleus was never conscious and never will be. It was, and still is, only interpreted, and every interpretation that comes anywhere near the hidden sense (or, from the point of view of the scientific intellect, nonsense, which comes to the same thing) has always, right from the beginning, laid claim not only to absolute truth and validity but to instant reverence and religious devotion. Archetypes were, and still are, living psychic forces that demand to be taken seriously, and they have a strange way of making sure of their effect. Always they were the bringers of protection and salvation, and their violation has as its consequence the "perils of the soul" known to us from the psychology of primitives. Moreover, they are the infallible causes of neurotic and even psychotic disorders, behaving exactly like neglected or maltreated physical organs or organic functional systems.

What an archetypal content is always expressing is first and foremost a parable. If it speaks of the sun and identifies with it the lion, the king, the hoard of gold guarded by the dragon, or the force that makes for the life and health of man, it is neither the one thing nor the other, but the unknown third thing that finds more or less adequate expression in all these similes, yet—to the perpetual vexation of the intellect—remains unknown and not to be fitted into a formula. For this reason the scientific intellect is always inclined to put on airs of en-

---

[6] The relevant material can be found only in the unpublished reports of the Psychological Seminar at the Federal Polytechnic Institute in Zürich, 1936–39, and in Dr. Michael Fordham's book *The Life of Childhood* (London, Kegan Paul, 1944).

lightenment in the hope of banishing the specter once and for all. Whether its endeavors were called Euhemerism, or Christian Apologetics, or Enlightenment in the narrow sense, or Positivism, there was always a myth hiding behind it, in new and disconcerting garb, which then, following the ancient and venerable pattern, gave itself out as ultimate truth. In reality we can never legitimately cut loose from our archetypal foundations unless we are prepared to pay the price of a neurosis, any more than we can rid ourselves of our body and its organs without committing suicide. If we cannot deny the archetypes or otherwise neutralize them, we are confronted, at every new stage in the differentiation of consciousness to which civilization attains, with the task of finding a new *interpretation* appropriate to this stage, in order to connect the life of the past that still exists in us with the life of the present, which threatens to slip away from it. If this link-up does not take place, a kind of rootless consciousness comes into being no longer orientated to the past, a consciousness which succumbs helplessly to all manner of suggestions and, is, in fact, susceptible to psychic epidemics. With the loss of the past which has become "insignificant," devalued, and incapable of revaluation, the savior is lost too, for *the savior is either the insignificant thing itself or else arises out of it.* Over and over again in the "Metamorphosis of the Gods" he rises up as the prophet or first-born of a new generation and appears unexpectedly in the most unlikely places (sprung from a stone, tree, furrow, water, etc.) and in ambiguous form (Tom Thumb, dwarf, child, animal, and so on).

This archetype of the "child-god" is extremely widespread and intimately bound up with all the other mythological aspects of the child-motif. It is hardly necessary to allude to the still living "Christ-child," who, in the legend of St. Christopher, also has the typical feature of being "smaller than small and bigger than big." In folklore the child-motif appears in the guise of the *dwarf* or the *elf* as personifications of the hidden forces of nature. To this sphere also belongs the little metal man of late antiquity, the *androparion* or *anthroparion*="manikin"[7] who, till far into the Middle Ages, on the one hand inhabited the mine shafts,[8] and on the other represented the alchemical metals,[9] above all, Mercury reborn in perfect form —as the hermaphrodite, *filius sapientiae*, or *infans noster*.[10] Thanks to the religious interpretation of the "child," a fair amount of evidence has come down to us from the Middle Ages, showing that the "child" was not merely a traditional figure, but a vision spontaneously experienced (as a so-called "irruption of the unconscious"). I am thinking of Meister Eckhart's vision of the "naked boy" and the dream of Brother Eustachius.[11] Interesting accounts of these spontaneous experiences are also to be found in English ghost stories, where we read of the vision of a "Radiant Boy" said to have been seen in a place where there are Roman remains.[12] This apparition was supposed to be of evil omen. It almost looks as though we were dealing with the figure of a *puer aeternus* who had become inauspicious through "metamorphosis," or in other words had shared the fate of the classical and Germanic gods, who have all become bugbears. The mystical character of the experience is also confirmed in Part II of Goethe's *Faust*, where Faust himself is transformed into a boy and admitted into the "choir of blessed youths," this being the "larval stage" of Dr. Marianus.[13]

In the strange tale called "Das Reich ohne Raum" by Bruno Goetz, a *puer aeternus* named Fo (=Buddha) appears with whole troops of "unholy" boys of evil significance. (Con-

---

[7] Berthelot, *Alchemistes Grecs*, III, XXXV.

[8] Georg Agricola, *De Animantibus Subterraneis* (1549); A. Kircher, *Mundus Subterraneus* (1678), VIII, 4.

[9] Mylius, *Philosophia Reformata* (1622).

[10] "Alleg. sup. Libr. Turbae" in *Artis Auriferae*, Vol. I, p. 161.

[11] *Texte aus der deutschen Mystik des 14. und 15. Jahrhunderts*, ed. Ad. Spamer, pp. 143, 150.

[12] John H. Ingram, *The Haunted Homes* (1897), pp. 43ff.

[13] There is an old alchemistic authority by name of Morienes, Morienus, Marianus (*De Composit. Alch.*, Manget, *Bibliotheca chemica curiosa*, I, pp. 509ff.). In view of the explicitly alchemistical character of *Faust*, Part II, a connection of this sort would not be surprising.

temporary parallels are better let alone.) I mention this instance only to demonstrate the enduring vitality of the child-archetype.

The child-motif not infrequently occurs in the field of psychopathology. The "imaginary" child is common among women with mental disorders and is usually interpreted in a Christian sense. Homunculi also appear, as in the famous Schreber case,[14] where they come in swarms and plague the sufferer. But the clearest and most significant manifestation of the child-motif in the therapy of neuroses is the maturation process of personality induced by the analysis of the unconscious, which I have termed the process of *individuation*.[15] Here we are confronted with pre-conscious processes which, in the form of more or less well-formed fantasies, gradually pass over into the conscious mind, or become conscious as dreams, or, lastly, are made conscious through the method of *active imagination*.[16] This material is rich in archetypal motifs, among them frequently that of the child. Often the child is formed after the Christian model; more often, though, it develops from earlier, altogether non-Christian levels—that is to say, out of chthonic animals such as crocodiles, dragons, serpents, or monkeys. Sometimes the child appears in the cup of a flower, or out of a golden egg, or as the center of a *mandāla*. In dreams it often occurs as the dreamer's son or daughter, as a boy, youth, or young girl; occasionally it seems to be of exotic origin, Indian or Chinese, with a dusky skin, or, appearing more cosmically, surrounded by stars or with a starry coronet; as the king's son or the witch's child with daemonic attributes. Seen as a special instance of "the treasure hard to attain" motif,[17] the child-motif is extremely protean and assumes all manner of shapes, such as the jewel, the pearl, the flower, the

[14] Schreber, *Denkwürdigkeiten eines Nervenkranken* (1903) [*Memoirs of My Nervous Sickness*].

[15] For a general presentation see *The Integration of Personality* (N. Y., 1939), Ch. 1. Specific phenomena in the following chapters, also in *Psychology and Alchemy* (Coll. Works, Vol. 12, Part II).

[16] "The Relations between the Ego and the Unconscious" in: *Two Essays on Analytical Psychology* (Coll. Works, Vol. 7).

[17] *Symbols of Transformation* (Coll. Works, Vol. 5), p. 259.

chalice, the golden egg, the quaternity, the golden ball, and so on. It can be interchanged with these and similar images almost without limit.

1. The Archetype as a Link with the Past

As to the *psychology* of our theme I must point out that every statement going beyond the purely phenomenal aspects of an archetype lays itself open to the criticism we have expressed above. Not for a moment dare we succumb to the illusion that an archetype can be finally explained and disposed of. Even the best attempts at explanation are only more or less successful translations into another metaphorical language. (Indeed, language itself is only a metaphor.) The most we can do is to *dream the myth onwards* and give it a modern dress. And whatever explanation or interpretation does to it, we do to our own souls as well, with corresponding results for our own well-being. The archetype—let us never forget this—is a psychic organ present in all of us. A bad explanation means a correspondingly bad attitude to this organ, which may thus be injured. But the ultimate sufferer is the bad interpreter himself. Hence the "explanation" should always be such that the functional significance of the archetype remains unimpaired, i.e., that an adequate and meaningful connection between the conscious mind and the archetypes is assured. For the archetype is an element of our psychic structure and thus a vital and necessary component in our psychic economy. It represents or personifies certain instinctive data of the dark, primitive psyche, the real but invisible *roots of consciousness*. Of what elementary importance the connection with these roots is, we see from the preoccupation of the primitive mentality with certain "magic" factors, which are nothing less than what we call archetypes. This original form of *religio* ("linking back") is the essence, the working basis, of all religious life even today, and always will be, whatever future form this life may take.

There is no "rational" substitute for the archetype any more than there is for the cerebellum or the kidneys. We can examine the physical organs anatomically, histologically, and embryologically. This would correspond to an outline of archetypal phenomenology and its presentation in historical and comparative terms. But we only arrive at the *meaning* of a physical organ when we begin to ask teleological questions. Hence the query arises: What is the biological purpose of the archetype? Just as physiology answers such a question for the body, so it is the business of psychology to answer it for the archetype.

Statements like "the child-motif is a vestigial memory of one's own childhood" and similar explanations merely beg the question. But if, giving this proposition a slight twist, we were to say: "The child-motif is a picture of certain *forgotten* things in our childhood," we are getting closer to the truth. Since, however, the archetype is always an image belonging to the whole human race and not merely to the individual, we might put it better this way: *"The child-motif represents the preconscious, childhood aspect of the collective psyche."*[18]

We shall not go wrong if we take this statement for the time being *historically*, on the analogy of certain psychologi-

---

[18] It may not be superfluous to point out that lay prejudice is always inclined to identify the child-motif with the concrete experience "child," as though the real child were the cause and precondition of the existence of the child-motif. In psychological reality, however, the empirical idea "child" is only the means (and not the only one) by which to express a psychic fact that cannot be formulated more exactly. Hence by the same token the mythological idea of the child is emphatically not a copy of the empirical child, but a *symbol* clearly recognizable as such: it is a wonder-child, a divine child, begotten, born, and brought up in quite extraordinary circumstances, and not—this is the point—a human child. Its deeds are as miraculous or monstrous as its nature and physical make-up. Simply and solely on account of these highly unempirical properties is it necessary to speak of a "child-motif" at all. Moreover, the mythological "child" has various forms: now a god, giant, Tom Thumb, animal, etc., and this points to a causality that is anything but rational or concretely human. The same is true of the "father" and "mother" archetypes which, mythologically speaking, are likewise irrational symbols.

cal experiences which show that certain phases in an individual's life can become autonomous, can personify themselves to such an extent that they result in a *vision of oneself*—for instance, one sees oneself as a child. Visionary experiences of this kind, whether they occur in dreams or in the waking state, are, as we know, conditional to a dissociation having previously taken place between past and present. Such dissociations come about because of various incompatibilities; for instance, a man's present state may have come into conflict with his childhood state, or he may have violently separated himself from his original character in the interests of some arbitrary *persona* more in keeping with his ambitions.[19] He has thus become unchildlike and artificial, and has lost his roots. All this presents a favorable opportunity for an equally vehement confrontation with the primary truth.

In view of the fact that men have never ceased their utterances on the subject of the child-god, we may perhaps extend the individual analogy to the life of mankind and say in conclusion that humanity, too, probably always comes into conflict with its childhood state, that is, with its original, unconscious, and instinctive state, and that the danger of the kind of conflict which induces the vision of the "child" actually exists. Religious observances, i.e., the retelling and ritual repetition of the mythical event, consequently serve the purpose of bringing the image of the child, and everything connected with it, again and again before the eyes of the conscious mind so that the link with the original condition may not be broken.

2. *The Function of the Archetype*

The child-motif represents not only something that existed in the distant past but also something that exists *now;* that is to say, it is not just a vestige but a system functioning in the present whose purpose is to compensate or correct, in a mean-

[19] *Psychological Types*, p. 590 and *Two Essays on Analytical Psychology*.

ingful manner, the inevitable one-sidednesses and extravagances of the conscious mind. It is in the nature of the conscious mind to concentrate on relatively few contents and to raise them to the highest pitch of clarity. A necessary result and condition of this is the exclusion of other potential contents of consciousness. The exclusion is bound to bring about a certain one-sidedness of conscious content. Since the differentiated consciousness of civilized man has been granted an effective instrument for the practical realization of its contents through the dynamics of his will, there is all the more danger, the more he trains his will, of his getting lost in one-sidedness and deviating further and further from the laws and roots of his being. This means, on the one hand, the possibility of human freedom, but on the other it is a source of endless transgressions against one's instincts. Accordingly, primitive man, being closer to his instincts, like the animal, is characterized by fear of novelty and adherence to tradition. To our way of thinking he is painfully backward, whereas we exalt progress. But our progressiveness, though it may result in a great many delightful wish-fulfillments, piles up an equally gigantic Promethean debt which has to be paid off from time to time in the form of hideous catastrophes. For ages man has dreamed of flying, and all we have got for it is saturation bombing! We smile today at the Christian hope of a life beyond the grave, and yet we often fall into chiliasms a hundred times more ridiculous than the notion of a happy Hereafter. Our differentiated consciousness is in continual danger of being uprooted; hence it needs compensation through the still existing state of childhood.

The symptoms of compensation are described, from the progressive point of view, in scarcely flattering terms. Since, to the superficial eye, it looks like a retarding operation, people speak of inertia, backwardness, skepticism, fault-finding, conservatism, timidity, petulance, and so on. But inasmuch as man has, in high degree, the capacity for cutting himself off from his own roots, he may also be swept uncritically to catastrophe by his dangerous one-sidedness. The retarding ideal is always more primitive, more natural (in the good sense as in the bad), and more "moral" in that it keeps faith with law and tradition. The progressive ideal is always more abstract, more unnatural, and less "moral" in that it demands disloyalty to tradition. Progress enforced by will is always convulsive. Backwardness may be closer to naturalness, but in its turn it is always menaced by painful awakenings. The older view of things realized that progress is only possible *Deo concedente*, thus proving itself conscious of the opposites and repeating the age-old *rites d'entrée et de sortie* on a higher plane. The more differentiated consciousness becomes, the greater the danger of severance from the root-condition. Complete severance comes when the *Deo concedente* is forgotten. Now it is an axiom of psychology that when a part of the psyche is split off from consciousness it is only *apparently* inactivated; in actual fact it brings about a possession of the personality with the result that the individual's aims are falsified in the interests of the split-off part. If, then, the childhood state of the collective psyche is repressed to the point of total exclusion, the unconscious content overwhelms the conscious aim and inhibits, falsifies, even destroys its realization. Viable progress only comes from the co-operation of both.

3. *The Futurity of the Archetype*

One of the essential features of the child-motif is its *futurity*. The child is potential future. Hence the occurrence of the child-motif in the psychology of the individual signifies as a rule an anticipation of future developments, even though at first sight it may seem like a retrospective configuration. Life is a flux, a flowing into the future, and not a stoppage or a backwash. It is therefore not surprising that so many of the mythological *saviors* are child-gods. This agrees exactly with our experience in the psychology of the individual, which shows that the "child" paves the way for a future change of personality. In the individuation process, it anticipates the figure that comes from the synthesis of conscious and unconscious elements in the personality. It is therefore a *unifying symbol* which unites the opposites;[20] a mediator, bringer of healing, that is, *one who makes whole*. Because it has this meaning, the child-motif is capable of the numerous transformations mentioned above: it can be expressed by roundness, the circle or sphere, or else by the quaternity as another form of wholeness.[21] I have called this wholeness that transcends consciousness the "self."[22] The purpose of the individuation process is the *synthesis* of the self. From another point of view the term "entelechy" might be preferable to "synthesis." There is an empirical reason why "entelechy" is, in certain conditions, more fitting: the symbols of wholeness frequently occur at the beginning of the individuation process; indeed they can often be observed in the first dreams of early infancy. This observation says much for the a priori existence of potential wholeness, and on this account the idea of *entelechy* instantly recommends itself. But in so far as the individuation process occurs, empirically speaking, as a *synthesis*, it looks, paradoxically enough, as if something already existent were being put together. From this point of view, the term "synthesis" is also applicable.

4. *Unity and Plurality of the Child-Motif*

In the manifold phenomenology of the "child" we have to distinguish between the *unity* and *plurality* of its respective manifestations. Where, for instance, numerous homunculi, dwarfs, boys, etc., appear, having no individual characteristics at all, there is the probability of a *dissociation*. Such forms are therefore found especially in schizophrenia, which is es-

[20] *Psychological Types*, pp. 234ff. *Vereinigendes Symbol* has been rendered in previous translations as "reconciling symbol," but is here translated, with Professor Jung's consent, by "unifying symbol," which is closer to the German *vereinigen*.—Ed.

[21] *Psychology and Alchemy* (Coll. Works, Vol. 12), pp. 215ff. and *Psychology and Religion* (New Haven, Yale University Press, 1938), pp. 78ff.

[22] *Two Essays on Analytical Psychology*.

sentially a fragmentation of personality. The many children then represent the products of its dissolution. But if the plurality occurs in normal people, then it is the representation of an as yet incomplete synthesis of personality. The personality (viz., the "self") is still in the *plural stage*, i.e., an ego may be present, but it cannot experience its wholeness within the framework of its own personality, only within the community of the family, tribe, or nation; it is still in the stage of unconscious identification with the plurality of the group. The Church takes due account of this widespread condition in her doctrine of the *Corpus Mysticum*, of which the individual is by nature a member.

If, however, the child-motif appears in the form of a unity, we are dealing with an unconscious and, for the time being, already complete synthesis of the personality, which, like everything unconscious, signifies no more than a possibility.

5. *Child-God and Child-Hero*

Sometimes the "child" looks more like a *child-god*, sometimes more like a young *hero*. Common to both types is the miraculous birth and the adversities of early childhood—abandonment and danger through persecution. The god is by nature wholly supernatural; the hero's nature is human but raised to the limit of the supernatural—he is "semi-divine." While the god, especially in his close affinity with the symbolic animal, personifies the collective unconscious which is not yet integrated in a human being, the hero's supernaturalness includes human nature and thus represents a synthesis of the ("divine," i.e., not yet humanized) unconscious and human consciousness. Consequently he signifies the potential anticipation of an individuation process which is approaching wholeness.

For this reason the various "child"-fates may be regarded as illustrating the kind of psychic event that occurs in the entelechy or genesis of the "self." The "miraculous birth" tries to depict the way in which this genesis is experienced. Since it is a psychic genesis, everything must happen non-empirically, e.g., by means of a virgin birth, or by miraculous conception, or by birth from unnatural organs. The motifs of "insignificance," exposure, abandonment, danger, etc., try to show how precarious is the psychic possibility of wholeness, that is, the enormous difficulties to be met with in attaining this "highest good." They also signify the powerlessness and helplessness of the life-urge which subjects every growing thing to the law of maximum self-fulfillment, while at the same time the environmental influences place all sorts of insuperable obstacles in the way of individuation. More especially the threat to one's inmost self coming from dragons and serpents points to the danger of the newly acquired consciousness being swallowed up again by the instinctive psyche, the unconscious. The lower vertebrates have from earliest times been favorite symbols of the collective psychic substratum,[23] which is localized anatomically in the sub-cortical centers, the cerebellum and the spinal cord. These organs constitute the snake.[24] Snake-dreams usually occur, therefore, when the conscious mind is deviating from its instinctual basis.

The motif of "smaller than small yet bigger than big" complements the impotence of the child by means of its equally miraculous deeds. This paradox is the essence of the hero and runs through his whole destiny like a red thread. He can cope with the greatest perils, yet, in the end, something quite insignificant is his undoing: Baldur perishes because of the mistletoe, Maui because of the laughter of a little bird, Siegfried because of his one vulnerable spot, Hercules because of his wife's gift, others because of common treachery, and so on.

The hero's main feat is to overcome the monster of darkness: it is the long-hoped-for and expected triumph of consciousness over the unconscious. Day and light are synonyms for consciousness, night and dark for the unconscious. The coming of consciousness was probably the most tremendous experience

---

[23] Higher vertebrates symbolize mainly affects.
[24] This interpretation of the snake is to be found as early as Hippolytus, *Refutatio omnium haeresium*, IV, 49–51 (ed. Wendland). Cf. also Leisegang, *Die Gnosis*, p. 146.

of primeval times, for with it a world came into being whose existence no one had suspected before. "And God said: 'Let there be light!'" is the projection of that immemorial experience of the separation of the conscious from the unconscious. Even among primitives today the possession of a soul is a precarious thing and the "loss of soul" a typical psychic malady which drives primitive medicine to all sorts of psychotherapeutic measures. Hence the "child" distinguishes itself by deeds which point to the conquest of the dark.

The Special Phenomenology of the Child Archetype

1. *The Abandonment of the Child*

Abandonment, exposure, danger, etc., are all elaborations of the "child's" *insignificant beginnings* and of its *mysterious and miraculous birth*. This statement describes a certain psychic experience of a creative nature, whose object is the emergence of a new and as yet unknown content. In the psychology of the individual there is always, at such moments, an agonizing situation of conflict from which there seems to be no way out—at least for the conscious mind, since as far as this is concerned, *tertium non datur*.[25] But out of this collision of opposites the unconscious psyche always creates a third thing of an irrational nature, which the conscious mind neither expects nor understands. It presents itself in a form that is neither a straight "yes" nor a straight "no," and is consequently rejected by both. For the conscious mind knows nothing beyond the opposites and, as a result, has no knowledge of the thing that unites them. Since, however, the solution of the conflict

[25] *Psychological Types*, p. 242.

through the union of opposites is of vital importance, and is moreover the very thing that the conscious mind is longing for, some inkling of the creative act, and of the significance of it, nevertheless gets through. From this comes the "numinous" character of the "child." A meaningful but unknown content always has a secret *fascination* for the conscious mind. The new configuration is a nascent whole; it is on the way to wholeness, at least in so far as it excels in "wholeness" the conscious mind when torn by opposites and thus surpasses it in integrity. For this reason all "uniting symbols" have a redemptive significance.

Out of this situation the "child" emerges as a symbolic content, manifestly separated or even isolated from its background (the mother), but sometimes including the mother in its perilous situation, threatened on the one hand by the negative attitude of the conscious mind and on the other by the *horror vacui* of the unconscious, which is quite ready to swallow up all its progeny, since it produces them only in play, and destruction is an inescapable part of its play. Nothing in all the world welcomes this new birth, although it is the most precious fruit of Mother Nature herself, the most pregnant with the future, signifying a higher stage of self-realization. That is why Nature, the world of the instincts, takes the "child" under its wing: it is nourished or protected by *animals*.

"Child" means something evolving towards independence. This it cannot do without detaching itself from its origins: abandonment is therefore a necessary condition, not just a concomitant symptom. The conflict is not to be overcome by the conscious mind remaining caught between the opposites, and for this very reason it needs a symbol to point out the necessity of freeing itself from its oirgins. Because the symbol of the "child" fascinates and grips the conscious mind, its *redemptive* effect passes over into consciousness and brings about that separation from the conflict-situation which the conscious mind by itself was unable to achieve. The symbol anticipates a nascent state of consciousness. So long as this is not actually in being, the "child" remains a mythological projection which requires religious repetition and renewal by ritual. The Christ

Child, for instance, is a religious necessity only so long as the majority of men are incapable of giving psychological reality to the saying: "Unless ye become as little children. . . ." Since all such developments and transactions are extraordinarily difficult and dangerous, it is no wonder that images of this kind persist for hundreds or even thousands of years. Everything that man should, and yet cannot, be or do—be it in a positive or negative sense—lives on as a mythological figure or an anticipation alongside his consciousness, either as a religious projection or—what is still more dangerous—as unconscious contents which then project themselves spontaneously into incongruous objects, e.g., hygienic and other "salvationist" doctrines or practices. All these are so many rationalized substitutes for mythology, and their unnaturalness does more harm than good.

The conflict-situation that offers no way out, the sort of situation that produces the "child" as the *irrational third*, is of course a formula appropriate only to a psychological, that is, modern, stage of development. It is not strictly applicable to the psychic life of primitives, if only because primitive man's childlike range of consciousness still excludes a whole world of possible psychic experiences. Seen on the nature-level of the primitive, our modern *moral* conflict is still an *objective* calamity that threatens life itself. Hence not a few child-figures are *culture-heroes* and thus identified with things that promote culture, e.g., fire,[26] metal, corn, maize, etc. As *bringers of light*, that is, enlargers of consciousness, they overcome darkness, which is to say that they overcome the earlier unconscious state. Higher consciousness, or knowledge going beyond our present-day consciousness is equivalent to being *all alone in the world*. This loneliness expresses the conflict between the bearer or symbol of higher consciousness and his surroundings. The conquerors of darkness go back far into primeval times, and, together with many other legends, prove that there once existed a state of *original psychic distress*,

---

[26] Even Christ is of a fiery nature (*"qui iuxta me est, iuxta ignem est,"* Origen in *Homilies on Jeremiah*, XX, 3), likewise the Holy Ghost.

namely, *unconsciousness*. Hence in all probability the "irrational" fear which primitive man has of the dark even today. I found a form of religion among a tribe living on Mount Elgon that corresponded to pantheistic optimism. Their optimistic mood was, however, always in abeyance between 6 o'clock in the evening and 6 o'clock in the morning, during which time it was replaced by fear, for in the night the dark being Ayik has his dominion—the "Maker of Fear." During the daytime there were no monster snakes anywhere in the vicinity, but at night they were lurking on every path. At night the whole of mythology was let loose.

2. *The Invincibility of the Child*

It is a striking paradox in all child-myths that the "child" is on the one hand delivered helpless into the power of terrible enemies and in continual danger of extinction, while on the other he possesses powers far exceeding those of ordinary humanity. This is closely related to the psychological fact that though the child may be "insignificant," unknown, "a mere child," he is also divine. From the conscious standpoint we seem to be dealing with an insignificant content that has no releasing, let alone redeeming, character. The conscious mind is caught in its conflict-situation, and the combatant forces seem so overwhelming that the "child," as an isolated content bears no relation to the conscious factors. It is therefore easily overlooked and falls back into the unconscious. At least, this is what we should have to fear if things turned out according to our conscious expectations. Myth, however, emphasizes that it is not so, but that the "child" is endowed with superior powers and, despite all dangers, will unexpectedly pull through. The "child" is born out of the womb of the unconscious, begotten out of the depths of human nature, or rather out of living Nature herself. It is a personification of vital forces quite outside the limited range of our conscious mind; of ways and possibilities of which our one-sided conscious mind knows nothing; a wholeness which embraces the very depths of Nature. It represents the strongest, the most ineluctable urge in every being, namely, the urge to realize itself. It is, as it were, an incarnation of *the inability to do otherwise, equipped with all the powers of nature and instinct,* whereas the conscious mind is always getting caught in its supposed ability to do otherwise. The urge and compulsion to self-realization is a *law of nature* and thus of invincible power, even though its effect, at the start, is insignificant and improbable. The power is revealed in the miraculous deeds of the child-hero, and later in the *athla* ("works") of the bondsman or *thrall* (of the Hercules type), where, although the hero has outgrown the impotence of the "child," he is still in a menial position. The figure of the thrall generally leads up to the real epiphany of the semi-divine hero. Oddly enough, we have a similar modulation of themes in alchemy—in the synonyms for the *lapis*. As the *materia prima*, it is the *lapis exilis et vilis*. As a substance in process of transmutation, it is *servus rubeus* or *fugitivus;* and finally, in its true apotheosis, it attains the dignity of a *filius sapientiae* or *deus terrenus*, a "light above all lights," a power that contains in itself all the powers of the upper and nether regions. It becomes a *corpus glorificatum* which enjoys everlasting incorruptibility and is therefore a panacea ("bringer of healing!").[27] The size and invincibility of the "child" is bound up in Hindu speculation with the nature of the atman which corresponds to the "smaller than small yet bigger than big" motif. As an individual phenomenon, the *self* is "smaller than small"; as the equivalent of the cosmos, it is "bigger than big." The self, regarded as the Counter-pole of the world, its "absolutely other," is the *sine qua non* of all empirical knowledge and consciousness of subject and object. Only because of this psychic "otherness" is consciousness possible at all. Identity does not make consciousness possible; it is only separation, detachment, and agonizing confrontation through opposition that produce consciousness and insight. Hindu introspection recognized this psychological fact very early and consequently

---

[27] The material is collected in *Psychology and Alchemy*, Parts I and II. For Mercurius as a servant, see the parable of Eirenaeus Philaletha: *Erklärung der Riplaeischen Werke* (1741), pp. 132ff.

equated the subject of cognition with the subject of ontology in general. In accordance with the predominantly introverted attitude of Indian thinking the object lost the attribute of absolute reality and, in some systems, became a mere illusion. The Greek-Occidental type of mind could not free itself from the conviction of the world's absolute existence. This, however, occurred at the cost of the cosmic significance of the self. Even today Western man finds it hard to see the psychological necessity for a transcendental subject of cognition as the counterpole of the empirical universe, although the postulate of a world-confronting self, at least as a *point of reflection,* is a logical necessity. Regardless of philosophy's perpetual attitude of dissent or only half-hearted assent, there is always a compensating tendency in our unconscious psyche to produce a symbol of the self in its cosmic significance. These efforts take on the archetypal forms of the hero-myth such as can be observed in almost any individuation process.

The phenomenology of the "child's" birth always points back to an original psychological state of nonrecognition, i.e., of darkness or twilight, of nondifferentiation between subject and object, of unconscious identity of man and the universe. This phase of nondifferentiation produces the *golden egg,* which is both man and universe and yet neither, but an irrational third. To the twilight consciousness of primitive man it seems as if the egg came out of the womb of the wide world and were, accordingly, a cosmic, objective, external occurrence. To a differentiated consciousness, on the other hand, it seems evident that this egg is nothing but a symbol thrown up by the psyche or—what is even worse—a fanciful speculation and therefore "nothing but" a primitive phantasm to which no "reality" of any kind attaches. Present-day medical psychology, however, thinks somewhat differently about these "phantasms." It knows only too well what dire disturbances of the bodily functions and what devastating psychic consequences can flow from "mere" fantasies. "Fantasies" are the natural expressions of the life of the unconscious. But since the unconscious is the psyche of all the body's autonomous functional complexes, its "fantasies" have an aetiological significance that is not to be despised. From the psychopathology of the individuation process we know that the formation of symbols is frequently associated with physical disorders of a psychic origin, which in some cases are felt as decidedly "real." In medicine, fantasies are *real things* with which the psychotherapist has to reckon very seriously indeed. He cannot therefore deprive of all justification those phantasms which, because of their realness, primitive man projects upon the external world. In the last analysis the human body, too, is built of the stuff of the world, the very stuff wherein fantasies become visible; indeed, without it they could not be experienced at all. Without this stuff they would be like a sort of abstract crystal lattice in a solution where the crystallization process had not yet started.

The symbols of the self arise in the depths of the body and they express its materiality every bit as much as the structure of the perceiving consciousness. The symbol is thus a living body, *corpus et anima;* hence the "child" is such an apt formula for the symbol. The uniqueness of the psyche is something that can never be made wholly real, it can only be realized approximately, though it still remains the absolute basis of all consciousness. The deeper "layers" of the psyche lose their individual uniqueness as they retreat further and further into darkness. "Lower down," that is to say as they approach the autonomous functional systems, they become increasingly collective until they are universalized and extinguished in the body's materiality, i.e., in chemical substances. The body's carbon is simply carbon. Hence "at bottom" the psyche is simply "world." In this sense I hold Kerényi to be absolutely right when he says that in the symbol the *world itself* is speaking. The more archaic and "deeper," that is the more *physiological*, the symbol is, the more collective and universal, the more "material" it is. The more abstract, differentiated, and specific it is, the more its nature approximates to conscious uniqueness and individuality, the more it sloughs off its universal character. Having finally attained full consciousness, it runs the risk of becoming a mere *allegory* which nowhere oversteps the bounds of conscious comprehension, and is then exposed to all sorts of attempts at rationalistic and therefore inadequate explanation.

3. *The Hermaphroditism of the Child*

It is a remarkable fact that perhaps the majority of cosmogonic gods are of a bisexual nature. The hermaphrodite means nothing less than a union of the strongest and most striking opposites. In the first place this union refers back to a primitive state of mind, a twilight where differences and contrasts were either barely separated or completely merged. With increasing clarity of consciousness, however, the opposites draw more and more distinctly and irreconcilably apart. If, therefore, the hermaphrodite were only a product of primitive nondifferentiation, we would have to expect that it would soon be eliminated with increasing civilization. This is by no means the case; on the contrary, man's imagination has been preoccupied with this idea over and over again on the high and even the highest levels of culture, as we can see from the late Greek and syncretic philosophy of Gnosticism. The hermaphroditic *rebis* has an important part to play in the natural philosophy of the Middle Ages. And in our own day we hear of Christ's androgyny in Catholic mysticism.[28]

We can no longer be dealing, then, with the continued existence of a primitive phantasm, or with an original contamination of opposites. Rather, as we can see from medieval writings,[29] the original idea has become a *symbol of the creative union of opposites*, a "unifying symbol" in the literal sense. In its functional significance the symbol no longer points back, but forward to a goal not yet reached. Notwithstanding its monstrosity, the hermaphrodite has gradually turned into a subduer of conflicts and a bringer of healing, and it acquired

---

[28] Georg Koepgen, *Die Gnosis des Christentums* (1939), pp. 315ff.

[29] For the *lapis* as mediator and medium, cf. *Tractatus aureus cum scholiis*, Manget, *Bibliotheca chemica curiosa*, I, 408 b, and *Artis auriferae* (1572), p. 641.

this meaning in relatively early phases of civilization. This vital meaning explains why the image of the hermaphrodite did not fade out in primeval times but, on the contrary, was able to assert itself with increasing profundity of symbolic content—for thousands of years. The fact that an idea so utterly archaic could rise to such exalted heights of meaning not only points to the toughness of archetypal ideas, it also demonstrates the rightness of the principle that the archetype, because of its power to unite opposites, mediates between the unconscious substratum and the conscious mind. It throws a bridge between present-day consciousness, always in danger of losing its roots, and the natural, unconscious, instinctive wholeness of primeval times. Through this mediation the uniqueness, peculiarity, and one-sidedness of our present individual consciousness is linked up again with its natural, racial roots. Progress and development are ideals not lightly to be rejected, but they lose all meaning if man only arrives at his new state as a fragment of himself, having left his essential hinterland behind him in the shadow of the unconscious, in a state of primitivity or, indeed, barbarism. The conscious mind, split off from its origins, incapable of realizing the meaning of the new state, then relapses all too easily into a situation far worse than the one from which the innovation was intended to free it—*exempla sunt odiosa!* It was Friedrich Schiller who first had an inkling of this problem; but neither his contemporaries nor his successors were capable of drawing any conclusions. Instead, people incline more than ever to educate *children* and nothing more. I therefore suspect that the *furor paedogogicus* is a godsent method of by-passing the central problem touched on by Schiller, namely, *the education of the educator*. Children are educated by what the grown-up *is* and not by what he says. The popular faith in words is a veritable disease of the mind, for a superstition of this sort always leads further and further away from man's foundations and seduces people into a disastrous identification of personality with the slogan that happens to be in vogue. Meanwhile everything that has been overcome and left behind by so-called "progress" sinks deeper and deeper into the unconscious, from which there re-emerges in the end the primitive condition of *identity with the mass*. Instead of the expected progress, this condition now becomes reality.

As civilization develops, the bisexual "primary being" turns into a symbol of the unity of personality, a symbol of the *self* where the war of opposites finds peace. In this way the primary being becomes the distant *goal* of man's self-development, having been from the very beginning a projection of unconscious wholeness. Man's wholeness consists in the union of the conscious and the unconscious personality. Just as every individual derives from masculine and feminine genes, and the sex is determined by the predominance of the corresponding genes, so in the psyche it is only the conscious mind, in a man, that has the masculine sign, while the unconscious is by nature feminine. The reverse is true in the case of a woman. All I have done in my anima-theory is to rediscover and reformulate this fact.[30] It had long been known.

The idea of the *coniunctio* of male and female, which became almost a technical concept in Hermetic philosophy, appears in Gnosticism as the *mysterium iniquitatis,* probably not uninfluenced by the Old Testament "divine marriage" as performed, for instance, by Hosea.[31] Such things are indicated not only by certain traditional customs,[32] but also by the quotation from the Gospels in the second letter of Clement: "When the two shall be one, the outer as the inner, and the male with the female, neither male nor female."[33] Clement of Alexandria introduces this logion with the words: "When ye have trod the cloak of shame (with thy feet) . . ."[34] which probably refers to the body; for Clement as well as Cassian (from whom the quotation was taken over), and the pseudo-Clement, too, interpreted the words in a spiritual sense, in contrast to the Gnostics, who would seem to have taken the *coniunctio* all too

---

[30] *Psychological Types,* def. 48, "Soul," p. 588; and *Two Essays on Analytical Psychology.*
[31] Hosea, 1: 2ff.
[32] Cf. Fendt, *Gnostische Mysterien* (1922).
[33] James, The Apocryphal New Testament, p. 11.
[34] Clement, *Stromateis,* III, 13, 92, 2.

literally. They took care, however, through the practice of abortion and other restrictions, that the biological meaning of their acts did not swamp the religious significance of the rite. While, in Church mysticism, the primordial image of the *hieros gamos* was sublimated on a lofty plane and only occasionally, as for instance with Mechthild von Magdeburg,[35] approached the physical sphere—in emotional intensity, for the rest of the world it remained very much alive and continued to be the object of especial psychic preoccupation. In this respect the symbolical drawings of Opicinus de Canistris[36] afford us an interesting glimpse of the way in which this primordial image was instrumental in uniting opposites even in a pathological state. On the other hand, in the Hermetic philosophy that throve in the Middle Ages the *coniunctio* was performed wholly in the physical realm in the admittedly abstract theory of the *coniugium solis et lunae,* which despite this drawback gave the creative imagination much occasion for anthropomorphic flights.

Such being the state of affairs, it is readily understandable that the primordial image of the hermaphrodite should reappear in modern psychology in the guise of the male-female antithesis, in other words as *male* consciousness and personified *female* unconscious. But the psychological process of bringing things to consciousness has complicated the picture considerably. Whereas the old science was almost exclusively a field in which only the man's unconscious could project itself, the new psychology had to acknowledge the existence of an autonomous female psyche as well. But here the case is reversed, and a feminine consciousness confronts a masculine personification of the unconscious, which can no longer be called the *anima* but the *animus.* This discovery also complicates the problem of the *coniunctio.*

Originally this archetype played its part entirely in the field of fertility magic and thus remained for a very long time a purely biological phenomenon with no other purpose than that of fecundation. But even in early antiquity the symbolical

[35] The flowing light of the Godhead.
[36] Richard Salomon, *Opicinus de Canistris* (1936).

meaning of the act seems to have increased. Thus, for example, the physical performance of the *hieros gamos* as a sacred rite not only became a mystery—it faded to a mere conjecture.[37] As we have seen, Gnosticism, too, endeavored in all seriousness to subordinate the physiological to the metaphysical. Finally, the Church severed the *coniunctio* from the physical realm altogether, and natural philosophy turned it into an abstract *theoria*. These developments meant the gradual transformation of the archetype into a psychological process which, in theory, we can call a combination of conscious and unconscious processes.[38] In practice, however, it is not so simple, because as a rule the feminine unconscious of a man is projected upon a feminine partner, and the masculine unconscious of a woman is projected upon a man. The elucidation of these problems is a special branch of psychology and has no part in a discussion of the mythological hermaphrodite.

4. *The Child as Beginning and End*

Faust, after his death, is received as a boy into the "choir of blessed youths." I do not know whether Goethe was referring, with this peculiar idea, to the *cupids* on antique gravestones. It is not unthinkable. The figure of the *cucullatus* points to the hooded, that is, the *invisible* one, the genius of the departed, who reappears in the childlike frolics of a new life, surrounded by the *sea-forms* of dolphins and tritons. The sea is the favorite symbol for the unconscious, the mother of all that lives. Just as the "child" is, in certain circumstances (e.g., in the case of Hermes and the Dactyls), closely related to the phallus, symbol of the begeter, so it comes up again in the sepulchral phallus, symbol of a renewed begetting.

[37] Cf. the accusation of Bishop Asterius (Foucart, *Mystères d' Eleusis*, Ch. XX). According to Hippolytus' account the hierophant actually made himself impotent by a draught of hemlock. The self-castration of priests in the worship of the Mother Goddess is of similar import.
[38] Cf. *Two Essays on Analytical Psychology*, Ch. 2.

The "child" is therefore *renatus in novam infantiam*. It is thus both beginning and end, an initial and a terminal creature. The initial creature existed before man was, and the terminal creature will be when man is not. Psychologically speaking, this means that the "child" symbolizes the pre-conscious and the post-conscious nature of man. His pre-conscious nature is the unconscious state of earliest childhood; his post-conscious nature is an anticipation by analogy of life after death. In this idea the all-embracing nature of psychic wholeness is expressed. Wholeness is never comprised within the compass of the conscious mind—it includes the indefinite and indefinable extent of the unconscious as well. Wholeness is therefore, empirically speaking of immeasurable extent, older and younger than consciousness and enfolding it in time and space. This is no speculation, but an immediate psychic experience. Not only is the conscious process continually accompanied, it is often guided, helped, or interrupted, by unconscious happenings. The child had a psychic life before it had consciousness. Even the adult still says and does things whose significance he realizes only later, if ever. And yet he said them and did them as if he knew what they meant. Our dreams are continually saying things beyond our conscious comprehension (which is why they are so useful in the therapy of neuroses). We have intimations and intuitions from unknown sources. Fears, moods, plans, and hopes befall us from invisible causes. These concrete experiences are at the bottom of our feeling that we know ourselves very little, at the bottom, too, of the painful conjecture that we might have surprises in store for ourselves.

Primitive man is no puzzle to himself. The question "What is man?" is the question that man has always kept until last. Primitive man has so much psyche outside his conscious mind that the experience of something psychic outside him is far more familiar to him than to us. Consciousness hedged about by psychic powers, sustained or threatened or deluded by them, is the age-old experience of mankind. This experience has projected itself into the archetype of the child, which expresses man's wholeness. The "child" is all that is abandoned and exposed and at the same time divinely powerful; the insignificant, dubious beginning, and the triumphal end. The "eternal child" in man is an indescribable experience, an incongruity, a disadvantage, and a divine prerogative; an imponderable that determines the ultimate worth or worthlessness of a personality.

Conclusion

I am aware that a psychological commentary on the child-archetype without detailed documentation must remain a mere sketch. But since this is virgin territory for the psychologist, my main endeavor has been to stake out the possible extent of the problems raised by our archetype and to describe, at least cursorily, its different aspects. Clear-cut distinctions and strict formulations are quite impossible in this field, seeing that a kind of fluid interpenetration belongs to the very nature of all archetypes. They can only be roughly circumscribed at best. Their living meaning comes out more from the presentation as a whole than from a single formulation. Every attempt to focus them more sharply is immediately punished by the intangible core of meaning losing its luminosity. No archetype can be reduced to a simple formula. It is a vessel which we can never empty, and never fill. It has a potential existence only, and when it takes shape in matter it is no longer what it was. It persists throughout the ages and requires interpreting ever anew. The archetypes are the imperishable elements of the unconscious, but they change their shape continually.

It is a well-nigh hopeless undertaking to tear a single archetype out of the living tissue of the psyche; but despite their interwoven meanings the archetypes do form units that are accessible to intuition. Psychology, as one of the many expressions of psychic life, operates with ideas which in their turn are derived from archetypal structures and thus generate a somewhat more abstract kind of myth. Psychology therefore translates the archaic speech of myth into a modern mythologem—not yet, of course, recognized as such—which constitutes one element of the myth "science." This "hopeless" activity is a *living and lived myth,* satisfying to persons of suitable temperament, indeed wholesome insofar as they have been cut off from their psychic origins by neurotic dissociation.

As a matter of experience, we meet the child-archetype in spontaneous and in therapeutically induced individuation processes. The first manifestation of the "child" is, as a rule, a totally unconscious phenomenon. Here the patient identifies himself with his personal infantilism. Then, under the influence of therapy, we get a more or less gradual separation from and objectification of the "child," that is, the identity breaks down and is accompanied by an intensification (sometimes technically induced) of fantasy, with the result that archaic or mythological features become increasingly apparent. Further transformations run true to the hero-myth. The theme of "mighty feats" is generally absent, but on the other hand the mythical dangers play all the greater part. At this stage there is usually another identification, this time with the hero, whose role is attractive for a variety of reasons. The identification is often extremely stubborn and dangerous to the psychic equilibrium. If it can be broken down and if consciousness can be reduced to human proportions, the figure of the hero can gradually be differentiated into a symbol of the self.

In practical reality, however, it is of course not enough for the patient merely to *know about* such developments; what counts is his *experience* of the various transformations. The initial stage of personal infantilism presents the picture of an "abandoned" or "misunderstood" and unjustly treated child with overweening pretensions. The epiphany of the hero (the second identification) shows itself in a corresponding inflation: the colossal pretension grows into a conviction that one is something extraordinary, or else the impossibility of the pretension ever being fulfilled only proves one's own inferiority, which is favorable to the role of the heroic sufferer (a negative inflation). In spite of their contradictoriness, both forms are identical, because unconscious compensatory inferiority tallies with conscious megalomania, and unconscious megalomania with conscious inferiority (you never get one without the other). Once the reef of the second identification has been successfully circumnavigated, conscious processes can be cleanly separated from the unconscious, and the latter observed objectively. This leads to the possibility of an accommodation with the unconscious, and thus to a possible synthesis of the conscious and unconscious elements of knowledge and action. This in turn leads to a shifting of the center of personality from the ego to the self.[39]

In this psychological framework the motifs of abandonment, invincibility, hermaphroditism, beginning and end take their place as distinct categories of experience and understanding.

[39] A more detailed account of these developments is to be found in *Two Essays on Analytical Psychology*.

Transformation Symbolism
in the Mass[1]

The Mass is a still-living mystery, the origins of which go back to early Christian times. It is hardly necessary to point out that it owes its vitality partly to its undoubted psychological efficacy, and is therefore a fit subject for psychological study. But it should be equally obvious that psychology can only approach the subject from the phenomenological angle, for the realities of faith lie outside the realm of psychology.

My exposition falls into four parts: in the introduction I indicate some of the New Testament sources of the Mass, with notes on its structure and significance. In section 2, I recapitulate the sequence of events in the rite. In 3, I cite a parallel

[1] The following account and examination of the principal symbol in the Mass is not concerned either with the Mass as a whole, or with its liturgy in particular, but solely with the ritual actions and texts which relate to the transformation process in the strict sense. In order to give the reader an adequate account of this, I had to seek professional help. I am especially indebted to the theologian Dr. Gallus Jud for reading through and correcting the first two sections. C. G. Jung

This study was first given by Dr. Jung in the form of two lectures in 1941. It represents a revised version translated by R. F. C. Hull and Monica Curtis, and published in "The Mysteries," Papers from the Eranos Yearbooks, edited by Joseph Campbell, Bollingen Series XXX (Pantheon Books, 1955), Vol. II.—Ed.

from pagan antiquity to the Christian symbolism of sacrifice and transformation: the visions of Zosimos. Finally, in 4, I attempt a psychological discussion of the sacrifice and transformation.

I. Introduction

The oldest account of the sacrament of the Mass is to be found in I Corinthians 11:23ff.:

> For the tradition which I have received of the Lord and handed down to you is that the Lord Jesus, on the night he was betrayed, took bread, gave thanks, broke it, and said: *This is my body for you; do this in remembrance of me. And after he had supped, he took the chalice also, and said: This chalice is the new testament in my blood. As often as you drink, do this in remembrance of me.* For as often as you eat this bread and drink the chalice, you declare the death of the Lord, until he comes.[2]

Similar accounts are to be found in Matthew, Mark, and Luke. In John the corresponding passage speaks of a "supper,"[3] but there it is connected with the washing of the disciples' feet. At this supper Christ utters the words which characterize the meaning and substance of the Mass (John 15:1, 4, 5): "I am the true vine." "Abide in me, and I in you." "I am the vine, ye are the branches." The correspondence between the liturgical accounts points to a traditional source outside the Bible.

---

[2] [This is a translation of the Karl von Weizsäcker version (1875) used here by Professor Jung. Elsewhere the Biblical quotations are taken from the Authorized Version. Following is the Latin (Vulgate) version of the italicized portion of this passage. —TRANS.] ". . . hoc est corpus meum, quod pro vobis tradetur: hoc facite in meam commemorationem. Similiter et calicem, postquam coenavit, dicens: Hic calix novum testamentum est in meo sanguine."

[3] *deipnon, coena.*

The Mass is a Eucharistic feast with an elaborately developed liturgy. It has the following structure:

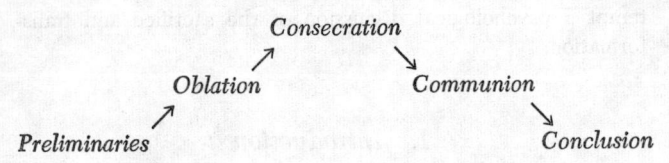

```
                    Consecration
                   ↗            ↘
          Oblation              Communion
         ↗                               ↘
Preliminaries                             Conclusion
```

In the sacrifice of the Mass two distinct ideas are blended together: the ideas of *deipnon* and *thysia*. *Thysia* comes from the verb θύειν, "to sacrifice" or "to slaughter"; but it also has the meaning of "blazing" or "flaring up." This refers to the leaping sacrificial fire by which the gift offered to the gods was consumed. Originally the food-offering was intended for the nourishment of the gods; the smoke of the burnt sacrifice carried the food up to their heavenly abode. At a later stage the smoke was conceived as a spiritualized form of food-offering; indeed, all through the Christian era up to the time of the Middle Ages, spirit (or *pneuma*) continued to be thought of as a fine, vaporous substance.[4]

Deipnon means "meal." In the first place it is a meal shared by those taking part in the sacrifice, at which the god was believed to be present. It is also a "sacred" meal at which "consecrated" food is eaten, and hence a *sacrifice* (from *sacrificare*, "to make sacred," "to consecrate").

The dual meaning of *deipnon* and *thysia* is implicitly contained in the words of the sacrament: "the body (which was given) for you."[5] This may mean either "which was given to you to eat" or, indirectly, "which was given for you to God." The idea of a meal immediately invests the word "body" with the meaning of *sarx*, "flesh" (as an edible substance). In Paul, *soma* and *sarx* are practically identical.[6]

Besides the authentic accounts of the institution of the sacra-

[4] This of course has nothing to do with the official conception of spirit by the Church.

[5] *"tō soma tō hyper hymōn."*

[6] Ernst Käsemann, *Leib und Leib Christi* (Beiträge zur historischen Theologie, 9; Tübingen, 1933), p. 120.

ment, we must also consider Hebrews 13:10–15 as a possible source for the Mass:

> We have an altar, whereof they have no right to eat which serve the tabernacle. For the bodies of those beasts, whose blood is brought into the sanctuary by the high priest for sin, are burned without the camp. Wherefore Jesus also, that he might sanctify the people with his own blood, suffered without the gate. Let us go forth therefore unto him without the camp, bearing his reproach. For here have we no continuing city, but we seek one to come. By him therefore let us offer the sacrifice of praise to God continually. . . .

As a further source we might mention Hebrews 7:17: "Thou art a priest for ever after the order of Melchisedec."[7] The idea of perpetual sacrifice and of an eternal priesthood is an essential component of the Mass. (Melchisedec, who according to Hebrews 7:3 was "without father, without mother, without descent, having neither beginning of days, nor end of life, but made like unto the Son of God," was believed to be a pre-Christian incarnation of the Logos.)

The idea of an eternal priesthood and of a sacrifice offered to God "continually" brings us to the true *mysterium fidei*, the transformation of the substances, which is the third aspect of the Mass. The ideas of *deipnon* and *thysia* do not in themselves imply or contain a mystery, although, in the burnt offering which is reduced to smoke and ashes by the fire, there is a primitive allusion to a transformation of substance in the sense of a spiritualization. But this aspect is of no practical importance in the Mass, where it only appears in subsidiary form in the censing, as an incense-offering. The *mysterium*, on the other hand, manifests itself clearly enough in the eternal priest "after the order of Melchisedec" and in the sacrifice which he offers to God "continually." The manifestation of an order out-

---

[7] Dr. Jud kindly drew my attention to the equally relevant passage in Malachi 1:10–11: "Who is there even among you that would shut the doors for nought? neither do ye kindle fire on mine altar for nought. . . . And in every place incense shall be offered unto my name, and a pure offering. . . ."

side time involves the idea of a *miracle* which takes place *"vere, realiter, substantialiter"* at the moment of transubstantiation, for the substances offered are no different from natural objects, and must in fact be definite commodities whose nature is known to everybody, namely, pure wheaten bread and wine. Furthermore, the officiating priest is an ordinary human being who, although he bears the indelible mark of the priesthood upon him and is thus empowered to offer sacrifice, is nevertheless not yet in a position to be the instrument of the divine self-sacrifice enacted in the Mass.[8] Nor is the congregation standing behind him yet purged from sin, consecrated, and itself transformed into a sacrificial gift. The ritual of the Mass takes this situation and transforms it step by step until the climax is reached—the Consecration, when Christ himself, as sacrificer and sacrificed, speaks the decisive words through the mouth of the priest. At that moment Christ is present in time and space. Yet his presence is not a reappearance, and therefore the inner meaning of the consecration is not a repetition of an event which occurred once in history, but the revelation of something existing in eternity, a rending of the veil of temporal and spatial limitations which separates the human spirit from the sight of the eternal. This event is necessarily a mystery, because it is beyond the power of man to conceive or imagine. In other words, the rite is necessarily and in every one of its parts a *symbol*. Now a symbol is not an arbitrary or intentional sign standing for a known and conceivable fact, but an admittedly anthropomorphic—hence limited and only partly valid—expression for something suprahuman and only partly

---

[8] That is to say, not before he has accomplished the preparatory part of the service. In offering these gifts the priest is not the "master" of the sacrifice. "Rather that which causes them to be sacrificed in the first place is sanctifying grace. For that is what their sacrifice means: their santification. The man who each time performs the sacred act is the servant of grace, and that is why the gifts and their sacrifice are always pleasing to God. The fact that the servant may be bad does not affect them in any way. The priest is only the servant, and even this he has from grace, not from himself." Joseph Kramp, S.J., *Die Opferanschauungen der römischen Messliturgie* (Regensburg, 1924), p. 148.

conceivable. It may be the best expression possible, yet it ranks below the level of the mystery it seeks to describe. The Mass is a symbol in this sense. Here I would like to quote the words of Father Kramp: "It is generally admitted that the sacrifice is a *symbolic* act, by which I mean that the offering of a material gift to God has no purpose in itself, but merely serves as a means to express an idea. And the choice of this means of expression brings a wide range of anthropomorphism into play: man confronts God as he confronts his own kind, almost as if God were a human being. We offer a gift to God as we offer it to a good friend or to an earthly ruler."[9]

In so far, then, as the Mass is an anthropomorphic symbol standing for something otherworldly and beyond our power to conceive, its symbolism is a legitimate subject for comparative psychology and analytical research. My psychological explanations are, of course, exclusively concerned with the symbolical expression.

II. *The Sequence of the Rite of Transformation*

The rite of transformation may be said to begin with the Offertory, an antiphon recited during the offering of the sacrificial gifts. Here we encounter the first ritual act relating to the transformation.[10]

1. OBLATION OF THE BREAD

The Host is lifted up towards the cross on the altar, and the priest makes the sign of the cross over it with the paten. The bread is thus brought into relation with Christ and his death on the cross; it is marked as a "sacrifice" and thereby becomes sacred. The elevation exalts it into the realm of the spiritual: it is a preliminary act of spiritualization. Justin makes the interesting remark that the presentation of the cleansed lepers

[9] Kramp, p. 17.
[10] In the account that follows I have made extensive use of Johannes Brinktrine, *Die Heilige Messe in ihrem Werden und Wesen* (2nd ed., Paderborn, 1934).

in the temple was an image of the Eucharistic bread.[11] This links up with the later alchemical idea of the imperfect or "leprous" substance which is made perfect by the *opus*. (*Quod natura relinquit imperfectum, arte perficitur.*)

2. PREPARATION OF THE CHALICE

This is still more solemn than that of the bread, corresponding to the "spiritual" nature of the wine, which is reserved for the priest.[12] Some water is mingled with the wine.

The mixing of water with the wine originally referred to the ancient custom of not drinking wine unless mixed with water. A drunkard was therefore called *akratopotes*, an "unmixed drinker." In modern Greek, wine is still called *krasi* (mixture). From the custom of the Monophysite Armenians, who did not add any water to the Eucharistic wine (so as to preserve the exclusively divine nature of Christ), it may be inferred that water has a hylical, or physical, significance and represents man's material nature. The mixing of water and wine in the Roman rite would accordingly signify that divinity is mingled with humanity as indivisibly as the wine with the water.[13] St. Cyprian (bishop of Carthage, d. 258) says that the wine refers to Christ, and the water to the congregation as the body of Christ. The significance of the water is explained by an allusion to the Book of Revelation 17:15: "The waters which thou sawest, where the whore sitteth, are peoples, and multitudes, and nations, and tongues." (In alchemy, *meretrix* the whore is a synonym for the *prima materia*, the *corpus imperfectum* which is sunk in darkness, like the man who wanders in the darkness unconscious and unredeemed. This idea is foreshadowed in the Gnostic image of Physis, who with passionate arms draws the Nous down from heaven and wraps him in her dark embrace.) As the water is an imperfect or even leprous substance,

---

[11] *Tupos ton arton tās heucharistias* = an image (or model) of the Eucharistic bread.

[12] That is, in the Roman rite. In the Greek Uniate rites, communion is received in bread *and* wine.

[13] This is the interpretation of Yves, bishop of Chartres (d. 1116).

it has to be blessed and consecrated before being mixed, so that only a purified body may be joined to the wine of the spirit, just as Christ is to be united only with a pure and sanctified congregation. Thus this part of the rite has the special significance of preparing a perfect body—the glorified body of resurrection.

At the time of St. Cyprian the communion was generally celebrated with water.[14] And, still later, St. Ambrose (bishop of Milan, d. 397) says: "In the shadow there was water from the rock, as if it were the blood of Christ."[15] The water communion is prefigured in John 7:37–39: "If any man thirst, let him come unto me, and drink. He that believeth on me, as the scripture hath said, out of his belly shall flow rivers of living water. (But this he spake of the Spirit, which they that believe on him should receive: for the Holy Ghost was not yet given, because that Jesus was not yet glorified.)" And also in John 4:14: "But whosoever drinketh of the water that I shall give him shall never thirst; but the water that I shall give him shall be in him a well of water springing up into everlasting life." The words "as the scripture hath said, out of his belly shall flow rivers of living water" do not occur anywhere in the Old Testament. They must therefore come from a writing which the author of the Johannine gospel obviously regarded as holy, but which is not known to us. It is just possible that they are based on Isaiah 58:11: "And the Lord shall guide thee continually, and satisfy thy soul in drought, and make fat thy bones: and thou shalt be like a watered garden, and like a spring of water, whose waters fail not." Another possibility is

---

[14] Cyprian attacks this heretical custom in his letter to Caecilius.
[15] "*In umbra erat aqua de petra quasi sanguis ex Christo.*" The *umbra*, "shadow," refers to the foreshadowing in the Old Testament, in accordance with the saying: "*Umbra in lege, imago in evangelio, veritas in coelestibus.*" Note that this remark of Ambrose does not refer to the Eucharist but to the water symbolism of early Christianity in general; and the same is true of the passages from John. St. Augustine himself says: "There the rock was Christ; for to us that is Christ which is placed on the altar of God" (*Tractatus in Johannem*, XLV, 9; tr. James Innes in *Works*, ed. Marcus Dods, Vol. XI, Edinburgh, 1874).

Ezekiel 47:1: "Afterward he brought me again unto the door of the house; and, behold, waters issued out from under the threshold of the house eastward . . . and the waters came down from under the right side of the house, at the south side of the altar." In the liturgy of Hippolytus (d. *ca.* 235) the water chalice is associated with the baptismal font, where the inner man is renewed as well as the body.[16] This interpretation comes very close to the baptismal *krater* of Poimandres[17] and to the Hermetic basin filled with *nous* which God gave to those seeking *ennoia* (thought, intent, design).[18] Here the water signifies the *pneuma*, i.e., the spirit of prophecy, and also the doctrine which a man receives and passes on to others.[19] The same image of the spiritual water occurs in the *Odes of Solomon:*[20]

> For there went forth a stream, and became a river great and broad; . . . and all the thirsty upon earth were given to drink of it; and thirst was relieved and quenched; for from the Most High the draught was given. Blessed then are the ministers of that draught who are entrusted with that water of His; they have assuaged the dry lips, and the will that had fainted they have raised up; and souls that were near departing they have caught back from death; and limbs that had fallen they straightened and set up; they gave strength for their feebleness and light to their eyes. For everyone knew them in the Lord, and they lived by the water of life for ever.[21]

[16] Edgar Hennecke, ed., *Neutestamentliche Apokryphen* (2nd ed., Tübingen, 1924), p. 580.

[17] Marcellin Berthelot, *Collection des anciens alchimistes grecs* (Paris, 1887–88), III, li, 8.

[18] *Corpus Hermeticum*, Lib. IV, 4, in *Hermetica*, ed. Walter Scott (Oxford, 1924–36), Vol. I, p. 151.

[19] H. L. Strack and Paul Billerbeck, *Kommentar zum Neuen Testament aus Talmud und Midrasch*, Vol. II (Munich, 1924), p. 492.

[20] A collection of Gnostic hymns from the 2nd century, in Hennecke, p. 441.

[21] Ode VI in *The Odes of Solomon*, ed. J. H. Bernard (Texts and Studies, VIII, 3; Cambridge, 1912), p. 55, after the J. Rendel

The fact that the Eucharist was also celebrated with water shows that the early Christians were mainly interested in the symbolism of the mysteries and not in the literal observance of the sacrament. (There were several other variants—"galactophagy," for instance—which all bear out this view.)

Another, very graphic, interpretation of the wine and water is the reference to John 19:34: "And forthwith came there out blood and water."

Deserving of special emphasis is the remark of St. John Chrysostom (patriarch of Constantinople, d. 407), that in drinking the wine Christ drank his own blood. (See below, p. 179.)

In this section of the Mass we meet the important prayer:

> O God, who in creating human nature, didst wonderfully dignify it, and hast still more wonderfully renewed it; grant that, by the mystery of this water and wine, we may be made partakers of his divinity who vouchsafed to become partaker of our humanity, Jesus Christ. . . .[22]

3. ELEVATION OF THE CHALICE

The lifting up of the chalice in the air prepares the spiritualization (i.e., volatilization) of the wine.[23] This is confirmed by the invocation to the Holy Ghost which immediately follows (*Veni sanctificator*), and it is even more evident in the Mozarabic[24] liturgy, which has *"Veni spiritus sanctificator."*

Harris version. Cf. the *hŭdōr thēon* (water of the gods), the *aqua permanens* of early alchemy, also the treatise of Komarios (Berthelot, IV, xx).

[22] *"Deus, qui humanae substantiae dignitatem mirabiliter condidisti, et mirabilius reformasti; da nobis per huius aquae et vini mysterium, eius divinitatis esse consortes, qui humanitatis nostrae fieri dignatus est particeps, Jesus Christus . . ."* [Here and throughout this essay the English translation is taken from *The Small Missal*, London, 1924 (?).—TRANS.]

[23] This is *my* interpretation and not that of the Church, which sees in this only an act of devotion.

[24] From Arabic *musta'rib*, "Arabianized," with reference to the Visigothic-Spanish form of ritual.

The invocation serves to infuse the wine with holy spirit, for it is the Holy Ghost who begets, fulfills, and transforms (cf. the "Obumbratio Mariae," Pentecostal fire). After the elevation, the chalice was, in former times, set down to the right of the Host, to correspond with the blood that flowed from the right side of Christ.

4. CENSING OF THE SUBSTANCES AND THE ALTAR

The priest makes the sign of the cross three times over the substances with the thurible, twice from right to left and once from left to right.[25] The counterclockwise movement (from right to left) corresponds psychologically to a circumambulation downwards, in the direction of the unconscious, while the clockwise (left-to-right) movement goes in the direction of consciousness. There is also a complicated censing of the altar.[26]

The censing has the significance of an incense offering and is therefore a relic of the original *thysia*. At the same time it signifies a transformation of the sacrificial gifts and of the altar, a spiritualization of all the physical substances subserving the rite. Finally, it is an apotropaic ceremony to drive away any daemonic forces that may be present, for it fills the air with the fragrance of the *pneuma* and renders it uninhabitable for evil spirits. The vapor also suggests the sublimated body, the *corpus volatile sive spirituale,* or wraithlike "subtle body." Rising up as a "spiritual" substance, the incense implements and represents the ascent of prayer—hence the *Dirigatur, Domine, oratio mea, sicut incensum, in conspectu tuo* ("Let my prayer, O Lord, ascend like incense in thy sight").

The censing brings the preparatory, spiritualizing rites to an end. The gifts have been sanctified and prepared for the actual transubstantiation. Priest and congregation are likewise purified by the prayers *Accendat in nobis Dominus ignem sui amoris* ("May the Lord enkindle in us the fire of his love")

---

[25] The circumambulation from left to right is strictly observed in Buddhism.

[26] The censing is only performed at High Mass.

and *Lavabo inter innocentes* ("I will wash my hands among the innocent"), and are made ready to enter into the mystic union of the sacrificial act which now follows.

5. THE EPICLESIS

The *Suscipe, sancta Trinitas*, like the *Orate, fratres*, the *Sanctus*, and the *Te igitur*, is a propitiatory prayer which seeks to ensure the acceptance of the sacrifice. Hence the Preface that comes after the Secret is called *Illatio* in the Mozarabic rite (the equivalent of the Greek *anaphora*=raising up), and in the old Gallican liturgy is known as *Immolatio* (in the sense of *oblatio*), with reference to the presentation of the gifts. The words of the *Sanctus*: "*Benedictus qui venit in nomine Domini*," point to the expected appearance of the Lord which has already been prepared, on the ancient principle that a "naming" has the force of a "summons." After the Canon there follows the "Commemoration of the Living," together with the prayers *Hanc igitur* and *Quam oblationem*. In the Mozarabic Mass these are followed by the Epiclesis (invocation): "*Adesto, adesto Jesu, bone Pontifex, in medio nostri: sicut fuisti in medio discipulorum tuorum.*" This naming likewise has the original force of a summons. It is an intensification of the *Benedictus qui venit*, and it may be, and sometimes was, regarded as the actual manifestation of the Lord, and hence as the culminating point of the Mass.

6. THE CONSECRATION

This, in the Roman Mass, is the climax, the transubstantiation of the bread and wine into the body and blood of Christ. The formula for the consecration of the bread runs:[27]

Qui pridie quam pateretur, accepit panem in sanctas ac venerabiles manus suas, et elevatis oculis in caelum ad te

[27] According to the edict of the Church these words ought not, on account of their sacredness, to be translated into any profane tongue. Although there are missals that sin against this wise edict, I would prefer the Latin text to stand untranslated.

Deum, Patrem suum omnipotentem, tibi gratias agens, benedixit, fregit, deditque discipulis suis, dicens: Accipite, et manducate ex hoc omnes. Hoc est enim Corpus meum.

And for the consecration of the chalice:

Simili modo postquam coenatum est, accipiens et hunc praeclarum Calicem in sanctas ac venerabiles manus suas, item tibi gratias agens, benedixit, deditque discipulis suis, dicens: Accipite, et bibite ex eo omnes. Hic est enim Calix Sanguinis mei, novi et aeterni testamenti: mysterium fidei: qui pro vobis et pro multis effundetur in remissionem peccatorum. Haec quotiescumque feceritis, in mei memoriam facietis.

The priest and congregation, as well as the substances and the altar, have now been progressively purified, consecrated, exalted, and spiritualized by means of the prayers and rites which began with the Preliminaries and ended with the Canon, and are thus prepared as a mystical unity for the divine epiphany. Hence the uttering of the words of the consecration signifies Christ himself speaking in the first person, his living presence in the *corpus mysticum* of priest, congregation, bread, wine, and incense, which together form the mystical unity offered for sacrifice. At this moment the eternal character of the one divine sacrifice is made evident: it is experienced at a particular time and a particular place, as if a window or a door had been opened upon that which lies beyond space and time. It is in this sense that we have to understand the words of St. Chrysostom: "And this word once uttered in any church, at any altar, makes perfect the sacrifice from that day to this, and till his Second Coming."[28] It is clear that only by our Lord's presence in his words, and by their virtue, is the imperfect body of the sacrifice made perfect, and not by the preparatory action of the priest. Were this the efficient cause, the rite would be no different from common magic. The

[28] "Et vox haec semel prolata in ecclesiis ad unamquamque mensam ab illo ad hodiernum usque tempus et usque ad adventum eius sacrificium perfectum efficit."

priest is only the *causa ministerialis* of the transubstantiation. The real cause is the living presence of Christ which operates spontaneously, as an act of divine grace.

Accordingly John of Damascus (d. 754) says that the words have a consecrating effect no matter by what priest they be spoken, as if Christ were present and uttering them himself.[29] And Duns Scotus (d. 1308) remarks that in the sacrament of the Last Supper, Christ, by an act of will, offers himself as a sacrifice in every Mass, through the agency of the priest.[30] This tells us plainly enough that the sacrificial act is not performed by the priest, but by Christ himself. The agent of transformation is nothing less than the divine will working through Christ. The Council of Trent declared that in the sacrifice of the Mass "the selfsame Christ is contained and bloodlessly sacrificed,"[31] although it is not a repetition of the historical sacrifice but a bloodless renewal of it. As the sacramental words have the power to accomplish the sacrifice, being an expression of God's will, they can be described metaphorically as the sacrificial knife or sword which, guided by his will, consummates the *thysia*. This comparison was first drawn by the Jesuit father Lessius (d. 1623), and has since gained acceptance as an ecclesiastical figure of speech. It is based on Hebrews 4:12: "For the word of God is quick, and powerful, and sharper than any two-edged sword," and perhaps even more on the Book of Revelation 1:16: "And out of his mouth went a sharp two-edged sword." The "mactation theory" first appeared in the sixteenth century. Its originator, Cuesta, bishop of Leon (d. 1560), declared that Christ was slaughtered by the priest.[32] So the sword metaphor followed quite natu-

[29] "Haec verba virtutem consecrativam sunt consecuta, a quocumque sacerdote dicantur, ac si Christus ea praesentialiter proferret."

[30] Ignaz Klug in *Theologie und Glaube* (Paderborn), XVIII (1926), 335f. Cited by Brinktrine, p. 192.

[31] ". . . idem ille Christus continetur et incruente immolatur."

[32] "Missa est sacrificium hac ratione quia Christus aliquo modo moritur et a sacerdote mactatur" (The Mass is a sacrifice because Christ after a certain fashion dies and is slaughtered by the priest).

rally.[33] Nicholas Cabasilas, archbishop of Thessalonica (d. *ca.* 1363), gives a vivid description of the corresponding rite in the Greek Orthodox Church:

> The priest cuts a piece of bread from the loaf, reciting the text: "As a lamb he was led to the slaughter." Laying it on the table he says: "The lamb of God is slain." Then a sign of the cross is imprinted on the bread and a small lance is stabbed into its side, to the text: "And one of the soldiers with a spear pierced his side, and forthwith came there out blood and water." With these words water and wine are mixed in the chalice, which is placed beside the bread.[34]

The *dōron* (gift) also represents the giver; that is to say, Christ is both the sacrificer and the sacrificed.

Kramp writes: "Sometimes the *fractio* and sometimes the *elevatio* which precedes the Pater noster was taken as symbolizing the death of Christ, sometimes the sign of the cross at the end of the *Supplices,* and sometimes the *consecratio;* but no one ever thought of taking a symbol like the 'mystical slaughter' as a sacrifice which constitutes the essence of the Mass. So it is not surprising that there is no mention of any 'slaughter' in the liturgy."[35]

7. THE GREATER ELEVATION

The consecrated substances are lifted up and shown to the congregation. The Host in particular represents a beatific vision of heaven, in fulfillment of Psalm 27:8: "Thy face, Lord, will I seek," for in it the Divine Man is present.

---

[33] The sword as a sacrificial instrument also occurs in the Zosimos visions (see below, pp. 174, 182ff.).
[34] Kramp, p. 114.
[35] *Ibid.,* p. 56.

8. POST-CONSECRATION

There now follows the significant prayer *Unde et memores*, which I give in full together with the *Supra quae* and *Supplices*:

> Wherefore, O Lord, we thy servants, as also thy holy people, calling to mind the blessed passion of the same Christ thy Son our Lord, his resurrection from hell, and glorious ascension into heaven, offer unto thy most excellent majesty, of thy gifts and grants, a pure Host, a holy Host, an immaculate Host, the holy bread of eternal life, and the chalice of everlasting salvation.
>
> Upon which vouchsafe to look down with a propitious and serene countenance, and to accept them, as thou wert graciously pleased to accept the gifts of thy just servant Abel, and the sacrifice of our patriarch Abraham, and that which thy high priest Melchisedec offered to thee, a holy sacrifice, an immaculate Host.
>
> We most humbly beseech thee, almighty God, command these things to be carried by the hands of thy holy angel to thy altar on high, in the sight of thy divine majesty, that as many of us as, by participation at this altar, shall receive the most sacred body and blood of thy Son, may be filled with all heavenly benediction and grace. Through the same Christ, our Lord. Amen.[36]

---

[36] "Unde et memores, Domine, nos servi tui, sed et plebs tua sancta, eiusdem Christi Filii tui, Domini nostri, tam beatae passionis, nec non et ab inferis resurrectionis, sed et in caelos gloriosae ascensionis: offerimus praeclarae majestati tuae de tuis donis ac datis, hostiam puram, hostiam sanctam, hostiam immaculatam, Panem sanctum vitae aeternae, et Calicem salutis perpetuae.

"Supra quae propitio ac sereno vultu respicere digneris: et accepta habere, sicuti accepta habere dignatus es munera pueri tui justi Abel, et sacrificium Patriarchae nostri Abrahae: et quod tibi obtulit summus sacerdos tuus Melchisedech, sanctum sacrificium, immaculatam hostiam.

"Supplices te rogamus, omnipotens Deus: jube haec perferri per manus sancti Angeli tui in sublime altare tuum, in conspectu

The first prayer shows that the transformed substances contain an allusion to the resurrection and glorification of our Lord, and the second prayer calls to mind the prefigurations in the Old Testament. Abel sacrificed a lamb; Abraham was to sacrifice his son, but a ram was substituted at the last moment. Melchisedec offers no sacrifice, but comes to meet Abraham with bread and wine. This sequence is probably not accidental and is a sort of crescendo. Abel is essentially the son, and sacrifices an animal; Abraham is essentially the father—indeed, the "tribal father"—and therefore on a higher level. He does not offer a choice possession merely, but is ready to sacrifice the best and dearest thing he has—his only son. Melchisedec ("teacher of righteousness"), is, according to Hebrews 7:1, king of Salem and "priest of the most high God," El 'Elyon. Philo Byblius mentions a *Helyon ha hypsistos* ('Elyon the highest) as a Canaanite deity,[37] but he cannot be identical with Jehovah. Abraham nevertheless acknowledges the priesthood of Melchisedec[38] by paying him "a tenth part of all." Sir Leonard Woolley gives a very interesting explanation of this in his report on the excavations at Ur.[39] By virtue of his priesthood, Melchisedec stands above the patriarch, and his feasting of Abraham has the significance of a priestly act. We must therefore attach a symbolical meaning to it, as is in fact suggested by the bread and wine. Consequently the symbolical offering ranks even higher than the sacrifice of a son, which is still the sacrifice of somebody else. Melchisedec's offering is thus a prefiguration of Christ's sacrifice of himself.

In the prayer *Supplices te rogamus* we beseech God to bring the gifts "by the hands of thy holy angel to thy altar on high." This singular request derives from the apocryphal *Epistolae*

---

divinae majestatis tuae: ut, quotquot ex hac altaris participatione sacrosanctum Filii tui corpus, et sanguinem sumpserimus, omni benedictione caelesti et gratia repleamur. Per eundem Christum, Dominum nostrum. Amen."

[37] Eusebius, *Evangelica praeparatio*, I, 10, 11.
[38] "Sidik" is a Phoenician name for God.
[39] *Abraham: Recent Discoveries and Hebrew Origins* (London, 1936).

Apostolorum, where there is a legend that Christ, before he became incarnate, bade the archangels take his place at God's altar during his absence.[40] This brings out the idea of the eternal priesthood which links Christ with Melchisedec.

9. END OF THE CANON

Taking up the Host, the priest makes the sign of the cross three times over the chalice, and says: "Through Him, and with Him, and in Him." Then he makes the sign of the cross twice between himself and the chalice. This establishes a relation of identity among Host, chalice, and priest, thus affirming once more the unity of all parts of the sacrifice. The union of Host and chalice signifies the union of the body and blood, i.e., the quickening of the body with a soul, for blood is equivalent to soul. Then follows the *Pater noster*.

10. BREAKING OF THE HOST ("FRACTIO")

The prayer "Deliver us, O Lord, we beseech thee, from all evils, past, present, and to come" lays renewed emphasis on the petition made in the preceding *Pater noster:* "but deliver us from evil." The connection between this and the sacrificial death of Christ lies in the descent into hell and the breaking of the infernal power. The breaking of the bread that now follows is symbolic of Christ's death. The Host is broken in two over the chalice. A small piece, the *particula,* is broken off from the left half and used for the rite of *consignatio* and *commixtio*. In the Byzantine rite the bread is divided into four, the four pieces being marked with letters as follows:

IS

NI   KA

KS

This means *Jesus kristōs nika*—"Jesus Christ is victorious." The peculiar arrangement of the letters obviously represents a quaternity, which as we know always has the character of

[40] Kramp, p. 98.

wholeness. This quaternity, as the letters show, refers to Christ glorified, king of glory and Pantokrator.

Still more complicated is the Mozarabic *fractio:* the Host is first broken into two, then the left half into five parts, and the right into four. The five are named *corporatio (incarnatio), nativitas, circumcisio, apparatio,* and *passio;* and the four *mors, resurrectio, gloria, regnum.* The first group refers exclusively to the human life of our Lord, the second to his existence beyond this world. According to the old view, five is the number of the natural ("hylical") man, whose outstretched arms and legs form, with the head, a pentagram. Four, on the other hand, signifies eternity and totality (as shown for instance by the Gnostic name "Barbelo," which is translated as "fourness is God"). This symbol, I would add in passing, seems to indicate that extension in space signifies God's suffering (on the cross) and, on the other hand, his dominion over the universe.

11. CONSIGNATIO

The sign of the cross is made over the chalice with the *particula,* and then the priest drops it into the wine.

12. COMMIXTIO

This is the mingling of bread and wine, as explained by Theodore of Mopsuestia (d. 428?): ". . . he combines them into one, whereby it is made manifest to everybody that although they are two they are virtually one." The text at this point says: "May this mixture and consecration [*commixtio et consecratio*] of the body and blood of our Lord help us," etc. The word "consecration" may be an allusion to an original consecration by contact, though that would not clear up the contradiction since a consecration of both substances has already taken place. Attention has therefore been drawn to the old custom of holding over the sacrament from one Mass to another, the Host being dipped in wine and then preserved in softened, or mixed, form. There are numerous rites that end with minglings of this kind. Here I would only mention the consecration by water, or the mixed drink of honey and milk which the neophytes were given after communion in the liturgy of Hippolytus.

The *Leonine Sacramentary* (seventh century) interprets the *commixtio* as a mingling of the heavenly and earthly nature of Christ. The later view was that it symbolizes the resurrection, since in it the blood (or soul) of our Lord is reunited with the body lying in the sepulcher. There is a significant reversal here of the original rite of baptism. In baptism, the body is immersed in water for the purpose of transformation; in the *commixtio*, on the other hand, the body, or *particula*, is steeped in wine, symbolizing spirit, and this amounts to a glorification of the body. Hence the justification for regarding the *commixtio* as a symbol of the resurrection.

13. CONCLUSION

On careful examination we find that the sequence of ritual actions in the Mass contains, sometimes clearly and sometimes by subtle allusions, a representation in condensed form of the life and sufferings of Christ. Certain phases overlap or are so close together that there can be no question of conscious and deliberate condensation. It is more likely that the historical evolution of the Mass gradually led to its becoming a concrete picture of the most important aspects of Christ's life. First of all (in the *Benedictus qui venit* and *Supra quae*) we have an anticipation and prefiguration of his coming. The uttering of the words of consecration corresponds to the incarnation of the Logos, and also to Christ's passion and sacrificial death, which appears again in the *fractio*. In the *Libera nos* there is an allusion to the descent into hell, while the *consignatio* and *commixtio* hint at resurrection.

In so far as the offered gift is the sacrificer himself, in so far as the priest and congregation offer themselves in the sacrificial gift, and in so far as Christ is both sacrificer and sacrificed, there is a mystical unity in all parts of the sacrificial act. The combination of offering and offerer in the single figure of Christ is implicit in the doctrine that just as bread is composed of many grains of wheat, and wine of many grapes, so the mystical body of the Church is made up of a multitude of believers. The mystical body, moreover, includes both sexes, represented by the bread and wine.[41] Thus the two substances —the masculine wine and the feminine bread—also signify the androgynous nature of the mystical Christ.

The Mass thus contains, as its essential core, the mystery and miracle of God's transformation taking place in the human sphere, his becoming Man, and his return to his absolute existence in and for himself. Man, too, by his devotion and self-sacrifice as a ministering instrument, is included in the mysterious process. God's offering of himself is a voluntary act of love, but the actual sacrifice was an agonizing and bloody death brought about by men *instrumentaliter et ministerialiter*. (The words *incruente immolatur*—"bloodlessly sacrificed"—refer only to the rite, not to the thing symbolized.) The terrors of death on the cross are an indispensable condition for transformation. This is in the first place a bringing to life of substances which are in themselves lifeless, and, in the second, a substantial alteration of them, a spiritualization, in accordance with the ancient conception of *pneuma* as a subtle material entity (the *corpus glorificationis*). This idea is expressed in the concrete participation in the body and blood of Christ in the Communion.

III. *A Parallel from Pagan Antiquity*

1. THE AZTEC "TEOQUALO"

Although the Mass itself is a unique phenomenon in the history of comparative religion, its symbolic content would be profoundly alien to man were it not rooted in the human psyche. But if it is so rooted, then we may expect to find similar patterns of symbolism both in the earlier history of mankind and in the world of pagan thought contemporary with

[41] Kramp, p. 55.

it. As the prayer *Supra quae* shows, the liturgy of the Mass contains allusions to the "prefigurations" in the Old Testament, and thus indirectly to ancient sacrificial symbolism in general. It is clear, then, that in Christ's sacrifice and the Communion one of the deepest chords in the human psyche is struck: human sacrifice and ritual anthropophagy. Unfortunately I cannot enter into the wealth of ethnological material in question here, so must content myself with mentioning the ritual slaying of the king to promote the fertility of the land and the prosperity of his people, the renewal and revivification of the gods through human sacrifice, and the totem meal, the purpose of which was to reunite the participants with the life of their ancestors. These hints will suffice to show how the symbols of the Mass penetrate into the deepest layers of the psyche and its history. They are evidently among the most ancient and most central of religious conceptions. Now with regard to these conceptions there is still a widespread prejudice, not only among laymen, but in scientific circles too, that beliefs and customs of this kind must have been "invented" at some time or other, and were then handed down and imitated, so that they would not exist at all in most places unless they had got there in the manner suggested. It is, however, always a risky business to draw conclusions from our modern, "civilized" mentality about the primitive state of mind. Primitive consciousness differs from that of the present-day white man in several very important respects. Thus, in primitive societies, "inventing" is a very different thing from what it is with us, where one novelty follows another. With primitives, life goes on in the same way for generations; nothing alters, except perhaps the language. But that does not mean that a new one is "invented." Their language is "alive" and can therefore change, a fact that has been an unpleasant discovery for many lexicographers of primitive languages. Similarly, no one "invents" the picturesque slang spoken in America; it just springs up in inexhaustible abundance from the fertile soil of colloquial speech. Religious rites and their stock of symbols must have developed in much the same way from beginnings now lost to us, and not just in one place only, but in many places at once, and also at different periods. They have grown spontaneously out of the basic conditions of human nature, which are never invented but are everywhere the same.

So it is not surprising that we find religious rites which come very close to Christian practices in a field quite untouched by classical culture. I mean the rites of the Aztecs, and in particular that of *teoqualo*, the "god-eating," as recorded by Fray Bernardino de Sahagún, who began his missionary work among the Aztecs in 1529, eight years after the conquest of Mexico. In this rite, a doughlike paste was made out of the crushed and pounded seeds of the prickly poppy (*Argemone mexicana*) and molded into the figure of the god Huitzilopochtli:

> And upon the next day the body of Huitzilopochtli died.
> And he who slew him was the priest known as Quetzalcoatl. And that with which he slew him was a dart, pointed with flint, which he shot into his heart.
>
> He died in the presence of Moctezuma and of the keeper of the god, who verily spoke to Huitzilopochtli—who verily appeared before him, who indeed could make him offerings; and of four masters of the youths, front rank leaders. Before all of them died Huitzilopochtli.
>
> And when he had died, thereupon they broke up his body of . . . dough. His heart was apportioned to Moctezuma.
>
> And as for the rest of his members, which were made, as it were, to be his bones, they were distributed and divided up among all. . . . Each year . . . they ate it. . . . And when they divided up among themselves his body made of . . . dough, it was broken up exceeding small, very fine, as small as seeds. The youths ate it.
>
> And of this which they ate, it was said: "The god is eaten." And of those who ate it, it was said: "They guard the god."[42]

[42] Bernardino de Sahagún, *General History of the Things of New Spain* (*Florentine Codex*), Book 3: *The Origin of the Gods*, tr. Arthur J. O. Anderson and Charles E. Dibble (Monographs of the School of American Research, 14, Part IV; Santa Fe, 1952), pp. 5f. (slightly modified).

The idea of a divine body, its sacrifice in the presence of the high priest to whom the god appears and with whom he speaks, the piercing with the spear, the god's death followed by ritual dismemberment, and the eating (*communio*) of a small piece of his body, are all parallels which cannot be overlooked and which caused much consternation among the worthy Spanish Fathers at the time.

In Mithraism, a religion that sprang up not long before Christianity, we find a special set of sacrificial symbols and, it would seem, a corresponding ritual which unfortunately is known to us only from dumb monuments. There is a *transitus*, with Mithras carrying the bull; a bull sacrifice for seasonal fertility; a stereotyped representation of the sacrificial act, flanked on either side by dadophores carrying raised and lowered torches; and a meal at which pieces of bread marked with crosses were laid on the table. They have even found small bells, and these probably have some connection with the bell which is sounded at Mass. The Mithraic sacrifice is essentially a self-sacrifice, since the bull is a world bull which was originally identical with Mithras himself. This may account for the singularly agonized expression on the face of the *tauroktonos*,[43] which bears comparison with Guido Reni's *Crucifixion*. The Mithraic *transitus* is a motif that corresponds to Christ carrying the cross, just as the transformation of the beast of sacrifice corresponds to the resurrection of the Christian God in the form of food and drink. The representations of the sacrificial act, the tauroctony (bull-slaying), recall the crucifixion between two thieves, one of whom is raised up to paradise while the other goes down to hell.

These few references to the Mithras cult are but one example of the wealth of parallels offered by the legends and rites of the various Near Eastern gods who die young, are mourned, and rise again. For anyone who knows these religions at all, there can be no doubt as to the basic affinity of the symbolic types and ideas.[44] At the time of primitive Chris-

---

[43] Franz Cumont, *Textes et monuments figurés relatifs aux mystères de Mithra* (Brussels, 1894–99), Vol. I, p. 182.
[44] Cf. Frazer's *The Golden Bough*, Part III: "The Dying God."

tianity and in the early days of the Church the pagan world was saturated with conceptions of this kind and with philosophical speculations based upon them, and it was against this background that the visionary ideas of the Gnostic philosophers were unfolded.

II. THE VISION OF ZOSIMOS

A characteristic representative of this school of thought was Zosimos of Panopolis, a natural philosopher and alchemist of the third century A.D., whose works have been preserved, though in corrupt state, in the famous alchemical Codex Marcianus, and were published in 1887 by Berthelot in his *Collection des anciens alchimistes grecs*. In various portions of his treatises[45] Zosimos relates a number of dream visions, all of which appear to go back to one and the same dream.[46] He was clearly a non-Christian Gnostic, and in particular—so one gathers from the famous passage about the *krater*[47]—an adherent of the Poimandres sect, and therefore a follower of Hermes. Although alchemical literature abounds in parables, I would hesitate to class these dream visions among them. Anyone acquainted with the language of the alchemists will recognize that their parables are mere allegories of ideas that were common knowledge. In the allegorical figures and actions, one can usually see at once what substances and what procedures are being referred to under a deliberately theatrical disguise. There is nothing of this sort in the Zosimos visions. Indeed, it comes almost as a surprise to find the alchemical interpretation, namely, that the dream and its impressive machinery are simply an illustration of the means for producing the "divine water," the famed solvent or tincture. Moreover a parable is a self-contained whole, whereas our vision varies and amplifies the theme just as a dream does. So far as one can assess the nature of these visions at all, I should say that the contents

[45] *Alchimistes*, III, i, 2, 3; III, v; III, vi.
[46] Cf. my paper "Einige Bemerkungen zu den Visionen des Zosimos," which gives a translation of the relevant passages.
[47] Berthelot, III, li, 8.

of an imaginative meditation have grouped themselves round the kernel of an actual dream and been woven into it. That there really was such a meditation is evident from the fragments of it that accompany the visions in the form of a commentary. As we know, meditations of this kind are often vividly pictorial, as if the dream were being continued on a level nearer to consciousness. In his *Lexicon alchemiae,* Martin Ruland, writing in Frankfort in 1612, defines the meditation that plays such an important part in alchemy as an "internal colloquy with someone else, who is nevertheless not seen, it may be with God, with oneself, or with one's good angel." The latter is a milder and less obnoxious form of the *paredros,* the familiar spirit of ancient alchemy, who was generally a planetary demon conjured up by magic. It can hardly be doubted that real visionary experiences originally lay at the root of these practices, and a vision is in the last resort nothing less than a dream which has broken through into the waking state. We know from numerous witnesses all through the ages that the alchemist, in the course of his imaginative work, was beset by visions of all kinds,[48] and was sometimes even threatened with madness.[49] So the visions of Zosimos are not something unusual or unknown in alchemical experience, though they are perhaps the most important self-revelations ever bequeathed to us by an alchemist.

I cannot reproduce here the text of the visions in full, but will give as an example the first vision, in Zosimos' own words:

> And while I said this I fell asleep, and I saw a sacrificial priest standing before me, high up on an altar, which was in the shape of a shallow bowl. There were fifteen steps leading up to the altar. And the priest stood there, and I heard a voice from above say to me: "Behold, I have completed the descent down the fifteen steps of darkness and I have completed the ascent up the steps of light. And he

[48] Cf. the examples given in *Psychology and Alchemy* (New York and London, 1953), pars. 347f.
[49] Olympiodorus says this is particularly the effect of lead. Cf. Berthelot, II, iv, 43.

who renews me is the priest, for he cast away the density of the body, and by compulsive necessity I am sanctified and now stand in perfection as a spirit [*pneuma*]." And I perceived the voice of him who stood upon the altar, and I inquired of him who he was. And he answered me in a fine voice, saying: "I am Ion, priest of the innermost hidden sanctuary, and I submit myself to an unendurable torment. For there came one in haste at early morning, who overpowered me and pierced me through with the sword and cut me in pieces, yet in such a way that the order of my limbs was preserved. And he drew off the scalp of my head with the sword, which he wielded with strength, and he put the bones and the pieces of flesh together and with his own hand burned them in the fire, until I perceived that I was transformed and had become spirit. And that is my unendurable torment." And even as he spoke this, and I held him by force to converse with me, his eyes became as blood. And he spewed out all his own flesh. And I saw how he changed into a manikin [*anthroparion* i.e., an homunculus] who has lost a part of himself. And he tore his flesh with his own teeth, and sank into himself.

In the course of the visions the Hiereus (priest) appears in various forms. At first he is split into the figures of the Hiereus and the Hierourgon, who is charged with the performance of the sacrifice. But these figures blend into one in so far as both suffer the same fate. The sacrificial priest submits voluntarily to the torture by which he is transformed. But he is also the sacrificer who is sacrificed, since he is pierced through with the sword and ritually dismembered.[50] The *deipnon* consists in his tearing himself to pieces with his own teeth and eating himself; the *thysia*, in his flesh being sacrificially burned on the altar.

He is the Hiereus in so far as he rules over the sacrificial

[50] The dismemberment motif belongs in the wider context of rebirth symbolism. Consequently it plays an important part in the initiation experiences of shamans and medicine men, who are dismembered and then put together again. For details, see Mircea Eliade, *Le Chamanisme* (Paris, 1951), pp. 47ff.

rite as a whole, and over the human beings who are transformed during the *thysia*. He calls himself a guardian of spirits. He is also known as the "Brazen Man" and as Xyrourgos, the barber. The brazen or leaden man is an allusion to the spirits of the metals, or planetary demons, as protagonists of the sacrificial drama. In all probability they are *paredroi* who were conjured up by magic, as may be deduced from Zosimos' remark that he "held the priest by force" to converse with him. The planetary demons are none other than the old gods of Olympus who finally expired only in the eighteenth century, as the "souls of the metals"—or rather, assumed a new shape, since it was in this same century that paganism openly arose for the first time (in the French Revolution).

Somewhat more curious is the term "barber," for there is no mention of cutting the hair or shaving. There is, however, a scalping, which in our context is closely connected with the ancient rites of flaying and their magical significance.[51] I need hardly mention the flaying of Marsyas, who is an unmistakable parallel to the son-lover of Cybele, namely, Attis, the dying god who rises again. In one of the old Attic fertility rites an ox was flayed, stuffed, and set up on its feet. Herodotus reports a number of flaying ceremonies among the Scythians, and especially scalpings.[52] In general, flaying signifies transformation from a worse state to a better, and hence renewal and rebirth. The best examples are to be found in the religion of ancient Mexico.[53] Thus, in order to renew the moon-god-

[51] Cf. Frazer's *The Golden Bough*, Part IV: *Adonis, Attis, Osiris* (2nd ed., London, 1907), pp. 242ff. and p. 405, and my *Symbols of Transformation* (New York and London, 1956), pars. 594f. Cf. also Colin Campbell, *The Miraculous Birth of King Amon-Hotep III* (London, 1912), p. 142, concerning the presentation of the dead man, Sen-nezem, before Osiris, Lord of Amentet: "In this scene the god is usually represented enthroned. Before and behind him, hanging from a pole, is the dripping skin of a slain bull that was slaughtered to yield up the soul of Osiris at his reconstruction, with the vase underneath to catch the blood."

[52] Book IV, 60.

[53] Cf. Eduard Seler's account in Hastings, *ERE*, Vol. VIII, pp. 615f.

dess a young woman was decapitated and skinned, and a youth then put the skin round him to represent the risen goddess. The prototype of this renewal is the snake casting its skin every year, a phenomenon round which primitive fantasy has always played. In our vision the skinning is restricted to the head, and this can probably be explained by the underlying idea of spiritual transformation. Since olden times shaving the head has been associated with consecration, that is, with spiritual transformation or initiation. The priests of Isis had their heads shaved quite bald, and the tonsure, as we know, is still in use at the present day. This "symptom" of transformation goes back to the old idea that the transformed one becomes like a new-born babe (neophyte, *quasimodogenitus*) with a hairless head. In the myth of the night sea journey the hero loses all his hair during his incubation in the belly of the monster, because of the terrific heat.[54] The custom of tonsure, which is derived from these primitive ideas, naturally presupposes the presence of a ritual barber. Curiously enough, we come across the barber in that old alchemical "mystery," the *Chymical Wedding* of 1616.[55] There the hero, on entering the mysterious castle, is pounced on by invisible barbers, who give him something very like a tonsure.[56] Here again the initiation and transformation process is accompanied by a shaving.[57]

---

[54] Leo Frobenius, *Das Zeitalter des Sonnengottes* (Berlin, 1904), p. 30.

[55] [The *Chymische Hochzeit*, dated 1459, actually published at Strasbourg, 1616. Signed "Christian Rosencreutz," but actually written by Johann Valentin Andreae, Professor Jung states elsewhere. The 1616 ed. was reprinted under the editorship of F. Maack, Berlin, 1913. Tr. by E. Foxcroft, *The Hermetick Romance; or, The Chymical Wedding* (London, 1690).—Ed.]

[56] As Andreae, the author of the *Chymical Wedding*, must have been a learned alchemist, he might very well have got hold of a copy of the Codex Marcianus and seen the writings of Zosimos. Manuscript copies exist in Gotha, Leipzig, Munich, and Weimar. I know of only one printed edition, published in Italy in the 16th century, which is very rare.

[57] Hence the "shaving of a man" and the "plucking of a fowl," mentioned further on among the magical sacrificial recipes. A

In one variant of these visions there is a dragon who is killed and sacrificed in the same manner as the priest, and therefore seems to be identical with him. This makes one think of those far from uncommon medieval pictures, not necessarily alchemical, in which a serpent is shown hanging on the Cross in place of Christ. (Note the comparison of Christ with the serpent of Moses in John 3:14.)

We have already mentioned the leaden homunculus as one of the names of the priest, and this is none other than the leaden spirit or planetary demon Saturn. In Zosimos' day Saturn was regarded as a Hebrew god, presumably on account of the keeping holy of the Sabbath—Saturday means "Saturn's Day"[58]—and also on account of the Gnostic parallel with the supreme archon Ialdabaoth ("child of chaos") who, as *leontōādās* (lion-like),[59] may be grouped together with Baal, Kronos, and Saturn.[60] The later Arabic designation of Zosimos as al-'Ibrî (the Hebrew) does not of course prove that he himself was a Jew, but it is clear from his writings that he was acquainted with Jewish traditions.[61] The parallel between the Hebrew god and Saturn is of considerable importance as regards the alchemical idea of the transformation of the God of

---

similar motif is suggested by the "changing of wigs" at the Egyptian judgment of the dead. Cf. the picture in the tomb of Sennezem (Campbell, p. 143). When the dead man is led before Osiris his wig is black; immediately afterwards (at the sacrifice in the Papyrus of Ani) it is white.

[58] Plutarch, *Quaestiones convivales*, IV, 5, and Diogenes Laertius, II, §112; Richard Reitzenstein, *Poimandres* (Leipzig, 1904), pp. 75f. and 112. In a text named "Ghâya al-hakîm," ascribed to Maslama al-Madjrîtî, the following instructions are given when invoking Saturn: "Arrive vêtu à la manière des Juifs, car il est leur patron." Reinhart Dozy and M. J. de Goeje, "Nouveaux documents pour l'étude de la religion des Harraniens," *Actes du Sixième Congrès international des Orientalistes*, 1883 (Leyden, 1885), p. 350.

[59] Origen, *Contra Celsum*, V, 31. *Pistis Sophia*, Ch. 31. Wilhelm Bousset, *Hauptprobleme der Gnosis* (Göttingen, 1907), pp. 351ff.

[60] Roscher, *Lexikon*, s.v. Kronos, 1496. The dragon and Kronos are often confused.

[61] E. O. von Lippmann, *Entstehung und Ausbreitung der Alchemie* (Berlin, 1919–31), Vol. II, p. 229.

the Old Testament into the God of the New. The alchemists naturally attached great significance to Saturn, for, besides being the outermost planet, the supreme archon (the Harranites named him "Primas"), and the demiurge Ialdabaoth, he was also the *spiritus niger* who lies captive in the darkness of matter, the deity or that part of the deity which has been swallowed up in his own creation. He is the dark god who reverts to his original luminous state in the mystery of alchemical transmutation. As the *Aurora consurgens* (Part I) says: "Blessed is he who has discovered this science and on whom the providence of Saturn flows."[62]

The later alchemists were familiar not only with the ritual slaying of a dragon but also with the slaying of a lion, which took the form of his having all four paws cut off.[63] Like the dragon, the lion devours himself,[64] and so is probably only a variant.

The vision itself indicates that the main purpose of the transformation process is the spiritualization of the sacrificing priest: he is to be changed into *pneuma*. We are also told that he would "change the bodies into blood, make the eyes to see and the dead to rise again." Later in the visions he appears in glorified form, shining white like the midday sun.

Throughout the visions it is clear that sacrificer and sacrificed are one and the same. This idea of the unity of the *prima* and *ultima materia*, of that which redeems and that which is to be redeemed, pervades the whole of alchemy from beginning to end. "Unus est lapis, una medicina, unum vas, unum regimen, unaque dispositio" is the key formula to its enigmatic language.[65] Greek alchemy expresses the same idea in the formula *hen tō pan* (one in all). Its symbol is the uroboros,

---

[62] "Beatus homo qui invenerit hanc scientiam et cui affluit providentia Saturni."

[63] See the illustration in Béroalde de Verville's *Pandora* (1588) and the frontispiece of his *Poliphile* (1600).

[64] Generally the pictures show two lions eating one another. The uroboros, too, is often pictured in the form of two dragons engaged in the same process (*Viridarium chymicum*, 1624).

[65] Cf. the "Rosarium philosophorum," in the *Artis auriferae* (Basel, 1593), Vol. II, p. 206.

the tail-eating serpent. In our vision it is the priest as sacrificer who devours himself as the sacrifice. This recalls the saying of St. John Chrysostom that in the Eucharist Christ drinks his own blood. By the same token, one might add, he eats his own flesh. The grisly repast in the dream of Zosimos reminds us of the orgiastic meals in the Dionysus cult, when sacrificial animals were torn to pieces and eaten. They represent Dionysus Zagreus being torn to pieces by the Titans, from whose mangled remains the *neos* Dionysus arises.[66]

Zosimos tells us that the vision represents or explains the "production of the waters." The visions themselves only show the transformation into *pneuma*. In the language of the alchemists, however, spirit and water are synonymous,[67] as they

---

[66] Cf. the Cretan fragment of Euripides (Albrecht Dieterich, *Eine Mithrasliturgie*, Leipzig, 1910, p. 105): living a holy life, since I have been initiated into the mysteries of the Idaean Zeus, and eaten raw the flesh of Zagreus, the night-wandering shepherd.

[67] "Est et coelestis aqua sive potius divina Chymistarum . . . pneuma, ex aetheris natura et essentia rerum quinta" (There is also the celestial, or rather the divine, water of the alchemists . . . the pneuma, having the nature of the pneuma and the quintessence of things).—Hermolaus Barbarus, *Coroll. in Dioscoridem*, cited in M. Maier, *Symbola aureae mensae* (Frankfort, 1617), p. 174.

"Spiritus autem in hac arte nihil aliud quam aquam indicari . . ." (In this art, spirit means nothing else but water).—Theobaldus de Hoghelande, in the *Theatrum chemicum*, Vol. I (Ursel, 1602), p. 196. Water is a "spiritus extractus," or a "spiritus qui in ventre (corporis) occultus est et fiet aqua et corpus absque spiritu: qui est spiritualis naturae" (spirit which is hidden in the belly [of the substance], and water will be produced and a substance without spirit, which is of a spiritual nature).—J. D. Mylius, *Philosophia reformata* (Frankfort, 1622), p. 150. This quotation shows how closely spirit and water were associated in the mind of the alchemist.

"Sed aqua coelestis gloriosa *scil.* aes nostrum ac argentum nostrum, sericum nostrum, totaque oratio nostra, quod est unum et idem *scil.* sapientia, quam Deus obtulit, quibus voluit" (But the glorious celestial water, namely our copper and our silver, our silk, and everything we talk about, is one and the same thing, namely the Wisdom, which God has given to whomsoever he wished).—"Consilium coniugii," in the *Ars chemica* (Strasbourg, 1566), p. 120.

are in the language of the early Christians, for whom water meant the *spiritus veritatis*. In the "Book of Krates" we read: "You make the bodies to liquefy, so that they mingle and become an homogeneous liquid; this is then named 'divine water.'"[68] The passage corresponds to the Zosimos text, which says that the priest would "change the bodies into blood." For the alchemists, water and blood are identical. This transformation is the same as the *solutio* or *liquefactio*, which is a synonym for the *sublimatio*, for "water" is also "fire": "Item ignis . . . est aqua et ignis noster est ignis et non ignis" (For fire . . . is water and our fire is the fire that is no fire). "Aqua nostra" is said to be "ignea" (fiery).[69]

The "secret fire of our philosophy" is said to be "our mystical water,"[70] and the "permanent water" is the "fiery form of the true water."[71] The permanent water (the *hy̆dōr thaon* of the Greeks) also signifies "spiritualis sanguis,"[72] and is identified with the blood and water that flowed from Christ's side. Heinrich Khunrath says of this water: "So there will open for thee an healing flood which issues from the heart of the son of the great world." It is a water "which the son of the great world pours forth from his body and heart, to be for us a true and natural Aqua Vitae."[73] Just as a spiritual water of grace and truth flows from Christ's sacrifice, so the "divine water" is produced by a sacrificial act in the Zosimos vision. It is mentioned in the ancient treatise entitled "Isis to Horus,"[74] where the angel Amnael brings it to the prophetess in a drinking vessel. As Zosimos was probably an adherent of the Poimandres sect, another thing to be considered here is the *krater* which

[68] M. Berthelot, *La Chimie au moyen âge* (Paris, 1893), Vol. III, p. 53.

[69] Mylius, pp. 121 and 123. For the blood–water–fire equation see George Ripley, *Opera omnia chemica* (Kassel, 1649), pp. 162, 197, 295, 427.

[70] Ripley, *Opera*, p. 62.

[71] "Rosarium," p. 264.

[72] Mylius, p. 42.

[73] H. C. Khunrath, *Von hylealischen . . . Chaos* (Magdeburg, 1597), pp. 274f.

[74] Berthelot, *Alchimistes*, I, xiii.

God filled with *nous* for all those seeking *ennoia*.[75] *Nous* is identical with the alchemical Mercurius. This is quite clear from the Ostanes quotation in Zosimos, which says: "Go to the streams of the Nile and there thou wilt find a stone which hath a spirit. Take and divide it, thrust in thy hand and draw out its heart, for its soul is in its heart." Commenting on this, Zosimos remarks that "having a spirit" is a metaphorical expression for the *exhydrargyrosis*, the expulsion of the quicksilver.[76]

During the first centuries after Christ the words *nous* and *pneuma* were used indiscriminately, and the one could easily stand for the other. Moreover the relation of Mercurius to "spirit" is an extremely ancient astrological fact. Like Hermes, Mercurius (or the planetary spirit Mercury) was a god of revelation, who discloses the secret of the art to the adepts. The *Liber quartorum*, which being of Harranite origin cannot be dated later than the tenth century, says of Mercurius: *"Ipse enim aperit clausiones operum cum ingenio et intellectu suo"* (For he opens with his genius and understanding the locked [insoluble] problems of the work).[77] He is also the "soul of the bodies," the *"anima vitalis,"*[78] and Ruland defines him as "spirit which has become earth."[79] He is a spirit that penetrates into the depths of the material world and transforms it. Like the *nous*, he is symbolized by the serpent. In Michael Maier he points the way to the earthly paradise.[80] Besides being identified with Hermes Trismegistus,[81] he is also called the

---

[75] *Ibid.*, III, li, 8, and *Hermetica*, ed. Scott, Vol. I, p. 151.

[76] Berthelot, *Alchimistes*, III, vi, 5.

[77] Of the later authors I will mention only Joannes Christophorus Steeb, *Coelum sephiroticum* (Mainz, 1679): *"Omnis intellectus acuminis auctor . . . a coelesti mercurio omnem ingeniorum vim provenire"* (The author of all deeper understanding . . . all the power of genius comes from the celestial Mercurius). For the astrological connection see Auguste Bouché-Leclercq, *L'Astrologie grecque* (Paris, 1899), pp. 312, 321–23.

[78] *Aurora consurgens*. In Mylius (p. 533) he is a giver of life.

[79] *Lexicon*.

[80] *Symbola*, p. 592.

[81] P. 600.

"mediator"[82] and, as the Original Man, the "Hermaphroditic Adam."[83] From numerous passages it is clear that Mercurius is as much a fire as a water, both of which aptly characterize the nature of spirit.

Killing with the sword is a recurrent theme in alchemical literature. The "philosophical egg" is divided with the sword, and with it the "King" is transfixed and the dragon or "corpus" dismembered, the latter being represented as the body of a man whose head and limbs are cut off.[84] The lion's paws are likewise cut off with the sword. For the alchemical sword brings about the *solutio* or *separatio* of the elements, thereby restoring the original condition of chaos, so that a new and more perfect body can be produced by a new *impressio formae*, or by a "new imagination." The sword is therefore that which "kills and vivifies," and the same is said of the permanent water or mercurial water. Mercurius is the giver of life as well as the destroyer of the old form. In ecclesiastical symbolism the sword which comes out of the mouth of the Son of Man in the Book of Revelation is, according to Hebrews 4:12, the Logos, the Word of God, and hence Christ himself. This analogy did not escape the notice of the alchemists, who were always struggling to give expression to their fantasies. Mercurius was their mediator and savior, their *filius macrocosmi* (contrasted with Christ the *filius microcosmi*),[85] the solver and separator. So he too is a sword, for he is a "penetrating spirit" ("more piercing than a two-edged sword"!). Gerhard Dorn, an alchemist of the sixteenth century, says that in our world the sword was changed into Christ our Saviour. He comments as follows:

After a long interval of time the Deus Optimus Maximus

[82] Ripley, *Opera*, Forward, and in Khunrath's *Chaos*. In Plutarch, Mercurius acts as a kind of world soul.

[83] Gerhard Dorn, "Congeries Paracelsicae chemicae . . . ," in the *Theatrum chemicum*, Vol. I, p. 589.

[84] Illustration in "Splendor solis," *Aureum vellus* (Rorschach, 1598).

[85] Cf. Khunrath, *Chaos*, and *Amphitheatrum sapientiae aeternae* . . . (Hanau, 1604).

immersed himself in the innermost of his secrets, and he decided, out of the compassion of his love as well as for the demands of justice, to take the sword of wrath from the hand of the angel. And having hung the sword on the tree, he substituted for it a golden trident, and thus was the wrath of God changed into love. . . . When peace and justice were united, the water of Grace flowed more abundantly from above, and now it bathes the whole world.[86]

This passage, which might well have occurred in an author like Rabanus Maurus or Honorius of Autun without doing them discredit, actually occurs in a context which throws light on certain esoteric alchemical doctrines, namely in a colloquy between Animus, Anima, and Corpus. There we are told that it is Sophia, the Sapientia, Scientia, or Philosophia of the al-

---

[86] Dorn, "Speculativae philosophiae," in the *Theatrum chemicum*, Vol. I, pp. 284ff. The whole passage runs as follows:

After man's first disobedience the Lord straitened this wide road into a very narrow and difficult path, as you see. At its entrance he placed an angel of the Cherubim, holding in his hand a double-edged sword with which he was to keep all from entering into Paradise. Turning from thence on account of the sin of their first parents, the sons of Adam built for themselves a broad left-hand path: this you have shunned. After a long interval of time the Deus Optimus Maximus immersed himself in the innermost of his secrets, and he decided, out of the compassion of his love as well as for the demands of justice, to take the sword of wrath from the hand of the angel. And having hung the sword on the tree, he substituted for it a golden trident, and thus was the wrath of God changed into love, and justice remained unimpaired. Previous to this, however, the river was not collected into one as it is now, but before the Fall it was spread equally over the whole world, like dew. But later it returned to the place of its origin. When peace and justice were united, the water of grace flowed more abundantly from above, and now it bathes the whole world. Some of those who take the left-hand path, on seeing the sword suspended from the tree, and knowing its history, pass it by, because they are too entangled in the affairs of this world; some, on seeing it, do not choose to inquire into its efficacy; others never see it and would not wish to see it. All these continue their pilgrimage into the valley, except for those who are drawn back to Mount Zion by the hook of repentance. Now in our age, which is an age of grace, the sword has become Christ our Saviour, who ascended the tree of the Cross for our sins.

chemists, *"de cuius fonte scaturiunt aquae"* (from whose fount the waters gush forth). This Wisdom is the *nous* that lies hidden and bound in matter, the *"serpens mercurialis"* or *"humidum radicale"* that manifests itself in the *"viventis aquae fluvius de montis apice"* (stream of living water from the summit of the mountain).[87] That is the water of grace, the "permanent" and "divine" water which "now bathes the whole world." The apparent transformation of the God of the Old Testament into the God of the New is in reality the transformation of the *deus absconditus* (i.e., the *natura abscondita*) into the *Medicina catholica* of alchemical wisdom.[88]

The divisive and separative function of the sword, which is of such importance in alchemy, is prefigured in the flaming sword of the angel that separated our first parents from paradise. Separation by a sword is a theme that can also be found in the Gnosis of the Ophites: the earthly cosmos is surrounded by a ring of fire which at the same time encloses paradise. But paradise and the ring of fire are separated by the "flaming sword."[89] An important interpretation of this flaming sword is given in Simon Magus:[90] there is an incorruptible essence potentially present in every human being, the divine *pneuma* "which is stationed above and below in the stream of water." Simon says of this *pneuma:* "I and thou, thou before me. I, who am after thee." It is a force "that generates itself, that causes itself to grow; it is its own mother, sister, bride, daughter; its own son, mother, father; a unity, a root of the whole." It is the very ground of existence, the procreative urge, which is of fiery origin. Fire is related to blood, which "is fashioned warm and ruddy like fire." Blood turns

---

[87] Another remark of Dorn's points in the same direction: "The sword was suspended from a tree over the bank of the river" (p. 288).

[88] A few pages later Dorn himself remarks: Know, brothers, that everything which has been said above and everything which will be said in what follows can also be understood of the alchemical preparations.

[89] Hans Leisegang, *Die Gnosis* (Leipzig, 1924), pp. 171f.

[90] The passage which follows occurs in Hippolytus, *Elenchos* (in *Werke*, ed. Paul Wendland, Vol. III; Leipzig, 1916), pp. 4f.

into semen in men, and in women into milk. This "turning" is interpreted as "the flaming sword which turned every way, to keep the way of the tree of life."[91] The operative principle in semen and milk turns into mother and father. The tree of life is guarded by the turning (i.e., transforming) sword, and this is the "seventh power" which begets itself. "For if the flaming sword turned not, then would that fair Tree be destroyed, and perish utterly; but if it turneth into semen and milk, and there be added the Logos and the place of the Lord where the Logos is begotten, he who dwelleth potentially in the semen and milk shall grow to full stature from the littlest spark, and shall increase and become a power boundless and immutable, like to an unchanging Aeon, which suffereth no more change until measureless eternity."[92] It is clear from these remarkable statements of Hippolytus concerning the teachings of Simon Magus that the sword is very much more than an instrument which divides; it is itself the force which "turns" from something infinitesimally small into the infinitely great: from water, fire, and blood it becomes the limitless aeon. What it means is the transformation of the vital spirit in man into the Divine. The natural being becomes the divine *pneuma*, as in the vision of Zosimos. Simon's description of the creative *pneuma*, the true arcane substance, corresponds in every detail to the uroboros or *serpens mercurialis* of the Latinists. It too is its own father, mother, son, daughter, brother, and sister from the earliest beginnings of alchemy right down to the end.[93] It begets and sacrifices itself and is its own instrument of sacrifice, for it is a symbol of the deadly and life-giving water.[94]

Simon's ideas also throw a significant light on the above-quoted passage from Dorn, where the sword of wrath is transformed into Christ. Were it not that the philosophemes of Hippolytus were first discovered in the nineteenth century, on Mount Athos, one might almost suppose that Dorn had made

---

[91] Genesis 3:24.
[92] Leisegang, p. 80.
[93] That is why it is called "Hermaphroditus."
[94] One of its symbols is the scorpion, which stings itself to death.

use of them. There are numerous other symbols in alchemy whose origin is so doubtful that one does not know whether to attribute them to tradition, or to a study of the heresiologists, or to spontaneous revival.[95]

The sword as the "proper" instrument of sacrifice occurs again in the old treatise entitled "Consilium coniugii de massa solis et lunae." This says: "Both must be killed with their own sword" ("both" referring to Sol and Luna).[96] In the still older "Tractatus Micreris,"[97] dating perhaps from the twelfth century, we find the "fiery sword" in a quotation from Ostanes: "The great Astanus [Ostanes] saith: Take an egg, pierce it with the fiery sword, and separate its soul from its body."[98] Here the sword is something that divides body and soul, corresponding to the division between heaven and earth, the ring of fire and paradise, or paradise and the first parents. In an equally old treatise, the "Allegoriae sapientum . . . supra librum Turbae," there is even mention of a sacrificial rite: "Take a fowl [*volatile*], cut off its head with the fiery sword, then pluck out its feathers, separate the limbs, and cook over a charcoal fire till it becomes of one color." Here we have a decapitation with the fiery sword, then a "clipping," or more accurately a "plucking," and finally a "cooking." The cock, which is probably what is meant here, is simply called "volatile," a fowl or winged creature, and this is a common term for spirit, but a spirit still nature-bound and imperfect, and in need of improvement. In another old treatise, with the very similar title "Al-

---

[95] So far I have come across only two authors who admit to having read any heresiologists. The silence of the alchemists in this matter is nothing to wonder at, since the mere proximity to heresy would have put them in danger of their lives. Thus even 90 years after the death of Trithemius of Spanheim, who was supposed to have been the teacher of Paracelsus, the abbot Sigismund of Sion had to compose a moving defense in which he endeavored to acquit Trithemius of the charge of heresy. Cf. *Trithemius sui-ipsius vindex* (Ingolstadt, 1616).

[96] *Ars chemica,* p. 256. Printed in J. J. Manget, *Bibliotheca chemica curiosa* (Geneva, 1702), Vol. II, p. 235.

[97] "Micreris" is probably a corruption of "Mercurius."

[98] *Theatrum chemicum,* Vol. V (1622), p. 103.

legoriae super librum Turbae,"[99] we find the following supplementary variants: "Kill the mother [the *prima materia*], tearing off her hands and feet." "Take a viper . . . cut off its head and tail." "Take a cock . . . and pluck it alive." "Take a man, shave him, and drag him over a [hot] stone till his body dies." "Take the glass vessel containing bridegroom and bride, throw them into the furnace, and roast them for three days, and they will be two in one flesh." "Take the white man from the vessel."

One is probably right in assuming that these recipes are instructions for magical sacrifices, not unlike the Greek magic papyri.[100] As an example of the latter I will give the recipe from the Mimaut Papyrus (li. 2ff.): "Take a tomcat and make an Osiris of him[101] [by immersing] his body in water. And when you proceed to suffocate him, talk into his back." Another example from the same papyrus (li. 425): "Take a hoopoe, tear out its heart, pierce it with a reed, then cut it up and throw it into Attic honey."

Such sacrifices really were made for the purpose of summoning up the *paredros*, the familiar spirit. That this sort of thing was practiced, or at any rate recommended, by the alchemists is clear from the "Liber Platonis quartorum," where it speaks of the *"oblationes et sacrificia"* offered to the planetary demon. A deeper and more somber note is struck in the following passage, which I give in the original (and generally very corrupt) text:[102]

> Vas . . . oportet esse rotundae figurae: Ut sit artifex huius mutator firmamenti et testae capitis, ut cum sit res, qua indigemus, res simplex, habens partes similes, necesse est ipsius generationem, et in corpore habente similes partibus . . . proiicies ex testa capitis, videlicet capitis elementi hominis et massetur totum cum urina. . . .

[99] *Artis auriferae*, Vol. I, pp. 139f.
[100] *Papyri Graecae Magicae*, tr. and ed. Karl Preisendanz (Leipzig, Berlin, 1928–31, 2 vols.).
[101] *apotheosis* = "sacrifice."
[102] *Theatrum chemicum*, Vol. V, p. 153.

(The vessel . . . must be round in shape. Thus the artifex must be the transformer of this firmament and of the brain-pan, just as the thing for which we seek is a simple thing having uniform parts. It is therefore necessary that you should generate it in a body [i.e., a vessel] of uniform parts . . . from the brain-pan, that is, from the head of the element Man, and that the whole should be macerated with urine. . . .)

One asks oneself how literally this recipe, with its implied human sacrifice,[103] is to be taken. The following story from the "Ghâya al-hakîm" is exceedingly enlightening in this connection:

The Jacobite patriarch Dionysius I set it on record that in the year 765, a man who was destined for the sacrifice, on beholding the bloody head of his predecessor, was so terrified that he took flight and lodged a complaint with Abbas, the prefect of Mesopotamia, against the priests of Harran, who were afterwards severely punished. The story goes on to say that in 830 the Caliph Mamun told the Harranite envoys: "You are without doubt the people of the head, who were dealt with by my father Rashid." We learn from the "ghâya" that a fair-haired man with dark-blue eyes was lured into a chamber of the temple, where he was immersed in a great jar filled with sesame oil. Only his head was left sticking out. There he remained for forty days, and during this time was fed on nothing but figs soaked in sesame oil. He was not given a drop of water to drink. As a result of this treatment his body became as soft as wax. The prisoner was repeatedly fumigated with incense, and magical formulae were pronounced over him. Eventually his head was torn off at the neck, the body remaining in the oil. The head was then placed in a niche on the ashes of burnt olives, and was packed round with cotton wool. More incense was burned before it, and the head would thereupon predict famines or good harvests, changes of dynasty, and other future events. Its eyes could see, though

[103] The preparation known in medieval alchemy as *mumia* had to be compounded of *fresh* human bones.

the lids did not move. It also revealed to people their inmost thoughts, and scientific and technical questions were likewise addressed to it.[104]

Even though it is possible that the real head was, in later times, replaced by a dummy, the whole idea of this ceremony, particularly when taken in conjunction with the above passage from the "Liber quartorum," seems to point to an original human sacrifice. The idea of a mysterious head is, however, considerably older than the school of Harran. As far back as Zosimos we find the philosophers described as "children of the golden head," and we also encounter the *"rotundum,"* which Zosimos says is the letter omega (Ω). This symbol may well be interpreted as the head, since the "Liber quartorum" also associates the round vessel with the head. Zosimos, moreover, refers on several occasions to the "whitest stone, which is in the head."[105] Probably all these ideas go back to the severed head of Osiris, which crossed the sea and was therefore associated with the idea of resurrection. The "head of Osiris" also plays an important part in medieval alchemy.

In this connection we might mention the legend that was current about Gerbert of Reims, afterwards Pope Sylvester II (d. 1003). He was believed to have possessed a golden head which spoke to him in oracles. Gerbert was one of the greatest savants of his time, and well known as the transmitter of Arabic science.[106] Can it be that the translation of the "Liber quartorum," which is of Harranite origin, goes back to this author? Unfortunately there is little prospect of our being able to prove this.

It has been conjectured that the Harranite oracle head may be connected with the ancient Hebrew teraphim. Rabbinic tradition considers the teraphim to have been originally either the decapitated head or skull of a human being, or else a

[104] Dozy and de Goeje, p. 365.

[105] *"Tōn panu lukōtaton lithon tōn engkephalon* (the brain is the very clearest stone)."—The importance of the cerebrum was also stressed by the medieval alchemists.

[106] Lynn Thorndike, *A History of Magic and Experimental Science*, Vol. I (New York, 1923), p. 705.

dummy head.[107] The Jews had teraphim about the house as a sort of lares and penates (who were plural spirits, like the Cabiri). The idea that they were heads goes back to I Samuel 19:13f., which describes how Michal, David's wife, put the teraphim in David's bed in order to deceive the messengers of Saul, who wanted to kill him. "Then Michal took an image and laid it on the bed and put a pillow of goats' hair at its head, and covered it with the clothes." The "pillow of goats' hair" is linguistically obscure and has even been interpreted as meaning that the teraphim were goats. But it may also mean something woven or plaited out of goats' hair, like a wig, and this would fit in better with the picture of a man lying in bed. Further evidence for this comes from a legend in a collection of midrashim from the twelfth century, printed in Bin Gorion's *Die Sagen der Juden*. There it is said:

> The teraphim were idols, and they were made in the following way. The head of a man, who had to be a firstborn, was cut off and the hair plucked out. The head was then sprinkled with salt and anointed with oil. Afterwards a little plaque, of copper or gold, was inscribed with the name of an idol and placed under the tongue of the decapitated head. The head was set up in a room, candles were lit before it, and the people made obeisance. And if any man fell down before it, the head began to speak, and answered all questions that were addressed to it.[108]

This is an obvious parallel to the Harranite ritual with the head. The tearing out of the hair seems significant, since it is an equivalent of scalping or shearing, and is thus a rebirth mystery. It is conceivable that in later times the bald skull was covered with a wig for a rite of renewal, as is also reported from Egypt.

It seems probable that this magical procedure is of primi-

---

[107] *Jewish Encyclopaedia* (New York, 1901–06), Vol. XII, s.v. "Teraphim."

[108] Micha Josef Bin Gorion, pseud., *Die Sagen der Juden* (Frankfort, 1935), p. 325. I am indebted to Dr. Riwkah Schärf for drawing my attention to this passage.

tive origin. I have to thank the South African writer, Laurens van der Post, for the following report from a lecture which he gave in Zurich in 1951:

> The tribe in question was an offshoot of the great Swazi nation—a Bantu people. When, some years ago, the old chief died, he was succeeded by his son, a young man of weak character. He soon proved to be so unsatisfactory a chief that his uncles called a meeting of the tribal elders. They decided that something must be done to strengthen their chief, so they consulted the witch doctors. The witch doctors treated him with a medicine which proved ineffective. Another meeting was held and the witch doctors were asked to use the strongest medicine of all on the chief because the situation was becoming desperate. A half brother of the chief, a boy of twelve, was chosen to provide the material for the medicine.
>
> One afternoon a sorcerer went up to the boy, who was tending cattle, and engaged him in conversation. Then, emptying some powder from a horn into his hand, he took a reed and blew the powder into the ears and nostrils of the boy. A witness told me that the lad thereupon began to sway like a drunken person and sank to the ground shivering. He was then taken to the river bed and tied to the roots of a tree. More powder was sprinkled round about, the sorcerer saying: "This person will no longer eat food but only earth and roots."
>
> The boy was kept in the river bed for nine months. Some people say a cage was made and put into the stream, with the boy inside it, for hours on end, so that the water should flow over him and make his skin white. Others reported seeing him crawling about in the river bed on his hands and knees. But all were so frightened that, although there was a mission school only one hundred yards away, no one except those directly concerned in the ritual would go near him. All are agreed that at the end of nine months this fat, normal, healthy boy was like an animal and quite white-

skinned. One woman said, "His eyes were white and the whole of his body was white as white paper."

On the evening that the boy was to be killed a veteran witch doctor was summoned to the chief's kraal and asked to consult the tribal spirits. This he did in the cattle kraal, and after selecting an animal for slaughter he retired to the chief's hut. There the witch doctor was handed parts of the dead boy's body: first the head in a sack, then a thumb and a toe. He cut off the nose and ears and lips, mixed them with medicine, and cooked them over a fire in a broken clay pot. He stuck two spears on either side of the pot. Then those present—twelve in all including the weak chief—leaned over the pot and deeply inhaled the steam. All save the boy's mother dipped their fingers in the pot and licked them. She inhaled but refused to dip her fingers in the pot. The rest of the body the witch doctor mixed into a kind of bread for doctoring the tribe's crops.

Although this magical rite is not actually a "head mystery," it has several things in common with the practices previously mentioned. The body is macerated or transformed by long immersion in water. The victim is killed, and the salient portions of the head form the main ingredient of the "strengthening" medicine which was concocted for the chief and his immediate circle. The body is kneaded into a sort of bread, and this is obviously thought of as a strengthening medicine for the tribe's crops as well. The rite is a transformation process, a sort of rebirth after nine months of incubation in the water. Laurens van der Post thinks that the purpose of the "whitening"[109] was to assimilate the mana of the white man, who has the political power. I agree with this view, and would add that painting with white clay often signifies transformation into ancestral spirits, in the same way as the neophytes are made invisible in the Nandi territory, in Kenya, where they walk about in portable, cone-shaped grass huts and demonstrate their invisibility to everyone.

Skull worship is widespread among primitives. In Melanesia

[109] Cf. the alchemical *albedo* and *homo albus*.

and Polynesia it is chiefly the skulls of the ancestors that are worshiped, because they establish connections with the spirits or serve as tutelary deities, like the head of Osiris in Egypt. Skulls also play a considerable role as sacred relics. It would lead us too far to go into this primitive skull worship, so I must refer the reader to the literature.[110] I would only like to point out that the cut-off ears, nose, and mouth can represent the head as parts that stand for the whole. There are numerous examples of this. Equally, the head or its parts (brain, etc.) can act as magical food or as a means for increasing the fertility of the land.

It is of special significance for the alchemical tradition that the oracle head was also known in Greece. Aelian[111] reports that Cleomenes of Sparta had the head of his friend Archonides preserved in a jar of honey, and that he consulted it as an oracle. The same was said of the head of Orpheus. Onians[112] rightly emphasizes the fact that the psyche, whose seat was in the head, corresponds to the modern "unconscious," and that at that stage of development consciousness was identified with *thumos* (heart) and *phrenes* (lungs), and was localized in the chest or heart region. Hence Pindar's expression for the soul—*eiōnos eidolōn* (image of Aion)—is extraordinarily apt, for the collective unconscious not only imparts "oracles" but forever represents the microcosm (i.e., the form of a physical man mirroring the Cosmos).

There is no evidence to show that any of the parallels we have drawn are historically connected with the Zosimos visions. It seems rather to be a case partly of parallel traditions (transmitted, perhaps, chiefly through the Harran school), and partly of spontaneous fantasies arising from the same archetypal background from which the traditions were derived in the first place. As my examples have shown, the imagery of the Zosimos visions, however strange it may be, is by no means isolated, but is interwoven with older ideas some of

---

[110] Hastings, *ERE*, Vol. VI, pp. 535f.
[111] *Varia Historia*, XII, 8.
[112] R. B. Onians, *The Origins of European Thought* (Cambridge, 1951), pp. 101ff.

which were certainly, and others quite possibly, known to Zosimos, as well as with parallels of uncertain date which continued to mold the speculations of the alchemists for many centuries to come. Religious thought in the early Christian era was not completely cut off from all contact with these conceptions;[113] it was in fact influenced by them, and in turn it fertilized the minds of the natural philosophers to an increasing degree during the next centuries. Towards the end of the sixteenth century the alchemical *opus* was even represented in the form of a Mass. The author of this tour de force was the Hungarian alchemist, Melchior Cibinensis. I have elaborated this parallel in my book *Psychology and Alchemy*.[114]

In conclusion, I would like to quote Zosimos' own commentary on his visions. He says:

Beautiful it is to speak and beautiful to hear, beautiful to give and beautiful to take, beautiful to be poor and beautiful to be rich. How does nature teach giving and taking? The brazen man gives, and the moist stone receives; the metal gives, and the plant receives; the stars give, and the flowers receive; the sky gives, and the earth receives; the thunderclaps give darting fire. And all things are woven together and all things are undone again, and all things are mingled with one another, and all things are composed, and all things are permeated with one another, and all things are decomposed again. And everything will be moistened and become desiccated again, and everything puts forth blossoms and everything withers again in the bowl of the altar. For each thing comes to pass with method and in fixed measure and according to the weighing of the four elements. The weaving together of all things and the undoing of all things and the whole fabric of things cannot come to pass without method. The method is natural, preserving due order in its inhaling and its exhaling; it brings increase and it brings stagnation. And to sum up: through

---

[113] Cf. my paper "Einige Bemerkungen zu den Visionen des Zosimos," *EJ 1937*, pp. 45ff.
[114] Pars. 480–89.

the harmonies of separating and combining, and if nothing of the method be neglected, all things bring forth nature. For nature applied to nature transforms nature. Such is the order of natural law throughout the whole cosmos, and thus all things hang together.

This commentary is a general philosophical conclusion drawn from the character of the visions, showing that the Hiereus who is transformed into *pneuma* represents the transformative principle at work in nature and the harmony of opposing forces. Chinese philosophy formulated this process as the enantiodromian interplay of Yin and Yang.[115] But the curious personifications which characterize not only these visions but alchemical literature in general show in the plainest possible terms that we are dealing with a psychic process that takes place mainly in the unconscious and therefore can come into consciousness only in the form of a dream or vision. At that time and until very much later no one had any idea of the unconscious; consequently all unconscious contents were projected into the object, or rather were found in nature as apparent objects or properties of matter and were not understood as purely internal psychic events. There is some evidence that Zosimos was well aware of the spiritual or mystical side of his art, but he believed that what he was concerned with was a spirit that dwelt in natural objects, and not something that came from the human psyche. It remained for modern science to despiritualize nature through its so-called objective knowledge of matter. All anthropomorphic projections were withdrawn from the object one after another, with a twofold result: firstly man's mystical identity with nature[116] was curtailed as never before, and secondly the projections falling back into the human soul caused such a terrific activation of

[115] The classical example being the *I Ching* or *Book of Changes* (tr. Richard Wilhelm; English tr. Cary F. Baynes; London and New York, 1950).
[116] Mystical or *unconscious* identity occurs in every case of projection, because the content projected upon the extraneous object creates an apparent relationship between it and the subject. [Note from 1954 version.]

the unconscious that in modern times man was compelled to postulate the existence of an unconscious psyche. The first beginnings of this can be seen in Leibniz and Kant, and then, with mounting intensity, in Schelling, Carus, and Von Hartmann, until finally modern psychology discarded the last metaphysical claims of the philosopher-psychologists and restricted the idea of the psyche's existence to the psychological statement, in other words, to its phenomenology.[117] The gods of Olympus were lost, but in exchange we have discovered the inner wealth of the psyche that lies buried in the heart of every man.

IV. *The Psychology of the Mass*

1. GENERAL REMARKS ON THE SACRIFICE

While discussing the transformation rite in section 2, I kept as far as possible to the ecclesiastical point of view; but in the present section I shall treat the Church's interpretation as a purely psychological statement. This method of procedure is simply a *modus considerandi* and does not imply any evaluation of the content of religious belief. It has nothing to do with that side of the question. Critical science is of course bound to adhere to the view that when something is held as an opinion, thought to be true, or believed, it does not posit the existence

---

[117] [Concluding sentence in 1954 version of the present paper:] So far as the dramatic course of the Mass represents the death, sacrifice and resurrection of a god and the inclusion and active participation of the priest and congregation, its phenomenology may legitimately be brought into line with other fundamentally similar, though more primitive, religious customs. This always involves the risk that sensitive people will find it unpleasant when "small things are compared with great." In fairness to the primitive psyche, however, I would like to emphasize that the "holy dread" of civilized man differs but little from the awe of the primitive, and that the God who is present and active in the mystery is a mystery for both. No matter how crass the outward differences, the similarity or equivalence of meaning should not be overlooked.

of any real fact other than a psychological one; but we must also bear in mind the legitimate criticism that in using the term "psychological" we are alluding to a "reality" about whose nature science knows little or nothing. At best—or at worst—we cannot know whether anything is "posited" or not by the fact that something is held to be true. We just cannot know how much stands or falls with the so-called "reality" of the psyche.

The ritual event that takes place in the Mass has a dual aspect, human and divine. From the human point of view, gifts are offered to God at the altar, signifying at the same time the self-oblation of the priest and the congregation. The ritual act consecrates both the gifts and the givers. It commemorates and represents the Last Supper which our Lord took with his disciples, the whole Incarnation, Passion, death, and resurrection of Christ. But from the point of view of the divine, this anthropomorphic action is only the outer shell or husk in which what is really happening is not a human action at all but a divine event. For an instant the life of Christ, eternally existent outside time, becomes visible and is unfolded in temporal succession, but in condensed form, in the sacred action: Christ incarnates as a man under the aspect of the offered substances, he suffers, is killed, is laid in the sepulcher, breaks the power of the underworld, and rises again in glory. In the utterance of the words of consecration the Godhead intervenes, Itself acting and truly present, and thus proclaims that the central event in the Mass is Its act of grace, in which the priest has only the significance of a minister. The same applies to the congregation and the offered substances: they are all ministering causes of the sacred event. The presence of Godhead binds all parts of the sacrificial act into a mystical unity, so that it is God himself who offers himself as a sacrifice in the substances, in the priest, and in the congregation, and who, in the human form of the Son, offers himself as an atonement to the Father.

Although this act is an eternal happening taking place within the divinity, man is nevertheless included in it as an essential component, firstly because God clothes himself in our human nature, and secondly because he needs the ministering co-operation of the priest and congregation, and even the material substances of bread and wine which have a special significance for man. Although God the Father is of one nature with God the Son, he appears in time on the one hand as the eternal Father and on the other hand as the Son of Man in a human body of limited duration. Mankind as a whole is included in God's human nature, which is why man is also included in the sacrificial act. Just as, in the sacrificial act, God is both *agens* and *patiens*, so too is man according to his limited capacity. The *causa efficiens* of the transubstantiation is a spontaneous act of God's grace. Ecclesiastical doctrine insists on this view and even tends to attribute the preparatory action of the priest, indeed the very existence of the rite, to divine prompting,[118] rather than to slothful human nature with its load of original sin. This view is of the utmost importance for a psychological understanding of the Mass. Wherever the magical aspect of a rite tends to prevail, it brings the rite nearer to satisfying the individual ego's blind greed for power, and thus breaks up the mystical body of the Church into separate units. Where, on the other hand, the rite is conceived as the action of God himself, the human participants have only an instrumental or "ministering" significance. The Church's view therefore presupposes the following psychological situation: human consciousness (represented by the priest and congregation) is confronted with an autonomous event which, taking place on a "divine" and "timeless" plane transcending consciousness, is in no way dependent on human action, but which impels man to act by seizing upon him as an instrument and making him the exponent of a "divine" happening. In the ritual action man places himself at the disposal of an autonomous and "eternal" agency operating outside the categories of human consciousness—*si parva licet componere magnis*—in much the same way that a good actor does not merely represent the drama, but allows himself to be overpowered by the genius of the dramatist. The beauty of the

[118] John 6:44: "No man can come to me, except the Father which hath sent me draw him."

ritual action is one of its essential properties, for man has not served God rightly unless he has also served him in beauty. Therefore the rite has no practical utility, for that would be making it serve a purpose—a purely human category. But everything divine is an end-in-itself, perhaps the only legitimate end-in-itself we know. How something eternal can "act" at all is a question we had better not touch, for it is simply unanswerable. Since man, in the action of the Mass, is a tool (though a tool of his own free will), he is not in a position to know anything about the hand which guides him. The hammer cannot discover within itself the power which makes it strike. It is something outside, something autonomous, which seizes and moves man. What happens in the consecration is essentially a miracle, and is meant to be so, for otherwise we should have to consider whether we were not conjuring up God by magic, or else lose ourselves in philosophical wonder how anything eternal can act at all, since action is a process in time with a beginning, a middle, and an end. It is necessary that the transubstantiation should be a cause of wonder and a miracle which man can in no wise comprehend. It is a *mysterium fidei*, a "mystery" in the sense of a *dromenon* and *dāknūmenon*, a secret that is acted and displayed. The ordinary man cannot find anything in himself that would cause him to perform a "mystery." He can only do so if and when *it* seizes upon *him*. This seizure, or rather the sensed or presumed existence of a power outside consciousness which seizes him, is the miracle par excellence, really and truly a miracle when one considers *what* is being represented. What is it that induces us to represent an absolute impossibility? What is it that for thousands of years has wrung from man the greatest spiritual effort, the loveliest works of art, the profoundest devotion, the most heroic self-sacrifice, and the most exacting service? What else but a miracle? It is a miracle which is not man's to command; for as soon as he tries to work it himself, or as soon as he philosophizes about it and tries to comprehend it intellectually, the bird is flown. A miracle is something that arouses man's wonder precisely because it seems inexplicable. And indeed, from what we know of human nature we could never explain why men are constrained to such statements and to such beliefs. (I am thinking here of the impossible statements made by all religions.) There must be some compelling reason for this, even though it is not to be found in ordinary experience. The very absurdity and impossibility of the statements proves the existence of this reason. That is the real ground for belief, as was formulated most brilliantly in Tertullian's *"prorsus credibile, quia ineptum."*[119] An improbable opinion has to submit sooner or later to correction. But the statements of religion are the most improbable of all and yet they persist for thousands of years.[120] Their wholly unexpected vitality proves the existence of a sufficient cause which has so far eluded scientific investigation. I can, as a psychologist, only draw attention to this fact and emphasize my belief that there are no facile "nothing but" explanations for psychic phenomena of this kind.

The dual aspect of the Mass finds expression not only in the contrast between human and divine action, but also in the dual aspect of God and the God-man, who, although they are by nature a unity, nevertheless represent a duality in the ritual drama. Without this "dichotomy of God," if I may use such a term, the whole act of sacrifice would be inconceivable and would lack actuality. According to the Christian view God has never ceased to be God, not even when he appeared in human form in the temporal order. The Christ of the Johannine gospel declares: "I and my Father are one. He that hath seen me hath seen the Father" (John 10:30, 14:9). And yet on the Cross Christ cries out: "My God, my God, why hast thou forsaken me?" This contradiction must exist if the formula "very God and very man" is psychologically true. And if it is true, then the different sayings of Christ are in no sense a con-

[119] *"Et mortuus est Dei filius, prorsus credibile est, quia ineptum est. Et sepultus resurrexit; certum est, quia impossibile est"* (And the Son of God is dead, which is to be believed because it is absurd. And buried He rose again, which is certain because it is impossible).

[120] The audacity of Tertullian's argument is undeniable, and so is its danger, but that does not militate against its psychological truth.

tradition. Being "very man" means being at an extreme remove and utterly different from God. *"De profundis clamavi ad te, Domine"*—this cry demonstrates both, the remoteness and the nearness, the outermost darkness and the dazzling spark of the Divine. God in his humanity is presumably so far from himself that he has to seek himself through absolute self-surrender. And where would God's wholeness be if he could not be the "wholly other"? Accordingly it is with some psychological justification, so it seems to me, that when the Gnostic Nous fell into the power of Physis he assumed the dark chthonic form of the serpent, and the Manichaean "Original Man" in the same situation actually took on the qualities of the Evil One. In Tibetan Buddhism all gods without exception have a peaceful and a wrathful aspect, for they reign over all the realms of being. The dichotomy of God into divinity and humanity and his return to himself in the sacrificial act hold out the comforting doctrine that in man's own darkness there is hidden a light that shall once again return to its source, and that this light actually *wanted* to descend into the darkness in order to deliver the Enchained One who languishes there, and lead him to light everlasting. All this belongs to the stock of pre-Christian ideas, being none other than the doctrine of the Anthropos, the "Man of Light," which the sayings of Christ in the gospels assume to be common knowledge.

II. THE PSYCHOLOGICAL MEANING OF SACRIFICE

(a) The Sacrificial Gifts

Kramp, in his book on the Roman liturgy, makes the following observations about the substances that symbolize the sacrifice:

> Now bread and wine are not only the ordinary means of subsistence for a large portion of humanity, they are also to be had all over the earth (which is of the greatest significance as regards the world-wide spread of Christianity). Further, the two together constitute the perfect food of man, who needs both solid and liquid sustenance. Because they

can be so regarded as the typical food of man, they are best fitted to serve as a symbol of human life and human personality, a fact which throws significant light on the gift-symbol.[121]

It is not immediately apparent why precisely bread and wine should be a "symbol of human life and human personality." This interpretation seems very likely a conclusion *a posteriori* from the special meaning which attaches to these substances in the Mass. In that case the meaning would be due to the liturgy and not to the substances themselves, for no one could imagine that bread and wine, in themselves, signify human life or human personality. But, in so far as bread and wine are important products of culture, they do express a vital human striving. They represent a definite cultural achievement which is the fruit of attention, patience, industry, devotion, and laborious toil. The words "our daily bread" express man's anxious care for his existence. By producing bread he makes his life secure. But in so far as he "does not live by bread alone," bread is fittingly accompanied by wine, whose cultivation has always demanded a special degree of attention and much painstaking work. Wine, therefore, is equally an expression of cultural achievement. Where wheat and the vine are cultivated, civilized life prevails. But where agriculture and vine-growing do not exist, there is only the uncivilized life of nomads and hunters.

So in offering bread and wine man is in the first instance offering up the products of his culture, the best, as it were, that human industry produces. But the "best" can be produced only by the best in man, by his conscientiousness and devotion. Cultural products can therefore easily stand for the psychological conditions of their production, that is, for those human virtues which alone make man capable of civilization.[122]

[121] *Die Opferanschauungen*, p. 55.
[122] My reason for saying this is that every symbol has an objective and a subjective—or psychic—origin, so that it can be interpreted on the "objective level" as well as on the "subjective level."

As to the special nature of these substances, bread is undoubtedly a food. There is a popular saying that wine "fortifies," though not in the same sense as food "sustains." It stimulates and "makes glad the heart of man" by virtue of a certain volatile substance which has always been called "spirit." It is thus, unlike innocuous water, an "inspiriting" drink, for a spirit or god dwells within it and produces the ecstasy of intoxication. The wine miracle at Cana was the same as the miracle in the temple of Dionysus, and it is profoundly significant that, on the Damascus Chalice, Christ is enthroned among vine tendrils like Dionysus himself.[123] Bread therefore represents the physical means of subsistence, and wine the spiritual. The offering up of bread and wine is the offering of both the physical and the spiritual fruits of civilization.

But, however sensible he was of the care and labor lavished upon them, man could hardly fail to observe that these cultivated plants grew and flourished according to an inner law of their own, and that there was a power at work in them which he compared to his own life breath or vital spirit. Frazer has called this principle, not unjustly, the "corn spirit." Human initiative and toil are certainly necessary, but even more necessary, in the eyes of primitive man, is the correct and careful performance of the ceremonies which sustain, strengthen, and propitiate the vegetation numen.[124] Grain and wine therefore have something in the nature of a soul, a specific life principle which makes them appropriate symbols not only of man's cultural achievements, but also of the seasonally dying and resurgent god who is their life spirit. Symbols are never simple—only signs and allegories are simple. The symbol always covers a complicated situation which is so far beyond the grasp of language that it cannot be expressed at all in any

---

This is a consideration of some importance in dream analysis. Cf. *Psychological Types* (New York and London, 1923), definitions 38 and 50.

[123] Further material in Robert Eisler, *Orpheus—the Fisher* (London, 1921), pp. 280f.

[124] Similarly, in hunting, the *rites d'entrée* are more important than the hunt itself, for on these rites the success of the hunt depends.

unambiguous manner.[125] Thus the grain and wine symbols have a fourfold layer of meaning:

1. as agricultural products;
2. as products requiring special processing (bread from grain, wine from grapes);
3. as expressions of psychological achievement (work, industry, patience, devotion, etc.) and of human vitality in general;
4. as manifestations of mana or of the vegetation daemon.

From this list it can easily be seen that a symbol is needed to sum up such a complicated physical and psychic situation. The simplest symbolical formula for this is "bread and wine," giving these words the original complex significance which they have always had for tillers of the soil.

(b) The Sacrifice

It is clear from the foregoing that the sacrificial gift is symbolic, and that it embraces everything which is expressed by the symbol, namely the physical product, the processed substance, the psychological achievement, and the autonomous, daemonic life principle of cultivated plants. The value of the gift is enhanced when it is the best or the first fruits. Since bread and wine are the best that agriculture can offer, they are by the same token man's best endeavor. In addition, bread symbolizes the visible manifestation of the divine numen which dies and rises again, and wine the presence of a pneuma which promises intoxication and ecstasy.[126] The classical world thought of this pneuma as Dionysus, particularly the suffering Dionysus Zagreus, whose divine substance is distributed throughout the whole of nature. In short, what is sacrificed under the forms of bread and wine is nature, man, and God, all combined in the unity of the symbolic gift.

The offering of so significant a gift at once raises the ques-

---

[125] Cf. *Psychological Types*, definition 51.
[126] Hans Leisegang, *Pneuma Hagion* (Leipzig, 1922), pp. 248ff.

tion: Does it lie within man's power to offer such a gift at all? Is he psychologically competent to do so? The Church says no, since she maintains that the sacrificing priest is Christ himself. But, since man is included in the gift—included, as we have seen, twice over—the Church also says yes, though with qualifications. On the side of the sacrificer there is an equally complicated, symbolic state of affairs, for the symbol is Christ himself, who is both the sacrificer and the sacrificed. This symbol likewise has several layers of meaning which I shall proceed to sort out in what follows.

The act of making a sacrifice consists in the first place in giving something which belongs to me. Everything which belongs to me bears the stamp of "mineness," that is, it has a subtle identity with my ego. This is vividly expressed in certain primitive languages, where the suffix of animation is added to an object—a canoe, for instance—when it belongs to me, but not when it belongs to somebody else. The affinity which all the things bearing the stamp of "mineness" have with my personality is aptly characterized by Lévy-Bruhl as *participation mystique*. It is an irrational, unconscious identity, arising from the fact that anything which comes into contact with me is not only itself, but also a symbol. This symbolization comes about firstly because every human being has unconscious contents, and secondly because every object has an unknown side. Your watch, for instance. Unless you are a watchmaker, you would hardly presume to say that you know how it works. Even if you do, you wouldn't know anything about the molecular structure of the steel unless you happened to be a mineralogist or a physicist. And have you ever heard of a scientist who knew how to repair his pocket watch? But where two unknowns come together, it is impossible to distinguish between them. The unknown in man and the unknown in the thing fall together into one. So there arises an unconscious identity which sometimes borders on the grotesque. No one is permitted to touch what is "mine," much less use it. One is affronted if "my" things are not treated with sufficient respect. I remember seeing two Chinese rickshaw boys engaged in furious argument. Just as they were about to come to blows, one of them gave the other's rickshaw a violent kick, thus putting an end to the quarrel. So long as they are unconscious our unconscious contents are always projected, and the projection fixes upon everything "ours," inanimate objects as well as animals and people. And to the extent that "our" possessions are projection carriers, they are *more* than what they are in themselves, and function as such. They have acquired several layers of meaning and are therefore symbolical, though this fact seldom or never reaches consciousness. In reality, our psyche spreads far beyond the confines of the conscious mind, as was apparently known long ago to the old alchemist who said that the soul was for the greater part outside the body.[127]

When, therefore, I give away something that is "mine," what I am giving is essentially a symbol, a thing of many meanings; but, owing to my unconsciousness of its symbolic character, it adheres to my ego, because it is part of my personality. Hence there is, explicitly or implicitly, a personal claim bound up with every gift. There is always an unspoken "give that thou mayest receive." Consequently the gift always carries with it a personal intention, for the mere giving of it is not a sacrifice. It only becomes a sacrifice if I give up the implied intention of receiving something in return. If it is to be a true sacrifice, the gift must be given as if it were being destroyed.[128] Only then is it possible for the egoistic claim to be given up. Were the bread and wine simply given without any consciousness of an egoistic claim, the fact that it was unconscious would be no excuse, but would on the contrary be sure proof of the existence of a *secret* claim. Because of its egoistic nature, the offering would then inevitably have the character of a magical act of propitiation, with the unavowed

[127] Michael Sendivogius, "Tractatus de sulphure" (16th cen.), in the *Musaeum hermeticum* (Frankfort, 1678), p. 617: "[Anima] quae extra corpus multa profundissima imaginatur" ([The soul] which imagines many things of the utmost profundity outside the body).

[128] The parallel to this is total destruction of the sacrificial gift by burning, or by throwing it into water or into a pit.

purpose and tacit expectation of purchasing the good will of the Deity. That is an ethically worthless simulacrum of sacrifice, and in order to avoid it the giver must at least make himself sufficiently conscious of his identity with the gift to recognize how far he is *giving himself up* in giving the gift. In other words, out of the natural state of identity with what is "mine" there grows the ethical task of sacrificing oneself, or at any rate that part of oneself which is identical with the gift. One ought to realize that when one gives or surrenders oneself there are corresponding claims attached, the more so the less one knows of them. The conscious realization of this alone guarantees that the giving is a real sacrifice. For if I know and admit that I am giving myself, forgoing myself, and do not want to be repaid for it, then I have sacrificed my claim, and thus a part of myself. Consequently, all absolute giving, a giving which is a total loss from the start, is a self-sacrifice. Ordinary giving for which no return is received is felt as a loss; but a sacrifice is meant to be like a loss, so that one may be sure that the egoistic claim no longer exists. Therefore the gift should be given as if it were being destroyed. But since the gift represents myself, I have in that case destroyed myself, given myself away without expectation of return. Yet, looked at in another way, this intentional loss is also a gain, for if you can give yourself it proves that you possess yourself. Nobody can give what he has not got. So anyone who can sacrifice himself and forgo his claim must have had it; in other words, he must have been conscious of the claim. This presupposes an act of considerable self-knowledge, lacking which one remains permanently unconscious of such claims. It is therefore quite logical that the confession of sin should come before the rite of transformation in the Mass. The self-examination is intended to make one conscious of the selfish claim bound up with every gift, so that it may be consciously given up; otherwise the gift is no sacrifice. The sacrifice proves that you possess yourself, for it does not mean just letting yourself be passively taken: it is a conscious and deliberate self-surrender, which proves that you have full control of yourself, that is, of your ego. The ego thus becomes the object of a moral act, for "I" am making a decision on behalf of an authority which is superordinate to my ego nature. I am, as it were, deciding against my ego and renouncing my claim. The possibility of self-renunciation is an established psychological fact whose philosophical implications I do not propose to discuss. Psychologically, it means that the ego is a relative quantity which can be subsumed under various superordinate authorities. What are these authorities? They are not to be equated outright with collective moral consciousness, as Freud wanted to do with his superego, but rather with certain psychic conditions which existed in man from the beginning and are not acquired by experience. Behind a man's actions there stands neither public opinion nor the moral code,[129] but the personality of which he is still unconscious. Just as a man still is what he always was, so he already is what he will become. The conscious mind does not embrace the totality of a man, for this totality consists only partly of his conscious contents, but for the other and far greater part, of his unconscious, which is of indefinite extent with no assignable limits. In this totality the conscious mind is contained like a smaller circle within a larger one. Hence it is quite possible for the ego to be made into an object, that is to say, for a more compendious personality to emerge in the course of development and take the ego into its service. Since this growth of personality comes out of the unconscious, which is by definition unlimited, the extent of the personality now gradually realizing itself cannot in practice be limited either. But, unlike the Freudian superego, it is still individual. It is in fact individuality in the highest sense, and therefore theoretically limited, since no individual can possibly display *every* quality. (I have called this process of realization the "indi-

[129] If there were really nothing behind him but collective standards of value on the one hand and natural instincts on the other, every breach of morality would be simply a rebellion of instinct. In that case valuable and meaningful innovations would be impossible, for the instincts are the oldest and most conservative element in man and beast alike. Such a view forgets the creative instinct which, although it can behave like an instinct, is seldom found in nature and is confined almost exclusively to Homo sapiens.

viduation process.") So far as the personality is still potential, it can be called transcendent, and so far as it is unconscious, it is indistinguishable from all those things that carry its projections—in other words, the unconscious personality merges with our environment. This fact is of the greatest practical importance because it renders intelligible the peculiar symbols through which this projected entity expresses itself in dreams. By this I mean the symbols of the outside world and the cosmic symbols. These form the psychological basis for the conception of man as a microcosm, whose fate, as we know, is bound up with the macrocosm through the astrological components of his character.

The term "self" seemed to me a suitable one for this unconscious substrate, whose actual exponent in consciousness is the ego. The ego stands to the self as the moved to the mover, or as object to subject, because the determining factors which radiate out from the self surround the ego on all sides and are therefore superordinate to it. The self, like the unconscious, is an a priori existent out of which the ego evolves. It is an unconscious prefiguration of the ego. It is not I who create myself, rather I happen to myself. This realization is of fundamental importance for the psychology of religious phenomena, which is why Ignatius Loyola started off his spiritual exercises with *"Homo creatus est"* as their *"fundamentum."* But, fundamental as it is, it can be only half the psychological truth. If it were the whole truth it would be tantamount to determinism, for if man were merely a creature that came into being as a result of something already existing unconsciously, he would have no freedom and there would be no point in consciousness. Psychology must reckon with the fact that despite the causal nexus man does enjoy a feeling of freedom, which is identical with autonomy of consciousness. However much the ego can be proved to be dependent and preconditioned, it cannot be convinced that it has no freedom. An absolutely preformed consciousness and a totally dependent ego would be a pointless farce, since everything would proceed just as well or even better unconsciously. The existence of ego consciousness has meaning only if it is free and autonomous.

By stating these facts we have, it is true, established an antinomy, but we have at the same time given a picture of things as they are. There are temporal, local, and individual differences in the degree of dependence and freedom. In reality both are always present: the supremacy of the self and the hybris of consciousness. If ego consciousness follows its own road exclusively, it is trying to become like a god or a superman. But exclusive recognition of its dependence only leads to a childish fatalism and to a world-negating and misanthropic spiritual arrogance.

This conflict between conscious and unconscious is at least brought nearer to a solution through our becoming aware of it. Such an act of realization is presupposed in the act of self-sacrifice. The ego must make itself conscious of its claim, and the self must cause the ego to renounce it. This can happen in two ways:

1. I renounce my claim in consideration of a general moral principle, namely that one must not expect repayment for a gift. In this case the "self" coincides with public opinion and the moral code. It is then identical with Freud's superego because it is projected, and therefore essentially unconscious and identical with environmental circumstances.

2. I renounce my claim because I feel impelled to do so for painful inner reasons which are not altogether clear to me. These reasons give me no particular moral satisfaction; on the contrary, I even feel some resistance to them. But I must yield to the power which suppresses my egoistic claim. Here the self is integrated; it is withdrawn from projection and has become perceptible as a determining psychic factor. The objection that in this case the moral code is simply unconscious must be ruled out, because I am perfectly well aware of the moral criticism against which I would have to assert my egoism. Where the ego wish clashes with the moral standard, it is not easy to show that the tendency which suppresses it is individual and not collective. But where it is a case of conflicting loyalties, or we find ourselves in a situation of which the classical example is Hosea's marriage with the harlot, then the ego wish coincides with the collective moral standard, and

Hosea would have been bound to accuse Jehovah of immorality. Similarly, the unjust steward would have had to admit his guilt.[130] Experiences of this kind make it clear that the self cannot be equated either with collective morality or with natural instinct, but must be conceived as a determining factor whose nature is individual and unique. The superego is a necessary and unavoidable substitute for the experience of the self.

These two ways of renouncing one's egoistic claim reveal not only a difference of attitude, but also a difference of situation. In the first case the situation need not affect me personally and directly; in the second, the gift must necessarily be a very personal one which seriously affects the giver and forces him to overcome himself. In the one case it is merely a question, say, of going to Mass; in the other it is more like Abraham's sacrifice of his son or Christ's decision in Gethsemane. The one may be felt very earnestly and experienced with all piety, but the other is the real thing.[131]

So long as the self is unconscious, it corresponds to Freud's superego and is a source of perpetual moral conflict. If, however, it is withdrawn from projection and is no longer identical with public opinion, then one is truly one's own yea and nay. The self then functions as a union of opposites and thus constitutes the most immediate experience of the Divine which it is psychologically possible to imagine.[132]

(c) *The Sacrificer*

What I sacrifice is my own selfish claim, and by doing this I

---

[130] Jesus took a different view. To the defiler of the Sabbath he said: "Man, if indeed thou knowest what thou doest, thou art blessed; but if thou knowest not, thou art cursed, and a transgressor of the law." M. R. James, *The Apocryphal New Testament* (Oxford, 1924), p. 33.

[131] In order to avoid misunderstandings, I must emphasize that I am speaking only of the personal experience of the Mass, and not of the mysterious reality which it has for the believer.

[132] Cf. the "uniting symbol" in *Psychological Types*, definition 51.

give up myself. Every sacrifice is therefore, to a greater or lesser degree, a self-sacrifice. The degree to which it is so depends on the significance of the gift. If it is of great value to me and touches my most personal feelings, I can be sure that in giving up my egoistic claim I shall challenge my ego personality to revolt. I can also be sure that the power which suppresses this claim, and thus suppresses me, must be the self. Hence it is the self that causes me to make the sacrifice; nay more, it compels me to make it.[133] The self is the sacrificer, and I am the sacrificed gift, the human sacrifice. Let us try for a moment to look into Abraham's soul when he was commanded to sacrifice his only son. Quite apart from the compassion he felt for his child, would not a father in such a position feel himself as the victim, and feel that he was plunging the knife into his own breast? He would be at the same time the sacrificer and the sacrificed.

Now, since the relation of the ego to the self is like that of the son to the father, we can say that when the self calls on us to sacrifice ourselves, it is really carrying out the sacrificial act on itself. We know more or less what this act means to us, but what it means to the self is not so clear. As the self can only be comprehended by us in particular acts, but remains concealed from us as a whole because it is more comprehensive than we are, all we can do is to draw conclusions from the little of the self that we can experience. We have seen that a sacrifice only takes place when we feel the self actually carrying it out on ourselves. We may also venture to surmise that in so far as the self stands to us in the relation of father to son, the self in some sort feels our sacrifice as a sacrifice of itself. From that sacrifice we gain ourselves—our "self" —for we only have what we give. But what does the self gain? We see it entering into manifestation, freeing itself from unconscious projection, and, as it grips us, entering into our lives

[133] In Indian philosophy we find a parallel in Prajapati and Purusha Narayana. Purusha sacrifices himself at the command of Prajapati, but at bottom the two are identical. Cf. the Shatapatha-Brahmana (*SBE*, Vol. XLIV, pp. 172ff.); also the Rig-Veda, X, 90.

and so passing from unconsciousness into consciousness, from potentiality into actuality. What it is in the diffuse unconscious state we do not know; we only know that in becoming ourself it has become man.

This process of becoming human is represented in dreams and inner images as the putting together of many scattered units, and sometimes as the gradual emergence and clarification of something that was always there.[134] The speculations of alchemy, and also of some Gnostics, revolve round this process. It is likewise expressed in Christian dogma, and more particularly in the transformation mystery in the Mass. The psychology of this process makes it easier to understand why, in the Mass, man appears as both the sacrificer and the sacrificed gift, and why it is not man who is these things, but God who is both; why God becomes the suffering and dying man, and why man, through partaking of the Glorified Body, gains the assurance of resurrection and becomes aware of his participation in Godhead.

As I have already suggested, the integration or humanization of the self is initiated from the conscious side by our making ourselves aware of our egoistic aims; we examine our motives and try to form as complete and objective a picture as possible of our own nature. It is an act of self-recollection, a gathering together of what is scattered, of all the things in us that have never been properly related, and a coming to terms with oneself with a view to achieving full consciousness.

---

[134] This contradiction is unavoidable because the concept of the self allows only of antinomial statements. The self is by definition conceived as an entity which is more comprehensive than the conscious personality. Consequently the latter cannot pass any comprehensive judgment on the self; any judgment and any statement about it is incomplete and has to be supplemented (but not nullified) by a conditioned negative. If I assert, "The self exists," I must supplement this by saying, "But it seems not to exist." For the sake of completeness I must also invert the proposition and say, "The self does not exist, but yet seems to exist." Actually, this inversion is superfluous in view of the fact that the self is not a philosophical concept like Kant's "thing-in-itself," but an empirical concept of psychology, and can therefore be hypostatized if the above precautions are taken.

(Unconscious self-sacrifice is merely an accident, not a moral act.) Self-recollection, however, is about the hardest and most repellent thing there is for man, who is predominantly unconscious. Human nature has an invincible dread of becoming more conscious of itself. What nevertheless drives us to it is the self, which demands sacrifice by sacrificing itself to us. Conscious realization or the bringing together of the scattered parts is in one sense an act of the ego's will, but in another sense it is a spontaneous manifestation of the self,[135] which was always there. Individuation appears, on the one hand, as the synthesis of a new unity which previously consisted of scattered particles, and on the other hand, as the revelation of something which existed before the ego and is in fact its father or creator and also its totality. Up to a point we create the self by making ourselves conscious of our unconscious contents, and to that extent it is our son. This is why the alchemists called their incorruptible substance—which means precisely the self—the *filius philosophorum*.[136] But we are forced to make this effort by the unconscious presence of the self, which is all the time urging us to overcome our unconsciousness. From that point of view the self is the father. This accounts for certain alchemical terms, such as Mercurius Senex (Hermes Trismegistus) and Saturnus, who in Gnosticism was regarded as a graybeard and a youth, just as Mercurius was in alchemy. These psychological connections are seen most clearly in the ancient conceptions of the Original Man, the Protanthropos, and the Son of Man. Christ as the Logos is from all eternity, but in his human form he is the "Son of Man."[137] As the Logos, he is the world-creating principle. This corresponds with the relation of the self to consciousness, without which no world could be perceived at all. The Logos

[135] In so far as it is the self that actuates the ego's self-recollection.

[136] Cf. *Psychology and Alchemy*, index, s.v.

[137] If I use the unhistorical term "self" for the corresponding processes in the psyche, I do so out of a conscious desire not to trespass on other preserves, but to confine myself exclusively to the field of empirical psychology.

is the real *principium individuationis*, because everything proceeds from it, and because everything which is, from crystal to man, exists only in individual form. In the infinite variety and differentiation of the phenomenal world is expressed the essence of the *auctor rerum*. As a correspondence we have, on the one hand, the indefiniteness and unlimited extent of the unconscious self (despite its individuality and uniqueness), its creative relation to individual consciousness, and, on the other hand, the individual human being as a mode of its manifestation. Ancient philosophy paralleled this idea with the legend of the dismembered Dionysus, who, as creator, is the *meristos* (undivided) *nous*, and, as the creature, the *memeris menos* (divided) *nous*.[138] Dionysus is distributed throughout the whole of nature, and just as Zeus once devoured the throbbing heart of the god, so his worshipers tore wild animals to pieces in order to reintegrate his dismembered spirit. The gathering together of the light-substance in Barbelognosis and in Manichaeism points in the same direction. The psychological equivalent of this is the integration of the self through conscious assimilation of the split-off contents. Self-recollection is a gathering together of the self. It is in this sense that we have to understand the instructions which Monoimos gives to Theophrastus:

> Seek him [God] from out yourself, and learn who it is that takes possession of everything in you, saying: *my* god, *my* spirit [*nous*], *my* understanding, *my* soul, *my* body; and learn whence come sorrow and gladness, and hate and love, and the unwished-for wakefulness and the unwished-for drowsiness, and the unwished-for anger and the unwished-for love. And when you examine all this closely, you will find him within yourself, the One and the Many, like that little speck, for it is from you that he has his origin.[139]

[138] Firmicus Maternus, *De errore profanarum religionum* (Corpus scriptorum ecclesiasticorum latinorum, Vol. II; Vienna, 1867), 7, 8.
[139] Hippolytus, *Elenchos*, VIII, 15.

Self-recollection or—what comes to the same thing—the urge to individuation gathers together what is scattered and multifarious, and exalts it to the original form of the One, the Primordial Man. In this way our existence as separate beings, our former ego nature, is abolished, the circle of consciousness is widened, and because the paradoxes have been made conscious the sources of conflict are dried up. This approximation to the self is a kind of repristination or apocatastasis, in so far as the self has an "incorruptible" or "eternal" character on account of its being pre-existent to consciousness.[140] This feeling is expressed in the words from the *Benedictio fontis*: "*Et quos aut sexus in corpore aut aetas discernit in tempore, omnes in unam pariat gratia mater infantiam*" (And may Mother Grace bring forth into one infancy all those whom sex has separated in the body, or age in time).

The figure of the divine sacrificer corresponds feature for feature to the empirical modes of manifestation of the archetype that lies at the root of almost all known conceptions of God. This archetype is not merely a static image, but dynamic, full of movement. It is always a drama, whether in heaven, on earth, or in hell.[141]

(d) The Archetype of Sacrifice

Comparing the basic ideas of the Mass with the imagery of the Zosimos visions, we find that, despite considerable differences, there is a remarkable degree of similarity. For the sake

---

[140] And also on account of the fact that the unconscious is only conditionally bound by space and time. The comparative frequency of telepathic phenomena proves that space and time have only a relative validity for the psyche. Evidence for this is furnished by Rhine's experiments. Cf. my paper on "synchronicity," in *The Interpretation of Nature and the Psyche* (London and New York, 1955), by W. Pauli and me.

[141] The word "hell" may strike the reader as odd in this connection. I would, however, recommend him to study the brothel scene in James Joyce's *Ulysses*, or James Hogg's *The Private Memoirs and Confessions of a Justified Sinner* (London, 1824; ed. with intro. by André Gide, London, 1947). [Note added.]

of clearness I give the similarities and differences in tabular form.

Zosimos	Mass

SIMILARITIES

1. The chief actors are two priests.
2. One priest slays the other.
3. Other human beings are sacrificed as well.
4. The sacrifice is a voluntary self-sacrifice.
5. It is a painful death.
6. The victim is dismembered.
7. There is a *thysia*.
8. The priest eats his own flesh.
9. He is transformed into spirit.
10. A shining white figure appears, like the midday sun.
11. Production of the "divine water."

---

1. There is the priest, and Christ the eternal priest.
2. The *Mactatio Christi* takes place as the priest pronounces the words of consecration.
3. The congregation itself is a sacrificial gift.
4. Christ offers himself freely as a sacrifice.
5. He suffers in the sacrificial act.
6. Breaking of the Bread.
7. Offering up of incense.
8. Christ drinks his own blood (St. Chrysostom).
9. The substances are transformed into the body and blood of Christ.
10. The Host is shown as the Beatific Vision ("*Quaesivi vultum tuum, Domine*") in the greater elevation.
11. The Grace conferred by the Mass; similarity of water chalice and font; water a symbol of grace.

DIFFERENCES

1. The whole sacrificial process is an individual dream vision, a fragment of the unconscious depicting itself in dream consciousness.

2. The dreamer is only a spectator of the symbolic action.

3. The action is a bloody and gruesome human sacrifice.

4. The sacrifice is accompanied by a scalping.

5. It is also performed on a dragon, and is therefore an animal sacrifice.

6. The flesh is roasted.

7. The meaning of the sacrifice is the production of the divine water, used for the transmutation of metals and, mystically, for the birth of the self.

8. What is transformed in the vision is presumably the planetary demon Saturn, the supreme Archon (who is related to the God of the Hebrews). It is the dark, heavy, material principle in man—*hyle*—which is transformed into *pneuma*.

---

1. The Mass is a conscious artifact, the product of many centuries and many minds.

2. Priest and congregation both participate in the mystery.

3. Nothing obnoxious; the *mactatio* itself is not mentioned. There is only the bloodless sacrifice of bread and wine (*incruente immolatur!*).

4. Nothing comparable.

5. Symbolic sacrifice of the Lamb.

6. The substances are spiritually transformed.

7. The meaning of the Mass is the communion of the living Christ with his flock.

8. What is transformed in the Mass is God, who as Father begat the Son in human form, suffered and died in that form, and rose up again to His origin.

The gross concretism of the vision is so striking that one might easily feel tempted, for esthetic and other reasons, to drop the comparison with the Mass altogether. If I nevertheless venture to bring out certain analogies, I do so not with the rationalistic intention of devaluing the sacred ceremony by putting it on a level with a piece of pagan nature worship. If I have any aim at all apart from scientific truth, it is to show that the most important mystery of the Catholic Church rests, among other things, on psychic conditions which are deeply rooted in the human soul.

The vision, which in all probability has the character of a dream, must be regarded as a spontaneous psychic product which was never consciously aimed at. Like all dreams, it is a product of nature. The Mass, on the other hand, is a product of man's mind or spirit, and is a definitely conscious proceeding. To use an old but not antiquated nomenclature, we can call the vision *psychic,* and the Mass *pneumatic.* The vision is undifferentiated raw material, while the Mass is a highly differentiated artifact. That is why the one is gruesome and the other beautiful. If the Mass is antique, it is antique in the best sense of the word, and its liturgy is therefore satisfying to the highest requirements of the present day. In contrast to this, the vision is archaic and primitive, but its symbolism points directly to the fundamental alchemical idea of the incorruptible substance, namely, to the self, which is beyond change. The vision is a piece of unalloyed naturalism, banal, grotesque, squalid, horrifying, and profound as nature herself. Its meaning is not clear, but it allows itself to be divined with the abysmal uncertainty and ambiguity that pertains to all things nonhuman, suprahuman, and subhuman. The Mass, on the other hand, represents and clearly expresses the Deity itself, and clothes it in the garment of the most beautiful humanity.

From all this it is evident that the vision and the Mass are two different things, so different as to be almost incommensurable. But if we could succeed in reconstructing the natural process in the unconscious on which the Mass is psychically based, we should probably obtain a picture which would be rather more commensurable with the vision of Zosimos. According to the view of the Church, the Mass is based on the historical events in the life of Jesus. From this "real" life we can single out certain details that add a few concretistic touches to our picture and thus bring it closer to the vision. For instance, I would mention the scourging, the crowning with thorns, and the clothing in a purple robe, which show Jesus as the archaic sacrificed king. This is further emphasized by the Barabbas episode (the name means "son of the father") which leads to the sacrifice of the king. Then there is the agony of death by crucifixion, a shameful and horrifying spectacle, far indeed from any *"incruente immolatur"*! The right pleural cavity and probably the right ventricle of the heart were cut open by the spear, so that blood clots and serum flowed out. If we add these details to the process which underlies the Mass, we shall see that they form a striking equivalent to certain archaic and barbarous features of the vision. There are also the fundamental dogmatic ideas to be considered. As is shown by the reference to the sacrifice of Isaac in the prayer *Unde et memores*, the sacrifice has the character not only of a human sacrifice, but the sacrifice of a son—and an *only* son. That is the cruelest and most horrible kind of sacrifice we can imagine, so horrible that, as we know, Abraham was not required to carry it out.[142] And even if he had carried it out, a stab in the heart with a knife would have been a quick and relatively painless death for the victim. Even the bloody Aztec ceremony of cutting out the heart was a swift death. But the

---

[142] How Jewish piety reacted to this sacrifice can be seen from the following Talmudic legend: "'And I,' cried Abraham, 'swear that I will not go down from the altar until you have heard me. When you commanded me to sacrifice my son Isaac you offended against your word, "in Isaac shall your descendants be named." So if ever my descendants offend against you, and you wish to punish them, then remember that you too are not without fault, and forgive them.' 'Very well, then,' replied the Lord, 'there behind you is a ram caught in the thicket with his horns. Offer up that instead of your son Isaac. And if ever your descendants sin against me, and I sit in judgment over them on New Year's Day, let them blow the horn of a ram, that I may remember my words, and temper justice with mercy.'" Jakob Frommer and Manuel Schnitzer, *Legenden aus dem Talmud* (Berlin, 1922), pp. 34f. [Note added.]

sacrifice of the son which forms the essential feature of the Mass began with scourging and mockery, and culminated in six hours of suspension on a cross to which the victim was nailed hand and foot—not exactly a quick death, but a slow and exquisite form of torture. As if that were not enough, crucifixion was regarded as a disgraceful death for slaves, so that the physical horror is balanced by the moral horror.

Leaving aside for the moment the unity of nature of Father and Son—which it is possible to do because they are two distinct Persons who are not to be confused with one another—let us try to imagine the feelings of a father who saw his son suffering such a death, knowing that it was he himself who had sent him into the enemy's country and deliberately exposed him to this danger. Executions of this kind were generally carried out as an act of revenge or as punishment for a crime, with the idea that both father and son should suffer. The idea of punishment can be seen particularly clearly in the crucifixion between two thieves. The punishment is carried out on God himself, and the model for this execution is the ritual slaying of the king. The king is killed when he shows signs of impotence, or when failure of the crops arouses doubts as to his efficacy. He is thus killed in order to improve the condition of his people, just as God is sacrificed for the salvation of mankind.

What is the reason for this "punishment" of God? Despite the almost blasphemous nature of this question—my arguments here are not for children—we must nevertheless ask it in view of the obviously punitive character of the sacrifice. The usual explanation is that Christ was punished for our sins.[143] The dogmatic validity of this answer is not in question here. As I am in no way concerned with the Church's explanation, but only wish to reconstruct the underlying psychic process, we must logically assume the existence of a guilt proportionate to the punishment. If mankind is the guilty party, logic surely demands that mankind should be punished. But if God takes

---

[143] Isaiah 53:5: "But he was wounded for our transgressions, he was bruised for our iniquities: the chastisement of our peace was upon him; and with his stripes we are healed."

the punishment on himself, he exculpates mankind, and we must then conjecture that it is not mankind who is guilty, but God (which would logically explain why he took the guilt on himself). For reasons that can readily be understood, a satisfactory answer is not to be expected from orthodox Christianity. But such an answer may be found in the Old Testament, in Gnosticism, and in late Catholic speculation. From the Old Testament we know that though Yahweh was a guardian of the law he was not just, and that he suffered from fits of rage which he had every occasion to regret.[144] And from certain Gnostic systems it is clear that the *auctor rerum* was a lower archon who falsely imagined that he had created a perfect world, whereas in fact it was woefully imperfect. On account of his Saturnine disposition this demiurgic archon has affinities with the Jewish Yahweh, who was likewise a world creator. His work was imperfect and did not prosper, but the blame cannot be placed on the creature any more than one can curse the pots for being badly turned out by the potter! This argument led to the Marcionite Reformation and to purging the New Testament of elements derived from the Old. Even as late as the seventeenth century the learned Jesuit, Nicolas Caussin, declared that the unicorn was a fitting symbol for the God of the Old Testament, because in his wrath he reduced the world to confusion like an angry rhinoceros (unicorn), until, overcome by the love of a pure virgin, he was changed in her lap into a God of Love.[145]

In these explanations we find the natural logic we missed in the answer of the Church. God's guilt consisted in the fact that, as creator of the world and king of his creatures, he was

---

[144] See my *Answer to Job* (London, 1954).
[145] Caussin, *De symbolica Aegyptiorum sapientia. Polyhistor symbolicus, Electorum symbolorum, et Parabolarum historicarum stromata* (Paris, 1618 and 1623), p. 348. Cf. also Philippus Picinelli, *Mundus symbolicus* (Cologne, 1680–81), Vol. I, p. 419: "Of a truth God, terrible beyond measure, appeared before the world peaceful and wholly tamed after dwelling in the womb of the most blessed Virgin. St. Bonaventura said that Christ was tamed and pacified by the most kindly Mary, so that he should not punish the sinner with eternal death."

inadequate and therefore had to submit to the ritual slaying. For primitive man the concrete king was perfectly suited to this purpose, but not for a higher level of civilization with a more spiritual conception of God. Earlier ages could still dethrone their gods by destroying their images or putting them in chains. At a higher level, however, one god could be dethroned only by another god, and when monotheism developed, God could only transform himself.

The psychic basis for this transformation is the process of transformation in the unconscious. One of the finest examples of this is the vision of Zosimos, which contains a whole series of archetypal transformation symbols expressed in the Gnostic-alchemical language of his time. A rich harvest of transformation symbols is to be found in alchemy generally, whether influenced by Christianity or not, in the initiation rites of all primitive peoples, and—last but not least—in the dreams of modern men and women. It would lead us too far to cite examples from any of these fields, which each demand a separate study. But I ought at least to mention Christian Rosencreutz's *Chymical Wedding*, which reads almost like a first draft of *Faust*, Part II, and the transformation symbol of the uroboros which I dealt with in my earlier paper on Zosimos.

Taken in this wider sense, the archetypal image of sacrifice is always one of transformation as well. The simplest and most striking example of this is the whale-dragon myth of Leo Frobenius. The archetype of transformation always appears when a psychologically unsatisfactory situation has to be replaced by a satisfactory one, no matter how great or small the issue may be. If only a minor change of attitude is involved, the dream does not use any obviously mythological language. For instance, instead of a dragon it is an automobile, instead of the dragon's belly a spooky cellar, instead of spiritualization an elevator, instead of the sacrificial knife a hypodermic syringe, instead of torture a tight squeeze or a difficult climb, instead of the dismemberment of a man a horse whose hooves are cut off, instead of the bleeding sacrificial wound a leaking gasoline tank, and so on.

If, however, it is a question of a fundamental change of personality or of one's general attitude, as was obviously the case with Zosimos (witness his advice to Theosebeia[146]), then mythological motifs appear, sometimes borrowed, sometimes spontaneously produced, which do not fail to suggest the most intense suffering, even at a time when the conscious mind is not aware of anything painful, except perhaps a vague sense of oppression or uneasiness. It is true that the onset of conscious suffering is not as a rule very long delayed. If the inner transformation enters more or less completely into consciousness, it becomes one of the vividest and most decisive experiences a man can have of his individual fate. The saying *"extra ecclesiam nulla salus"*—there is no salvation outside the Church—is no doubt a profound truth; but the grace of God, it seems to me, is profounder still.

[146] Berthelot, *Alchimistes*, III, li, 8.

Foreword to the *I Ching* or *Book of Changes*[1]

Since I am not a sinologue, a foreword to the *Book of Changes* from my hand must be a testimonial of my individual experience with this great and singular book. It also affords me a welcome opportunity to pay tribute again to the memory of my late friend, Richard Wilhelm. He himself was profoundly aware of the cultural significance of his translation of the *I Ching*, a version unrivaled in the West.

If the meaning of the *Book of Changes* were easy to grasp, the work would need no foreword. But this is far from being the case, for there is so much that is obscure about it that Western scholars have tended to dispose of it as a collection

[1] This foreword was written for Professor Richard Wilhelm's translation into German of the ancient Chinese book of wisdom entitled *I Ching* or *Book of Changes*. The book is regarded as one of the five classics of Confucianism and as having provided a common source for both Confucianism and Taoist philosophy. Its central theme is the continuous change and transformation underlying all existence. The *I Ching* teaches that these changes take place in accordance with universal laws. The work has been rendered into English by Cary F. Baynes, and published as Bollingen Series XXIX, through Pantheon Books, 1956.—Ed.

of "magic spells," either too abstruse to be intelligible, or of no value whatsoever. Legge's translation of the *I Ching*, up to now the only version available in English, has done little to make the work accessible to Western minds.[2] Wilhelm, however, has made every effort to open the way to an understanding of the symbolism of the text. He was in a position to do this because he himself was taught the philosophy and the use of the *I Ching* by the venerable sage Lao Nai Hsüan; moreover, he had over a period of many years put the peculiar technique of the oracle into practice. His grasp of the living meaning of the text gives his version of the *I Ching* a depth of perspective that an exclusively academic knowledge of Chinese philosophy could never provide.

I am greatly indebted to Wilhelm for the light he has thrown upon the complicated problem of the *I Ching*, and for insight as regards its practical application as well. For more than thirty years I have interested myself in this oracle technique, or method of exploring the unconscious, for it has seemed to me of uncommon significance. I was already fairly familiar with the *I Ching* when I first met Wilhelm in the early 1920s; he confirmed for me then what I already knew, and taught me many things more.

I do not know Chinese and have never been in China. I can assure my reader that it is not altogether easy to find the right access to this monument of Chinese thought, which departs so completely from our ways of thinking. In order to understand what such a book is all about, it is imperative to cast off certain prejudices of the Western mind. It is a curious fact that such a gifted and intelligent people as the Chinese have never developed what we call science. Our science, however, is based upon the principle of causality, and causality is considered to be an axiomatic truth. But a great change in our standpoint is setting in. What Kant's *Critique of Pure Reason* failed to do, is being accomplished by modern physics. The axioms of causality are being shaken to their foundations: we know now that what we term natural laws

[2] *The Sacred Books of the East*, Vol. XVI, *The Yi King*, 2d ed., Oxford: Clarendon Press, 1899.

are merely statistical truths and thus must necessarily allow for exceptions. We have not sufficiently taken into account as yet that we need the laboratory with its incisive restrictions in order to demonstrate the invariable validity of natural law. If we leave things to nature, we see a very different picture: every process is partially or totally interfered with by chance, so much so that under natural circumstances a course of events absolutely conforming to specific laws is almost an exception.

The Chinese mind, as I see it at work in the *I Ching*, seems to be exclusively preoccupied with the chance aspect of events. What we call coincidence seems to be the chief concern of this peculiar mind, and what we worship as causality passes almost unnoticed. We must admit that there is something to be said for the immense importance of chance. An incalculable amount of human effort is directed to combating and restricting the nuisance or danger represented by chance. Theoretical considerations of cause and effect often look pale and dusty in comparison to the practical results of chance. It is all very well to say that the crystal of quartz is a hexagonal prism. The statement is quite true in so far as an ideal crystal is envisaged. But in nature one finds no two crystals exactly alike, although all are unmistakably hexagonal. The actual form, however, seems to appeal more to the Chinese sage than the ideal one. The jumble of natural laws constituting empirical reality holds more significance for him than a causal explanation of events that, moreover, must usually be separated from one another in order to be properly dealt with.

The manner in which the *I Ching* tends to look upon reality seems to disfavor our causalistic procedures. The moment under actual observation appears to the ancient Chinese view more of a chance hit than a clearly defined result of concurring causal chain processes. The matter of interest seems to be the configuration formed by chance events in the moment of observation, and not at all the hypothetical reasons that seemingly account for the coincidence. While the Western mind carefully sifts, weighs, selects, classifies, isolates, the Chinese picture of the moment encompasses everything down to the minutest nonsensical detail, because all of the ingredients make up the observed moment.

Thus it happens that when one throws the three coins, or counts through the forty-nine yarrow stalks, these chance details enter into the picture of the moment of observation and form a part of it—a part that is insignificant to us, yet most meaningful to the Chinese mind. With us it would be a banal and almost meaningless statement (at least on the face of it) to say that whatever happens in a given moment possesses inevitably the quality peculiar to that moment. This is not an abstract argument but a very practical one. There are certain connoisseurs who can tell you merely from the appearance, taste, and behavior of a wine the site of its vineyard and the year of its origin. There are antiquarians who with almost uncanny accuracy will name the time and place of origin and the maker of an *objet d'art* or piece of furniture on merely looking at it. And there are even astrologers who can tell you, without any previous knowledge of your nativity, what the position of sun and moon was and what zodiacal sign rose above the horizon in the moment of your birth. In the face of such facts, it must be admitted that moments can leave long-lasting traces.

In other words, whoever invented the *I Ching* was convinced that the hexagram worked out in a certain moment coincided with the latter in quality no less than in time. To him the hexagram was the exponent of the moment in which it was cast—even more so than the hours of the clock or the divisions of the calendar could be—inasmuch as the hexagram was understood to be an indicator of the essential situation prevailing in the moment of its origin.

This assumption involves a certain curious principle that I have termed synchronicity, a concept that formulates a point of view diametrically opposed to that of causality. Since the latter is a merely statistical truth and not absolute, it is a sort of working hypothesis of how events evolve one out of another, whereas synchronicity takes the coincidence of events in space and time as meaning something more than mere chance, namely, a peculiar interdependence of objective events among themselves as well as with the subjective (psychic) states of the observer or observers.

The ancient Chinese mind contemplates the cosmos in a way comparable to that of the modern physicist, who cannot deny that his model of the world is a decidedly psychophysical structure. The microphysical event includes the observer just as much as the reality underlying the *I Ching* comprises subjective, i.e., psychic, conditions in the totality of the momentary situation. Just as causality describes the sequence of events, so synchronicity to the Chinese mind deals with the coincidence of events. The causal point of view tells us a dramatic story about how D came into existence: it took its origin from C, which existed before D, and C in its turn had a father, B, etc. The synchronistic view on the other hand tries to produce an equally meaningful picture of coincidence. How does it happen that A', B', C', D', etc., appear all in the same moment and in the same place? It happens in the first place because the physical events A' and B' are of the same quality as the psychic events C' and D', and further because all are the exponents of one and the same momentary situation. The situation is assumed to represent a legible or understandable picture.

Now the sixty-four hexagrams of the *I Ching* are the instrument by which the meaning of sixty-four different yet typical situations can be determined. These interpretations are equivalent to causal explanations. Causal connection is statistically necessary and can therefore be subjected to experiment. Inasmuch as situations are unique and cannot be repeated, experimenting with synchronicity seems to be impossible under ordinary conditions.[3] In the *I Ching*, the only criterion of the validity of synchronicity is the observer's opinion that the text of the hexagram amounts to a true rendering of his psychic condition. It is assumed that the fall of the coins or the result of the division of the bundle of yarrow stalks is what it necessarily must be in a given "situation," inasmuch as anything happening in that moment belongs to it as an

[3] Cf. J. B. Rhine, *The Reach of the Mind*, 1947.

indispensable part of the picture. If a handful of matches is thrown to the floor, they form the pattern characteristic of that moment. But such an obvious truth as this reveals its meaningful nature only if it is possible to read the pattern and to verify its interpretation, partly by the observer's knowledge of the subjective and objective situation, partly by the character of subsequent events. It is obviously not a procedure that appeals to a critical mind used to experimental verification of facts or to factual evidence. But for someone who likes to look at the world at the angle from which ancient China saw it, the *I Ching* may have some attraction.

My argument as outlined above has of course never entered a Chinese mind. On the contrary, according to the old tradition, it is "spiritual agencies," acting in a mysterious way, that make the yarrow stalks give a meaningful answer.[4] These powers form, as it were, the living soul of the book. As the latter is thus a sort of animated being, the tradition assumes as much as that one can put questions to the *I Ching* and expect to receive intelligent answers. Thus it occurred to me that it might interest the uninitiated reader to see the *I Ching* at work. For this purpose I made an experiment strictly in accordance with the Chinese conception: I personified the book in a sense, asking its judgment about its present situation, i.e., my intention to present it to the Western mind.

Although this procedure is well within the premises of Taoist philosophy, it appears exceedingly odd to us. However, not even the strangeness of insane delusions or of primitive superstition has ever shocked me. I have always tried to remain unbiased and curious—*rerum novarum cupidus*. Why not venture a dialogue with an ancient book that purports to be animated? There can be no harm in it, and the reader may watch a psychological procedure that has been carried out time and again throughout the millennia of Chinese civilization, representing to a Confucius or a Lao-tse both a supreme expression of spiritual authority and a philosophical enigma.

[4] They are *shên*, that is, "spirit-like." "Heaven produced the 'spirit-like things'" (Legge, *op. cit.*, p. 41).

I made use of the coin method, and the answer obtained was hexagram 50, Ting, THE CALDRON.

In accordance with the way my question was phrased, the text of the hexagram must be regarded as though the *I Ching* itself were the speaking person. Thus it describes itself as a caldron,[5] that is, as a ritual vessel containing cooked food. Here the food is to be understood as spiritual nourishment. Wilhelm says about this:

> The *ting*, as a utensil pertaining to a refined civilization, suggests the fostering and nourishing of able men, which redounded to the benefit of the state. . . . Here we see civilization as it reaches its culmination in religion. The *ting* serves in offering sacrifice to God. . . . The supreme revelation of God appears in prophets and holy men. To venerate them is true veneration of God. The will of God, as revealed through them, should be accepted in humility.

Keeping to our hypothesis, we must conclude that the *I Ching* is here testifying concerning itself.

When any of the lines of a given hexagram have the value of six or nine, it means that they are specially emphasized and hence important in the interpretation.[6] In my hexagram the "spiritual agencies" have given the emphasis of a nine to the lines in the second and in the third place. The text says:

> Nine in the second place means:
>
> There is food in the *ting*.
> My comrades are envious,
> But they cannot harm me.
> Good Fortune.

Thus the *I Ching* says of itself: "I contain (spiritual) nourishment." Since a share in something great always arouses envy, the chorus of the envious[7] is part of the picture. The

---

[5] [Chinese *ting*.]

[6] See the explanation of the method in Wilhelm's text, p. 392.

[7] For example, the *invidi* ("the envious") are a constantly recurring image in the old Latin books on alchemy, especially in the *Turba philosophorum* (eleventh or twelfth century).

envious want to rob the *I Ching* of its great possession, that is, they seek to rob it of meaning, or to destroy its meaning. But their enmity is in vain. Its richness of meaning is assured; that is, it is convinced of its positive achievements, which no one can take away. The text continues:

> Nine in the third place means:
> The handle of the *ting* is altered.
> One is impeded in his way of life.
> The fat of the pheasant is not eaten.
> Once rain falls, remorse is spent.
> Good fortune comes in the end.

The handle [German *Griff*] is the part by which the *ting* can be grasped [*gegriffen*]. Thus it signifies the concept[8] (*Begriff*) one has of the *I Ching* (the *ting*). In the course of time this concept has apparently changed, so that today we can no longer grasp (*begreifen*) the *I Ching*. Thus "one is impeded in his way of life." We are no longer supported by the wise counsel and deep insight of the oracle; therefore we no longer find our way through the mazes of fate and the obscurities of our own natures. The fat of the pheasant, that is, the best and richest part of a good dish, is no longer eaten. But when the thirsty earth finally receives rain again, that is, when this state of want has been overcome, "remorse," that is, sorrow over the loss of wisdom, is ended, and then comes the longed-for opportunity. Wilhelm comments: "This describes a man who, in a highly evolved civilization, finds himself in a place where no one notices or recognizes him. This is a severe block to his effectiveness." The *I Ching* is complaining, as it were, that its excellent qualities go unrecognized and hence lie fallow. It comforts itself with the hope that it is about to regain recognition.

The answer given in these two salient lines to the question I put to the *I Ching* requires no particular subtlety of interpretation, no artifices, no unusual knowledge. Anyone with a

---

[8] From the Latin *concipere*, "to take together," e.g., in a vessel: *concipere* derives from *capere*, "to take," "to grasp."

little common sense can understand the meaning of the answer; it is the answer of one who has a good opinion of himself, but whose value is neither generally recognized nor even widely known. The answering subject has an interesting notion of itself: it looks upon itself as a vessel in which sacrificial offerings are brought to the gods, ritual food for their nourishment. It conceives of itself as a cult utensil serving to provide spiritual nourishment for the unconscious elements or forces ("spiritual agencies") that have been projected as gods—in other words, to give these forces the attention they need in order to play their part in the life of the individual. Indeed, this is the original meaning of the word *religio*—a careful observation and taking account of (from *relegere*[9]) the numinous.

The method of the *I Ching* does indeed take into account the hidden individual quality in things and men, and in one's own unconscious self as well. I have questioned the *I Ching* as one questions a person whom one is about to introduce to friends: one asks whether or not it will be agreeable to him. In answer the *I Ching* tells me of its religious significance, of the fact that at present it is unknown and misjudged, of its hope of being restored to a place of honor—this last obviously with a sidelong glance at my as yet unwritten foreword,[10] and above all at the English translation. This seems a perfectly understandable reaction, such as one could expect also from a person in a similar situation.

But how has this reaction come about? Because I threw three small coins into the air and let them fall, roll, and come to rest, heads up or tails up as the case might be. This odd fact that a reaction that makes sense arises out of a technique seemingly excluding all sense from the outset, is the great achievement of the *I Ching*. The instance I have just given is not unique; meaningful answers are the rule. Western sinologues and distinguished Chinese scholars have been at pains to inform me that the *I Ching* is a collection of obsolete "magic spells." In the course of these conversations my in-

---

[9] This is the classical etymology. The derivation of *religio* from *religare*, "binding to," originated with the Church Fathers.
[10] I made this experiment before I actually wrote the foreword.

formant has sometimes admitted having consulted the oracle through a fortune teller, usually a Taoist priest. This could be "only nonsense" of course. But oddly enough, the answer received apparently coincided with the questioner's psychological blind spot remarkably well.

I agree with Western thinking that any number of answers to my question were possible, and I certainly cannot assert that another answer would not have been equally significant. However, the answer received was the first and only one; we know nothing of other possible answers. It pleased and satisfied me. To ask the same question a second time would have been tactless and so I did not do it: "the master speaks but once." The heavy-handed pedagogic approach that attempts to fit irrational phenomena into a preconceived rational pattern is anathema to me. Indeed, such things as this answer should remain as they were when they first emerged to view, for only then do we know what nature does when left to herself undisturbed by the meddlesomeness of man. One ought not to go to cadavers to study life. Moreover, a repetition of the experiment is impossible, for the simple reason that the original situation cannot be reconstructed. Therefore in each instance there is only a first and single answer.

To return to the hexagram itself. There is nothing strange in the fact that all of Ting, THE CALDRON, amplifies the themes announced by the two salient lines.[11] The first line of the hexagram says:

> A *ting* with legs upturned.
> Furthers removal of stagnating stuff.
> One takes a concubine for the sake of her son.
> No blame.

A *ting* that is turned upside down is not in use. Hence the *I Ching* is like an unused caldron. Turning it over serves to remove stagnating matter, as the line says. Just as a man takes a concubine when his wife has no son, so the *I Ching* is called

[11] The Chinese interpret only the changing lines in the hexagram obtained by use of the oracle. I have found all the lines of the hexagram to be relevant in most cases.

upon when one sees no other way out. Despite the quasi-legal status of the concubine in China, she is in reality only a somewhat awkward makeshift; so likewise the magic procedure of the oracle is an expedient that may be utilized for a higher purpose. There is no blame, although it is an exceptional recourse.

The second and third lines have already been discussed. The fourth line says:

> The legs of the *ting* are broken.
> The prince's meal is spilled
> And his person is soiled.
> Misfortune.

Here the *ting* has been put to use, but evidently in a very clumsy manner, that is, the oracle has been abused or misinterpreted. In this way the divine food is lost, and one puts oneself to shame. Legge translates as follows: "Its subject will be made to blush for shame." Abuse of a cult utensil such as the *ting* (i.e., the *I Ching*) is a gross profanation. The *I Ching* is evidently insisting here on its dignity as a ritual vessel and protesting against being profanely used.

The fifth line says:

> The *ting* has yellow handles, golden carrying rings.
> Perseverance furthers.

The *I Ching* has, it seems, met with a new, correct (yellow) understanding, that is, a new concept (*Begriff*) by which it can be grasped. This concept is valuable (golden). There is indeed a new edition in English, making the book more accessible to the Western world than before.

The sixth line says:

> The *ting* has rings of jade.
> Great good fortune.
> Nothing that would not act to further.

Jade is distinguished for its beauty and soft sheen. If the carrying rings are of jade, the whole vessel is enhanced in beauty, honor, and value. The *I Ching* expresses itself here as being not only well satisfied but indeed very optimistic. One can only await further events and in the meantime remain content with the pleasant conclusion that the *I Ching* approves of the new edition.

I have shown in this example as objectively as I can how the oracle proceeds in a given case. Of course the procedure varies somewhat according to the way the question is put. If, for instance, a person finds himself in a confusing situation, he may himself appear in the oracle as the speaker. Or, if the question concerns a relationship with another person, that person may appear as the speaker. However, the identity of the speaker does not depend entirely on the manner in which the question is phrased, inasmuch as our relations with our fellow beings are not always determined by the latter. Very often our relations depend almost exclusively on our own attitudes, though we may be quite unaware of this fact. Hence, if an individual is unconscious of his role in a relationship, there may be a surprise in store for him; contrary to expectation, he himself may appear as the chief agent, as is sometimes unmistakably indicated by the text. It may also occur that we take a situation too seriously and consider it extremely important, whereas the answer we get on consulting the *I Ching* draws attention to some unsuspected other aspect implicit in the question.

Such instances might at first lead one to think that the oracle is fallacious. Confucius is said to have received only one inappropriate answer, i.e., hexagram 22, GRACE—a thoroughly esthetic hexagram. This is reminiscent of the advice given to Socrates by his demon—"You ought to make more music"— whereupon Socrates took to playing the flute. Confucius and Socrates compete for first place as far as reasonableness and a pedagogic attitude to life are concerned; but it is unlikely that either of them occupied himself with "lending grace to the beard on his chin," as the second line of this hexagram advises. Unfortunately, reason and pedagogy often lack charm and grace, and so the oracle may not have been wrong after all.

To come back once more to our hexagram. Though the *I*

Ching not only seems to be satisfied with its new edition, but even expresses emphatic optimism, this still does not foretell anything about the effect it will have on the public it is intended to reach. Since we have in our hexagram two yang lines stressed by the numerical value nine, we are in a position to find out what sort of prognosis the *I Ching* makes for itself. Lines designated by a six or a nine have, according to the ancient conception, an inner tension so great as to cause them to change into their opposites, that is, yang into yin, and vice versa. Through this change we obtain in the present instance hexagram 35, Chin, PROGRESS.

The subject of this hexagram is someone who meets with all sorts of vicissitudes of fortune in his climb upward, and the text describes how he should behave. The *I Ching* is in this same situation: it rises like the sun and declares itself, but it is rebuffed and finds no confidence—it is "progressing, but in sorrow." However, "one obtains great happiness from one's ancestress." Psychology can help us to elucidate this obscure passage. In dreams and fairy tales the grandmother, or ancestress, often represents the unconscious, because the latter in a man contains the feminine component of the psyche. If the *I Ching* is not accepted by the conscious, at least the unconscious meets it halfway, and the *I Ching* is more closely connected with the unconscious than with the rational attitude of consciousness. Since the unconscious is often represented in dreams by a feminine figure, this may be the explanation here. The feminine person might be the translator, who has given the book her maternal care, and this might easily appear to the *I Ching* as a "great happiness." It anticipates general understanding, but is afraid of misuse—"Progress like a hamster." But it is mindful of the admonition, "Take not gain and loss to heart." It remains free of "partisan motives." It does not thrust itself on anyone.

The *I Ching* therefore faces its future on the American book market calmly and expresses itself here just about as any reasonable person would in regard to the fate of so controversial a work. This prediction is so very reasonable and full of common sense that it would be hard to think of a more fitting answer.

All of this happened before I had written the foregoing paragraphs. When I reached this point, I wished to know the attitude of the *I Ching* to the new situation. The state of things had been altered by what I had written, inasmuch as I myself had now entered upon the scene, and I therefore expected to hear something referring to my own action. I must confess that I had not been feeling too happy in the course of writing this foreword, for, as a person with a sense of responsibility toward science, I am not in the habit of asserting something I cannot prove or at least present as acceptable to reason. It is a dubious task indeed to try to introduce to a critical modern public a collection of archaic "magic spells," with the idea of making them more or less acceptable. I have undertaken it because I myself think that there is more to the ancient Chinese way of thinking than meets the eye. But it is embarrassing to me that I must appeal to the good will and imagination of the reader, inasmuch as I have to take him into the obscurity of an age-old magic ritual. Unfortunately I am only too well aware of the arguments that can be brought against it. We are not even certain that the ship that is to carry us over the unknown seas has not sprung a leak somewhere. May not the old text be corrupt? Is Wilhelm's translation accurate? Are we not self-deluded in our explanations?

The *I Ching* insists upon self-knowledge throughout. The method by which this is to be achieved is open to every kind of misuse, and is therefore not for the frivolous-minded and immature; nor is it for intellectualists and rationalists. It is appropriate only for thoughtful and reflective people who like to think about what they do and what happens to them— a predilection not to be confused with the morbid brooding of the hypochondriac. As I have indicated above, I have no answer to the multitude of problems that arise when we seek to harmonize the oracle of the *I Ching* with our accepted scientific canons. But needless to say, nothing "occult" is to be inferred. My position in these matters is pragmatic, and the great disciplines that have taught me the practical usefulness of this viewpoint are psychotherapy and medical psychology. Probably in no other field do we have to reckon with so many unknown quantities, and nowhere else do we become more accustomed to adopting methods that work even though for a long time we may not know why they work. Unexpected cures may arise from questionable therapies and unexpected failures from allegedly reliable methods. In the exploration of the unconscious we come upon very strange things, from which a rationalist turns away with horror, claiming afterward that he did not see anything. The irrational fullness of life has taught me never to discard anything, even when it goes against all our theories (so short-lived at best) or otherwise admits of no immediate explanation. It is of course disquieting, and one is not certain whether the compass is pointing true or not; but security, certitude, and peace do not lead to discoveries. It is the same with this Chinese mode of divination. Clearly the method aims at self-knowledge, though at all times it has also been put to superstitious use.

I of course am thoroughly convinced of the value of self-knowledge, but is there any use in recommending such insight, when the wisest of men throughout the ages have preached the need of it without success? Even to the most biased eye it is obvious that this book represents one long admonition to careful scrutiny of one's own character, attitude, and motives. This attitude appeals to me and has induced me to undertake the foreword. Only once before have I expressed myself in regard to the problem of the *I Ching:* this was in a memorial address in tribute to Richard Wilhelm.[12] For the rest I have maintained a discreet silence. It is by no means easy to feel one's way into such a remote and mysterious mentality as that underlying the *I Ching*. One cannot easily disregard such great minds as Confucius and Lao-tse, if one is at all able to appreciate the quality of the thoughts they represent; much less can one overlook the fact that the *I Ching*

---

[12] [Cf. R. Wilhelm and C. G. Jung, *The Secret of the Golden Flower* (London: Routledge and Kegan Paul, 1931), in which this address appears as an appendix. The book did not appear in English until a year after Wilhelm's death.—TRANS.]

was their main source of inspiration. I know that previously I would not have dared to express myself so explicitly about so uncertain a matter. I can take this risk because I am now in my eighth decade, and the changing opinions of men scarcely impress me any more; the thoughts of the old masters are of greater value to me than the philosophical prejudices of the Western mind.

I do not like to burden my reader with these personal considerations; but, as already indicated, one's own personality is very often implicated in the answer of the oracle. Indeed, in formulating my question I even invited the oracle to comment directly on my action. The answer was hexagram 29, K'an, THE ABYSMAL. Special emphasis is given to the third place by the fact that the line is designated by a six. This line says:

> Forward and backward, abyss on abyss.
> In danger like this, pause at first and wait,
> Otherwise you will fall into a pit in the abyss.
> Do not act in this way.

Formerly I would have accepted unconditionally the advice, "Do not act in this way," and would have refused to give my opinion of the *I Ching*, for the sole reason that I had none. But now the counsel may serve as an example of the way in which the *I Ching* functions. It is a fact that if one begins to think about it, the problems of the *I Ching* do represent "abyss on abyss," and unavoidably one must "pause at first and wait" in the midst of the dangers of limitless and uncritical speculation; otherwise one really will lose his way in the darkness. Could there be a more uncomfortable position intellectually than that of floating in the thin air of unproved possibilities, not knowing whether what one sees is truth or illusion? This is the dreamlike atmosphere of the *I Ching*, and in it one has nothing to rely upon except one's own so fallible subjective judgment. I cannot but admit that this line represents very appropriately the feelings with which I wrote the foregoing passages. Equally fitting is the comforting beginning of this hexagram—"If you are sincere, you have success in your heart" —for it indicates that the decisive thing here is not the outer danger but the subjective condition, that is, whether one believes oneself to be "sincere" or not.

The hexagram compares the dynamic action in this situation to the behavior of flowing water, which is not afraid of any dangerous place but plunges over cliffs and fills up the pits that lie in its course (K'an also stands for water). This is the way in which the "superior man" acts and "carries on the business of teaching."

K'an is definitely one of the less agreeable hexagrams. It describes a situation in which the subject seems in grave danger of being caught in all sorts of pitfalls. Just as in interpreting a dream one must follow the dream text with utmost exactitude, so in consulting the oracle one must hold in mind the form of the question put, for this sets a definite limit to the interpretation of the answer. The first line of the hexagram notes the presence of the danger: "In the abyss one falls into a pit." The second line does the same, then adds the counsel: "One should strive to attain small things only." I apparently anticipated this advice by limiting myself in this foreword to a demonstration of how the *I Ching* functions in the Chinese mind, and by renouncing the more ambitious project of writing a psychological commentary on the whole book.

The fourth line says:

> A jug of wine, a bowl of rice with it;
> Earthen vessels
> Simply handed in through the window.
> There is certainly no blame in this.

Wilhelm makes the following comment here:

> Although as a rule it is customary for an official to present certain introductory gifts and recommendations before he is appointed, here everything is simplified to the utmost. The gifts are insignificant, there is no one to sponsor him, he introduces himself; yet all this need not be humiliating if only there is the honest intention of mutual help in danger.

It looks as if the book were to some degree the subject of this line.

The fifth line continues the theme of limitation. If one studies the nature of water, one sees that it fills a pit only to the rim and then flows on. It does not stay caught there:

The abyss is not filled to overflowing,
It is filled only to the rim.

But if, tempted by the danger, and just because of the uncertainty, one were to insist on forcing conviction by special efforts, such as elaborate commentaries and the like, one would only be mired in the difficulty, which the top line describes very accurately as a tied-up and caged-in condition. Indeed, the last line often shows the consequences that result when one does not take the meaning of the hexagram to heart.

In our hexagram we have a six in the third place. This yin line of mounting tension changes into a yang line and thus produces a new hexagram showing a new possibility or tendency. We now have hexagram 48, Ching, THE WELL. The water hole no longer means danger, however, but rather something beneficial, a well:

Thus the superior man encourages the people at their work,
And exhorts them to help one another.

The image of people helping one another would seem to refer to the reconstruction of the well, for it is broken down and full of mud. Not even animals drink from it. There are fishes living in it, and one can shoot these, but the well is not used for drinking, that is, for human needs. This description is reminiscent of the overturned and unused *ting* that is to receive a new handle. Moreover, this well, like the *ting*, is cleaned. But no one drinks from it:

This is my heart's sorrow,
For one might draw from it.

The dangerous water hole or abyss pointed to the *I Ching*, and so does the well, but the latter has a positive meaning: it contains the waters of life. It should be restored to use. But one has no concept (*Begriff*) of it, no utensil with which to carry the water; the jug is broken and leaks. The *ting* needs new handles and carrying rings by which to grasp it, and so also the well must be newly lined, for it contains "a clear, cold spring from which one can drink." One may draw water from it, because "it is dependable."

It is clear that in this prognosis the speaking subject is again the *I Ching*, representing itself as a spring of living water. The preceding hexagram described in detail the danger confronting the person who accidentally falls into the pit within the abyss. He must work his way out of it, in order to discover that it is an old, ruined well, buried in mud, but capable of being restored to use again.

I submitted two questions to the method of chance represented by the coin oracle, the second question being put after I had written my analysis of the answer to the first. The first question was directed, as it were, to the *I Ching*: what had it to say about my own action, that is, about the situation in which I was the acting person, the situation described by the first hexagram I obtained? To the first question the *I Ching* replied by comparing itself to a caldron, a ritual vessel in need of renovation, a vessel that was finding only doubtful favor with the public. To the second question the reply was that I had fallen into a difficulty, for the *I Ching* represented a deep and dangerous water hole in which one might easily be mired. However, the water hole proved to be an old well that needed only to be renovated in order to be put to useful purposes once more.

These four hexagrams are in the main consistent as regards theme (vessel, pit, well); and as regards intellectual content, they seem to be meaningful. Had a human being made such replies, I should, as a psychiatrist, have had to pronounce him of sound mind, at least on the basis of the material presented. Indeed, I should not have been able to discover anything delirious, idiotic, or schizophrenic in the four answers. In view of the *I Ching's* extreme age and its Chinese origin, I cannot consider its archaic, symbolic, and flowery language abnormal. On the contrary, I should have had to congratulate this hypothetical person on the extent of his insight into my unexpressed state of doubt. On the other hand, any person of clever and versatile mind can turn the whole thing around and show how I have projected my subjective contents into the symbolism of the hexagrams. Such a critique, though catastrophic from the standpoint of Western rationality, does no harm to the function of the *I Ching*. On the contrary, the Chinese sage would smilingly tell me: "Don't you see how useful the *I Ching* is in making you project your hitherto unrealized thoughts into its abstruse symbolism? You could have written your foreword without ever realizing what an avalanche of misunderstanding might be released by it."

The Chinese standpoint does not concern itself as to the attitude one takes toward the performance of the oracle. It is only we who are puzzled, because we trip time and again over our prejudice, viz., the notion of causality. The ancient wisdom of the East lays stress upon the fact that the intelligent individual realizes his own thoughts, but not in the least upon the way in which he does it. The less one thinks about the theory of the *I Ching*, the more soundly one sleeps.

It would seem to me that on the basis of this example an unprejudiced reader would now be in a position to form at least a tentative judgment on the operation of the *I Ching*. More cannot be expected from a simple introduction. If by means of this demonstration I have succeeded in elucidating the psychological phenomenology of the *I Ching*, I shall have carried out my purpose. As to the thousands of questions, doubts, and criticisms that this singular book stirs up—I cannot answer these. The *I Ching* does not offer itself with proofs and results; it does not vaunt itself, nor is it easy to approach. Like a part of nature, it waits until it is discovered. It offers neither facts nor power, but for lovers of self-knowledge, of wisdom—if there be such—it seems to be the right book. To one person its spirit appears as clear as day; to another, shadowy as twilight; to a third, dark as night. He who is not pleased by it does not have to use it, and he who is against it is not obliged to find it true. Let it go forth into the world for the benefit of those who can discern its meaning.

C. G. JUNG

Zurich, 1949

Two Chapters from: *The Interpretation of Nature and the Psyche*

III. Forerunners of the Idea of Synchronicity[1]

The causality principle asserts that the connection between cause and effect is a necessary one. The synchronicity principle asserts that the terms of a meaningful coincidence are connected by *simultaneity* and *meaning*. So if we assume that the ESP experiments and numerous other observations are established facts, we must conclude that besides the connection between cause and effect there is another factor in nature which expresses itself in the arrangement of events and appears to us as meaning. Although meaning is an anthropomorphic interpretation it nevertheless forms the indispensable criterion of synchronicity. What that factor which appears to us as "meaning" may be in itself we have no possibility of knowing. As an hypothesis, however, it is not quite so impossible as may appear at first sight. We must remember that the rationalistic attitude of the West is not the only possible one and

[1] This chapter forms a part of Dr. Jung's treatise on "Synchronicity: An Acausal Connecting Principle," translated by R. F. C. Hull. It appeared in the Bollingen Series XLVIII (Pantheon Books, 1955), entitled "Interpretation of Nature and the Psyche," and was produced in co-authorship with the physicist W. Pauli.—Ed.

is not all-embracing, but is in many ways a prejudice and a bias that ought perhaps to be corrected. The very much older civilization of the Chinese has always thought differently from us in this respect, and we have to go back to Heraclitus if we want to find something similar in our civilization, at least where philosophy is concerned. Only in astrology, alchemy, and the mantic procedures do we find no differences of principle between our attitude and the Chinese. That is why alchemy developed along parallel lines in East and West and why in both ambits it strove towards the same goal with more or less identical ideas.[2]

In Chinese philosophy one of the oldest and most central ideas is that of Tao, which the Jesuits translated as "God." But that is correct only for the Western way of thinking. Other translations, such as "Providence" and the like, are mere makeshifts. Richard Wilhelm brilliantly interprets it as "meaning."[3] The concept of Tao pervades the whole philosophical thought of China. Causality occupies this paramount position with us, but it acquired its importance only in the course of the last two centuries, thanks to the levelling influence of the statistical method on the one hand and the unparalleled success of the natural sciences on the other, which brought the metaphysical view of the world into disrepute.

Lao-tzu gives the following description of Tao in his celebrated *Tao Teh Ching*:[4]

There is something formless yet complete
That existed before heaven and earth.

[2] Cf. my *Psychology and Alchemy* (London and New York, 1953), p. 343, and *Symbolik des Geistes* (Zurich, 1948), p. 115. Also the doctrine of *chen-yen* in Wei Po-yang ("An Ancient Chinese Treatise on Alchemy Entitled Ts'ang T'ung Ch'i," trans. by Lu-ch'iang Wu, *Isis*, Bruges, XVIII, 1932, 241, 251) and in Chuang-tzu.

[3] Wilhelm and Jung, *The Secret of the Golden Flower* (6th imp., London, 1945), p. 94, and Wilhelm, *Chinesische Lebensweisheit* (Darmstadt, 1922).

[4] [Quotations from Arthur Waley's *The Way and Its Power* (London, 1934), with occasional slight changes to fit Wilhelm's reading.—TRANS.]

How still! how empty!
Dependent on nothing, unchanging,
All pervading, unfailing.
One may think of it as the mother of all things under heaven.
I do not know its name,
But I call it "Meaning."
If I had to give it a name, I should call it "The Great."
[Ch. XXV.]

Tao "covers the ten thousand things like a garment but does not claim to be master over them" (Ch. XXXIV). Lao-tzu describes it as "Nothing,"[5] by which he means, says Wilhelm, only its "contrast with the world of reality." Lao-tzu describes its nature as follows:

We put thirty spokes together and call it a wheel;
But it is on the space where there is nothing that the utility
    of the wheel depends.
We turn clay to make a vessel;
But it is on the space where there is nothing that the utility
    of the vessel depends.
We pierce doors and windows to make a house;
And it is on these spaces where there is nothing that the
    utility of the house depends.
Therefore just as we take advantage of what is, we should recognize the utility of what is not. [Ch. XI.]

"Nothing" is evidently "meaning" or "purpose," and it is only called Nothing because it does not manifest itself in the world of the senses, but is only its organizer.[6] Lao-tzu says:

Because the eye gazes but can catch no glimpse of it,
It is called elusive.
Because the ear listens but cannot hear it,
It is called the rarefied.

[5] Tao is the contingent, which Andreas Speiser defines as "pure nothing" ("Über die Freiheit," *Basler Universitätsreden*, XXVIII, 1950).
[6] Wilhelm, *Chinesische Lebensweisheit*, p. 15: "The relation between meaning (Tao) and reality cannot be conceived, either, under the category of cause and effect."

> Because the hand feels for it but cannot find it,
> It is called the infinitesimal. . . .
> These are called the shapeless shapes,
> Forms without form,
> Vague semblances.
> Go towards them, and you can see no front;
> Go after them, and you see no rear. [Ch. XIV.]

Wilhelm describes it as "a borderline conception lying at the extreme edge of the world of appearances." In it, the opposites "cancel out in non-discrimination," but are still potentially present. "These seeds," he continues, "point to something that corresponds firstly to *the visible*, i.e., something in the nature of an image; secondly to *the audible*, i.e., something in the nature of words; thirdly to *extension in space*, i.e., something with a form. But these three things are not clearly distinguished and definable, they are a non-spatial and non-temporal unity, having no above and below or front and back." As the *Tao Teh Ching* says:

> Incommensurable, impalpable,
> Yet latent in it are forms;
> Impalpable, incommensurable,
> Yet within it are entities.
> Shadowy it is and dim. [Ch. XXI.]

Reality, thinks Wilhelm, is conceptually knowable because according to the Chinese view there is in all things a latent "rationality."[7] This is the basic idea underlying meaningful coincidence: it is possible because both sides have the same meaning. Where meaning prevails, order results:

> Tao is eternal, but has no name;
> The Uncarved Block, though seemingly of small account,
> Is greater than anything under heaven.
> If the kings and barons would but possess themselves of it,
> The ten thousand creatures would flock to do them homage;
> Heaven and earth would conspire
> To send Sweet Dew;

[7] *Ibid.*, p. 19.

Without law or compulsion men would dwell in harmony.
  [Ch. XXXII.]

Tao never does;
Yet through it all things are done. [Ch. XXXVII.]

Heaven's net is wide;
Coarse are the meshes, yet nothing slips through.
  [Ch. LXXIII.]

Chuang-tzu (a contemporary of Plato's) says of the psychological premises on which Tao is based: "The state in which ego and non-ego are no longer opposed is called the pivot of Tao."[8] It sounds almost like a criticism of our scientific view of the world when he remarks that "Tao is obscured when you fix your eye on little segments of existence only", or "Limitations are not originally grounded in the meaning of life. Originally words had no fixed meanings. Differences only arose through looking at things subjectively." The sages of old, says Chuang-tzu, "took as their starting-point a state when the existence of things had not yet begun. That is indeed the extreme limit beyond which you cannot go. The next assumption was that though things existed they had not yet begun to be separated. The next, that though things were separated in a sense, affirmation and negation had not yet begun. When affirmation and negation came into being, Tao faded. After Tao faded, then came one-sided attachments." "Outward hearing should not penetrate further than the ear; the intellect should not seek to lead a separate existence, thus the soul can become empty and absorb the whole world. It is Tao that fills this emptiness." If you have insight, says Chuang-tzu, "you use your inner eye, your inner ear, to pierce to the heart of things, and have no need of intellectual knowledge." This is obviously an allusion to the absolute knowledge of the unconscious, and to the presence in the microcosm of macrocosmic events.

This Taoistic view is typical of Chinese thinking. It is,

[8] *Das wahre Buch vom südlichen Blütenland*, trans. by R. Wilhelm (Jena, 1912).

whenever possible, *a thinking in terms of the whole,* a point also brought out by Marcel Granet,[9] the eminent authority on Chinese psychology. This peculiarity can be seen in ordinary conversation with the Chinese: what seems to us a perfectly straightforward, precise question about some detail evokes from the Chinese thinker an unexpectedly elaborate answer, as though one had asked him for a blade of grass and got a whole meadow in return. With us details are important for their own sakes; for the Oriental mind they always complete a total picture. In this totality, as in primitive or in our own medieval, pre-scientific psychology (still very much alive!), are included things which seem to be connected with one another only "by chance," by a coincidence whose meaningfulness appears altogether arbitrary. This is where the theory of *correspondentia*[10] comes in, which was propounded by the natural philosophers of the Middle Ages, and particularly the classical idea of the *sympathy of all things*.[11] Hippocrates says:

> There is one common flow, one common breathing, all things are in sympathy. The whole organism and each one of its parts are working in conjunction for the same purpose . . . the great principle extends to the extremest part, and from the extremest part it returns to the great principle, to the one nature, being and not-being.[12]

The universal principle is found even in the smallest particle, which therefore corresponds to the whole.

---

[9] *La Pensée chinoise* (Paris, 1934); also Lily Abegg, *The Mind of East Asia* (London and New York, 1952). The latter gives an excellent account of the synchronistic mentality of the Chinese.

[10] Professor W. Pauli kindly calls my attention to the fact that Niels Bohr used "correspondence" as a mediating term between the representation of the discontinuum (particle) and the continuum (wave). Originally (1913–18) he called it the "principle of correspondence," but later (1927) it was formulated as the "argument of correspondence."

[11] *"sympatheia tōn holōn."*

[12] "De alimento," a tract ascribed to Hippocrates. (Trans. by John Precope in *Hippocrates on Diet and Hygiene,* London, 1952, p. 174, modified.)

In this connection there is an interesting idea in Philo (25 B.C.–A.D. 42):

> God, being minded to unite in intimate and loving fellowship the beginning and end of created things, made heaven the beginning and man the end, the one the most perfect of imperishable objects of sense, the other the noblest of things earthborn and perishable, being, in very truth, a miniature heaven. He bears about within himself, like holy images, endowments of nature that correspond to the constellations. . . . For since the corruptible and the incorruptible are by nature contrary the one to the other, God assigned the fairest of each sort to the beginning and the end, heaven (as I have said) to the beginning, and man to the end.[13]

Here the great principle or beginning, heaven, is infused into man the microcosm, who reflects the starlike natures and thus, as the smallest part and end of the work of Creation, contains the whole.

According to Theophrastus (371–288 B.C.) the supersensuous and the sensuous are joined by a bond of community. This bond cannot be mathematics, so must presumably be God. Similarly in Plotinus the individual souls born of the one World Soul are related to one another by sympathy or antipathy, regardless of distance.[14] Similar views are to be found in Pico della Mirandola:

> Firstly there is the unity in things whereby each thing is at one with itself, consists of itself, and coheres with itself. Secondly there is the unity whereby one creature is united with the others and all parts of the world constitute one world. The third and most important (unity) is that

---

[13] *De opificio mundi*, 82 (trans. by F. H. Colson and G. H. Whitaker in the Loeb Classical Library ed. of Philo, London and Cambridge, Mass., I, 1929), p. 67.

[14] *Enneads*, IV, 3, 8 and 4, 32 (in A. C. H. Drews, *Plotin und der Untergang der antiken Weltanschauung*, Jena, 1907), p. 179.

whereby the whole universe is one with its Creator, as an army with its commander.[15]

By this threefold unity Pico means a simple unity which, like the Trinity, has three aspects; "a unity distinguished by a threefold character, yet in such a way as not to depart from the simplicity of unity." For him the world is *one* being, a visible God, in which everything is naturally arranged from the very beginning like the parts of a living organism. The world appears as the *corpus mysticum* of God, just as the Church is the *corpus mysticum* of Christ, or as a well-disciplined army can be called a sword in the hand of the commander. The view that all things are arranged according to God's will is one that leaves little room for causality. Just as in a living body the different parts work in harmony and are meaningfully adjusted to one another, so events in the world stand in a meaningful relationship which cannot be derived from any immanent causality. The reason for this is that in either case the behavior of the parts depends on a central control which is superordinate to them.

In his treatise *De hominis dignitate* Pico says: "The Father implanted in man at birth seeds of all kinds and the germs of original life."[16] Just as God is the "copula" of the world, so, within the created world, is man. "Let us make man in our image, who is not a fourth world or anything like a new nature, but is rather the fusion and synthesis of three worlds (the supercelestial, the celestial, and the sublunary)."[17] In body and spirit man is "the little God of the world," the microcosm.[18] Like God, therefore, man is a center of events, and all things revolve about him.[19] This thought, so utterly

[15] *Heptaplus*, VI, prooem., in *Opera omnia* (Basel, 1557), pp. 40f.

[16] *Opera omnia*, p. 315.

[17] *Heptaplus*, V, vi, in *ibid.*, p. 38.

[18] "God . . . placed man in the centre [of the world] after his image and the similitude of forms."

[19] Pico's doctrine is a typical example of the medieval correspondence theory. A good account of cosmological and astrological correspondence is to be found in Alfons Rosenberg, *Zeichen am Himmel: Das Weltbild der Astrologie* (Zurich, 1949).

strange to the modern mind, dominated man's picture of the world until a few generations ago, when natural science proved man's subordination to nature and his extreme dependence on causes. The idea of a correlation between events and meaning (now assigned exclusively to man) was banished to such a remote and benighted region that the intellect lost track of it altogether. Schopenhauer remembered it somewhat belatedly after it had formed one of the chief items in Leibniz's scientific explanations.

By virtue of his microcosmic nature man is a son of the firmament or macrocosm. "I am a star travelling together with you," the initiate confesses in the Mithraic liturgy.[20] In alchemy the microcosmos has the same significance as the *rotundum*, a favorite symbol since the time of Zosimos of Panopolis, which was also known as the Monad.

The idea that the inner and outer man together form the whole, the *oulomeliā* of Hippocrates, a microcosm or smallest part wherein the "great principle" is undividedly present, also characterizes the thought of Agrippa von Nettesheim. He says:

> It is the unanimous consent of all Platonists, that as in the archetypal World, all things are in all; so also in this corporeal world, all things are in all, albeit in different ways, according to the receptive nature of each. Thus the Elements are not only in these inferiour bodies, but also in the Heavens, in Stars, in Demons, in Angels, and lastly in God, the maker, and archetype of all things.[21]

The ancients had said: "All things are full of gods." These gods were "divine powers which are diffused in things." Zoroaster had called them "divine allurements," and Synesius "symbolic inticements."[22] This latter interpretation comes very

---

[20] Albrecht Dieterich, *Eine Mithrasliturgie* (Leipzig, 1903), p. 9.

[21] Henricus Cornelius Agrippa von Nettesheim, *De occulta philosophia Libri tres* (Cologne, 1533). Trans. by "J. F." as *Three Books of Occult Philosophy* (London, 1651), p. 20; republished under the editorship of W. F. Whitehead (Chicago, 1898; Book I only), p. 55.

[22] "symbolicae illecebrae." [In J. F. original ed., p. 32; Whitehead ed., p. 69.—TRANS.]

close indeed to the idea of archetypal projections in modern psychology, although from the time of Synesius until quite recently there was no epistemological criticism, let alone the newest form of it, namely psychological criticism. Agrippa shares with the Platonists the view that there is an "immanent power in the things of the lower world which makes them agree to a large extent with the things of the upper world," and that as a result the animals are connected with the "divine bodies" (i.e., the stars) and exert an influence on them.[23] Here he quotes Virgil: "I for my part do not believe that they [the rooks] are endowed with divine spirit or with a foreknowledge of things greater than the oracle."[24]

Agrippa is thus suggesting that there is an inborn "knowledge" or "imagination" in living organisms, an idea which recurs in our own day in Hans Driesch.[25] Whether we like it or not, we find ourselves in this embarrassing position as soon as we begin seriously to reflect on the teleological processes in biology or to investigate the compensatory function of the unconscious, not to speak of trying to explain the phenomenon of synchronicity. Final causes, twist them how we will, postulate a *foreknowledge of some kind*. It is certainly not a knowledge that could be connected with the ego, and hence not a conscious knowledge as we know it, but rather a self-subsistent "unconscious" knowledge which I would prefer to call "absolute knowledge." It is not cognition but, as Leibniz so excellently calls it, a "perceiving" which consists—or to be more cautious, seems to consist—of images, of subjectless "simulacra." These postulated images are presumably the same as my archetypes, which can be shown to be formal factors in spontaneous fantasy products. Expressed in modern language, the microcosm which contains "the images of all

[23] *De occulta philosophia*, lv, p. 69. (J. F. ed., p. 117; Whitehead ed., p. 169.) Similarly in Paracelsus.

[24] "Haud equidem credo, quia sit divinius illis
   Ingenium aut rerum fato prudentia maior."
                                   —*Georgics*, I.

[25] *Die "Seele" als elementarer Naturfaktor* (Leipzig, 1903), pp. 80, 82.

creation" would be the collective unconscious.[26] By the *spiritus mundi*, the *ligamentum animae et corporis*, the *quinta essentia*,[27] which he shares with the alchemists, Agrippa probably means what we would call the unconscious. The spirit that "penetrates all things," or shapes all things, is the World Soul: "The soul of the world therefore is a certain only thing, filling all things, bestowing all things, binding, and knitting together all things, that it might make one frame of the world. . . ."[28] Those things in which this spirit is particularly powerful therefore have a tendency to "beget their like," in other words, to produce correspondences or meaningful coincidences.[29] Agrippa gives a long list of these correspondences, based on the numbers 1 to 12. A similar but more alchemical table of correspondences can be found in a treatise of Aegidius de Vadis.[30] Of these I would only mention the *scala unitatis*, because it is especially interesting from the point of view of the history of symbols: "Iod [the first letter of the tetragrammaton, the divine name]—anima mundi—sol—lapis philosophorum—cor—Lucifer."[31] I must content myself with saying that this is an attempt to set up a hierarchy of archetypes, and that tendencies in this direction can be shown to exist in the unconscious.

[26] Cf. "The Spirit of Psychology," in *Spirit and Nature* (Papers from the Eranos Yearbooks, 1; New York, 1954; London, 1955).

[27] Agrippa says of this: "That which we call the quintessence: because it is not from the four Elements, but a certain fifth thing, having its being above, and besides them."

[28] *Loc. cit.* (J. F. ed., p. 331): "Est itaque anima mundi, vita quaedam unica omnia replens, omnia perfundens, omnia colligens et connectens, ut unam reddat totius mundi machinam. . . ."

[29] The zoologist A. C. Hardy reaches similar conclusions: "Perhaps our ideas on evolution may be altered if something akin to telepathy—unconscious no doubt—were found to be a factor in moulding the patterns of behaviour among members of a species. If there was such a non-conscious group-behaviour plan, distributed between, and linking, the individuals of the race, we might find ourselves coming back to something like those ideas of subconscious racial memory of Samuel Butler, but on a group rather than an individual basis." *Discovery* (London), X (Oct. 1949).

[30] "Dialogus inter naturam et filium philosophiae," *Theatrum chemicum* (Ursel, 1602), II, p. 123.

[31] Cited in Agrippa, *op. cit.*

Agrippa was an older contemporary of Theophrastus Paracelsus and is known to have had a considerable influence on him.[32] So it is not surprising if the thinking of Paracelsus proves to be steeped in the idea of correspondence. He says:

> If a man will be a philosopher without going astray, he must lay the foundations of his philosophy by making heaven and earth a microcosm, and not be wrong by a hair's breadth. Therefore he who will lay the foundations of medicine must also guard against the slightest error, and must make from the microcosm the revolution of heaven and earth, so that the philosopher does not find anything in heaven and earth which he does not also find in man, and the physician does not find anything in man which heaven and earth do not have. And these two differ only in outward form, and yet the form on both sides is understood as pertaining to one thing.[33]

The *Paragranum* has some pointed psychological remarks to make about physicians:

> For this reason, [we assume] not four, but one arcanum, which is, however, four-square, like a tower facing the four winds. And as little as a tower may lack a corner, so little may the physician lack one of the parts. . . . At the same [time he] knows how the world is symbolized [by] an egg in its shell, and how a chick with all its substance lies hidden within it. Thus everything in the world and in man must lie hidden in the physician. And just as the hens, by their brooding, transform the world prefigured in the shell into a chick, so Alchemy brings to maturity the philosophical arcana lying in the physician. . . . Herein lies the error of those who do not understand the physician aright.[34]

[32] Cf. my *Paracelsica* (Zurich, 1942), pp. 47ff.
[33] *Das Buch Paragranum*, ed. by Franz Strunz (Leipzig, 1903), pp. 35f.
[34] Similar ideas in Jakob Böhme, *The Signature of All Things,* trans. by John Ellistone and ed. by Clifford Bax (Everyman's Library, London, 1912), p. 10: "Man has indeed the forms of all the three worlds in him, for he is a complete image of God, or

What this means for alchemy I have shown in some detail in my *Psychology and Alchemy*.

Johannes Kepler thought in much the same way. He says in his *Tertius interveniens* (1610):[35]

> This [viz., a geometrical principle underlying the physical world] is also, according to the doctrine of Aristotle, the strongest tie that links the lower world to the heavens and unifies it therewith so that all its forms are governed from on high; for in this lower world, that is to say the globe of the earth, there is inherent a spiritual nature, capable of *Geometria*, which *ex instinctu creatoris, sine ratiocinatione* comes to life and stimulates itself into a use of its forces through the geometrical and harmonious combination of the heavenly rays of light. Whether all plants and animals as well as the globe of the earth have this faculty in themselves I cannot say. But it is not an unbelievable thing. . . . For, in all these things [e.g., in the fact that flowers have a definite colour, form, and number of petals] there is at work the *instinctus divinus, rationis particeps*, and not at all man's own intelligence. That man, too, through his soul and its lower faculties, has a like affinity to the heavens as has the soil of the earth can be tested and proven in many ways.

Concerning the astrological "Character," i.e., astrological synchronicity, Kepler says:

> This *Character* is received, not into the body, which is much too inappropriate for this, but into the soul's own nature, which behaves like a point (for which reason it can also be transformed into the point of the *confluxus radiorum*). This [nature of the soul] not only partakes of their reason (on account of which we human beings are called reasonable above other living creatures) but also has another, innate reason [enabling it] to apprehend instantane-

---

of the Being of all beings. . . ." (*De signatura rerum*, Amsterdam, 1635, I, 7.)

[35] *Joannis Kepleri Astronomi Opera omnia*, ed. by C. Frisch (Frankfort on the Main and Erlangen, 1858ff.), I, pp. 605ff.

ously, without long learning, the *Geometriam* in the *radiis* as well as in the *vocibus*, that is to say, in *Musica*.

Thirdly, another marvellous thing is that the nature which receives this *Characterem* also induces a certain correspondence *in constellationibus coelestibus* in its relatives. When a mother is great with child and the natural time of delivery is near, nature selects for the birth a day and hour which correspond, on account of the heavens [scil., from an astrological point of view], to the nativity of the mother's brother or father, and this *non qualitative, sed astronomice et quantitative*.

Fourthly, so well does each nature know not only its *characterem coelestem* but also the celestial *configurationes* and courses of every day that, whenever a planet moves *de praesenti* into its *characteris ascendentem* or *loca praecipua*, especially into the *Natalitia*,[36] it responds to this and is affected and stimulated thereby in various ways.

Kepler supposes that the secret of the marvellous correspondence is to be found in the *earth*, because the earth is animated by an *anima telluris*, for whose existence he adduces a number of proofs. Among these are the constant temperature below the surface of the earth; the peculiar power of the earth-soul to produce metals, minerals, and fossils, namely the *facultas formatrix*, which is similar to that of the womb and can bring forth in the bowels of the earth shapes that are otherwise found only outside—ships, fishes, kings, popes, monks, soldiers, etc.; further the practice of geometry, for it produces the five geometrical bodies and the six-cornered figures in crystals. The *anima telluris* has all this from an original impulse, independent of the reflection and ratiocination of man.[37]

---

[36] ["in die Natalitia" = "into those [positions presiding] at birth," if "in die" is construed as German. The *Gesammelte Werke*, ed. by M. Caspar and F. Hammer (Munich, 1941), IV, p. 211, has "in die Natalitio" = "in the day of birth," the words "in die" being construed as Latin.—TRANS.]

[37] Kepler, *Opera*, ed. by Frisch, V, p. 254; cf. also II, pp. 270f. and VI, pp. 178f.

The seat of astrological synchronicity is not in the planets but in the earth; not in matter, but in the *anima telluris*. Therefore every kind of natural or living power in bodies has a certain "divine similitude."

Such was the intellectual background when Gottfried Wilhelm von Leibniz (1646–1716) appeared with his idea of *pre-established harmony*, that is, an absolute synchronism of psychic and physical events. This theory finally petered out in the concept of "psychophysical parallelism." Leibniz's pre-established harmony and the above-mentioned idea of Schopenhauer's, that the unity of the primal cause produces a simultaneity and interrelationship of events not in themselves causally connected, are at bottom only a repetition of the old peripatetic view, with a modern deterministic coloring in the case of Schopenhauer and a partial replacement of causality by an antecedent order in the case of Leibniz. For him God is the creator of order. He compares soul and body to two synchronized clocks[38] and uses the same simile to express the

---

[38] G. W. Leibniz, "Second Explanation of the System of the Communication between Substances" (*The Philosophical Works of Leibniz*, a selection trans. by G. M. Duncan, New Haven, 1890, pp. 90–91): "From the beginning God has made each of these two substances of such a nature that merely by following its own peculiar laws, received with its being, it nevertheless accords with the other, just as if there were a mutual influence or as if God always put his hand thereto in addition to his general co-operation."

As Professor Pauli has kindly pointed out, it is possible that Leibniz took his idea of the synchronized clocks from the Flemish philosopher Arnold Geulincx (1625–99). In his *Metaphysica vera, Part III*, there is a note to "Octava scientia" (*Opera philosophica*, The Hague, 1892, Vol. II, p. 195), which says (p. 296): "the clock of our will is synchronized with the clock of our physical movement." Another note (p. 297) explains: "Our will has no influence, no causative or determinative power, and no effect of any kind on our movement. . . . If we examine our thoughts carefully, we find in ourselves no idea or concept of determination. . . . There remains, therefore, only God as the prime mover and only mover, because he arranges and orders movement and freely co-ordinates it with our will, so that our will wishes simultaneously to throw the feet forward into walking, and simultaneously the forward move-

relations of the monads or entelechies with one another. Although the monads cannot influence one another directly because, as he says, they "have no windows"[39] (relative abolition of causality!), they are so constituted that they are always in accord without having knowledge of one another. He conceives each monad to be a "little world" or "active indivisible mirror."[40] Not only is man a microcosm enclosing the whole in himself, but every entelechy or monad is in effect such a microcosm. Each "simple substance" has connections "which express all the others." It is "a perpetual living mirror of the universe."[41] He calls the monads of living organisms "souls": "the soul follows its own laws, and the body its own likewise, and they accord by virtue of the harmony pre-established among all substances, since they are all representations of one and the same universe." This clearly expresses the idea that man is a microcosm. "Souls in general," says Leibniz, "are the living mirrors or images of the universe of created things." He distinguishes between minds on the one hand, which are "images of the Divinity . . . capable of knowing the system of the universe, and of imitating something of it by architectonic patterns, each mind being as it were a little divinity in

---

ment and the walking takes place." A note to "Nona scientia" adds (p. 298): "Our mind . . . is totally independent of the body . . . everything we know about the body is already in the body, before our thought. So that we can, as it were, read ourselves in our body, but not imprint ourselves on it. Only God can do that." This idea anticipates Leibniz's clock comparison.

[39] *Monadology*, § 7 (*Leibniz: Philosophical Writings*, selected and trans. by Mary Morris, Everyman's Library, London, 1934, p. 3): "Monads have no windows, by which anything could come in or go out. . . . Thus neither substance nor accident can enter a monad from without."

[40] Rejoinder to the remarks in Bayle's Dictionary, from the *Kleinere philosophische Schriften* (ed. by R. Habs, Leipzig, 1883), XI, p. 105.

[41] *Monadology*, § 56 (Morris ed., p. 12): "Now this connection or adaptation of all created things with each, and of each with all the rest, means that each simple substance has relations which express all the others, and that consequently it is a perpetual living mirror of the universe."

its own department,"[42] and bodies on the other hand, which "act according to the laws of efficient causes by motions," while the souls act "according to the laws of final causes by appetitions, ends, and means." In the monad or soul alterations take place whose cause is the "appetition." "The passing state, which involves and represents a plurality within the unity or simple substance, is nothing other than what is called perception," says Leibniz. Perception is the "inner state of the monad representing external things," and it must be distinguished from conscious apperception. "For perception is unconscious."[43] Herein lay the great mistake of the Cartesians, "that they took no account of perceptions which are not apperceived."[44] The perceptive faculty of the monad corresponds to the *knowledge,* and its appetitive faculty to the *will,* that is in God.[45]

It is clear from these quotations that besides the causal connection Leibniz postulates a complete pre-established parallelism of events both inside and outside the monad. The synchronicity principle thus becomes the absolute rule in all cases where an inner event occurs simultaneously with an outside one. As against this, however, it must be borne in mind that the synchronistic phenomena which can be verified empirically, far from constituting a rule, are so exceptional that most people doubt their existence. They certainly occur much more frequently in reality than one thinks or can prove, but we still do not know whether they occur so frequently and so regularly in any field of experience that we could speak of them as conforming to law.[46] We only know that there must

---

[42] *Ibid.,* § 83 (p. 18); cf. *Theodicy,* § 147 (trans. by E. M. Huggard, ed. by Austin Farrer, New Haven, 1952, pp. 215f).

[43] "Principles of Nature and of Grace, Founded on Reason," § 4 (Morris ed., p. 22).

[44] *Monadology,* § 14 (p. 5).

[45] *Monadology,* § 48 (p. 11); *Theodicy,* § 149.

[46] I must again stress the possibility that the relation between body and soul may yet be understood as a synchronistic one. Should this conjecture ever be proved, my present view that synchronicity is a relatively rare phenomenon would have to be corrected.

be an underlying principle which might possibly explain all such (related) phenomena.

The primitive as well as the classical and medieval views of nature postulate the existence of some such principle alongside causality. Even in Leibniz, causality is neither the only view nor the predominant one. Then, in the course of the eighteenth century, it became the exclusive principle of natural science. With the rise of the physical sciences in the nineteenth century the correspondence theory vanished completely from the surface, and the magical world of earlier ages seemed to have disappeared once and for all until, towards the end of the century, the founders of the Society for Psychical Research indirectly opened up the whole question again through their investigation of telepathic phenomena.

The medieval attitude of mind I have described above underlies all the magical and mantic procedures which have played an important part in man's life since the remotest times. The medieval mind would regard Rhine's laboratory-arranged experiments as magical performances, whose effect for this reason would not seem so very astonishing. It was interpreted as a "transmission of energy," which is still commonly the case today, although, as I have said, it is not possible to form any empirically verifiable conception of the transmitting medium.

I need hardly point out that for the primitive mind synchronicity is a self-evident fact; consequently at this stage there is no such thing as chance. No accident, no illness, no death is ever fortuitous or attributable to "natural" causes. Everything is somehow due to magical influence. The crocodile that catches a man while he is bathing has been sent by a magician; illness is caused by some spirit or other; the snake that was seen by the grave of somebody's mother is obviously her soul; etc. On the primitive level, of course, synchronicity does not appear as an idea by itself, but as "magical" causality. This is an early form of our classical idea of causality, while the development of Chinese philosophy produced from the connotation of the magical the "concept" of Tao, of meaningful coincidence, but no causality-based science.

Synchronicity postulates a meaning which is a priori in relation to human consciousness and apparently exists outside man.[47] Such an assumption is found above all in the philosophy of Plato, which takes for granted the existence of transcendental images or models of empirical things, the *eidā* (forms, species), whose reflections *eidōla* (images) we see in the phenomenal world. This assumption not only presented no difficulty to earlier centuries but was on the contrary perfectly self-evident. The idea of an a priori meaning may also be found in the older mathematics, as in the mathematician Jacobi's paraphrase of Schiller's poem "Archimedes and His Pupil." He praises the calculation of the orbit of Uranus and closes with the lines:

> What you behold in the cosmos is only the light of God's glory;
> In the Olympian host Number eternally reigns.

The great mathematician Gauss is the putative author of the saying: "God does arithmetic."[48]

The idea of synchronicity and of a self-subsistent meaning, which forms the basis of classical Chinese thinking and of the naïve views of the Middle Ages, seems to us an archaic assumption that ought at all costs to be avoided. Though the West has done everything possible to discard this antiquated hypothesis, it has not quite succeeded. Certain mantic procedures seem to have died out, but astrology, which in our own day has attained an eminence never known before, remains

---

[47] In view of the possibility that synchronicity is not only a psychophysical phenomenon but might also occur without the participation of the human psyche, I should like to point out that in this case we should have to speak not of *meaning* but of equivalence or conformity.

[48] "*hō theos arithmatidzā.*" But in a letter of 1830 Gauss says: "We must in all humility admit that if number is *merely* a product of our mind, space has a reality outside our mind." (Leopold Kronecker, *Über den Zahlenbegriff*, in his *Werke*, III, 1899, p. 252.) Hermann Weyl likewise takes number as a product of reason. ("Wissenschaft als symbolische Konstruktion des Menschen," *Eranos-Jahrbuch 1948*, p. 375). Markus Fierz, on the other hand, inclines more to the Platonic idea. ("Zur physikalischen Erkenntnis," *Eranos-Jahrbuch 1948*, p. 434.)

very much alive. Nor has the determinism of a scientific epoch been able to extinguish altogether the persuasive power of the synchronicity principle. For in the last resort it is not so much a question of superstition as of a truth which remained hidden for so long only because it had less to do with the physical side of events than with their psychic aspects. It was modern psychology and parapsychology which proved that causality does not explain a certain class of events and that in this case we have to consider a formal factor, namely synchronicity, as a principle of explanation.

For those who are interested in psychology I should like to mention here that the peculiar idea of a self-subsistent meaning is suggested in dreams. Once when this idea was being discussed in my circle somebody remarked: "The geometrical square does not occur in nature except in crystals." A lady who had been present had the following dream that night: *In the garden there was a large sandpit in which layers of rubbish had been deposited. In one of these layers she discovered thin, slaty plates of green serpentine. One of them had black squares on it, arranged concentrically. The black was not painted on, but was ingrained in the stone, like the markings in an agate. Similar marks were found on two or three other plates, which Mr. A (a slight acquaintance) then took away from her.*[49] Another dream motif of the same kind is the following: *The dreamer was in a wild mountain region where he found contiguous layers of triassic rock. He loosened the slabs and discovered to his boundless astonishment that they had human heads on them in low relief.* This dream was repeated several times at long intervals.[50] Another time the dreamer *was traveling through the Siberian tundra and found an animal he had long been looking for. It was a more than lifesize cock, made of what looked like*

[49] According to the rules of dream interpretation this Mr. A would represent the animus, who, as a personification of the unconscious, takes back the designs because the conscious mind has no use for them and regards them only as *lusus naturae*.

[50] The recurrence of the dream expresses the persistent attempt of the unconscious to bring the dream content before the conscious mind.

thin, colorless glass. But it was alive and had just sprung by chance from a microscopic unicellular organism which had the power to turn into all sorts of animals (not otherwise found in the tundra) or even into objects of human use, of whatever size. The next moment each of these chance forms vanished without trace. Here is another dream of the same type: *The dreamer was walking in a wooded mountain region. At the top of a steep slope he came to a ridge of rock honeycombed with holes, and there he found a little brown man of the same color as the iron oxide with which the rock was coated.*[51] *The little man was busily engaged in hollowing out a cave, at the back of which a cluster of columns could be seen in the living rock. On the top of each column was a dark brown human head with large eyes, carved with great care out of some very hard stone, like lignite. The little man freed this formation from the amorphous conglomerate surrounding it. The dreamer could hardly believe his eyes at first, but then had to admit that the columns were continued far back into the living rock and must therefore have come into existence without the help of man. He reflected that the rock was at least half a million years old and that the artefact could not possibly have been made by human hands.*[52]

These dreams seem to point to the presence of a formal factor in nature. They describe not just a *lusus naturae,* but the meaningful coincidence of an absolutely natural product with a human idea apparently independent of it. This is what the dreams are obviously saying,[53] and what they are trying to bring nearer to consciousness through repetition.

[51] An Anthroparion or "metallic man."
[52] Cf. Kepler's theories quoted above.
[53] Those who find the dreams unintelligible will probably suspect them of harboring quite a different meaning which is more in accord with their preconceived opinions. One can indulge in wishful thinking about dreams just as one can about anything else. For my part I prefer to keep as close to the dream statement as possible, and to try to formulate it in accordance with its manifest meaning. If it proves impossible to relate this meaning to the conscious situation of the dreamer, then I frankly admit that I do not understand the dream, but I take good care not to juggle it into line with some preconceived theory.

IV. Conclusion

I do not regard these statements as in any way a final proof of my views, but simply as a conclusion from empirical premises which I would like to submit to the consideration of my reader. From the material before us I can derive no other hypothesis that would adequately explain the facts (including the ESP experiments). I am only too conscious that synchronicity is a highly abstract and "irrepresentable" quantity. It ascribes to the moving body a certain psychoid property which, like space, time, and causality, forms a criterion of its behavior. We must completely give up the idea of the psyche's being somehow connected with the brain, and remember instead the "meaningful" or "intelligent" behavior of the lower organisms, which are without a brain. Here we find ourselves much closer to the formal factor which, as I have said, has nothing to do with brain activity.

If that is so, then we must ask ourselves whether the relation of soul and body can be considered from this angle, that is to say whether the co-ordination of psychic and physical processes in a living organism can be understood as a synchronistic phenomenon rather than as a causal relation. Both Geulincx and Leibniz regarded the co-ordination of the psychic and the physical as an act of God, of some principle standing outside empirical nature. The assumption of a causal relation between psyche and physis leads on the other hand to conclusions which it is difficult to square with experience: either there are physical processes which cause psychic happenings, or there is a pre-existent psyche which organizes matter. In the first case it is hard to see how chemical processes can ever produce psychic processes, and in the second case one wonders how an immaterial psyche could ever set matter in motion. It is not necessary to think of Leibniz's pre-established harmony or anything of that kind, which would have to be absolute and would manifest itself in a universal correspondence and sympathy, rather like the meaningful coincidence of time-points lying on the same degree of latitude in Schopenhauer.

The synchronicity principle possesses properties that may help to clear up the body-soul problem. Above all it is the fact of causeless order, or rather, of meaningful orderedness, that may throw light on psychophysical parallelism. The "absolute knowledge" which is characteristic of synchronistic phenomena, a knowledge not mediated by the sense organs, supports the hypothesis of a self-subsistent meaning, or even expresses its existence. Such a form of existence can only be transcendental, since, as the knowledge of future or spatially distant events shows, it is contained in a psychically relative space and time, that is to say in an irrepresentable space-time continuum.

It may be worth our while to examine more closely, from this point of view, certain experiences which seem to indicate the existence of psychic processes in what are commonly held to be unconscious states. Here I am thinking chiefly of the remarkable observations made during deep syncopes resulting from acute brain injuries. Contrary to all expectations, a severe head injury is not always followed by a corresponding loss of consciousness. To the observer, the wounded man seems apathetic, "in a trance," and not conscious of anything. Subjectively, however, consciousness is by no means extinguished. Sensory communication with the outside world is in a large measure restricted, but is not always completely cut off, although the noise of battle, for instance, may suddenly give way to a "solemn" silence. In this state there is sometimes a very distinct and impressive feeling or hallucination of levitation, the wounded man seeming to rise into the air in the same position he was in at the moment he was wounded. If he was wounded standing up, he rises in a standing position, if lying down, he rises in a lying position, if sitting, he rises in a sitting position. Occasionally his surroundings seem to rise with him —for instance the whole bunker in which he finds himself at the moment. The height of the levitation may be anything from eighteen inches to several yards. All feeling of weight is lost. In a few cases the wounded think they are making swimming movements with their arms. If there is any perception of their surroundings at all, it seems to be mostly imaginary, i.e., composed of memory images. During levitation the mood is predominantly euphoric. "'Buoyant, solemn, heavenly, serene, relaxed, blissful, expectant, exciting' are the words used to describe it. . . . There are various kinds of 'ascension experiences.'"[54] Jantz and Beringer rightly point out that the wounded can be roused from their syncope by remarkably small stimuli, for instance if they are addressed by name or touched, whereas the most terrific bombardment has no effect.

Much the same thing can be observed in deep comas resulting from other causes. I would like to give an example from my own medical experience: A woman patient, whose reliability and truthfulness I have no reason to doubt, told me that her first birth was very difficult. After thirty hours of fruitless labor the doctor considered that a forceps delivery was indicated. This was carried out under light narcosis. She was badly torn and suffered great loss of blood. When the doctor, her mother, and her husband had gone, and everything was cleared up, the nurse wanted to eat, and the patient saw her turn round at the door and ask, "Do you want anything before I go to supper?" She tried to answer, but couldn't. She had the feeling that she was sinking through the bed into a bottomless void. She saw the nurse hurry to the bedside and seize her hand in order to take her pulse. From the way she moved her fingers to and fro the patient thought it must be almost imperceptible. Yet she herself felt quite all right, and was slightly amused at the nurse's alarm. She was not in the least frightened. That was the last she could remember for a long time. The next thing she was aware of was that, without feeling her body and its position, she was *looking down* from a point in the ceiling and could see everything going on in the room below her: she saw herself lying in the bed, deadly pale, with closed eyes. Beside her stood the nurse. The doctor paced up and down the room excitedly, and it seemed to her that he had lost his head and didn't know what to do. Her relatives crowded to the door. Her mother and her husband came in

[54] Hubert Jantz and Kurt Beringer, "Das Syndrom des Schwebeerlebnisses unmittelbar nach Kopfverletzungen," *Der Nervenarzt* (Berlin), XVII (1944).

and looked at her with frightened faces. She told herself it was too stupid of them to think she was going to die, for she would certainly come round again. All this time she knew that behind her was a glorious, park-like landscape shining in the brightest colors, and in particular an emerald green meadow with short grass, which sloped gently upwards beyond a wrought-iron gate leading into the park. It was spring, and little gay flowers such as she had never seen before were scattered about in the grass. The whole demesne sparkled in the sunlight, and all the colors were of an indescribable splendor. The sloping meadow was flanked on both sides by dark green trees. It gave her the impression of a clearing in the forest, never yet trodden by the foot of man. "I knew that this was the entrance to another world, and that if I turned round to gaze at the picture directly, I should feel tempted to go in at the gate, and thus step out of life." She did not actually *see* this landscape, as her back was turned to it, but she *knew* it was there. She felt there was nothing to stop her from entering in through the gate. She only knew that she would turn back to her body and would not die. That was why she found the agitation of the doctor and the distress of her relatives stupid and out of place.

The next thing that happened was that she awoke from her coma and saw the nurse bending over her in bed. She was told that she had been unconscious for about half an hour. The next day, some fifteen hours later, when she felt a little stronger, she made a remark to the nurse about the incompetent and "hysterical" behavior of the doctor during her coma. The nurse energetically denied this criticism in the belief that the patient had been completely unconscious at the time and could therefore have known nothing of the scene. Only when she described in full detail what had happened during the coma was the nurse obliged to admit that the patient had perceived the events exactly as they happened in reality.

One might conjecture that this was simply a psychogenic twilight state in which a split-off part of consciousness still continued to function. The patient, however, had never been hysterical and had suffered a genuine heart collapse followed by syncope due to cerebral anemia, as all the outward and evidently alarming symptoms indicated. She really was in a coma and ought to have had a complete psychic black-out and been altogether incapable of clear observation and sound judgment. The remarkable thing was that it was not an immediate perception of the situation through indirect or unconscious observation, but she saw the whole situation from *above*, as though "her eyes were in the ceiling," as she put it.

Indeed, it is not easy to explain how such unusually intense psychic processes can take place, and be remembered, in a state of severe collapse, and how the patient could observe actual events in concrete detail with closed eyes. One would expect such obvious cerebral anemia to militate against or prevent the occurrence of highly complex psychic processes of that kind.

Sir Auckland Geddes presented a very similar case before the Royal Medical Society on February 26, 1927, though here the ESP went very much further. During a state of collapse the patient noted the splitting off of an integral consciousness from his bodily consciousness, the latter gradually resolving itself into its organ components. The other consciousness possessed verifiable ESP.[55]

These experiences seem to show that in swoon states, where by all human standards there is every guarantee that conscious activity and sense perception are suspended, consciousness, reproducible ideas, acts of judgment, and perceptions can still continue to exist. The accompanying feeling of levitation, alteration of the angle of vision, and extinction of hearing and of coenaesthetic perceptions indicate a shift in the localization of consciousness, a sort of separation from the body, or from the cerebral cortex or cerebrum which is conjectured to be the seat of conscious phenomena. If we are correct in this assumption, then we must ask ourselves whether there is some other nervous substrate in us, apart from the cerebrum, that can think and perceive, or whether the psychic processes that go

[55] Cf. G. N. M. Tyrrell's report in *The Personality of Man* (London, 1947), pp. 197f. There is another case of this kind on pp. 199f.

on in us during loss of consciousness are synchronistic phenomena, i.e., events which have no causal connection with organic processes. This last possibility cannot be rejected out of hand in view of the existence of ESP, i.e., of perceptions independent of space and time which cannot be explained as processes in the biological substrate. Where sense perceptions are impossible from the start, it can hardly be a question of anything but synchronicity. But where there are spatial and temporal conditions which would make perception and apperception possible in principle, and only the activity of consciousness, or the cortical function, is extinguished, and where, as in our example, a conscious phenomenon like perception and judgment nevertheless occurs, then the question of a nervous substrate might well be considered. It is well nigh axiomatic that conscious processes are tied to the cerebrum, and that the lower centers contain nothing but chains of reflexes which in themselves are unconscious. This is particularly true of the sympathetic system. Hence the insects, which have no cerebrospinal nervous system at all, but only a double chain of ganglia, are regarded as reflex automata.

This view has recently been challenged by the researches which von Frisch, of Graz, made into the life of bees. It turns out that bees not only tell their comrades, by means of a peculiar sort of dance, that they have found a feeding-place, but that they also indicate its direction and distance, thus enabling the beginners to fly to it directly.[56] This kind of message is no different in principle from information conveyed by a human being. In the latter case we would certainly regard such behavior as a conscious and intentional act and can hardly imagine how anyone could prove in a court of law that it had taken place unconsciously. We could, at a pinch, admit on the basis of psychiatric experiences that objective information can in exceptional cases be communicated in a twilight state, but would expressly deny that communications of this kind are normally unconscious. Nevertheless it would be possible to suppose that in bees the process is unconscious. But that

[56] Karl von Frisch, *The Dancing Bees*, trans. by Dora Ilse (New York and London, 1954), pp. 112ff.

would not help to solve the problem, because we are still faced with the fact that the ganglionic system apparently achieves exactly the same result as our cerebral cortex. Nor is there any proof that bees are unconscious.

Thus we are driven to the conclusion that a nervous substrate like the sympathetic system, which is absolutely different from the cerebrospinal system in point of origin and function, can evidently produce thoughts and perceptions just as easily as the latter. What then are we to think of the sympathetic system in vertebrates? Can it also produce or transmit specifically psychic processes? Von Frisch's observations prove the existence of transcerebral thought and perception. One must bear this possibility in mind if we want to account for the existence of some form of consciousness during an unconscious coma. During a coma the sympathetic system is not paralyzed and could therefore be considered as a possible carrier of psychic functions. If that is so, then one must ask whether the normal state of unconsciousness in sleep, and the potentially conscious dreams it contains, can be regarded in the same light—whether, in other words, dreams are produced not so much by the activity of the sleeping cortex, as by the unsleeping sympathetic system, and are therefore of a transcerebral nature.

Outside the realm of psychophysical parallelism, which we cannot at present pretend to understand, synchronicity is not a phenomenon whose regularity it is at all easy to demonstrate. One is as much impressed by the disharmony of things as one is surprised by their occasional harmony. In contrast to the idea of a pre-established harmony, the synchronistic factor merely claims the existence of an intellectually necessary principle which could be added as a fourth to the recognized triad of space, time, and causality. These factors are necessary but not absolute—most psychic contents are non-spatial, time and causality are psychically relative—and in the same way the synchronistic factor proves to be only conditionally valid. But unlike causality, which reigns despotically over the whole picture of the macrophysical world and whose universal rule is shattered only in certain lower orders of magnitude, synchronicity is a phenomenon that seems to be primarily connected with psychic conditions, that is to say, with processes in the unconscious. Synchronistic phenomena are found to occur—experimentally—with some degree of regularity and frequency in the intuitive, "magical" procedures, where they are subjectively convincing but are extremely difficult to verify objectively and cannot be statistically evaluated (at least at present).

On the organic level it might be possible to regard biological morphogenesis in the light of the synchronistic factor. Professor A. M. Dalcq (of Brussels) understands form, despite its tie with matter, as a "continuity that is superordinate to the living organism."[57] Sir James Jeans reckons radioactive decay among the causeless events which, as we have seen, include synchronicity. He says: "Radioactive break-up appeared to be an effect without a cause, and suggested that the ultimate laws of nature were not even causal."[58] This highly paradoxical formula, coming from the pen of a physicist, is typical of the intellectual dilemma with which radioactive decay confronts us. It, or rather the phenomenon of "half-life," appears as an instance of acausal orderedness—a conception which also includes synchronicity and to which I shall revert below.

Synchronicity is not a philosophical view but an empirical concept which postulates an intellectually necessary principle. This cannot be called either materialism or metaphysics. No serious investigator would assert that the nature of what is observed to exist, and of that which observes, namely, the psyche, are known and recognized quantities. If the latest conclusions of science are coming nearer and nearer to a unitary idea of being, characterized by space and time on the one hand and by causality and synchronicity on the other, that has nothing to do with materialism. Rather it seems to show

---

[57] "La Morphogénèse dans la cadre de la biologie générale," *Verhandlungen der Schweizerischen Naturforschenden Gesellschaft* (129th Annual Meeting, at Lausanne; pub. Aarau, 1949). Cf. above, the similar conclusion reached by the zoologist A. C. Hardy.

[58] *Physics and Philosophy* (Cambridge, 1942), p. 127; cf. also p. 151.

that there is some possibility of getting rid of the incommensurability between the observed and the observer. The result, in that case, would be a unity of being which would have to be expressed in terms of a new conceptual language—a "neutral language," as W. Pauli once called it.

Space, time, and causality, the triad of classical physics, would then be supplemented by the synchronicity factor and become a tetrad, a *quaternio* which makes possible a whole judgment:

$$\text{Causality} \quad\text{---}\quad \begin{array}{c} Space \\ | \\ Time \end{array} \quad\text{---}\quad Synchronicity$$

Here synchronicity is to the three other principles as the one-dimensionality of time[59] is to the three-dimensionality of space, or as the recalcitrant "Fourth" in the *Timaeus*, which, Plato says, can only be added "by force" to the other three.[60] Just as the introduction of time as the fourth dimension in modern physics postulates an irrepresentable space-time continuum, so the idea of synchronicity with its inherent quality of meaning produces a picture of the world so irrepresentable as to be quite baffling.[61] The advantage, however, of adding this concept is that it makes possible a view which includes the psychoid factor in our description and knowledge of nature—an a priori meaning or "equivalence." The problem that runs like a red thread through the speculations of alchemists for fifteen hundred years thus repeats and solves itself, the so-called axiom of Maria the Jewess (or Copt): "Out of the

---

[59] I am not counting P. A. M. Dirac's multi-dimensionality of time.

[60] Cf. my "Versuch einer psychologischen Deutung des Trinitätsdogmas," in *Symbolik des Geistes* (Zurich, 1948), pp. 323ff.

[61] Sir James Jeans (*Physics and Philosophy*, p. 215) thinks it possible "that the springs of events in this substratum include our own mental activities, so that the future course of events may depend in part on these mental activities." The causalism of this argument does not seem to me altogether tenable.

Third comes the One as the Fourth."[62] This cryptic observation confirms what I said above, that in principle new points of view are not as a rule discovered in territory that is already known, but in out-of-the-way places that may even be avoided because of their bad name. The old dream of the alchemists, the transmutation of chemical elements, this much-derided idea, has become a reality in our own day, and its symbolism, which was no less an object of ridicule, has turned out to be a veritable gold mine for the psychology of the unconscious. Their dilemma of three and four, which began with the story that serves as a setting for the *Timaeus* and extends all the way to the Cabiri scene in *Faust*, Part II, is recognized by a sixteenth-century alchemist, Gerhard Dorn, as the decision between the Christian Trinity and the *serpens quadricornutus*, the four-horned serpent who is the Devil. As though in anticipation of things to come he anathematizes the pagan quaternity which was ordinarily so beloved of the alchemists, on the ground that it arose from the binarius (the number 2) and is thus something material, feminine, and devilish.[63] Dr. von Franz has demonstrated this emergence of trinitarian thinking in the *Parable* of Bernard of Treviso, in Khunrath's *Amphitheatrum*, in Michael Maier, and in the anonymous author of the *Aquarium sapientum*.[64] W. Pauli calls attention to the polemical writings of Kepler and of Robert Fludd, in which Fludd's correspondence theory was the loser and had to make room for Kepler's theory of three principles.[65] The decision in favor of freedom, which in certain respects ran counter to the alchemical tradition, was followed by a scientific epoch that knew nothing of correspondence and clung with passionate insistence to a triadic view of the world—a continuation of the trinitarian type of thinking—which described and

[62] "*ek ton triton to hen tetarton.*" Cf. *Psychology and Alchemy* (New York and London, 1953), p. 23.

[63] "De tenebris contra naturam," in *Theatrum chemicum* (Ursel, 1602), I, pp. 540ff.

[64] Marie-Louise von Franz, "Die Parabel von der Fontina des Grafen von Tarvis" (unpublished MS.).

[65] See Pauli's contribution to the present volume (*Synchronicity: An Acausal Connecting Principle*).

explained everything in terms of space, time, and causality.

The revolution brought about by the discovery of radioactivity has considerably modified the classical views of physics. So great is the change of standpoint that we have to revise the classical schema I made use of above. As I was able, thanks to the friendly interest which Professor Pauli evinced in my work, to discuss these questions of principle with a professional physicist who could at the same time appreciate my psychological arguments, I am in a position to put forward a suggestion that takes modern physics into account. Pauli suggested replacing the opposition of space and time in the classical schema by (conservation of) energy and the space-time continuum. This suggestion led me to a closer definition of the other pair of opposites—causality and synchronicity—with a view to establishing some kind of connection between these two heterogeneous concepts. We finally agreed on the following *quaternio:*

Indestructible Energy

Constant Connection through Effect (Causality) — *Inconstant Connection through Contingency, Equivalence, or "Meaning" (Synchronicity)*

Space-Time Continuum

This schema satisfies on the one hand the postulates of modern physics, and on the other hand those of psychology. The psychological point of view needs clarifying. A causalistic explanation of synchronicity seems out of the question for the reasons given above. It consists essentially of "chance" equivalences. Its *tertium comparationis* rests on the psychoid factors I call archetypes. These are *indefinite,* that is to say they can be known and determined only approximately. Although associated with causal processes, or "carried" by them, they continually go beyond their frame of reference, an infringement to which I would give the name "transgressivity," because the archetypes are not found exclusively in the psychic sphere, but can occur just as much in circumstances that are not psychic (equivalence of an outward physical process with a psychic one). Archetypal equivalences are *contingent* to causal determination, that is to say there exist between them and the causal processes no relations that conform to law. They seem, therefore, to represent a special instance of randomness or chance, or of that "random state" which "runs through time in a way that fully conforms to law," as Andreas Speiser says.[66] It is an initial state which is "not governed by mechanistic law" but is the precondition of law, the chance substrate on which law is based. If we consider synchronicity or the archetypes as the contingent, then the latter takes on the specific aspect of a modality that has the functional significance of a world-constituting factor. The archetype represents *psychic probability,* since it portrays ordinary instinctual events in the form of *types.* It is a special psychic instance of probability in general, which "is made up of the laws of chance and lays down rules for nature just as the laws of mechanics do."[67] We must agree with Speiser that although in the realm of pure intellect the contingent is "a formless substance," it reveals itself to psychic introspection—so far as inward perception can grasp it at all—as an image, or rather a type which underlies not only the psychic equivalences but, remarkably enough, the psychophysical equivalences too.

It is difficult to divest conceptual language of its causalistic coloring. Thus the word "underlying," despite its causalistic connotation, does not refer to anything causal, but simply to an existing quality, an irreducible contingency which is "Just-So." The meaningful coincidence or equivalence of a psychic and a physical state that have no causal relationship to one another means, in general terms, that it is a modality without a cause, an "acausal orderedness." The question now arises whether our definition of synchronicity with reference to the equivalence of psychic and physical processes is capable of expansion, or rather, requires expansion. This requirement seems to force itself on us when we consider the above, wider conception of synchronicity as an "acausal orderedness." Into this category come all "acts of creation," a priori factors such

[66] Über die Freiheit," *Basler Universitätsreden,* XXVIII (1950).
[67] *Ibid.,* p. 6.

as the properties of natural numbers, the discontinuities of modern physics, etc. Consequently we would have to include constant and experimentally reproducible phenomena within the scope of our expanded concept, though this does not seem to accord with the nature of the phenomena included in synchronicity narrowly understood. The latter are mostly individual cases which cannot be repeated experimentally. This is not of course altogether true, as Rhine's experiments show and numerous other experiences with clairvoyant individuals. These facts prove that even in individual cases which have no common measure there are certain regularities and therefore constant factors, from which we must conclude that our narrower conception of synchronicity is probably too narrow and really needs expanding. I incline in fact to the view that synchronicity in the narrower sense is only a particular instance of general acausal orderedness—that, namely, of the equivalence of psychic and physical processes where the observer is in the fortunate position of being able to recognize the *tertium comparationis*. But as soon as he perceives the archetypal background he is tempted to trace the mutual assimilation of independent psychic and physical processes back to a (causal) effect of the archetype, and thus to overlook the fact that they are merely contingent. This danger is avoided if one regards synchronicity as a special instance of general acausal orderedness. In this way we also avoid multiplying our principles of explanation illegitimately, for the archetype *is* the introspectively recognizable form of a priori psychic orderedness. If an external synchronistic process now associates itself with it, it falls into the same basic pattern—in other words, it too is "ordered." This form of orderedness differs from that of the properties of natural numbers or the discontinuities of physics in that the latter have existed from eternity and occur regularly, whereas the forms of psychic orderedness are *acts of creation in time.* That, incidentally, is precisely why I have stressed the element of time as being characteristic of these phenomena and called them *synchronistic*.

The modern discovery of discontinuity (e.g., the orderedness of energy quanta, of radium decay, etc.) has put an end to the sovereign rule of causality and thus to the triad of principles. The territory lost by the latter belonged earlier to the sphere of correspondence and sympathy, concepts which reached their greatest development in Leibniz's idea of pre-established harmony. Schopenhauer knew far too little about the empirical foundations of correspondence to realize how hopeless his causalistic attempt at explanation was. Today, thanks to the ESP experiments, we have a great deal of empirical material at our disposal. We can form some conception of its reliability when we learn from G. E. Hutchinson[68] that the ESP experiments conducted by S. G. Soal and K. M. Goldney have a probability of $1:10^{35}$, this being equivalent to the number of molecules in 250,000 tons of water. There are relatively few experiments in the field of the natural sciences whose results come anywhere near so high a degree of certainty. The exaggerated skepticism in regard to ESP is really without a shred of justification. The main reason for it is simply the ignorance which nowadays, unfortunately, seems to be the inevitable accompaniment of specialism and screens off the necessarily limited horizon of specialist studies from all higher and wider points of view in the most undesirable way. How often have we not found that the so-called "superstitions" contain a core of truth that is well worth knowing! It may well be that the originally magical significance of the word "wish," which is still preserved in "wishing-rod" (divining rod, or magic wand) and expresses not just wishing in the sense of desire but a magical action,[69] and the traditional belief in

---

[68] S. G. Soal, "Science and Telepathy," *Enquiry* (London), I (1948): 2, p. 6.

[69] Jacob Grimm, *Teutonic Mythology*, trans. by J. S. Stallybrass (London, 1883–88), I, p. 137. Wish-objects are magic implements forged by dwarfs, such as Odin's spear Gungnir, Thor's hammer Mjollnir, and Freya's sword (II, p. 870). Wishing is "gotes kraft" (divine power). "Got hât an sie den wunsch geleit und der wünschelruoten hort" (God has bestowed the wish on her and the treasure of [*or:* found by] the wishing-rod). "Beschoenen mit wunsches gewalte" (to make beautiful with the power of the wish) (IV, p. 1329). "Wish" = Sanskrit *manoratha*, literally, "car of the mind" or of the psyche, i.e., wish, desire, fancy. (A. A. Macdonell, *A Practical Sanskrit Dictionary*, London, 1924, s.v.)

the efficacy of prayer, are both based on the experience of concomitant synchronistic phenomena.

Synchronicity is no more baffling or mysterious than the discontinuities of physics. It is only the ingrained belief in the sovereign power of causality that creates intellectual difficulties and makes it appear unthinkable that causeless events exist or could ever occur. But if they do, then we must regard them as *creative acts,* as the continuous creation[70] of a pattern that exists from all eternity, repeats itself sporadically, and is not derivable from any known antecedents. We must of course guard against thinking of every event whose cause is unknown as "causeless." This, as I have already stressed, is admissible only when a cause is not even thinkable. But thinkability is itself an idea that needs the most rigorous criticism. Had the atom[71] corresponded to the original philosophical conception of it, its fissionability would be unthinkable. But once it proves

---

[70] Continuous creation is to be thought of not only as a series of successive acts of creation, but also as the eternal presence of the *one* creative act, in the sense that God "was always the Father and always generated the Son" (Origen, *De principiis*, I, 2, 3), or that he is the "eternal Creator of minds" (Augustine, *Confessions*, XI, 31, trans. F. J. Sheed, London, 1943, p. 273). God is contained in his own creation, "nor does he stand in need of his own works, as if he had place in them where he might abide; but endures in his own eternity, where he abides and creates whatever pleases him, both in heaven and earth" (Augustine, on Ps. 113:14, in *Expositions on the Book of Psalms*, Library of Fathers of the Holy Catholic Church, Vol. V, Oxford, 1853). What happens successively in time is simultaneous in the mind of God: "An immutable order binds mutable things into a pattern, and in this order things which are not simultaneous in time exist simultaneously outside time" (Prosper of Aquitaine, *Sententiae ex Augustino delibatae* [Migne, Jacques Paul (ed.) *Patrologiae cursus completus*, Latin Series, Paris, 1844–80, 221 vols., Vol. LI, col. 433]). "Temporal succession is time in the eternal wisdom of God" (LVII [Migne, col. 455]). Before the Creation there was no time—time only began with created things: "Rather did time arise from the created than the created from time" (CCLXXX [Migne, col. 468]). "There was no time before time, but time was created together with the world" (Anon., *De triplici habitaculo*, VI [Migne, XL, col. 995]).

[71] [From *atmos*, "indivisible, that cannot be cut."—Trans.]

to be a measurable quantity, its non-fissionability becomes unthinkable. Meaningful coincidences are thinkable as pure chance. But the more they multiply and the greater and more exact the correspondence is, the more their probability sinks and their unthinkability increases, until they can no longer be regarded as pure chance but, for lack of a causal explanation, have to be thought of as meaningful arrangements. As I have already said, however, their "inexplicability" is not due to the fact that the cause is unknown, but to the fact that a cause is not even thinkable in intellectual terms. This is necessarily the case when space and time lose their meaning or have become relative, for under those circumstances a causality which presupposes space and time for its continuance can no longer be said to exist and becomes altogether unthinkable.

For these reasons it seems to me necessary to introduce, alongside space, time, and causality, a category which not only enables us to understand synchronistic phenomena as a special class of natural events, but also takes the contingent partly as a universal factor existing from all eternity, and partly as the sum of countless individual acts of creation occurring in time.

Résumé

I have been informed that many readers find it difficult to follow my argument. Acausality and the idea of synchronicity as such, and also the astrological experiment, seem to present especial difficulties to their understanding, and for this reason I should like to make a few additional remarks in order to sum up these three points.

1. ACAUSALITY. If natural law were an absolute truth, then of course there could not possibly be any processes that deviate from it. But since causality is a *statistical* truth, it holds good only on average and thus leaves room for *exceptions* which must somehow be experienceable, that is to say, *real*. I try to regard synchronistic events as acausal exceptions of this kind. They prove to be relatively independent of space and time; they relativize space and time in so far as space presents in

principle no obstacle to their passage and the sequence of events in time is inverted, so that it looks as if an event which has not yet occurred were causing a perception in the present. But if space and time are relative, then causality too loses its validity, since the sequence of cause and effect is either relativized or abolished.

2. SYNCHRONICITY. Despite my express warning I see that this concept has already been confused by the critics with *synchronism*. By synchronicity I mean the occurrence of a *meaningful coincidence in time*. It can take three forms:

a) The coincidence of a certain psychic content with a corresponding objective process which is perceived to take place simultaneously.

b) The coincidence of a subjective psychic state with a phantasm (dream or vision) which later turns out to be a more or less faithful reflection of a "synchronistic," objective event that took place more or less simultaneously, but at a distance.

c) The same, except that the event perceived takes place in the future and is represented in the present only by a phantasm that corresponds to it.

Whereas in the first case an objective event coincides with a subjective content, the synchronicity in the other two cases can only be verified subsequently, though the synchronistic event as such is formed by the coincidence of a neutral psychic state with a phantasm (dream or vision).

Psychological Commentary on *The Tibetan Book of the Dead*[1]

Before embarking upon the psychological commentary, I should like to say a few words about the text itself. The Tibetan Book of the Dead, or the *Bardo Thödol*, is a book of instructions for the dead and dying. Like The Egyptian Book of the Dead, it is meant to be a guide for the dead man during the period of his *Bardo* existence, symbolically described as an intermediate state of forty-nine days' duration between death and rebirth. The text falls into three parts. The first part, called *Chikhai Bardo*, describes the psychic happenings at the moment of death. The second part, or *Chönyid Bardo*, deals with the dream-state which supervenes immediately after death, and with what are called "karmic illusions." The third part, or *Sidpa Bardo*, concerns the onset of the birth-instinct

[1] Dr. Jung's commentary on the ancient Tibetan *Bardo Thödol* is here presented through the courtesy of the Oxford University Press, which has put at my disposal the galley proofs of the volume which is being prepared for a revised reprinting. The commentary was written by Dr. Jung for the German translation of this book, and has not previously appeared in English. The translator of Jung's commentary is R. F. C. Hull.—Ed.

and of prenatal events. It is characteristic that supreme insight and illumination, and hence the greatest possibility of attaining liberation, are vouchsafed during the actual process of dying. Soon afterward, the "illusions" begin which lead eventually to reincarnation, the illuminative lights growing ever fainter and more multifarious, and the visions more and more terrifying. This descent illustrates the estrangement of consciousness from the liberating truth as it approaches nearer and nearer to physical rebirth. The purpose of the instruction is to fix the attention of the dead man, at each successive stage of delusion and entanglement, on the ever-present possibility of liberation, and to explain to him the nature of his visions. The text of the *Bardo Thödol* is recited by the *lāma* in the presence of the corpse.

I do not think I could better discharge my debt of thanks to the two previous translators of the *Bardo Thödol*, the late Lāma Kazi Dawa-Samdup and Dr. Evans-Wentz, than by attempting, with the aid of a psychological commentary, to make the magnificent world of ideas and the problems contained in this treatise a little more intelligible to the Western mind. I am sure that all who read this book with open eyes, and who allow it to impress itself upon them without prejudice, will reap a rich reward.

The *Bardo Thödol*, fitly named by its editor, Dr. W. Y. Evans-Wentz, The Tibetan Book of the Dead, caused a considerable stir in English-speaking countries at the time of its first appearance in 1927. It belongs to that class of writings which are not only of interest to specialists in Mahāyāna Buddhism, but which also, because of their deep humanity and their still deeper insight into the secrets of the human psyche, make an especial appeal to the layman who is seeking to broaden his knowledge of life. For years, ever since it was first published, the *Bardo Thödol* has been my constant companion, and to it I owe not only many stimulating ideas and discoveries but also many fundamental insights. Unlike The Egyptian Book of the Dead, which always prompts one to say too much or too little, the *Bardo Thödol* offers one an intelligible philosophy addressed to human beings rather than to gods or primitive savages. Its philosophy contains the quintessence of Buddhist psychological criticism; and, as such, one can truly say that it is of an unexampled superiority. Not only the "wrathful" but also the "peaceful" deities are conceived as *sangsāric* projections of the human psyche, an idea that seems all too obvious to the enlightened European, because it reminds him of his own banal simplifications. But though the European can easily explain away these deities as projections, he would be quite incapable of positing them at the same time as real. The *Bardo Thödol* can do that, because, in certain of its most essential metaphysical premises, it has the enlightened as well as the unenlightened European at a disadvantage. The ever-present, unspoken assumption of the *Bardo Thödol* is the antinomial character of all metaphysical assertions, and also the idea of the qualitative difference of the various levels of consciousness and of the metaphysical realities conditioned by them. The background of this unusual book is not the niggardly European "either-or," but a magnificently affirmative "both-and." This statement may appear objectionable to the Western philosopher, for the West loves clarity and unambiguity; consequently, one philosopher clings to the position "God is," while another clings equally fervently to the negation "God is not." What would these hostile brethren make of an assertion like the following:

> "Recognizing the voidness of thine own intellect to be Buddhahood, and knowing it at the same time to be thine own consciousness, thou shalt abide in the state of the divine mind of the Buddha."

Such an assertion is, I fear, as unwelcome to our Western philosophy as it is to our theology. The *Bardo Thödol* is in the highest degree psychological in its outlook; but, with us, philosophy and theology are still in the medieval, pre-psychological stage where only the assertions are listened to, explained, defended, criticized and disputed, while the authority that makes them has, by general consent, been deposed as outside the scope of discussion.

Metaphysical assertions, however, are *statements of the*

psyche, and are therefore psychological. To the Western mind, which compensates its well-known feelings of resentment by a slavish regard for "rational" explanations, this obvious truth seems all too obvious, or else it is seen as an inadmissible negation of metaphysical "truth." Whenever the Westerner hears the word "psychological," it always sounds to him like *"only* psychological." For him the "soul" is something pitifully small, unworthy, personal, subjective, and a lot more besides. He therefore prefers to use the word "mind" instead, though he likes to pretend at the same time that a statement which may in fact be very subjective indeed is made by the "mind," naturally by the "Universal Mind," or even—at a pinch—by the "Absolute" itself. This rather ridiculous presumption is probably a compensation for the regrettable smallness of the soul. It almost seems as if Anatole France had uttered a truth which was valid for the whole Western world when, in his *Penguin Island,* Cathérine d'Alexandrie offers this advice to God: *Donnez-leur une ame, mais une petite!* ["Give them a soul, but a little one!"]

It is the psyche which, by the divine creative power inherent in it, makes the metaphysical assertion; it posits the distinctions between metaphysical entities. Not only is it the condition of all metaphysical reality, it *is* that reality.

With this great psychological truth the *Bardo Thödol* opens. The book is not a ceremonial of burial, but a set of instructions for the dead, a guide through the changing phenomena of the *Bardo* realm, that state of existence which continues for forty-nine days after death until the next incarnation. If we disregard for the moment the supra-temporality of the soul—which the East accepts as a self-evident fact—we, as readers of the *Bardo Thödol,* shall be able to put ourselves without difficulty in the position of the dead man, and shall consider attentively the teaching set forth in the opening section, which is outlined in the quotation above. At this point, the following words are spoken, not presumptuously, but in a courteous manner:

"O nobly born (so and so), listen. Now thou art experiencing the Radiance of the Clear Light of Pure Reality. Recognize it. O nobly-born, thy present intellect, in real nature void, not formed into anything as regards characteristics or color, naturally void, is the very Reality, the All-Good.

"Thine own intellect, which is now voidness, yet not to be regarded as of the voidness of nothingness, but as being the intellect itself, unobstructed, shining, thrilling, and blissful, is the very consciousness, the All-good Buddha."

This realization is the *Dharma-Kāya* state of perfect enlightenment; or, as we should express it in our own language, the creative ground of all metaphysical assertion is consciousness, as the invisible, intangible manifestation of the soul. The "Voidness" is the state transcendent over all assertion and all predication. The fullness of its discriminative manifestations still lies latent in the soul.

The text continues:

"Thine own consciousness, shining, void, and inseparable from the Great Body of Radiance, hath no birth, nor death, and is the Immutable Light—Buddha Amitābha."

The soul is assuredly not small, but the radiant Godhead itself. The West finds this statement either very dangerous, if not downright blasphemous, or else accepts it unthinkingly and then suffers from a theosophical inflation. Somehow we always have a wrong attitude to these things. But if we can master ourselves far enough to refrain from our chief error of always wanting to *do* something with things and put them to practical use, we may perhaps succeed in learning an important lesson from these teachings, or at least in appreciating the greatness of the *Bardo Thödol*, which vouchsafes to the dead man the ultimate and highest truth, that even the gods are the radiance and reflection of our own souls. No sun is thereby eclipsed for the Oriental as it would be for the Christian, who would feel robbed of his God; on the contrary, his soul is the light of the Godhead, and the Godhead is the soul. The East can sustain this paradox better than the unfortunate

Angelus Silesius, who even today would be psychologically far in advance of his time.

It is highly sensible of the *Bardo Thödol* to make clear to the dead man the primacy of the psyche, for that is the one thing which life does not make clear to us. We are so hemmed in by things which jostle and oppress that we never get a chance, in the midst of all these "given" things, to wonder by whom they are "given." It is from this world of "given" things that the dead man liberates himself; and the purpose of the instruction is to help him towards this liberation. We, if we put ourselves in his place, shall derive no lesser reward from it, since we learn from the very first paragraphs that the "giver" of all "given" things dwells within us. This is a truth which in the face of all evidence, in the greatest things as in the smallest, is never known, although it is often so very necessary, indeed vital, for us to know it. Such knowledge, to be sure, is suitable only for contemplatives who are minded to understand the purpose of existence, for those who are Gnostics by temperament and therefore believe in a saviour who, like the saviour of the Mandaeans, is called "knowledge of life" (*manda d'hajie*). Perhaps it is not granted to many of us to see the world as something "given." A great reversal of standpoint, calling for much sacrifice, is needed before we can see the world as "given" by the very nature of the psyche. It is so much more straightforward, more dramatic, impressive, and therefore more convincing, to see that all the things happen to me than to observe how I make them happen. Indeed, the animal nature of man makes him resist seeing himself as the maker of his circumstances. That is why attempts of this kind were always the object of secret initiations, culminating as a rule in a figurative death which symbolized the total character of this reversal. And, in point of fact, the instruction given in the *Bardo Thödol* serves to recall to the dead man the experiences of his initiation and the teachings of his *guru*, for the instruction is, at bottom, nothing less than an initiation of the dead into the *Bardo* life, just as the initiation of the living was a preparation for the Beyond. Such was the case, at least, with all the mystery cults in ancient civilizations from the time of the Egyptian and Eleusinian mysteries. In the initiation of the living, however, this "Beyond" is not a world beyond death, but a reversal of the mind's intentions and outlook, a psychological "Beyond" or, in Christian terms, a "redemption" from the trammels of the world and of sin. Redemption is a separation and deliverance from an earlier condition of darkness and unconsciousness, and leads to a condition of illumination and releasedness, to victory and transcendence over everything "given."

Thus far the *Bardo Thödol* is, as Dr. Evans-Wentz also feels, an initiation process whose purpose it is to restore to the soul the divinity it lost at birth. Now it is a characteristic of oriental religious literature that the teaching invariably begins with the most important item, with the ultimate and highest principles which, with us, would come last—as for instance in Apuleius, where Lucius is worshipped as Helios only right at the end. Accordingly, in the *Bardo Thödol*, the initiation is a series of diminishing climaxes ending with rebirth in the womb. The only "initiation process" that is still alive and practiced today in the West is the analysis of the unconscious as used by doctors for therapeutic purposes. This penetration into the ground-layers of consciousness is a kind of rational maieutics in the Socratic sense, a bringing forth of psychic contents that are still germinal, subliminal, and as yet unborn. Originally, this therapy took the form of Freudian psychoanalysis and was mainly concerned with sexual fantasies. This is the realm that corresponds to the last and lowest region of the *Bardo*, known as the *Sidpa Bardo*, where the dead man, unable to profit by the teachings of the *Chikhai* and *Chönyid Bardo*, begins to fall a prey to sexual fantasies and is attracted by the vision of mating couples. Eventually he is caught by a womb and born into the earthly world again. Meanwhile, as one might expect, the Oedipus complex begins to function. If his *karma* destines him to be reborn as a man, he will fall in love with his mother-to-be and will find his father hateful and disgusting. Conversely, the future daughter will be highly attracted by her father-to-be and repelled by her mother. The

European passes through this specifically Freudian domain when his unconscious contents are brought to light under analysis, but he goes in the reverse direction. He journeys back through the world of infantile-sexual fantasy to the womb. It has even been suggested in psychoanalytical circles that the trauma par excellence is the birth-experience itself—nay more, psychoanalysts even claim to have probed back to memories of intra-uterine origin. Here Western reason reaches its limit, unfortunately. I say "unfortunately" because one rather wishes that Freudian psychoanalysis could have happily pursued these so-called intra-uterine experiences still further back; had it succeeded in this bold undertaking, it would surely have come out beyond the *Sidpa Bardo* and penetrated from behind into the lower reaches of the *Chönyid Bardo*. It is true that with the equipment of our existing biological ideas such a venture would not have been crowned with success; it would have needed a wholly different kind of philosophical preparation from that based on current scientific assumptions. But, had the journey back been consistently pursued, it would undoubtedly have led to the postulate of a pre-uterine existence, a true *Bardo* life, if only it had been possible to find at least some trace of an experiencing subject. As it was, the psychoanalysts never got beyond purely conjectural traces of intra-uterine experiences, and even the famous "birth trauma" has remained such an obvious truism that it can no longer explain anything, any more than can the hypothesis that life is a disease with a bad prognosis because its outcome is always fatal.

Freudian psychoanalysis, in all essential aspects, never went beyond the experiences of the *Sidpa Bardo;* that is, it was unable to extricate itself from sexual fantasies and similar "incompatible" tendencies which cause anxiety and other affective states. Nevertheless, Freud's theory is the first attempt made by the West to investigate, as if from below, from the animal sphere of instinct, the psychic territory that corresponds in Tantric Lāmaism to the *Sidpa Bardo*. A very justifiable fear of metaphysics prevented Freud from penetrating into the sphere of the "occult." In addition to this, the *Sidpa* state, if we are to accept the psychology of the *Sidpa Bardo*, is characterized by the fierce wind of *karma*, which whirls the dead man along until he comes to the "womb-door." In other words, the *Sidpa* state permits of no going back, because it is sealed off against the *Chönyid* state by an intense striving downwards, towards the animal sphere of instinct and physical rebirth. That is to say, anyone who penetrates into the unconscious with purely biological assumptions will become stuck in the instinctual sphere and be unable to advance beyond it, for he will be pulled back again and again into physical existence. It is therefore not possible for Freudian theory to reach anything except an essentially negative valuation of the unconscious. It is a "nothing-but." At the same time, it must be admitted that this view of the psyche is typically Western, only it is expressed more blatantly, more plainly, and more ruthlessly than others would have dared to express it, though at bottom they think no differently. As to what "mind" means in this connection, we can only cherish the hope that it will carry conviction. But, as even Max Scheler noted with regret, the power of this "mind" is, to say the least of it, doubtful.

I think, then, we can state it as a fact that with the aid of psychoanalysis the rationalizing mind of the West has pushed forward into what one might call the neuroticism of the *Sidpa* state, and has there been brought to an inevitable standstill by the uncritical assumption that everything psychological is subjective and personal. Even so, this advance has been a great gain, inasmuch as it has enabled us to take one more step behind our conscious lives. This knowledge also gives us a hint of how we ought to read the *Bardo Thödol*—that is, backwards. If, with the help of our Western science, we have to some extent succeeded in understanding the psychological character of the *Sidpa Bardo*, our next task is to see if we can make anything of the preceding *Chönyid Bardo*.

The *Chönyid* state is one of "*karmic* illusion"—that is to say, illusions which result from the psychic residua of previous existences. According to the Eastern view, *karma* implies a sort of psychic theory of heredity based on the hypothesis of reincarnation, which in the last resort is an hypothesis of the supra-temporality of the soul. Neither our scientific knowledge nor our reason can keep in step with this idea. There are too many if's and but's. Above all, we know desperately little about the possibilities of continued existence of the individual soul after death, so little that we cannot even conceive how anyone could prove anything at all in this respect. Moreover, we know only too well, on epistemological grounds, that such a proof would be just as impossible as the proof of God. Hence we may cautiously accept the idea of *karma* only if we understand it as *psychic heredity* in the very widest sense of the word. Psychic heredity does exist—that is to say, there is inheritance of psychic characteristics such as predisposition to disease, traits of character, special gifts, and so forth. It does no violence to the psychic nature of these complex facts if natural science reduces them to what appear to be physical aspects (nuclear structures in cells, and so on). They are essential phenomena of life which express themselves, in the main, psychically, just as there are other inherited characteristics which express themselves, in the main, physiologically, on the physical level. Among these inherited psychic factors there is a special class which is not confined either to family or to race. These are the universal dispositions of the mind, and they are to be understood as analogous to Plato's forms (*eidola*), in accordance with which the mind organizes its contents. One could also describe these forms as *categories* analogous to the logical categories which are always and everywhere present as the basic postulates of reason. Only, in the case of our "forms," we are not dealing with categories of reason but with categories of the *imagination*. As the products of imagination are always in essence visual, their forms must, from the outset, have the character of images and moreover of *typical* images, which is why, following St. Augustine, I call them "archetypes." Comparative religion and mythology are rich mines of archetypes, and so is the psychology of dreams and psychoses. The astonishing parallelism between these images and the ideas they serve to express has frequently given rise to the wildest migration theories, although it would have been far more natural to think of the remarkable similarity of the human psyche at all times and in all places. Archetypal fantasy-forms are, in fact, reproduced spontaneously anytime and anywhere, without there being any conceivable trace of direct transmission. The original structural components of the psyche are of no less surprising a uniformity than are those of the visible body. The archetypes are, so to speak, organs of the pre-rational psyche. They are eternally inherited forms and ideas which have at first no specific content. Their specific content only appears in the course of the individual's life, when personal experience is taken up in precisely these forms. If the archetypes were not pre-existent in identical form everywhere, how could one explain the fact, postulated at almost every turn by the *Bardo Thödol*, that the dead do not know that they are dead, and that this assertion is to be met with just as often in the dreary, half-baked literature of European and American Spiritualism? Although we find the same assertion in Swedenborg, knowledge of his writings can hardly be sufficiently widespread for this little bit of information to have been picked up by every small-town "medium." And a connection between Swedenborg and the *Bardo Thödol* is completely unthinkable. It is a primordial, universal idea that the dead simply continue their earthly existence and do not know that they are disembodied spirits—an archetypal idea which enters into immediate, visible manifestation whenever anyone sees a ghost. It is significant, too, that ghosts all over the world have certain features in common. I am naturally aware of the unverifiable spiritualistic hypothesis, though I have no wish to make it my own. I must content myself with the hypothesis of an omnipresent, but differentiated, psychic structure which is inherited and which necessarily gives a certain form and direction to all experience. For just as the organs of the body are not mere lumps of indifferent, passive matter, but are dynamic, functional complexes which assert themselves with imperious urgency, so also the archetypes, as organs of the psyche, are dynamic, instinctual complexes which determine psychic life to an extraordinary degree. That is why I also call them *dominants* of the unconscious. The layer of unconscious psyche which is made up of these universal dynamic forms I have termed the *collective unconscious*.

So far as I know, there is no inheritance of individual prenatal, or pre-uterine, memories, but there are undoubtedly inherited archetypes which are, however, devoid of content, because, to begin with, they contain no personal experiences. They only emerge into consciousness when personal experiences have rendered them visible. As we have seen, Sidpa psychology consists in wanting to live and to be born. (The *Sidpa Bardo* is the "Bardo of Seeking Rebirth.") Such a state, therefore, precludes any experience of transsubjective psychic realities, unless the individual refuses categorically to be born back again into the world of consciousness. According to the teachings of the *Bardo Thödol*, it is still possible for him, in each of the *Bardo* states, to reach the *Dharma-Kāya* by transcending the four-faced Mount Meru, provided that he does not yield to his desire to follow the "dim lights." This is as much as to say that the dead man must desperately resist the dictates of reason, as we understand it, and give up the supremacy of egohood, regarded by reason as sacrosanct. What this means in practice is complete capitulation to the objective powers of the psyche, with all that this entails; a kind of symbolical death, corresponding to the Judgment of the Dead in the *Sidpa Bardo*. It means the end of all conscious, rational, morally responsible conduct of life, and a voluntary surrender to what the *Bardo Thödol* calls "karmic illusion." *Karmic* illusion springs from belief in a visionary world of an extremely irrational nature, which neither accords with nor derives from our rational judgments but is the exclusive product of uninhibited imagination. It is sheer dream or "fantasy," and every well-meaning person will instantly caution us against it; nor indeed can one see at first sight what is the difference between fantasies of this kind and the phantasmagoria of a lunatic. Very often only a slight *abaissement du niveau mental* is needed to unleash this world of illusion. The terror and darkness of this moment has its equivalent in the experiences described in the opening sections of the *Sidpa Bardo*. But the contents of this *Bardo* also reveal the archetypes, the *karmic* images which appear first in their terrifying form. The *Chönyid* state is equivalent to a deliberately induced psychosis.

One often hears and reads about the dangers of *yoga*, particularly of the ill-reputed *Kundalini yoga*. The deliberately induced psychotic state, which in certain unstable individuals might easily lead to a real psychosis, is a danger that needs to be taken very seriously indeed. These things really are dangerous and ought not to be meddled with in our typically Western way. It is a meddling with fate, which strikes at the very roots of human existence and can let loose a flood of sufferings of which no sane person ever dreamed. These sufferings correspond to the hellish torments of the *Chönyid* state, described in the text as follows:

> "Then the Lord of Death will place round thy neck a rope and drag thee along; he will cut off thy head, tear out thy heart, pull out thy intestines, lick up thy brain, drink thy blood, eat thy flesh, and gnaw thy bones; but thou wilt be incapable of dying. Even when thy body is hacked to pieces, it will revive again. The repeated hacking will cause intense pain and torture."

These tortures aptly describe the real nature of the danger: it is a disintegration of the wholeness of the *Bardo* body, which is a kind of "subtle body" constituting the visible envelope of the psychic self in the after-death state. The psychological equivalent of this dismemberment is psychic dissociation. In its deleterious form it would be schizophrenia (split mind). This most common of all mental illnesses consists essentially in a marked *abaissement du niveau mental* which abolishes the normal checks imposed by the conscious mind and thus gives unlimited scope to the play of the unconscious "dominants."

The transition, then, from the *Sidpa* state to the *Chönyid* state is a dangerous reversal of the aims and intentions of the conscious mind. It is a sacrifice of the ego's stability and a surrender to the extreme uncertainty of what must seem like a chaotic riot of phantasmal forms. When Freud coined the phrase that the ego was "the true seat of anxiety," he was giving voice to a very true and profound intuition. Fear of self-sacrifice lurks deep in every ego, and this fear is often only the precariously controlled demand of the unconscious forces to burst out in full strength. No one who strives for selfhood (individuation) is spared this dangerous passage, for that which is feared also belongs to the wholeness of the self—the subhuman, or suprahuman, world of psychic "dominants" from which the ego originally emancipated itself with enormous effort, and then only partially, for the sake of a more or less illusory freedom. This liberation is certainly a very necessary and very heroic undertaking, but it represents nothing final: it is merely the creation of a *subject*, who, in order to find fulfillment, has still to be confronted by an *object*. This, at first sight, would appear to be the world, which is swelled out with projections for that very purpose. Here we seek and find our difficulties, here we seek and find our enemy, here we seek and find what is dear and precious to us; and it is comforting to know that all evil and all good is to be found out there, in the visible object, where it can be conquered, punished, destroyed, or enjoyed. But nature herself does not allow this paradisal state of innocence to continue forever. There are, and always have been, those who cannot help but see that the world and its experiences are in the nature of a symbol, and that it really reflects something that lies hidden in the subject himself, in his own transsubjective reality. It is from this profound intuition, according to *lamaist* doctrine, that the *Chönyid* state derives its true meaning, which is why the *Chönyid Bardo* is entitled "The *Bardo* of the Experiencing of Reality."

The reality experienced in the *Chönyid* state is, as the last section of the corresponding *Bardo* teaches, the reality of thought. The "thought-forms" appear as realities, fantasy takes on real form, and the terrifying dream evoked by *karma* and played out by the unconscious "dominants" begins. The first to appear (if we read the text backwards) is the all-destroying God of Death, the epitome of all terrors; he is followed by the twenty-eight "power-holding" and sinister goddesses and the fifty-eight "blood-drinking" goddesses. In spite of their daemonic aspect, which appears as a confusing chaos of terrifying attributes and monstrosities, a certain order is already discernible. We find that there are companies of gods and goddesses who are arranged according to the four directions and are distinguished by typical mystic colors. It gradually becomes clearer that all these deities are organized into *mandālas*, or circles, containing a cross of the four colors. The colors are co-ordinated with the four aspects of wisdom:

1. White=the light-path of the mirrorlike wisdom;
2. Yellow=the light-path of the wisdom of equality;
3. Red=the light-path of the discriminative wisdom;
4. Green=the light-path of the all-performing wisdom.

On a higher level of insight, the dead man knows that the real thought-forms all emanate from himself, and that the four light-paths of wisdom which appear before him are the radiations of his own psychic faculties. This takes us straight to the psychology of the *lāmaistic mandāla*, which I have already discussed in the book I brought out with the late Richard Wilhelm, *The Secret of the Golden Flower*.

Continuing our ascent backwards through the region of the *Chönyid Bardo*, we come finally to the vision of the Four Great Ones: the green Amogha-Siddhi, the red Amitābha, the yellow Ratna-Sambhava, and the white Vajra-Sattva. The ascent ends with the effulgent blue light of the *Dharma-Dhātu*, the Buddha-body, which glows in the midst of the *mandāla* from the heart of Vairochana.

With this final vision the *karmic* illusions cease; consciousness, weaned away from all form and from all attachment to objects, returns to the timeless, inchoate state of the *Dharma-Kāya*. Thus (reading backwards) the *Chikhai* state, which appeared at the moment of death, is reached.

I think these few hints will suffice to give the attentive reader some idea of the psychology of the *Bardo Thödol*. The book describes a way of initiation in reverse, which, unlike the eschatological expectations of Christianity, prepares the soul for a descent into physical being. The thoroughly intellectualistic and rationalistic worldly-mindedness of the European makes it advisable for us to reverse the sequence of the *Bardo Thödol* and to regard it as an account of Eastern initiation experiences, though one is perfectly free, if one chooses, to substitute Christian symbols for the gods of the *Chönyid Bardo*. At any rate, the sequence of events as I have described it offers a close parallel to the phenomenology of the European unconscious when it is undergoing an "initiation process," that is to say, when it is being analyzed. The transformation of the unconscious that occurs under analysis makes it the natural analogue of the religious initiation ceremonies, which do, however, differ in principle from the natural process in that they forestall the natural course of development and substitute for the spontaneous production of symbols a deliberately selected set of symbols prescribed by tradition. We can see this in the *Exercitia* of Ignatius Loyola, or in the *yoga* meditations of the Buddhists and Tantrists.

The reversal of the order of the chapters, which I have suggested here as an aid to understanding, in no way accords with the original intention of the *Bardo Thödol*. Nor is the psychological use we make of it anything but a secondary intention, though one that is possibly sanctioned by *lāmaist* custom. The real purpose of this singular book is the attempt, which must seem very strange to the educated European of the twentieth century, to enlighten the dead on their journey through the regions of the *Bardo*. The Catholic Church is the only place in the world of the white man where any provision is made for the souls of the departed. Inside the Protestant camp, with its world-affirming optimism, we only find a few mediumistic "rescue circles," whose main concern is to make the dead aware of the fact that they *are* dead. But, generally speaking, we have nothing in the West that is in any way comparable to the *Bardo Thödol*, except for certain secret writings which are inaccessible to the wider public and to the ordinary scientist. According to tradition, the *Bardo Thödol*, too, seems to have been included among the "hidden" books, as Dr. Evans-Wentz makes clear in his Introduction. As such, it forms a special chapter in the magical "cure of the soul" which extends even beyond death. This cult of the dead is rationally based on the belief in the supra-temporality of the soul, but its irrational basis is to be found in the psychological need of the living to do something for the departed. This is an elementary need which forces itself upon even the most "enlightened" individuals when faced by the death of relatives and friends. That is why, enlightenment or no enlightenment, we still have all manner of ceremonies for the dead. If Lenin had to submit to being embalmed and put on show in a sumptuous mausoleum like an Egyptian pharaoh, we may be quite sure it was not because his followers believed in the resurrection of the body. Apart, however, from the Masses said for the soul in the Catholic Church, the provisions we make for the dead are rudimentary and on the lowest level, not because we cannot convince ourselves of the soul's immortality, but because we have rationalized the above-mentioned psychological need out of existence. We behave as if we did not have this need, and because we cannot believe in a life after death we prefer to do nothing about it. Simpler-minded people follow their own feelings, and, as in Italy, build themselves funeral monuments of gruesome beauty. The Catholic Masses for the soul are on a level considerably above this, because they are expressly intended for the psychic welfare of the deceased and are not a mere gratification of lachrymose sentiments. But the highest application of spiritual effort on behalf of the departed is surely to be found in the instructions of the *Bardo Thödol*. They are so detailed and thoroughly adapted to the apparent changes in the dead man's condition that every serious-minded reader must ask himself whether these wise old *lāmas* might not, after all, have caught a glimpse of the fourth dimension and twitched the veil from the greatest of life's secrets.

Even if the truth should prove to be a disappointment, one feels tempted to concede at least some measure of reality to the vision of life in the *Bardo*. At any rate, it is unexpectedly original, if nothing else, to find the after-death state, of which our religious imagination has formed the most grandiose conceptions, painted in lurid colors as a terrifying dream-state of a progressively degenerative character. The supreme vision comes not at the end of the *Bardo,* but right at the beginning, in the moment of death; what happens afterward is an ever-deepening descent into illusion and obscuration, down to the ultimate degradation of new physical birth. The spiritual climax is reached at the moment when life ends. Human life, therefore, is the vehicle of the highest perfection it is possible to attain; it alone generates the *karma* that makes it possible for the dead man to abide in the perpetual light of the Voidness without clinging to any object, and thus to rest on the hub of the wheel of rebirth, freed from all illusion of genesis and decay. Life in the *Bardo* brings no eternal rewards or punishments, but merely a descent into a new life which shall bear the individual nearer to his final goal. But this eschatological goal is what he himself brings to birth as the last and highest fruit of the labors and aspirations of earthly existence. This view is not only lofty, it is manly and heroic.

The degenerative character of *Bardo* life is corroborated by the spiritualistic literature of the West, which again and again gives one a sickening impression of the utter inanity and banality of communications from the "spirit world." The scientific mind does not hesitate to explain these reports as emanations from the unconscious of the "mediums" and of those taking part in the séance, and even to extend this explanation to the description of the Hereafter given in The Tibetan Book of the Dead. And it is an undeniable fact that the whole book is created out of the archetypal contents of the unconscious. Behind these there lie—and in this our Western reason is quite right—no physical or metaphysical realities, but "merely" the reality of psychic facts, the data of psychic experience. Now whether a thing is "given" subjectively or objectively, the fact remains that it *is*. The *Bardo Thödol* says no more than this, for its five Dhyāni Buddhas are themselves no other than psychic data. That is just what the dead man has to recognize, if it has not already become clear to him during life that his own psychic self and the giver of all data are one and the same. The world of gods and spirits is truly "nothing but" the collective unconscious inside me. To turn this sentence round so that it reads: The collective unconscious is the world of gods and spirits outside me, no intellectual acrobatics are needed, but a whole human lifetime, perhaps even many lifetimes of increasing *completeness*. Notice that I do not say "of increasing perfection," because those who are "perfect" make another kind of discovery altogether.

The *Bardo Thödol* began by being a "closed" book, and so it has remained, no matter what kind of commentaries may be written upon it. For it is a book that will only open itself to spiritual understanding, and this is a capacity which no man is born with, but which he can only acquire through special training and special experience. It is good that such to all intents and purposes "useless" books exist. They are meant for those "queer folk" who no longer set much store by the uses, aims, and meaning of present-day "civilization."

Commentary on
The Secret of the Golden Flower[1]

Introduction

1. DIFFICULTIES ENCOUNTERED BY A EUROPEAN IN TRYING TO UNDERSTAND THE EAST

A thorough Westerner in feeling, I am necessarily deeply impressed by the strangeness of this Chinese text. It is true

[1] Dr. Jung's commentary on "The Secret of the Golden Flower" forms part of a book first published by Kegan Paul, Trench, Trubner and Co., Ltd., London, in 1931, and written in conjunction with the German sinologist Richard Wilhelm. The book is concerned with an ancient esoteric Chinese teaching, the origins of which, according to Professor Wilhelm's explanations, reach back to the days of Lao-Tzu. Its contents represent an account of the religion named "The Golden Elixir of Life." They were transmitted orally until the eighth century A.D., when Liü Yen, the well-known Taoist adept, founded a sect based upon its principles. The first printing is from the Ch'ien-Lung period (18th century). Wilhelm's translation is based upon a private reprinting done in Peking in 1920, motivated by a new religious movement growing out of the exigencies then prevailing in China. As both Wilhelm's and Jung's commentaries indicate, the text expresses the conviction that the psyche and the cosmos are related to each other like the inner

COMMENTARY ON THE SECRET OF THE GOLDEN FLOWER

that some knowledge of Eastern religions and philosophies aids my intellect and intuition in understanding these ideas to a certain extent, just as I can understand the paradoxes of primitive beliefs in terms of "ethnology," or in terms of the "comparative history of religions." Indeed, this is the Western way of hiding one's heart under the cloak of so-called scientific understanding. We do it partly because of the *misérable vanité des savants* which fears and rejects with horror any sign of living sympathy, and partly because a sympathetic understanding might permit contact with an alien spirit to become a serious experience. So-called scientific objectivity would have reserved this text for the philological acuity of sinologues, and would have guarded it jealously from any other interpretation. But Richard Wilhelm penetrated into the secret and mysterious life of Chinese wisdom too deeply to have allowed such a pearl of intuitive insight to disappear in the pigeonholes of the specialists. I am greatly honored that his choice of a psychological commentator has fallen upon me.

This entails the risk, though, that this unique treasure will be swallowed by still another special science. Nonetheless, anyone seeking to minimize the merits of Western science and scholarship is undermining the main support of the European mind. Science is not, indeed, a perfect instrument, but it is a superior and indispensable one that works harm only when taken as an end in itself. Scientific method must serve; it errs when it usurps a throne. It must be ready to serve all branches of science, because each, by reason of its insufficiency, has need of support from the others. Science is the tool of the Western mind and with it more doors can be opened than with bare hands. It is part and parcel of our knowledge and only obscures our insight when it holds that the understanding given by it is the only kind there is. The East has taught us another, wider, more profound, and higher understanding,

---

and outer worlds. Jung's commentary represents a meditation upon this theme and upon the specific features which characterize it in the particular philosophy expressed in the text. I am indebted to Mrs. Cary F. Baynes for her kind permission to use her sensitively revised translation, which she has only recently completed.—Ed.

that is, understanding through life. We know this way only vaguely, as a mere shadowy sentiment culled from religious terminology, and therefore we gladly dispose of Eastern "wisdom" in quotation marks, and relegate it to the obscure territory of faith and superstition. But in this way we lose sight of the "realism" of the East. This text, for instance, does not consist of exaggerated sentiment or overwrought mystical intuitions bordering on the pathological and emanating from ascetic cranks and recluses. It is based on the practical wisdom of the Chinese mind, which we have not the slightest justification for undervaluing.

This assertion may seem bold, perhaps, and is likely to be met with disbelief, but that is not surprising, considering how little is known about the material. Moreover, the strangeness of the material is so arresting that our embarrassment as to how and where the Chinese world of thought might be joined to ours is quite understandable. When faced with this problem of grasping the ideas of the East, the usual mistake of Western man is like that of the student in Faust. Misled by the Devil, he contemptuously turns his back on science, and, carried away by Eastern occultism, takes over yoga practices quite literally and becomes a pitiable imitator. (Theosophy is our best example of this mistake.) And so he abandons the one safe foundation of the Western mind, and loses himself in a mist of words and ideas which never would have originated in European brains, and which can never be profitably grafted upon them.

An ancient adept has said: "If the wrong man uses the right means, the right means work in the wrong way." This Chinese saying, unfortunately all too true, stands in sharp contrast to our belief in the "right" method irrespective of the man who applies it. In reality, in such matters everything depends on the man and little or nothing on the method. For the method is merely the path, the direction taken by a man. The way he acts is the true expression of his nature. If it ceases to be this, then the method is nothing more than an affectation, something artificially added and rootless, serving only the illegitimate goal of self-deception. It becomes a means of fooling oneself and of evading what may perhaps be the implacable law of one's being. This is far removed from the earthborn quality and sincerity of Chinese thought. On the contrary, it is the denial of one's own being, self-betrayal to strange and unclean gods, a cowardly trick for the purpose of usurping psychic superiority, everything in fact which is profoundly contrary to the meaning of the Chinese "method." For these insights result from a way of life that is complete, genuine, and true in the fullest sense; they are insights coming from that ancient, cultural life of China which has grown consistently and coherently from the deepest instincts, and which, for us, is forever remote and inimitable.

Western imitation of the East is doubly tragic in that it comes from an unpsychological misunderstanding as sterile as are the modern escapades in Taos, the blissful South Sea Islands, and Central Africa, where "primitivity" is earnestly being played at while Western civilized man evades his menacing duties, his *Hic Rhodus hic salta*. It is not a question of our imitating, or worse still, becoming missionaries for what is organically foreign, but rather a question of building up our own Western culture, which sickens with a thousand ills. This has to be done on the spot, and by the real European as he is in his Western commonplaceness, with his marriage problems, his neuroses, his social and political delusions, and his whole philosophical disorientation.

We should do well to confess at once, that, fundamentally speaking, we do not understand the complete detachment from the world of a text like this, indeed, that we do not want to understand it. Have we, perhaps, an inkling that a mental attitude which can direct the glance inward to this extent can bring about such detachment only because these people have so completely fulfilled the instinctive demands of their natures that little or nothing prevents them from viewing the invisible essence of the world? Can it be, perhaps, that the premise of such vision is liberation from those ambitions and passions which bind us to the visible world, and does not this liberation result from the sensible fulfillment of instinctive demands, rather than from the premature or fear-born repression of them? Is it that our eyes are opened to the spirit only when the laws of earth are obeyed? Anybody who knows the history of Chinese culture, and has also carefully studied the *I Ching*, that book of wisdom which for thousands of years has permeated all Chinese thought, will not pass over these questions lightly. He will know, moreover, that the views set forth in our text are nothing extraordinary from the Chinese point of view, but are actually inescapable, psychological conclusions.

In our Christian culture, spirit, and the passion of the spirit, were for a long time the greatest values and the things most worth striving for. Only after the decline of the Middle Ages, that is, in the course of the nineteenth century, when spirit began to degenerate into intellect, did a reaction set in against the unbearable dominance of intellectualism. This movement, it is true, committed the pardonable mistake of confusing intellect with spirit, and blaming the latter for the misdeeds of the former (Klages). Intellect does, in fact, harm the soul when it dares to possess itself of the heritage of the spirit. It is in no way fitted to do this, because spirit is something higher than intellect in that it includes not only the latter, but the feelings as well. It is a direction or principle of life that strives toward attaining suprahuman heights. In opposition to it stands the dark, the earthbound principle (yin, the feminine) with its emotionality and instinctiveness that reach far back into the depths of time, and into the roots of physiological continuity. Without a doubt, these concepts are purely intuitive insights, but one cannot very well dispense with them if one is trying to understand the nature of the human soul. China could not do without them because, as the history of Chinese philosophy shows, it has never strayed so far from central psychic facts as to lose itself in a one-sided overdevelopment and overvaluation of a single psychic function. Therefore, the Chinese have never failed to recognize the paradoxes and the polarity inherent in what is alive. The opposites always balanced one another—a sign of high culture. Onesidedness, though it lends momentum, is a mark of barbarism. The reaction which is now beginning in the West against the intellect in favor of feeling, or in favor of intuition, seems to me a mark of cultural advance, a widening of consciousness beyond the narrow limits set by a tyrannical intellect.

I have no wish to undervalue the tremendous differentiation of Western intellect; measured by it, Eastern intellect can be described as childish. (Obviously this has nothing to do with intelligence.) If we should succeed in elevating another, or even a third psychic function to the dignity accorded to the intellect, then the West might expect to surpass the East by a very great margin. Therefore it is sad indeed when the European departs from his own nature and imitates the East or "affects" it in any way. The possibilities open to him would be so much greater if he would remain true to himself and develop out of his own nature all that the East has brought forth from its inner being in the course of the centuries.

In general, and looked at from the incurably external point of view of the intellect, it would seem as if the things so highly valued by the East were nothing desirable for us. Intellect alone cannot fathom at first the practical importance which Eastern ideas might have for us, and that is why it can classify these ideas as philosophical and ethnological curiosities and nothing more. The lack of comprehension goes so far that even learned sinologues have not understood the practical application of the *I Ching,* and have therefore looked on the book as a collection of abstruse magic spells.

2. MODERN PSYCHOLOGY OFFERS A POSSIBILITY OF UNDERSTANDING

Observations made in my practice have opened to me a quite new and unexpected approach to Eastern wisdom. But it must be well understood that I did not have a knowledge, however inadequate, of Chinese philosophy as a starting point. On the contrary, when I began my life-work in the practice of psychiatry and psychotherapy, I was completely ignorant of Chinese philosophy, and only later my professional experience showed me that in my technique I had been unconsciously led along that secret way which has been the preoccupation of the best minds of the East for centuries. This could be taken for a subjective fancy—one reason for my previous hesitation to publish anything on the subject—but Richard Wilhelm, that great interpreter of the soul of China, has fully confirmed the parallel for me. Thus he has given me the courage to write about a Chinese text which belongs entirely to the mysterious shadows of the Eastern mind. At the same time, and this is the extraordinary thing, it is a living parallel to the course of psychic development in my patients, none of whom is Chinese.

In order to make this strange fact more intelligible to the reader, it must be pointed out that just as the human body shows a common anatomy over and above all racial differences, so too, the psyche possesses a common substratum transcending all differences in culture and consciousness. I have called this substratum the collective unconscious. This unconscious psyche, common to all mankind, does not consist merely of contents capable of becoming conscious, but of latent dispositions toward identical reactions. Thus the fact of the collective unconscious is simply the psychic expression of the identity of brain-structure irrespective of all racial differences. This explains the analogy, sometimes even identity, between various myth-motifs and symbols, and the possibility of human understanding in general. The various lines of psychic development start from one common stock whose roots reach back into all the strata of the past. This also is the origin of psychological parallelisms with animals.

Taken purely psychologically, it means that we have common instincts of imagination, and of action. All conscious imagination and action have developed over these unconscious prototypes, and always remain bound up with them. Especially is this the case when consciousness has not attained any high degree of clarity, that is, when, in all its functions, it is more dependent on the instincts than on the conscious will, more governed by affect than by rational judgment. This condition ensures a primitive health of the psyche, which, however, immediately becomes lack of adaptation as soon as circumstances arise calling for a higher moral effort. Instincts suffice only for the individual embedded in nature which, on the whole, remains always the same. An individual who is more often guided by unconscious than by conscious choice tends therefore toward marked psychic conservatism. This is the reason the primitive does not change in the course of thousands of years, and it is also the reason why he fears everything strange and unusual. It might lead him to maladaptation, and thus to the greatest of psychic dangers, namely, a kind of neurosis. A higher and wider consciousness which only comes by means of assimilating the unfamiliar, tends toward autonomy, toward revolution against the old gods who are nothing other than those powerful, unconscious, primal images which, up to this time, have held consciousness in thrall.

The more powerful and independent consciousness, and with it the conscious will, becomes, the more the unconscious is forced into the background. When this happens, it is easily possible for the conscious structures to detach themselves from the unconscious images. Gaining thus in freedom, they break the chains of mere instinctiveness, and finally arrive at a state that is deprived of, or contrary to, instinct. Consciousness thus is torn from its roots and no longer able to appeal to the authority of the primal images; it has Promethean freedom, it is true, but also a godless hybris. It does indeed soar above the earth, even above mankind, but the danger of an upset is there, not for every individual, to be sure, but collectively for the weak members of such a society, who then, again like Prometheus, are chained to the rock by the unconscious. The wise Chinese would say in the words of the *I Ching:* When yang has reached its greatest strength, the dark power of yin is born within its depths, for night begins at midday when yang breaks up and begins to change into yin.

A physician is in a position to see this peripeteia enacted literally in life. He sees, for instance, a successful businessman attaining all his desires regardless of death and the devil, and then, having withdrawn from activity at the height of his success, falling in a short time into a neurosis, which changes him into a querulous old woman, fastens him to his bed, and thus finally destroys him. The picture is complete even to the change from a masculine to a womanish attitude. An exact parallel to this is the legend of Nebuchadnezzar in the Book of Daniel, and indeed, the Caesarean madness in general. Similar cases of one-sided exaggeration in the conscious standpoint, and of the corresponding yin reaction of the unconscious, form no small part of the practice of psychiatrists in our time which so overvalues the conscious will as to believe that "where there is a will there is a way." Not that I wish to detract in the least from the high moral value of conscious willing; consciousness and will may well continue to be considered the highest cultural achievements of humanity. But of what use is a morality that destroys the human being? To bring will and capacity into harmony seems to me to be a better thing than morality. Morality *à tout prix* is a sign of barbarism—more often wisdom is better—but perhaps I look at this through the professional glasses of the physician who has to mend the ills following in the wake of an exaggerated cultural achievement.

Be that as it may. In any case, it is a fact that consciousness, heightened by a necessary one-sidedness, gets so far out of touch with the primal images that a breakdown follows. Long before the actual catastrophe, the signs of error announce themselves as absence of instinct, nervousness, disorientation, and entanglement in impossible situations and problems. When the physician comes to investigate, he finds an unconscious which is in complete rebellion against the values of the conscious, and which, therefore, cannot possibly be assimilated to the conscious, while the reverse of course is altogether out of the question. We are then confronted with an apparently irreconcilable conflict with which human reason cannot deal by sham solutions or dubious compromises. If both of these evasions are rejected, we are faced with the question as to what has become of the much needed unity of personality, and with the necessity of seeking it. And here we come to the path traveled by the East from time immemorial. Quite obviously, the Chinese owe the finding of this path to the fact that they were never able to force the opposites in human nature so far apart that all conscious connection between them was lost. The Chinese have such an all-inclusive consciousness because, as in the case of primitive mentality, the yea and the nay have remained in their original proximity. Nonetheless, they could not escape feeling the collision of the opposites, and therefore they sought out a way of life in which they would be what the Hindu terms *nirdvandva*, free of the opposites.

Our text is concerned with this way, and this same problem comes up with my patients also. There could be no greater mistake than for a Westerner to take up the direct practice of Chinese yoga, for then it would still be a matter of his will and his consciousness, bringing about the very effect to be avoided. The neurosis would then simply be intensified. It cannot be sufficiently strongly emphasized that we are not Orientals, and therefore have an entirely different point of departure in these things. It would also be a great mistake to assume that this is the path every neurotic must travel, or that it is the solution to be sought at every stage of the neurotic problem. It is appropriate only in those cases where the conscious has reached an abnormal degree of development, and has therefore diverged too far from the unconscious. This high degree of consciousness is the *conditio sine qua non*. It would be wrong to wish to open this way to neurotics who are ill because of the undue predominance of the unconscious. For the same reason, this way of development has scarcely any meaning before the middle of life (normally between the ages of thirty-five and forty); in fact, if entered upon too soon, it can be decidedly injurious.

As has been indicated, the reason for looking for a new way was the fact that the fundamental problem of the patient seemed insoluble to me unless violence was done to the one or the other side of his nature. I always worked with the temperamental conviction that fundamentally there are no insoluble problems, and experience justified me in so far as I have often seen individuals simply outgrow a problem which had destroyed others. This "outgrowing," as I formerly called it, on further experience was seen to consist in a new level of consciousness. Some higher or wider interest arose on the person's horizon, and through this widening of his view, the insoluble problem lost its urgency. It was not solved logically in its own terms, but faded out when confronted with a new and stronger life-tendency. It was not repressed and made unconscious, but merely appeared in a different light, and so itself became different. What, on a lower level, had led to the wildest conflicts and to panicky emotions, viewed from the higher level of the personality, now seemed like a storm in the valley seen from a high mountain top. This does not mean that the thunderstorm is robbed of its reality, but instead of being in it, one is now above it. However, since we are both valley and mountain with respect to the psyche, it might seem a vain illusion to feel oneself beyond what is human. One certainly does feel the affect and is shaken and tormented by it, yet at the same time one is aware of a higher consciousness, which prevents one from becoming identical with the affect, a consciousness which takes the affect objectively, and can say, "I know that I suffer." What our text says of laziness: "Laziness of which a man is conscious and laziness of which he is unconscious are a thousand miles apart," holds true in the highest degree of affect also.

Here and there it happened in my practice that a patient grew beyond himself because of unknown potentialities, and this became an experience of prime importance to me. I had learned in the meanwhile that the greatest and most important problems of life are all in a certain sense insoluble. They must be so because they express the necessary polarity inherent in every self-regulating system. They can never be solved, but only outgrown. I therefore asked myself whether this possibility of outgrowing, that is, further psychic development, was not the normal thing, and therefore remaining stuck in a conflict was what was pathological. Everyone must possess that higher level, at least in embryonic form, and in favorable circumstances must be able to develop this possibility. When I examined the way of development of those persons who quietly, and as if unconsciously, grew beyond themselves, I saw that their fates had something in common. The new thing came to them out of obscure possibilities either outside or inside themselves; they accepted it and developed further by means of it. It seemed to me typical that some took the new thing from outside themselves, others from within; or rather that it grew into some persons from without, and into others from within. But it was never something that came exclusively either from within or from without. If it arose from outside, it became a deeply subjective experience; if it arose from within, it became an outer event. But in no case was it conjured into existence through purpose and conscious willing, but rather seemed to be borne on the stream of time.

We are so greatly tempted to turn everything into purpose and method that I deliberately express myself in very abstract terms in order to avoid causing a prejudice in one direction or another. The new thing must not be pigeonholed under any heading, for then it becomes a recipe to be applied mechanically, and it would again be a case of the "right means" in the hands of the wrong man." I have been deeply impressed with the fact that the new thing presented by fate seldom or never corresponds to conscious expectation. And still more remarkable, though the new thing contradicts deeply rooted instincts as we know them, it is a singularly appropriate expression of the total personality, an expression which one could not imagine in a more nearly complete form.

What did these people do in order to achieve the development that liberated them? As far as I could see they did nothing (*wu wei*)[2] but let things happen. As Master Lü-tse teaches in our text, the light rotates according to its own law, if one does not give up one's ordinary occupation. The art of letting things happen, action in nonaction, letting go of oneself, as taught by Meister Eckhart, became for me the key opening the door to the way. We must be able to let things happen in the psyche. For us, this actually is an art of which few people know anything. Consciousness is forever interfering, helping, correcting, and negating, and never leaving the simple growth of the psychic processes in peace. It would be simple enough, if only simplicity were not the most difficult of all things. To begin with, the task consists solely in objectively

---

[2] [Action in nonaction.—Trans.]

observing a fragment of a fantasy in its development. Nothing could be simpler, and yet right here the difficulties begin. No fantasy-fragment seems to appear—or yes, one does—but it is too stupid—hundreds of good excuses are thought up. One cannot concentrate on it—it is too boring—what would it amount to—it is "nothing but," et cetera. The conscious mind raises prolific objections; in fact, it often seems bent upon blotting out the spontaneous fantasy-activity in spite of real insight, even of firm determination on the part of the individual to allow the psychic processes to go forward without interference. Often a veritable cramp of consciousness exists.

If one is successful in overcoming the initial difficulties, criticism is still likely to start in afterwards and attempt to interpret the fantasy, to classify, to estheticize, or to depreciate it. The temptation to do this is almost irresistible. After a complete and faithful observation, free rein can be given to the impatience of the conscious mind; in fact it must be given, else obstructing resistances develop. But each time the fantasy material is to be produced, the activity of consciousness must again be put aside.

In most cases the results of these efforts are not very encouraging at first. They usually consist of webs of fantasy which yield no clear knowledge of their origin or goal. Also, the way of getting at the fantasies is individually different. For many people, it is easiest to write them, others visualize them, and others again draw and paint them with or without visualization. In cases of a high degree of conscious cramp, oftentimes the hands alone can fantasy; they model or draw figures that are often quite foreign to the conscious mind.

These exercises must be continued until the cramp in the conscious mind is released, or, in other words, until one can let things happen, which was the immediate goal of the exercise. In this way, a new attitude is created, an attitude which accepts the nonrational and the incomprehensible, simply because it is what is happening. This attitude would be poison for a person who has already been overwhelmed by things that just happen, but it is of the highest value for one who chooses, with an exclusively conscious critique, only the things acceptable to his consciousness from among the things that happen, and thus is gradually drawn out of the stream of life into a stagnant backwater.

At this point, the way traveled by the two types mentioned above seems to be separate. Both have learned to accept what comes to them. (As Master Lü-tse teaches: "When occupations come to us we must accept them; when things come to us we must understand them from the ground up.") One man will chiefly take what comes to him from without, and the other what comes from within, and, according to the law of life, the one will have to take from the outside something he never could accept before from outside, and the other will accept from within things that he would always have excluded before.

This reversal of one's being means an enlargement, heightening, and enrichment of the personality when the previous values are retained along with the change, provided, of course, that these values are not mere illusions. If the values are not retained, the individual goes over to the other side, and passes from fitness to unfitness, from adaptation to the lack of it, from sense to nonsense, and even from rationality to mental disturbance. The way is not without danger. Everything good is costly, and the development of the personality is one of the most costly of all things. It is a question of yea-saying to oneself, of taking oneself as the most serious of tasks, of being conscious of everything one does, and keeping it constantly before one's eyes in all its dubious aspects—truly a task that taxes us to the utmost.

The Chinese can fall back upon the authority of his entire culture. If he starts on the long way, he does what is recognized as being the best of all the things he could do. But the Westerner who wishes to start upon this way, if he is truly serious, has all authority against him—intellectual, moral, and religious. That is why it is infinitely easier for a man to imitate the Chinese method, and leave behind the troublesome European, or else, to seek again the way back to the medievalism of the Christian Church, and build up once more the European wall intended to separate true Christians from the poor heathen and the ethnographic curiosities dwelling outside. Esthetic or intellectual flirtations with life and fate come to an abrupt end here. The step to higher consciousness leads us out and away from all rear-guard cover and from all safety measures. The individual must give himself to the new way completely, for it is only by means of his integrity that he can go further, and only his integrity can guarantee that his way does not turn out to be an absurd adventure.

Whether a person receives his fate from without or from within, the experiences and events of the way remain the same. Therefore I need say nothing about the manifold outer and inner events, the endless variety of which I could never exhaust in any case. To do so, moreover, would be irrelevant to the text under discussion. But there is much to be said of the psychic states that accompany the further development. These psychic states are expressed symbolically in our text, and in the very symbols which for many years have been familiar to me in my practice.

The Fundamental Concepts

1. TAO

The great difficulty in interpreting this and similar texts[3] for the European mind is due to the fact that the Chinese author always starts from the central point, from the point we would call his objective or goal; in a word, he begins with the ultimate insight he has set out to attain. Thus the Chinese author begins his work with ideas that demand such a comprehensive understanding that a person of discriminating mind must feel that he would be guilty of ridiculous pretension, or even of utter nonsense, if he should embark on an intellectual discourse on the most subtle psychic experiences of the great-

[3] Compare Liu Hua-yang: *Hui Ming Ching, Das Buch vom Bewusstsein und Leben* (*The Book of Consciousness and Life*), translated into German by L. C. Lo, *Chinesische Blätter*, No. 1, Vol. 3, published by Richard Wilhelm.

est minds of the East. For example, our text begins: "That which exists through itself, is called tao." The *Hui Ming Ching* begins with the words: "The most subtle secret of tao is essence and life."

It is characteristic of the Western mind that it has no concept for tao. The Chinese character is made up of the character for "head," and that for "going." Wilhelm translates tao by *Sinn* (Meaning). Others translate it as "way," "providence," or even as "God," as the Jesuits do. This shows the difficulty. "Head" can be taken as consciousness,[4] and "to go" as traveling a way; thus the idea would be: to go consciously, or the conscious way. This agrees with the fact that "the light of heaven" which "dwells between the eyes" as the "heart contained in the "light of heaven," and according to Liu Huayang, are the most important secrets of tao. Now "light" is the symbolical equivalent of consciousness, and the nature of consciousness is expressed by analogies with light. The *Hui Ming Ching* is introduced with the verse:

"If thou wouldst complete the diamond body without outflowing,
Diligently heat the roots of consciousness[5] and life.
Kindle light in the blessed country ever close at hand,
And, there hidden, let thy true self forever dwell."

These verses contain a sort of alchemestic instruction, a method or way of creating the "diamond body" which is also meant by our text. "Heating" is necessary; that is, there must be an intensification of consciousness in order that the dwelling place of the spirit may be "illumined." But not only consciousness, life itself must be intensified. The union of these two produces "conscious life." According to the *Hui Ming Ching*, the ancient sages knew how to bridge the gap between consciousness and life because they cultivated both. In this

[4] The head is also the "seat of heavenly light."
[5] In the *Hui Ming Ching*, "essence" and "consciousness" are used interchangeably.

way the *shêli*, the immortal body, is "melted out," and in this way "the great tao is completed."[6]

If we take tao to be the method or conscious way by which to unite what is separated, we have probably come close to the psychological content of the concept. In any case, the separation of consciousness from life cannot very well be understood to mean anything but what I have described above as a deviation, or deracination, of consciousness. Without doubt also, the realization of the opposite hidden in the unconscious, i.e., the "reversal" signifies reunion with the unconscious laws of being, and the purpose of this reunion is the attainment of conscious life, or, expressed in Chinese terms, the bringing about of tao.

2. THE CIRCULAR MOVEMENT AND THE CENTER

As has already been pointed out, the union of the opposites[7] on a higher level of consciousness is not a rational thing, nor is it a matter of will; it is a psychic process of development which expresses itself in symbols. Historically, this process has always been represented in symbols, and today the development of individual personality still presents itself in symbolical figures. This fact was revealed to me in the following observations. The spontaneous fantasy products we mentioned above become more profound and concentrate themselves gradually around abstract structures which apparently represent "principles," true Gnostic *archai*. When the fantasies are chiefly expressed in thoughts, the results are intuitive formulations of dimly felt laws or principles, which at first tend to be dramatized or personified. (We shall come back to these again later.) If the fantasies are expressed in drawings, symbols appear which are chiefly of the so-called mandāla[8] type. *Mandāla* means a circle, more especially a magic circle, and

[6] *Loc. cit.*, p. 104.
[7] Compare my discussion in *Psychological Types*, Chap. v.
[8] [For a discussion of the mandāla, see Heinrich Zimmer, *Kunstform und Yoga im Indischen Kultbild*, Berlin, 1926.—TRANS.]

COMMENTARY ON THE SECRET OF THE GOLDEN FLOWER   319

this symbol is not only to be found all through the East, but also among us; mandālas are amply represented in the Middle Ages. The early Middle Ages are especially rich in Christian mandālas, and for the most part show Christ in the center, with the four evangelists, or their symbols, at the cardinal points. This conception must be a very ancient one, for the Egyptians[9] represented Horus with his four sons in the same way. (It is known that Horus with his four sons has close connections with Christ and the four evangelists.) Later there is to be found an unmistakable and very interesting mandāla in Jacob Boehme's book on the soul.[10] This latter mandāla, it is clear, deals with a psycho-cosmic system strongly colored by Christian ideas. Boehme calls it the "philosophical eye,"[11] or the "mirror of wisdom," which obviously means a summa of secret knowledge. For the most part, the mandāla form is that of a flower, cross, or wheel, with a distinct tendency toward quadripartite structure. (One is reminded of the *tetraktys*, the fundamental number in the Pythagorean system.) Mandālas of this sort are also to be found in the sand paintings used in the ceremonies of the Pueblo and Navajo Indians.[12] But the most beautiful mandālas are, of course, those of the East, especially those belonging to Tibetan Buddhism. The symbols of our text are represented in these mandālas. I have also found mandāla drawings among the mentally ill, and indeed among persons who certainly did not have the least idea of any of the connections we have discussed.[13]

Among my patients I have come across cases of women who did not draw mandālas but who danced them instead. In India this type is called mandāla *nrithya*, or mandāla dance, and

[9] Compare Wallis Budge, *The Gods of the Egyptians*.

[10] *For the Questions of the Soule*, 1602, first English translation.

[11] Compare the Chinese concept of the heavenly light between the eyes.

[12] Matthews, *The Mountain Chant*. Fifth Annual Report of the Bureau of Ethnology, 1883–84, and Stevenson, *Ceremonial of Hasjelti Dailjiis*, Eighth Annual Report of the Bureau of Ethnology, 1886–87.

[13] I have published the mandāla of a somnambulist in *Collected Papers on Analytical Psychology*.

the dance figures express the same meanings as the drawings. My patients can say very little about the meaning of the symbols but are fascinated by them and find them in some way or other expressive and effective with respect to their psychic condition.

Our text promises to "reveal the secret of the Golden Flower of the Great One." The Golden Flower is the light, and the light of heaven is tao. The Golden Flower is a mandāla symbol which I have often met with in the material brought me by my patients. It is drawn either seen from above as a regular geometric ornament or as a blossom growing from a plant. The plant is frequently a structure in brilliant fiery colors growing out of a bed of darkness, and carrying the blossom of light at the top, a symbol similar to that of the Christmas tree. A drawing of this kind also expresses the origin of the Golden Flower, for according to the *Hui Ming Ching*, the "germinal vesicle" is nothing other than the "yellow castle," the "heavenly heart," the "terrace of life," the "square inch field of the square foot house," the "purple hall of the city of jade," the "dark pass," the "space of former heaven," the "dragon castle at the bottom of the sea." It is also called the "border region of the snow mountains," the "primal pass," the "realm of the greatest joy," the "land without boundaries," and the "altar upon which consciousness and life are made." "If a dying man does not know this seed place," says the *Hui Ming Ching*, "he will not find the unity of consciousness and life in a thousand births and ten thousand aeons."

The beginning, in which everything is still one, and which therefore appears as the highest goal, lies at the bottom of the sea in the darkness of the unconscious. In the germinal vesicle, life and consciousness (for "essence" and "life," hsing-ming) are still a "unity,"[14] "inseparably mixed like the seed of fire in the refining furnace." "Inside the germinal vesicle is the fire of the ruler." "In the germinal vesicle all wise men have begun their work." Note the fire analogies. I know a series of European mandāla drawings in which something like

[14] *Hui Ming Ching*, p. 105.

a plant seed surrounded by its coverings is shown floating in water, and from the depths below, fire penetrating the seed, makes it grow, and causes the formation of a large golden flower from within the germinal vesicle.

This symbolism refers to a sort of alchemical process of refining and ennobling; darkness gives birth to light; out of the "lead of the water-region," grows the noble gold; what is unconscious becomes conscious in the form of a process of life and growth. (Hindu Kundalini yoga[15] affords a complete analogy.) In this way the union of consciousness and life takes place.

When my patients produce these mandāla pictures it is, of course, not through suggestion; similar pictures were being made long before I knew their meaning or their connection with the practices of the East, which, at that time, were wholly unfamiliar to me. The pictures came quite spontaneously and from two sources. One source is the unconscious, which spontaneously produces such fantasies; the other source is life, which, if lived with complete devotion, brings an intuition of the self, the individual being. Awareness of the individual self is expressed in the drawing, while the unconscious exacts devotedness to life. For quite in accord with the Eastern conception, the mandāla symbol is not only a means of expression, but works an effect. It reacts upon its maker. Very ancient magical effects lie hidden in this symbol for it derives originally from the "enclosing circle," the "charmed circle," the magic of which has been preserved in countless folk-customs.[16] The image has the obvious purpose of drawing a *sulcus primigenius*, a magical furrow around the center, the *templum*, or temenos (sacred precinct), of the innermost personality, in order to prevent "flowing out," or to guard by apotropaeic means against deflections through external influences. The magical practices are nothing but the projections of psychic events, which are here applied in reverse to the psyche, like a kind of spell on one's own personality. That is

---

[15] A. Avalon, *The Serpent Power* (London, 1931).
[16] See the excellent collection of E. F. Knuchel, *Die Umwandlung in Kult, Magie und Rechtsgebrauch* (Basel 1919).

to say, by means of these concrete performances, the attention, or better said, the interest, is brought back to an inner, sacred domain, which is the source and goal of the soul. This inner domain contains the unity of life and consciousness, which, though once possessed, has been lost, and must now be found again.

The unity of these two, life and consciousness, is tao, whose symbol would be the central white light (compare the Bardo Thödol).[17] This light dwells in the "square inch," or in the "face," that is, between the eyes. It is the image of the creative point, a point having intensity without extension, thought of as connected with the space of the "square inch," the symbol for that which has extension. The two together make tao. Essence, or consciousness (hsing), is expressed in light symbolism, and is therefore intensity, while life (ming), would coincide with extensity. The first has the character of the yang principle, the latter of the yin. The above-mentioned mandāla of a somnambulist girl, fifteen-and-a-half years old, whom I had under observation thirty years ago, shows in its center, a "spring of life-force" without extension, which in its emanations collides directly with a contrary space-principle—a perfect analogy with the fundamental idea of the Chinese text.

The "enclosure," or *circumambulatio,* is expressed in our text by the idea of a "circulation." The "circulation" is not merely motion in a circle, but means, on the one hand, the marking off of the sacred precinct, and, on the other, fixation and concentration. The sun wheel begins to run; that is to say, the sun is animated, and begins to take its course, or, in other words, tao begins to work and to take over the leadership. Action is reversed into nonaction; all that is peripheral is subjected to the command of what is central. Therefore it is said: "Movement is only another name for mastery." Psychologically, this circulation would be the "turning in a circle around oneself," whereby, obviously, all sides of the personality become involved. "The poles of light and darkness are made to rotate," that is, day and night alternate.

[17] W. Y. Evans-Wentz, *The Tibetan Book of the Dead* (London, 1927).

> *"Es wechselt Paradieseshelle
> Mit tiefer, schauervoller Nacht."*[18]

Thus the circular movement also has the moral significance of activating all the light and the dark forces of human nature, and with them, all the psychological opposition of whatever kind they may be. It is self-knowledge by means of self-incubation (Hindu *tapas*). A similar archetypal concept of a perfect being is that of the Platonic man, round on all sides and uniting within himself the two sexes.

One of the finest parallels to what has been said here is the description of his central experience given by Edward Maitland, the co-worker of Anna Kingsford.[19] He had discovered that during reflection on an idea, related ideas became visible, so to speak, in a long series apparently reaching back to their source, which to him was the divine spirit. By means of concentration on this series, he tried to penetrate to their origin. He says: "I was absolutely without knowledge or expectation when I yielded to the impulse to make the attempt. I simply experimented on a faculty . . . being seated at my writing-table the while in order to record the results as they came, and resolved to retain my hold on my outer and circumferential consciousness, no matter how far towards my inner and central consciousness I might go. For I knew not whether I should be able to regain the former if I once quitted my hold of it, or to recollect the facts of the experience. At length I achieved my object, though only by a strong effort, the tension occasioned by the endeavor to keep both extremes of the consciousness in view at once being very great.

"Once well started on my quest, I found myself traversing a succession of spheres or belts . . . the impression produced being that of mounting a vast ladder stretching from the circumference towards the center of a system, which was at once my own system, the solar system, and the universal system, the three systems being at once diverse and identical. . . .

---

[18] ["The radiance of Paradise alternates with deep, dreadful night" (Faust).—Trans.]

[19] Edward Maitland, *Anna Kingsford, Her Life, Letters, Diary, and Work* (London, 1896).

Presently, by a supreme, and what I felt must be a final effort . . . I succeeded in polarizing the whole of the convergent rays of my consciousness into the desired focus. And at the same instant, as if through the sudden ignition of the rays thus fused into a unity, I found myself confronted with a glory of unspeakable whiteness and brightness, and of a lustre so intense as well-nigh to beat me back. . . . But though feeling that I had to explore further, I resolved to make assurance doubly sure by piercing if I could the almost blinding lustre, and seeing what it enshrined. With a great effort I succeeded, and the glance revealed to me that which I had felt must be there. . . . It was the dual form of the Son . . . the unmanifest made manifest, the unformulate formulate, the unindividuate individuate, God as the Lord, proving through His duality that God is Substance as well as Force, Love as well as Will, Feminine as well as Masculine, Mother as well as Father." He found that God is two in one like man. Besides this, he noticed something that our text also emphasizes, namely, "suspension of breathing." He says ordinary breathing stopped and was replaced by an internal respiration, "as if by breathing of a distinct personality within and other than the physical organism." He took this being to be the entelechy of Aristotle, and the inner Christ of the Apostle Paul, the "spiritual and substantial individuality engendered within the physical and phenomenal personality, and representing, therefore, the rebirth of man on a plane transcending the material."

This genuine[20] experience contains all the essential symbols of our text. The phenomenon itself, that is, the vision of light, is an experience common to many mystics, and one that is undoubtedly of the greatest significance, because in all times and places it appears as the unconditional thing, which unites in itself the greatest power and the profoundest meaning. Hil-

---

[20] Such experiences are genuine, but their genuineness does not prove that all the conclusions or convictions forming their context are necessarily sound. Even in cases of lunacy one comes across perfectly valid psychic experiences.

[The above note was added by the author to the English translation.—TRANS.]

degarde of Bingen, an outstanding personality quite apart from her mysticism, expresses herself about her central vision in a similar way. "Since my childhood," she says, "I always see a light in my soul, but not with the outer eyes, nor through the thoughts of my heart; neither do the five outer senses take part in this vision. . . . The light I perceive is not of a local kind, but is much brighter than the cloud which bears the sun. I cannot distinguish height, breadth, or length in it. . . . What I see or learn in such a vision stays long in my memory. I see, hear, and know in the same moment. . . . I cannot recognize any sort of form in this light, although I sometimes see in it another light that is known to me as the living light. . . . While I am enjoying the spectacle of this light, all sadness and sorrow disappear from my memory. . . ."

I know a few individuals who are familiar with this phenomenon from personal experience. As far as I have been able to understand it, the phenomenon seems to have to do with an acute state of consciousness, as intensive as it is abstract, a "detached" consciousness (see below), which, as Hildegarde pertinently remarks, brings up to consciousness regions of psychic events ordinarily covered with darkness. The fact that the general bodily sensations disappear during such an experience shows that their specific energy has been withdrawn from them, and apparently has gone toward heightening the clarity of consciousness. As a rule, the phenomenon is spontaneous, coming and going on its own initiative. Its effect is astonishing in that it almost always brings about a solution of psychic complications, and thereby frees the inner personality from emotional and intellectual entanglements, creating thus a unity of being, which is universally felt as "liberation."

The conscious will cannot attain such a symbolic unity because the conscious is partisan in this case. Its opponent is the collective unconscious which does not understand the language of the unconscious. Therefore it is necessary to have the magic of the symbol which contains those primitive analogies that speak to the unconscious. The unconscious can only be reached and expressed by symbols, which is the reason why the process of individuation can never do without the symbol.

The symbol is the primitive expression of the unconscious, but at the same time it is also an idea corresponding to the highest intuition produced by consciousness.

The oldest mandāla drawing known to me is a palaeolithic so-called "sun wheel," recently discovered in Rhodesia. It also is based on the principle of four. Things reaching so far back in human history naturally touch upon the deepest layers of the unconscious and affect the latter where conscious speech shows itself to be quite impotent. <u>Such things cannot be thought up but must grow again from the forgotten depths</u>, if they are to express the deepest insights of consciousness and the loftiest intuitions of the spirit. Coming from these depths they blend together the uniqueness of present-day consciousness with the age-old past of life.

Phenomena of the Way

1. THE DISINTEGRATION OF CONSCIOUSNESS

Whenever the narrowly delimited, but intensely clear, individual consciousness meets the immense expansion of the collective unconscious, there is danger because the latter has a definitely disintegrating effect on consciousness. Indeed, according to the exposition of the *Hui Ming Ching*, this effect belongs to the peculiar phenomena of Chinese yoga practice. It is said there[21]: "Every thought-fragment takes shape and becomes visible in color and form. All the powers of the soul unfold their traces."[22] One of the illustrations accompanying the book shows a sage sunk in contemplation, his head surrounded by tongues of fire, out of which five human figures emerge: these five split up again into twenty-five smaller figures. This would be a schizophrenic process if it were to become a permanent state. Therefore the instructions, as though

[21] *Loc. cit.*, p. 112.
[22] Cf. the recurrent memories of earlier incarnations that arise during contemplation.

warning the adept, say: "Figures formed out of the fire of the spirit, are only empty colors and forms. The light of the essence streams back to primal truth."

Thus it is understandable that the text returns to the protecting figure of the "enclosing circle." It is intended to prevent "outflowing," and to protect the unity of consciousness from being split apart by the unconscious. Moreover, the Chinese concept points a way toward lessening the disintegrating effect of the unconscious; it describes the "thought-figures" or "thought-fragments" as "empty colors and shapes," and thus depotentializes as much as possible. This idea runs through the whole of Buddhism (especially the *Mahāyāna* form), and, in the instructions to the dead in *The Tibetan Book of the Dead*, it is even pushed to the point of explaining favorable as well as unfavorable gods as illusions still to be overcome. It certainly is not within the competence of the psychologist to establish the metaphysical truth or falsity of this idea; he must be content to determine wherever possible what has psychic effect. In doing this, he need not bother himself as to whether the shape in question is a transcendental illusion or not, since faith, not science, has to decide this point. We are working here in a field which for a long time has seemed to be outside the domain of science, and which has therefore been looked upon as wholly illusory. But there is no scientific justification for such an assumption, for the substantiality of these things is not a scientific problem since it would lie beyond the power of human perception and judgment, in any case, and therefore beyond any possibility of proof. The psychologist is not concerned with the substance of these complexes, but with the psychic experience. Without a doubt they are psychic contents which can be experienced, and which have an indisputable autonomy. They are fragmentary psychic systems which either appear spontaneously in ecstatic states and, under certain circumstances, elicit powerful impressions and effects, or else become fixed as mental disturbances in the form of delusions and hallucinations, thus destroying the unity of the personality.

The psychiatrist is prone to believe in toxins and the like, and to explain schizophrenia (splitting of the mind in a psychosis) in these terms, and to put no emphasis on the psychic contents. On the other hand, in psychogenetic disturbances (hysteria, compulsion neurosis, etc.), where the question of toxic effects and cell degeneration cannot possibly arise, spontaneous split-off complexes are to be found, in somnambulistic states for example. Freud, it is true, would like to explain these as due to unconscious repression of sexuality, but this explanation is by no means valid for all cases, because contents which the conscious cannot assimilate can evolve spontaneously out of the unconscious, and the repression hypothesis is inadequate in such cases. Moreover, the essential autonomy of these elements can be observed in the affects of daily life which obstinately obtrude themselves against our wills, and then, in spite of our earnest efforts to repress them, overwhelm the ego and force it under their control. No wonder that the primitive sees in these moods either a state of possession, or sets them down to a loss of soul. Our colloquial speech reflects the same thing when we say: "I don't know what has got into him today"; "He is ridden by the devil"; "He is beside himself"; "He behaves as if possessed." Even legal practice recognizes a degree of diminished responsibility in a state of affect. <u>Autonomic psychic contents thus are quite common experiences for us. Such contents have a disintegrating effect on the conscious mind.</u>

Besides the ordinary, familiar effects, there are subtler, more complex emotional states which can no longer be described as affects pure and simple but which are complicated, fragmentary psychic systems. The more complicated they are, the more they have the character of personalities. As constituent factors of the psychic personality, they necessarily have the character of "persons." Such fragmentary systems appear especially in mental diseases, in cases of psychogenetic splitting of the personality (double personality), and of course in mediumistic phenomena. They are also encountered in religious phenomena. Many of the earlier gods have evolved out of "persons" into personified ideas, and finally into abstract ideas, for, activated unconscious contents always appear first as projections upon the outside world. In the course of mental development, consciousness gradually assimilates them as projections in space and reshapes them into conscious ideas which then forfeit their originally autonomous and personal character. As we know, some of the old gods have become mere descriptive attributes via astrology (martial, jovial, saturnine, erotic, logical, lunatic, and so on).

The instructions of *The Tibetan Book of the Dead* in particular enable us to see how greatly the conscious is threatened with disintegration through these figures. Again and again, the dead are instructed not to take these shapes for truth, and not to confuse their murky appearance with the pure white light of *Dharma-Kāya* ("the divine body of truth"). The meaning is that they are not to project the one light of highest consciousness into concretized figures, and in such a way dissolve it into a plurality of autonomous fragmentary systems. If there were no danger of this, and if these systems were not menacingly autonomous and divergent, such urgent instructions would not be necessary. If we consider the simpler, polytheistically orientated attitude of the Eastern mind, these instructions would almost be the equivalent of warnings to a Christian not to let himself be blinded by the illusion of a personal God, not to mention a Trinity and innumerable angels and saints.

If tendencies toward disassociation were not inherent in the human psyche, parts never would have been split off; in other words, neither spirits nor gods would ever have come to exist. That is the reason, too, that our time is so utterly godless and profane, for we lack knowledge of the unconscious psyche, and pursue a cult of consciousness to the exclusion of all else. Our true religion is a monotheism of consciousness, a possession by it, coupled with a fanatical denial that there are parts of the psyche which are autonomous. But we differ from the Buddhist yoga doctrine in that we even deny that such autonomous parts are experienceable. A great psychic danger arises here, because the parts then behave like any other repressed contents: they necessarily induce wrong attitudes, for the repressed material appears again in consciousness in a spurious form. This fact, which is so striking in every case of neurosis, holds true also for collective psychic phenomena. In this respect, our time is caught in a fatal error; we believe we can criticize religious facts intellectually; we think, for instance, like Laplace, that God is a hypothesis which can be subjected to intellectual treatment, to affirmation or denial. It is completely forgotten that the reason mankind believes in the "daemon" has nothing whatever to do with outside factors, but is due to simple perception of the powerful inner effect of the autonomous parts. This effect is not nullified by criticizing its name intellectually, nor by describing it as false. The effect is collectively always present; the autonomous systems are always at work, because the fundamental structure of the unconscious is not touched by the fluctuations of a transitory consciousness.

If we deny the existence of the autonomous systems, imagining that we have got rid of them by a critique of the name, then their effect which nevertheless continues cannot be understood, and they can no longer be assimilated to consciousness. Then they become an inexplicable factor of disturbance which we finally assume must exist somewhere or other outside of ourselves. In this way, a projection of the autonomous systems results, and at the same time, a dangerous situation is created, because the disturbing effects are now attributed to bad will outside ourselves which of course is not to be found anywhere but at our neighbor's—*de l'autre côté de la rivière*. This leads to collective delusions, political "incidents," and revolution, in a word, to destructive mass psychoses.

Insanity is possession by an unconscious content which, as such, is not assimilated to consciousness; nor can it be assimilated, since the conscious mind has denied the existence of such contents. Expressed in terms of religion, the attitude is equivalent to saying: "We no longer have any fear of God and believe that everything is to be judged by human standards." This *hybris*, that is, this narrowness of consciousness, is always the shortest way to the insane asylum. I recommend the excellent presentation of this problem in H. G. Wells' novel, *Christina Alberta's Father,* and Schreber's *Denkwürdigkeiten eines Nervenkranken.*[23]

The enlightened European is likely to be relieved when it is said in the *Hui Ming Ching* that the "shapes formed from the fire of the spirit are only empty colors and forms." That sounds quite European and seems to suit our reason excellently. Indeed, we think we can flatter ourselves at having already reached these heights of clarity because we imagine we have left such phantoms of gods far behind. But what we have outgrown are only the word-ghosts, not the psychic facts which were responsible for the birth of the gods. We are still as possessed by our autonomous psychic contents as if they were gods. Today they are called phobias, compulsions, and so forth, or in a word, neurotic symptoms. The gods have become diseases; not Zeus but the solar plexus now rules Olympus and causes the curious symptoms of the physician's consulting room, or disturbs the brains of the politicians and journalists who then unwittingly release mental epidemics.

So it is better for Western man if at the start he does not know too much about the secret insight of Eastern wise men, for it would be a case of the "right means in the hands of the wrong man." Instead of allowing himself to be convinced once more that the daemon is an illusion, the Westerner ought again to experience the reality of this illusion. He ought to learn to recognize these psychic powers again, and not wait until his moods, nervous states and hallucinations make clear to him in the most painful way possible that he is not the only master in his house. The products of the splitting tendencies are actual psychic personalities of relative reality. They are real when they are not recognized as such and are therefore projected; relatively real when they are related to the conscious (in religious terms: when a cult exists); but they are unreal to the extent that consciousness has begun to detach itself from its contents. However, this is only the case when life has been lived so exhaustively, and with such devotedness, that no more unfulfilled obligations to life exist, when, therefore, no

[23] Trans. "Memoirs of my Nervous Illness" (London, 1955).

desires that cannot be sacrificed unhesitatingly stand in the way of inner detachment from the world. It is futile to lie to ourselves about this. Wherever we are still attached, we are still possessed; and when one is possessed, it means the existence of something stronger than oneself. ("Truly from thence thou wilt ne'er come forth until thou hast paid the last farthing.") It is not a matter of indifference whether one calls something a "mania" or a "god." To serve a mania is detestable and undignified; to serve a god is decidedly more meaningful and more productive because it means an act of submission to a higher, spiritual being. The personification enables one to see the relative reality of the autonomous psychic part, and thus makes its assimilation possible and depotentializes the forces of fate. Where the god is not acknowledged, ego-mania develops, and out of this mania comes illness.

Yoga teaching takes the acknowledgement of the gods for granted. Its secret instruction is therefore only intended for him whose light of consciousness is on the point of disentangling itself from the powers of fate, in order to enter into the ultimate undivided unity, into the "center of emptiness," where "dwells the god of utmost emptiness and life," as our text says. "To hear such a teaching is difficult to attain in thousands of aeons." Clearly the veil of *Maya* cannot be lifted by a mere decision of reason, but demands the most thoroughgoing and persevering preparation consisting in the full payment of all debts to life. For as long as unconditional attachment through *cupiditas* exists, the veil is not lifted, and the heights of a consciousness free of contents and free of illusion are not reached; nor can any trick nor any deceit bring this about. It is an ideal that can be "finally" realized only in death. Until then there "exist" real and relatively real figures of the unconscious.

2. ANIMUS AND ANIMA

According to our text there among the figures of the unconscious are not only gods but also the animus and anima. The word *hun* is translated by Wilhelm as animus. Indeed, the concept "animus" seems appropriate for *hun*, the character for which is made up of the character for "clouds" and that for "daemon." Thus *hun* means "cloud-daemon," a higher "breath-soul" belonging to the yang principle and therefore masculine. After death, *hun* rises upward and becomes *shên*, the "expanding and self-revealing" spirit or god. "Anima," called *p'o*, and written with the characters for "white," and for "daemon," that is, "white ghost," belongs to the lower, earth-bound, bodily soul, the yin principle, and is therefore feminine. After death, it sinks downward and becomes *kuei* (daemon), often explained as the "one who returns" (i.e., to earth), a revenant, a ghost. The fact that the animus and the anima part after death and go their ways independently shows that, for the Chinese consciousness, they are distinguishable psychic factors which have markedly different effects, and, despite the fact that originally they are united in "one effective true essense," in the "house of the Creative," they are two. "The animus is in the heavenly heart; by day it lives in the eyes [that is, consciousness]; at night it dreams in the liver." It is that "which we have received from the great emptiness, that which is identical in form with the primal beginning." The anima, on the other hand, is the "power of what is heavy and murky"; it clings to the bodily, fleshly heart. "Desires, and impulses to anger" are its effects. "Whoever is sombre and moody on waking, is fettered by the anima."

Many years ago, before Wilhelm made me acquainted with this text, I used the concept "anima"[24] in a way quite analogous to the Chinese definition of *p'o*, and of course entirely apart from any metaphysical premise. To the psychologist, the anima is not a transcendental being but something quite within the range of experience. For as the Chinese definition also makes clear, affective conditions are immediate experiences. But why does one speak of anima and not simply of moods? The reason is that affects have an autonomous character, and therefore most people are under their power. But, as we have seen, affects are delimitable contents of consciousness, parts of the personality. As parts of the personality, they

[24] I refer the reader to the comprehensive presentation in my book, *Two Essays on Analytical Psychology*. (New York, 1953.)

partake of its character, and can therefore be easily personified, a process which is still going on today, as the examples cited above have shown. The personification is not an idle invention, inasmuch as the individual stirred by affect does not show a neutral character, but a quite distinct one, different from his ordinary character. Careful investigation has shown that the affective character in a man has feminine traits. This psychological fact has given rise to the Chinese teaching of the *p'o*-soul, as well as to my concept of the anima. Deeper introspection, or ecstatic experience, reveals the existence of a feminine figure in the unconscious, therefore the feminine name, anima, psyche, or soul. The anima can also be defined as an imago, or archetype, or as the resultant of all the experiences of man with woman. This is the reason the anima, as a rule, is projected on the woman. As we know, poetry has often described and celebrated the anima.[25] The connection of anima with ghost in the Chinese concept is of interest to parapsychologists inasmuch as the "controls" are very often of the opposite sex.

Although Wilhelm's translation of *hun* as "animus" seems justified to me, nonetheless I had important reasons for choosing "logos" for a man's spirit, for masculine clarity of consciousness and reason, rather than the otherwise appropriate expression "animus." Chinese philosophers are spared certain difficulties which burden Western psychologists, because Chinese philosophy, like all mental and spiritual activity of ancient times, is exclusively a constituent of the masculine world. Its concepts are never taken psychologically, and have therefore never been examined as to how far they also apply to the feminine psyche. But the psychologist cannot possibly ignore the existence of woman and her peculiar psychology. The reasons I prefer to translate *hun* as it appears in man by logos are connected with this fact. Wilhelm in his translation uses logos for the Chinese concept *hsing*, which could also be translated as essence, or creative consciousness. After death, *hun* becomes *shên*, spirit, which is very close, in the philosophical sense, to

[25] *Psychological Types* (London, 1923), Chap. V.

hsing. Since the Chinese concepts are not logical in our sense, but are intuitive ideas, their meaning can only be fathomed through the ways in which they are used, and by noting the constitution of the written characters, or further, by such relationships as that of *hun* to *shên*. *Hun,* then, would be the discriminating light of consciousness and of reason in man, originally coming from the *logos spermatikos* of *hsing,* and returning after death through *shên* to tao. For this use, the expression "logos" ought to be especially appropriate, since it includes the idea of a universal being, and therefore covers the fact that man's clarity of consciousness and capacity for reason are universal rather than something individually unique; moreover it is not personal, but in the deepest sense impersonal, and thus in sharp contrast to the anima, which is a personal daemon expressing itself in thoroughly personal moods (therefore animosity!).

In consideration of these psychological facts, I have reserved the term "animus" for women exclusively because, to answer a famous question, *mulier non habet animam, sed animum.* Feminine psychology contains an element analogous to the anima of man. Primarily, it is not of an affective nature, but is a quasi-intellectual element best described by the word "prejudice." The conscious side of woman corresponds to the emotional side of man, not to his "mind." Mind makes up the "soul," or better, the "animus" of woman, and just as the anima of the man consists of inferior relatedness, full of affect, so the animus of woman consists of inferior judgments, or better said, opinions. (For further details I must refer my reader to my essay cited above, for here I can only touch upon the general aspects.) The animus of the woman consists in a plurality of preconceived opinions, and is therefore not so susceptible of personification by one figure, but appears more often as a group or crowd. (A good example of this from parapsychology is the so-called "Imperator" group in the case of Mrs. Piper.)[26] On a low level, the animus is an inferior logos, a caricature of the differentiated masculine mind, just as the

---

[26] Compare Hyslop, *Science and a Future Life.*

anima, on a low level, is a caricature of the feminine eros. Following the parallelism further, we can say that just as *hun* corresponds to *hsing*, translated by Wilhelm as logos, so the eros of woman corresponds to *ming*, which is translated as fate, *fatum*, destiny, and is interpreted by Wilhelm as eros. Eros is an interweaving; logos is differentiating knowledge, clarifying light; eros is relatedness; logos is discrimination and detachment. Thus the inferior logos in the woman's animus appears as something quite unrelated, and therefore as an inaccessible prejudice, or as an opinion which, irritatingly enough, has nothing to do with the essential nature of the object.

I have often been reproached for personifying the anima and animus as mythology does, but this reproach would be justified only if it were proved that in my psychological use of these terms I concretize them in the same way that mythology does. I must declare once and for all that the personification is not an invention of mine, but is inherent in the nature of the phenomena. It would be unscientific to overlook the fact that the anima is a psychic and therefore a personal autonomous system. None of the people who make the charge against me would hesitate a second to say: "I dreamed of Mr. X," whereas, strictly speaking, he only dreamed of the representation of Mr. X. The anima is nothing but a representation of the personal nature of the autonomous system in question. What the nature of this autonomous system is, in a transcendental sense, that is to say, beyond the boundaries of experience, we cannot know.

I have defined the anima in a man as a personification of the unconscious in general, and have therefore taken it to be a bridge to the unconscious, that is, to be the function of relationship to the unconscious. There is an interesting point in our text in this connection. The text says that consciousness (that is, personal consciousness) comes from the anima. Since the Western mind is based wholly on the standpoint of consciousness, it must define anima in the way I have done, but the East, based as it is on the standpoint of the unconscious, sees consciousness as an effect of the anima! Without a doubt, consciousness originally arises out of the unconscious. This is something we forget too often, and therefore we are always attempting to identify the psyche with consciousness, or at least attempting to represent the unconscious as a derivative, or an effect of the conscious (as, for example, in the Freudian repression theory). But for the reasons discussed above, it is essential that nothing be taken away from the reality of the unconscious, and that the figures of the unconscious should be understood as active quantities. The person who has understood what is meant by psychic reality need have no fear that he has fallen back into primitive daemonology. If indeed the unconscious figures are not taken seriously as spontaneously active factors, we become victims of a one-sided faith in conscious mind, which finally leads to a state of overtension. Catastrophes are then bound to occur, because, despite all our consciousness, the dark psychic powers have been overlooked. It is not we who personify them; they have a personal nature from the very beginning. Only when this is thoroughly recognized can we think of depersonalizing them, that is of "subjugating the anima," as our text expresses it.

Here again we find a great difference between Buddhism and our Western attitude of mind, and again there is a dangerous semblance of agreement. Yoga teaching rejects all fantasy contents and we do the same, but the East does it on quite different grounds. In the East, conceptions and teachings prevail which express the creative fantasy in richest measure; in fact, protection is required against the excess of fantasy. We, on the other hand, look upon fantasy as insignificant, subjective reverie. Naturally the figures of the unconscious do not appear as abstractions stripped of all imaginative trappings; on the contrary, they are embedded and interwoven in a web of fantasies of extraordinary variety and bewildering abundance. The East can reject these fantasies because it has long ago extracted their essence and condensed it in profound teachings. But we have never even experienced these fantasies, much less extracted their quintessence. Here we have a large portion of experience to catch up with, and only when we have found the sense in apparent nonsense can we separate the valuable from the worthless. We may rest assured that what we extract from our experiences will differ from what the East offers us today. The East came to its knowledge of inner things in relative ignorance of the external world. We, on the other hand, will investigate the psyche and its depths, supported by a tremendously extensive historical and scientific knowledge. At this present moment, it is true, knowledge of the external world is the greatest obstacle to introspection, but the psychological distress will overcome all obstructions. We are already building up a psychology, that is, a science, which gives us a key to things to which the East has found entrance only through abnormal psychic states.

The Detachment of Consciousness from the Object

By understanding the unconscious we free ourselves from its domination. This is really also the purpose of the instructions in our text. The pupil is taught to concentrate on the light of the inmost region, and, while doing so, to free himself from all outer and inner entanglement. His life-impulse is guided toward a consciousness without content which none the less permits all contents to exist. The *Hui Ming Ching* says about this detachment:

"A radiance surrounds the world of the spirit.
We forget one another, still and pure, all-powerful and empty.
Emptiness is illumined by the radiance of the heart of heaven.
The sea is smooth and mirrors the moon on its surface.
The clouds vanish in blue space.
The mountains shine clear.
Consciousness dissolves itself in contemplation.
The disk of the moon floats alone in the sky."

This description of fulfillment pictures a psychic state which perhaps can best be characterized as a detachment of consciousness from the world, and a withdrawal of it to an extramundane point, so to speak. Thus consciousness is at the same time empty and not empty. It is no longer preoccupied with the images of things but merely contains them. The fullness of the world which heretofore pressed upon consciousness has lost none of its richness and beauty, but it no longer dominates consciousness. The magical claim of things has ceased because the original interweaving of consciousness with the world has come to an end. The unconscious is no longer projected, and so the primal *participation mystique* with things is abolished. Consciousness is no longer preoccupied with compulsive intentions, but turns into contemplative vision, as the Chinese text very aptly says.

How did this effect come about? (We assume, of course, that the Chinese author was first of all not a liar; secondly, that he was of sound mind; and, thirdly, that he was an extraordinarily intelligent man.) To understand or explain the detachment described in the text our mentality requires a somewhat roundabout approach. There is no use in our mimicking Eastern sensibility; for nothing would be more childish than to wish to estheticize a psychic condition such as this. This detachment is something I am familiar with in my practice; it is the therapeutic effect *par excellence* for which I labor with my students and patients, that is, the dissolution of *participation mystique*. With a stroke of genius, Lévy-Bruhl[27] has established *participation mystique* as being the hall-mark of primitive mentality. As described by him it is simply the indefinitely large remnant of nondifferentiation between subject and object, still so great among primitives that it cannot fail to strike European man, identified as he is with the conscious standpoint. In so far as the difference between subject and object does not become conscious, unconscious identity prevails. The unconscious is projected into the object, and the object is introjected into the subject, that is, psychologized. Then plants and animals behave like men; men are at the same time themselves and animals also, and everything is alive with ghosts and gods. Naturally, civilized man regards himself as immeasurably above these things. He is instead often identi-

[27] *Primitive Mentality* (London, 1923).

fied with his parents throughout his life, or he is identified with his affects and prejudices, and shamelessly accuses others of the things he will not see in himself. In a word, even he is afflicted with a remnant of primal unconsciousness, or nondifferentiation between subject and object. By virtue of this unconsciousness, he is held in thrall by countless people, things, and circumstances, that is, unconditionally influenced. His mind, nearly as much as the primitive's, is full of disturbing contents and he uses just as many apotropaeic charms. He no longer works the magic with medicine bags, amulets, and animal sacrifices, but with nerve remedies, neuroses, "progress," the cult of will power, and so forth.

But if the unconscious can be recognized as a co-determining quantity along with the conscious, and if we can live in such a way that conscious and unconscious, or instinctive demands are given recognition as far as possible, the center of gravity of the total personality shifts its position. It ceases to be in the ego which is merely the center of consciousness, and instead is located in a hypothetical point between the conscious and the unconscious which might be called the self. If such a transposition succeeds, it results in doing away with *participation mystique,* and a personality develops that suffers only in the lower stories, so to speak, but in the upper stories is singularly detached from painful as well as joyful events.

The creation and birth of this superior personality is what is meant by our text when it speaks of the "holy fruit," the "diamond body," or refers in other ways to an indestructible body. These expressions are psychologically symbolical of an attitude which is out of reach of intense emotional involvement and therefore safe from absolute shock; they symbolize a consciousness detached from the world. I have reasons for believing that this sets in after the middle of life and is actually a natural preparation for death. To the psyche death is just as important as birth and, like it, is an integral part of life. What happens to the detached consciousness in the end is a question the psychologist cannot be expected to answer. Whatever theoretical position he assumed, he would hopelessly overstep the boundaries set him by science. He can only point out that the views of our text with respect to the timelessness of the detached consciousness are in harmony with the religious thought of all times, and with the thought of the overwhelming majority of mankind. A person thinking differently would stand outside the human order in some way, and therefore would be suffering from a disturbed psychic equilibrium. Thus, as a physician I make a great effort to fortify the belief in immortality as far as I can, especially in my older patients for whom such questions are crucial. If viewed in the psychological sense, death is not an end but a goal, and therefore life toward death begins as soon as the meridian is passed.

Chinese yoga philosophy bases itself upon the fact of this instinctive preparation for death as a goal, and, following the analogy with the goal of the first half of life, namely, begetting and reproduction, the means towards perpetuation of physical life, it takes as the purpose of spiritual existence, the begetting and perpetuation of a psychic spirit-body ("subtle body"), which ensures the continuity of the detached consciousness. It is the pneumatic man, known to the European from antiquity, which he, however, seeks to produce by quite other symbols and magical practices, by faith and a Christian way of life. Here again we stand on a foundation quite different from that of the East. Again the text sounds as though it were not very far from Christian ascetic morality, but nothing could be more mistaken than to assume that it is actually dealing with the same thing. Back of our text is a culture thousands of years old, one which has built organically upon primitive instincts and which, therefore, knows nothing of the arbitrary morality violating the instincts, characteristic of us as recently civilized barbarians. For this reason, the Chinese are without that impulse toward violent repression of the instincts which hysterically exaggerates and poisons our spirituality. The man who lives his instincts can also detach from them, and in just as natural a way as he lived them. Any idea of heroic self-conquest would be entirely foreign to the sense of our text, but that is what it certainly would amount to if we followed the Chinese instructions literally.

We must never forget our historical premises. Only a little more than a thousand years ago, we stumbled from the crudest beginnings of polytheism into the midst of a highly developed oriental religion which lifted the imaginative minds of half-savages to a height that did not correspond to their degree of spiritual development. In order to maintain this height in some fashion or other, the instinctual sphere inevitably had to be repressed to a great extent. Thus religious practice and morality took on a markedly violent, almost malicious, character. The repressed elements naturally do not develop, but vegetate further in their original barbarism in the unconscious. We would like to scale the heights of a philosophical religion, but are, in fact, incapable of it. To grow up to it is the most we can hope for. The Amfortas wound and the Faustian split in the Germanic man are not yet healed; his unconscious is still loaded with contents which must first become conscious before he can be liberated from them. Recently I received a letter from a former patient which pictures the necessary transformation in simple but pertinent words. She writes: "Out of evil, much good has come to me. By keeping quiet, repressing nothing, remaining attentive, and by accepting reality—taking things as they are, and not as I wanted them to be—by doing all this, unusual knowledge has come to me, and unusual powers as well, such as I could never have imagined before. I always thought that when we accepted things they overpowered us in some way or other. This turns out not to be true at all, and it is only by accepting them that one can define an attitude toward them.[28] So now I intend playing the game of life, being receptive to whatever comes to me, good and bad, sun and shadow that are for ever shifting, and, in this way, also accepting my own nature with its positive and negative sides. Thus everything becomes more alive to me. What a fool I was! How I tried to force everything to go according to the way I thought it ought to!"

Only on the basis of such an attitude, which renounces none of the values won in the course of Christian development, but

[28] Dissolution of *participation mystique*.

which, on the contrary, tries with Christian charity and forbearance to accept even the humblest things in oneself, will a higher level of consciousness and culture be possible. This attitude is religious in the truest sense, and therefore therapeutic, for all religions are therapies for the sorrows and disorders of the soul. The increasing development of Western intellect and will has given us an almost fiendish capacity for aping such an attitude, with apparent success, despite the protests of the unconscious. But it is only a matter of time until the counter position forces recognition of itself one way or another. Aping an attitude always produces an unstable situation, which can be overthrown by the unconscious at any time. A safe foundation is found only when the instinctive premises of the unconscious win the same consideration as the viewpoints of the conscious mind. No one need delude himself that this necessity of giving due consideration to the unconscious does not stand in violent opposition to the occidental, and especially the Protestant cult of consciousness. Although the new always seems hostile to the old, if we feel a deep desire to understand, we cannot fail to discover that without the most serious application of the Christian values we have acquired, the new integration can never take place.

The Fulfillment

The growing acquaintance with the spiritual East should be no more to us than the symbolical expression of the fact that we are entering into connection with the elements in ourselves which are still strange to us. Denial of our own historical premises would be sheer folly and would be the best way to bring about another deracination. Only by standing firmly on our own soil can we assimilate the spirit of the East.

Describing the people who do not know where the true springs of secret powers lie, the old master, Ku Tê, says: "Worldly people lose the roots and cling to the tree-tops." The spirit of the East has come out of the yellow earth, and our spirit can, and should, come only out of our own earth. It is for this reason that I approach these problems in a way that has often been criticized as being "psychologism." If "psychology" were meant, I should be flattered, because it is really my purpose to push aside without mercy the metaphysical claims of all esoteric teaching; the secret objective of gaining power through words ill accords with our profound ignorance —which we should have the modesty to confess. It is my firm intention to bring things which have a metaphysical sound into the daylight of psychological understanding, and to do my best to prevent the public from believing in obscure words of power. Let the convinced Christian believe, for that is the duty he has taken upon himself. The non-Christian has forfeited the grace of faith. (Perhaps he was cursed from birth in not being able to believe, but only to know.) Therefore, he has no right to put his faith elsewhere. One cannot grasp anything metaphysically, but it can be done psychologically. Therefore I strip things of their metaphysical wrappings in order to make them objects of psychology. In this way, I can at least extract something understandable from them, and can avail myself of it. Moreover, I learn to know psychological conditions and processes which before were veiled in symbols and out of reach of my understanding. In doing this I also may be able to follow a simliar path and to have similar experiences; if finally there should still be an ineffable metaphysical element, it would have the best opportunity of revealing itself.

My admiration for the great Eastern philosophers is as genuine as my attitude toward their metaphysics is irreverent.[29] I suspect them of being symbolical psychologists, to whom no greater wrong could be done than to take them literally. If it were really metaphysics that they mean, it would be useless to try to understand them. But if it is psychology, we can not only understand them, but we can profit greatly by them, for then the so-called "metaphysical" comes within the range of experience. If I accept the fact that a god is absolute and beyond all human experience, he leaves me cold. I do not af-

[29] [The Chinese philosophers—in contrast to the dogmatists of the West—are only grateful for such an attitude, because they are masters of their gods also.—TRANS.]

fect him, nor does he affect me. But if I know that a god is a powerful impulse of my soul, at once I must concern myself with him, for then he can become important, even unpleasantly so, and even in practical ways which sounds horribly banal—like everything belonging to the sphere of reality.

The reproach of "psychologism" applies only to a fool who thinks he has his soul in his pocket; there are certainly more than enough such fools, because, although we know how to use big words about the "soul," the depreciation of psychic things is still a typical Western prejudice. If I make use of the concept "autonomous psychic complex," my reader immediately comes up with the prejudice, "nothing but a psychic complex." How can we be so sure that the soul is "nothing but?" It is as if we did not know, or else continually forgot, that everything of which we are conscious is an image, and that image *is* psyche. The people who think God is depreciated if he is understood as something moved in the psyche, as well as the moving force of the psyche, that is, understood as an "autonomous complex," these same people can be so afflicted by uncontrollable affects and neurotic states of mind that their wills and their whole philosophy of life fail miserably. Is that proof of the impotence of the psyche? Should Meister Eckhart also be reproached with "psychologism" when he says: "God must be brought to birth in the soul again and again"? I think the accusation of "psychologism" is only justified in the case of the type of intellect which denies the nature of the autonomous complex, and seeks to explain it rationally as the consequence of known causes, that is, as derived, as not existing in its own right. This latter judgment is just as arrogant as the "metaphysical" assertion which, overstepping human limitations, seeks to entrust a deity outside the range of our experience with the bringing about of our psychic states. "Psychologism" is simply the counterpart of metaphysical encroachment, and just as childish as the latter. It seems to me far more reasonable, indeed, to accord the psyche the same validity as the empirical world, and to admit that the former has just as much "reality" as the latter. As I see it, the psyche is a world in which the ego is contained.

Perhaps there are also fishes who believe that they contain the sea. We must rid ourselves of this habitual illusion of ours if we wish to consider metaphysical statements from the standpoint of psychology.

A metaphysical assertion of this kind is the idea of the "diamond body," the indestructible breath-body which develops in the Golden Flower, or in the square-inch space.[30] This body, like everything else, is a symbol for a remarkable psychological fact, which, because it is objective, first appears projected in forms experienced in by organic life, that is, as

---

[30] True, our test is somewhat unclear as to whether by "continuation of life" a survival after death or a prolongation of physical existence is meant. Expressions such as life-elixir and the like are deceptively ambiguous. Indeed, it is evident in the later additions that the yoga instructions are also understood in a purely physical sense. To a more primitive mind, there is nothing disturbing in this odd mixture of the physical and the spiritual, because to it life and death are by no means the complete opposites they are to us. (Particularly interesting in this connection, besides the well-known ethnological material, are the "communications" of the English "rescue circles" with their thoroughly archaic ideas.) The same ambiguity with respect to survival after death is present in early Christianity also where it depends on similar assumptions, that is, on the idea of a "breath body," the essential carrier of life. (Geley's para-psychological theory would be the latest reincarnation of this ancient idea.) But since in our text we also have warnings against superstitious use of it, for example, warnings against trying to make gold, we can confidently insist without contradiction to the sense of the text on the spiritual meaning of the instructions. In the conditions which the instructions seek to produce, the physical body plays an increasingly inessential role because it is replaced by the "breath body" (hence the importance of breathing in yoga practice in general). The "breath body" is not "spiritual" in our sense. It is characteristic of Western man that he has split apart the physical and the spiritual sides of life for the purpose of gaining knowledge, but these opposites exist together in the psyche, and psychology must recognize the fact. "Psychic" means physical _and_ mental. The ideas in our text all deal with this "in-between" world which seems unclear and confused to us because the concept of psychic reality is not yet current among us, although it defines our sphere of life. Without soul, mind is as dead as matter, because both are artificial abstractions; whereas man originally regarded mind as a volatile body, and matter as not lacking in soul.

fruit, embryo, child, living body, and so on. This psychological fact could best be expressed in the words: It is not I who live, it lives me. The illusion as to the superior powers of the conscious leads to the belief: I live. If the recognition of the unconscious shatters this illusion, the former appears as something objective in which the ego is included. The attitude toward the unconscious is then analogous to the feeling of the primitive to whom the existence of a son guarantees continuation of life. This characteristic feeling can assume grotesque forms even as in the case of the old Negro, who, angered at his disobedient son, cried out: "There he stands with my body, but does not even obey me!"

The change in inner feeling is similar to that experienced by a father to whom a son has been born; it is a change also known to us through the testimony of the Apostle Paul: "Not I [live], but Christ liveth in me." The symbol "Christ" as the "son of man" is an analogous psychic experience: a higher, spiritual being of human form is invisibly born in the individual, a spiritual body, which is to serve us as a future dwelling, a body which, as Paul expresses himself, is put on like a garment. ("For as many of you as have been baptised into Christ have put on Christ.") Obviously it is always a difficult thing to express, in intellectual terms, subtle feelings which are, nonetheless, infinitely important for the life and well-being of the individual. In a certain sense, the thing we are trying to express is the feeling of having been "replaced," but without the connotation of having been "deposed." It is as if the direction of the affairs of life had gone over to an invisible center. Nietzsche's metaphor, "in most loving bondage, free,"[31] would be appropriate here. Religious speech is full of imagery picturing this feeling of free dependence, of calm and devotion.

In this remarkable experience I see a phenomenon resulting from the detachment of consciousness, through which the subjective "I live" becomes the objective "It lives me." This state is felt to be higher than the earlier one; it is really as if it

[31] *"Frei in liebevollstem Muss."*

were a sort of release from compulsion and impossible responsibility which are the inevitable results of *participation mystique*. This feeling of liberation fills Paul completely. It is the consciousness of being a child of God which frees one from the spell of the blood. It is also a feeling of reconciliation with all that happens, and that is the reason that, according to the *Hui Ming Ching*, the glance of "one who has attained fulfillment returns to the beauty of nature."

In the Pauline Christ symbol the deepest religious experience of the West and the East meet. Christ the sorrow-laden hero, and the Golden Flower that blooms in the purple hall of the city of jade—what a contrast, what an infinity of difference, what an abyss of history! A problem fit to test the powers of a future psychologist!

Among the great religious problems of the present is one which has received scant attention, but which, in fact, is the main problem of our day: the problem of the progress of the religious spirit.[32] If we are to discuss it, we must emphasize the difference between East and West in their treatment of the "jewel," that is, the central symbol. The West emphasizes the human incarnation, and even the personality and historicity of Christ, while the East says: "Without beginning, without end, without past, without future."[33] In accordance with his conception, the Christian subordinates himself to the superior, divine person in expectation of His grace; but the Eastern man knows that redemption depends on the "work" the individual does upon himself. Tao grows out of the individual. The *Imitatio Christi* has this disadvantage: in the long run we worship as a divine example a man who embodied the deepest meaning of life, and then, out of sheer imitation, we forget to make real our own deepest meaning. As a matter of fact, it is not altogether uncomfortable to renounce one's own real meaning. Had Jesus done this, he would probably have become a respectable carpenter, and not the religious

[32] [For the sake of clarity the author has amplified the above sentence for this translation—TRANS.]
[33] *Hui Ming Ching*, p. 108.

rebel to whom, obviously, there would happen today the same thing that happened then.

Imitation of Christ might well be understood in a deeper way. It might be taken as the duty to give reality to one's best conviction, always the fullest expression of individual temperament, with the same courage and the same self-sacrifice shown by Jesus. Happily—we must say—not everyone has the task of being a leader of mankind, or a great rebel, and so it might be possible for each to realize himself in his own way. This honesty might even become an ideal. Since great innovations always begin in the most unlikely place, the fact, for example, that a person today is not nearly as ashamed of his nakedness as he used to be, might be the beginning of a recognition of himself as he is. Hard upon this will follow the recognition of many other things that were formerly strictly taboo, because the reality of the earth will not forever remain veiled like the *virgines velandae* of Tertullian. Moral unmasking is only one step further in the same direction, and behold, there stands a man as he is, and confesses to himself to be as he is. If he does this in a meaningless way, he is a muddled fool, but if he knows the significance of what he does, he can belong to a higher order of man who makes real the Christian symbol, regardless of suffering. It can often be observed that wholly concrete taboos or magical rites in an early stage of a religion, become in the next stage psychic, or even wholly spiritual symbols. An external law, in the course of development, becomes an inner conviction. Thus it might easily happen to contemporary man, especially the Protestant, that the person Jesus, now existing outside in the realm of history, might become the superior man within himself. Then we would have attained, in a European way, the psychological state corresponding to "enlightenment" in the Eastern sense.

All this is a step in the development of a higher human consciousness on the way toward unknown goals, and is not metaphysics in the ordinary sense. Thus far, it is only "psychology," but also thus far it can be experienced, it is intelligible, and —thank God—it is real, a reality with which something can be done, a reality containing possibilities and therefore alive. The fact that I restrict myself to what can be psychically experienced, and reject the metaphysical, does not mean, as anyone with insight can understand, a skeptic or agnostic gesture against faith or trust in higher powers; what I intend to say is approximately the same thing Kant meant when he called "the thing in itself," a "merely negative boundary-concept." [Grenzbegriff] Every statement about the transcendental is to be avoided because it is invariably a laughable presumption on the part of the human mind, which is unconscious of its limitations. Therefore, when God or tao is termed an impulse of the soul, or a state of the soul, something has been said about the knowable only, but nothing about the unknowable, about which nothing can be determined.

Conclusion

The purpose of my commentary is the attempt to build a bridge of psychological understanding between East and West. The basis of every real understanding is man, and therefore I had to speak of human things. This must be my excuse for having dealt only with general aspects, and for not having entered into technical details. Technical directions are valuable for those who know, for example, what a camera is, or a combustion engine, but they are useless for anyone who has no idea of such apparatus. Western man for whom I write is in an analogous position; he has no idea of the psyche. Therefore it seemed to me important above all to emphasize the agreement between the psychic states and the symbolism of East and West. By means of these analogies an entrance is opened to the inner chambers of the Eastern mind, an entrance that does not require the sacrifice of our own nature and hence does not threaten us with being torn from our roots. Nor is it an intellectual telescope or microscope offering a view fundamentally of no concern to us because it does not touch us. It is rather an atmosphere of suffering, seeking, and striving common to all civilized peoples; it is the tremendous experiment of becoming conscious, which nature has laid upon man kind, and which unites the most diverse cultures in a common task.

Western consciousness is by no means consciousness in general; it is a historically conditioned and geographically limited factor, representative of only one part of mankind. The widening of our consciousness ought not to proceed at the expense of other kinds of consciousness, but ought to take place through the development of those elements of our psyche which are analogous to those of an alien psyche, just as the East cannot do without our technology, science, and industry. The European invasion of the East was a deed of violence on a grand scale, and it has left us the duty—*noblesse oblige*—of understanding the mind of the East. This is perhaps more necessary than we realize at present.

BIBLIOGRAPHICAL NOTE

The publication of the first complete collected edition, in English, of the works of C. G. Jung has been undertaken by Routledge and Kegan Paul, Ltd., in England and by the Bollingen Foundation, through Pantheon Books, Inc., in the United States. This uniform edition contains newly revised versions of works originally written in English and in general, new translations of the major body of Professor Jung's writings. The author has supervised the textual revision which in some cases is extensive. To date, Volumes 1, 5, 7, 11, 12, 16 and 17 have been published.

Editions of earlier translations of Jung's works still in print are given at the end of this list of the Collected Works. The dates are those of first publication; references in italic type are to the volumes of the Collected Works in which the respective material will be found, in many cases revised or differently arranged.

The Collected Works of C. G. Jung

1. PSYCHIATRIC STUDIES

On the Psychology and Pathology of So-Called Occult Phenomena: A Psychiatric Study
On Hysterical Parapraxes in Reading
Cryptomnesia
On Manic Alteration
A Case of Hysterical Stupor in a Prisoner Awaiting Trial
On Simulated Insanity
A Medical Opinion on a Case of Simulated Insanity
A Third and Conclusive Opinion on Two Contradictory Psychiatric Diagnoses
On the Psychological Determination of Facts

2. EXPERIMENTAL RESEARCHES

STUDIES IN WORD ASSOCIATION

The Association of Normal Subjects (by Jung and Riklin)
Experimental Observations on Memory
On the Determination of Facts by Psychological Means
Analysis of the Associations of an Epileptic
The Association Method
Reaction-Time in Association Experiments
On Disturbances in Reproduction in Association Experiments
The Significance of Association Experiments for Psychopathology
Psychoanalysis and Association Experiments
Association, Dream, and Hysterical Symptoms

PSYCHOPHYSICAL RESEARCHES

On Psychophysical Relations of the Association Experiment
Psychophysical Investigations with the Galvanometer and Pneumograph in Normal and Insane Individuals (by Peterson and Jung)
Further Investigations on the Galvanic Phenomenon and Respirations in Normal and Insane Individuals (by Ricksher and Jung)

3. PSYCHOGENESIS IN MENTAL DISEASE

The Psychology of Dementia Praecox
The Content of the Psychoses
Complexes and the Cause of Illness in Dementia Praecox (by Bleuler and Jung)
A Criticism of Bleuler's "Theory of Schizophrenic Negativism"
On Psychological Understanding
On the Importance of the Unconscious in Psychopathology
On the Problem of Psychogenesis in Mental Disease
Mental Disease and the Psyche
On the Psychogenesis of Schizophrenia

4. FREUD AND PSYCHOANALYSIS

Freud's Theory of Hysteria
The Analysis of Dreams
The Significance of the Father in the Destiny of the Individual
A Contribution to the Psychology of Rumour
On the Significance of Number Dreams
On Some Crucial Points in Psychoanalysis: A Correspondence between Dr. Jung and Dr. Loy
The Theory of Psychoanalysis
On Psychoanalysis
Psychoanalysis
Freud and Jung: Contrasts
Appendix: Freud's Theory of Hysteria; Critical Remarks on Morton Prince's "Mechanism and Interpretation of Dreams"; Introduction to Kranefeldt's "Psychoanalysis"

5. SYMBOLS OF TRANSFORMATION

Illustrated

PART I
Introduction
Two Kinds of Thinking
The Miller Fantasies: Anamnesis
The Hymn of Creation
The Song of the Moth

PART II
Introduction
The Concept of Libido
The Transformation of Libido
The Origin of the Hero
Symbols of the Mother and of Rebirth
The Battle for Deliverance from the Mother
The Dual Mother Role
The Sacrifice
Epilogue

6. PSYCHOLOGICAL TYPES

PART I
Introduction
The Problem of Types in the History of Classical and Medieval Thought
Schiller's Ideas upon the Type Problem
The Apollonian and the Dionysian
The Type Problem in the Discernment of Human Character
The Problem of Types in Poetry
The Type Problem in Psychiatry
The Problem of Typical Attitudes in Aesthetics
The Problem of Types in Modern Philosophy
The Type Problem in Biography

PART II
General Description of the Types
Definitions
Conclusion
Four Papers on Psychological Typology

7. TWO ESSAYS ON ANALYTICAL PSYCHOLOGY

The Psychology of the Unconscious
The Relations between the Ego and the Unconscious
Appendix: New Paths in Psychology; The Structure of the Unconscious

8. THE STRUCTURE AND DYNAMICS OF THE PSYCHE

On Psychic Energy
A Review of the Complex Theory
General Aspects of Dream Psychology
The Nature of Dreams
Instinct and Unconscious
The Psychological Foundation of Belief in Spirits
The Structure of the Psyche
Basic Postulates of Analytical Psychology

The Real and the Surreal
The Soul and Death
Analytical Psychology and Weltanschauung
The Stages of Life
Spirit and Life
On the Nature of the Psyche
Synchronicity: An Acausal Connecting Principle
The Significance of Heredity and Constitution in Psychology
Psychological Factors Determining Human Behavior

9. PART I. ARCHETYPES AND THE
COLLECTIVE UNCONSCIOUS

Illustrated

The Concept of the Collective Unconscious
Archetypes of the Collective Unconscious
Concerning the Archetypes, with Special Reference to the Anima Concept
Psychological Aspects of the Mother Archetype
Concerning Rebirth
The Psychology of the Child Archetype
The Psychological Aspects of the Kore
The Phenomenology of the Spirit in Fairy Tales
On the Psychology of the Trickster Figure
The Conscious Mind, the Unconscious, and the Individuation
A Study in the Process of Individuation
Concerning Mandāla Symbolism

9. PART II. AION: CONTRIBUTIONS TO THE
SYMBOLISM OF THE SELF

Illustrated

The Ego
The Shadow
The Syzygy: Anima and Animus
The Self
Christ, a Symbol of the Self
The Sign of the Fishes

The Prophecies of Nostradamus
The Historical Significance of the Fish
The Ambivalence of the Fish Symbol
The Fish in Alchemy
The Alchemical Interpretation of the Fish
General Considerations on the Psychology of Christian Alchemical Symbolism
Gnostic Symbols of the Self
Structure and Dynamics of the Self
Epilogue

10. CIVILIZATION IN TRANSITION

GENERAL CONSIDERATIONS
The Role of the Unconscious
Archaic Man
The Meaning of Psychology for Modern Man
Mind and Earth
The Spiritual Problem of Modern Man

THE EUROPEAN CRISIS
The Fight with the Shadow
Woman in Europe
The Love Problem of the Student
The Swiss Line in the European Spectrum
Wotan
The State of Psychotherapy Today
After the Catastrophe
Epilogue to "Essays on Contemporary Events"

REVIEWS AND SHORT ARTICLES
Complications of American Psychology
The Rise of a New World: Review of Keyserling's "America Set Free"
The Dreamlike World of India
What India Can Teach Us
Review of Keyserling's "La Révolution Mondiale"
Contemporary Events (A Rejoinder to Dr. Bally's Article)

11. PSYCHOLOGY AND RELIGION

WESTERN RELIGION
Psychology and Religion
A Psychological Approach to the Dogma of the Trinity
Transformation Symbolism in the Mass
Foreword to White's "God and the Unconscious"
Introduction to Werblowsky's "Lucifer and Prometheus"
Bruder Klaus
Psychotherapists or the Clergy
Psychoanalysis and the Cure of Souls
Answer to Job

EASTERN RELIGION
Psychological Commentary on "The Tibetan Book of the Dead"
Psychological Commentary on "The Book of the Great Liberation"
Yoga and the West
Foreword to Suzuki's "Introduction to Zen Buddhism"
The Psychology of Eastern Meditation
The Holy Men of India: Introduction to Zimmer's "Der Weg zum Selbst"
Foreword to the "I Ching"

12. PSYCHOLOGY AND ALCHEMY
Illustrated

Introduction to the Religious and Psychological Problems of Alchemy
Individual Dream Symbolism in Relation to Alchemy
Religious Ideas in Alchemy
Epilogue

13. ALCHEMICAL STUDIES
Illustrated

Commentary on "The Secret of the Golden Flower"
The Spirit Mercurius
Some Observations on the Visions of Zosimos

Paracelsus as a Spiritual Phenomenon
The "Arbor philosophica"
The Riddle of Bologna

14. MYSTERIUM CONIUNCTIONIS

The Components of the *Coniunctio*
The Paradox
The Personification of Opposites:
  Introduction; Sol; Sulphur; Luna; Sal; Rex; Regina; Adam and Eve
The Conjunction

15. THE SPIRIT IN MAN, ART, AND LITERATURE

Paracelsus
Paracelsus the Physician
Sigmund Freud: A Cultural Phenomenon
Sigmund Freud: An Obituary
Richard Wilhelm: An Obituary
Psychology and Literature
On the Relation of Analytical Psychology to the Poetic Art
Picasso
"Ulysses"

16. THE PRACTICE OF PSYCHOTHERAPY
ESSAYS ON THE PSYCHOLOGY OF THE
TRANSFERENCE AND OTHER SUBJECTS

Illustrated

GENERAL PROBLEMS OF PSYCHOTHERAPY
Principles of Practical Psychotherapy
What Is Psychotherapy?
Some Aspects of Modern Psychotherapy
Aims of Modern Psychotherapy
Problems of Modern Psychotherapy
Psychotherapy and a Philosophy of Life
Medicine and Psychotherapy
Psychotherapy Today

Fundamental Questions of Psychotherapy

SPECIFIC PROBLEMS OF PSYCHOTHERAPY
The Therapeutic Value of Abreaction
The Practical Use of Dream Analysis
Psychology of the Transference

17. THE DEVELOPMENT OF PERSONALITY

Psychic Conflicts in a Child
Introduction to Wickes' "Analyse der Kinderseele"
Child Development and Education
Analytical Psychology and Education: Three Lectures
The Gifted Child
The Significance of the Unconscious in Individual Education
The Development of Personality
Marriage as a Psychological Relationship

Final Volume. MISCELLANEOUS WORKS, BIBLIOGRAPHY, AND GENERAL INDEX

REVIEWS, SHORT ARTICLES, ETC., OF THE PSYCHOANALYTICAL PERIOD
LATER INTRODUCTIONS, ETC.
BIBLIOGRAPHY OF C. G. JUNG'S WRITINGS
GENERAL INDEX OF THE COLLECTED WORKS

Earlier Translations

PSYCHOLOGY OF THE UNCONSCIOUS. Translated by Beatrice M. Hinkle. London: Routledge and Kegan Paul; New York: Dodd, Mead. [1916] The German original of this work has been revised and enlarged by the author and published as SYMBOLE DER WANDLUNG (Zurich: Rascher Verlag, 1952), which is translated as *Volume 5* of the Collected Works.

PSYCHOLOGICAL TYPES. THE PSYCHOLOGY OF INDIVIDUA-

TION. Translated with an introduction by H. G. Baynes. London: Routledge and Kegan Paul. [1923] *Volume 6.*

CONTRIBUTIONS TO ANALYTICAL PSYCHOLOGY. Translated by H. G. and C. F. Baynes. London: Routledge and Kegan Paul. [1928] *Volumes 6, 8, 10, 15, 16, 17.*

THE SECRET OF THE GOLDEN FLOWER. Translated into German and explained by Richard Wilhelm, with a European commentary by C. G. Jung. The whole translated into English by Cary F. Baynes. London: Routledge and Kegan Paul. [1931] *Volume 13.*

MODERN MAN IN SEARCH OF A SOUL. Translated by C. F. Baynes and Stanley Dell. London: Routledge and Kegan Paul; New York: Harcourt, Brace (in Harvest Books as a paperback reprint, 1955). [1933] *Volumes 4, 6, 8, 10, 11, 15, 16.*

THE PSYCHOLOGY OF DEMENTIA PRAECOX. Translated by A. A. Brill. New York and Washington: Nervous and Mental Disease Publishing Company. [1936] *Volume 3.*

PSYCHOLOGY AND RELIGION. THE TERRY LECTURES. New Haven: Yale University Press; London: Oxford University Press. [1938] *Volume 11.*

THE INTEGRATION OF THE PERSONALITY. Translated by Stanley Dell. London: Routledge and Kegan Paul. [1939] *Volumes 9, part i, 12, 17.*

ESSAYS ON A SCIENCE OF MYTHOLOGY. (With C. Kerényi.) Translated by R. F. C. Hull. Bollingen Series XXII. New York: Pantheon Books. (Same translation, entitled INTRODUCTION TO A SCIENCE OF MYTHOLOGY. London: Routledge and Kegan Paul.) [1949] *Volume 9, part i.*

ANSWER TO JOB. Translated by R. F. C. Hull. London: Routledge and Kegan Paul. [1954] *Volume 11.*

The following volumes contain contributions by C. G. Jung, translated by R. F. C. Hull:

SPIRIT AND NATURE. PAPERS FROM THE ERANOS YEARBOOKS, 1. London: Routledge and Kegan Paul; New York: Pantheon Books (Bollingen Series XXX · 1). [1954] Contains "The Phenomenology of the Spirit in Fairy Tales," *Volume 9, part i;* and "The Spirit of Psychology," a version of "On the Nature of the Psyche," *Volume 8.*

THE MYSTERIES. PAPERS FROM THE ERANOS YEARBOOKS, 2. London: Routledge and Kegan Paul; New York: Pantheon Books (Bollingen Series XXX · 2). [1955] Contains "Transformation Symbolism in the Mass," *Volume 11.*

INTERPRETATION OF NATURE AND THE PSYCHE. London: Routledge and Kegan Paul; New York: Pantheon Books (Bollingen Series XLVIII). [1955] Contains "Synchronicity: An Acausal Connecting Principle," *Volume 8.*

ANCHOR BOOKS

PSYCHOLOGY

THE BROKEN IMAGE: MAN, SCIENCE, AND SOCIETY—Floyd W. Matson, A506

THE CHALLENGE OF YOUTH (YOUTH: CHANGE AND CHALLENGE)—Erik H. Erikson, ed., A438

CHILDREN AND THE DEATH OF A PRESIDENT: Multi-Disciplinary Studies—ed. by Martha Wolfenstein and Gilbert Kliman, A543

DOGMA OF CHRIST—Erich Fromm, A500

AN ELEMENTARY TEXTBOOK OF PSYCHOANALYSIS—Charles Brenner, A102

EMOTIONAL PROBLEMS OF THE STUDENT—ed. by Graham B. Blaine, Jr. and Charles McArthur; Introduction by Erik H. Erikson, A527

ESSAYS IN PHILOSOPHICAL PSYCHOLOGY—Donald F. Gustafson, ed., A417

FREUD: THE MIND OF THE MORALIST—Philip Rieff, A278

THE FUTURE OF AN ILLUSION—Sigmund Freud, James Strachey, trans., A381

A GENERAL SELECTION FROM THE WORKS OF SIGMUND FREUD—John Rickman, M.D., ed., A115

HAMLET AND OEDIPUS—Ernest Jones, A31

HERRING GULL'S WORLD—A Study of the Social Behavior of Birds—Niko Tinbergen, A567

THE HIDDEN DIMENSION—Edward T. Hall, A609

THE HUMAN CONDITION—Hannah Arendt, A182

INTERACTION RITUAL: Essays on Face-to-Face Behavior—Erving Goffman, A596

THE LIFE AND WORK OF SIGMUND FREUD—Ernest Jones, ed. and abridged in one volume by Lionel Trilling and Steven Marcus, A340

THE NATURE OF PREJUDICE—Gordon Allport, A169

PAUL AND MARY: Two Case Histories from Truants from Life—Bruno Bettelheim, A237

THE POSITIVE THINKERS: A Study of the American Quest for Health, Wealth and Personal Power from Mary Baker Eddy to Norman Vincent Peale—Donald Meyer, A525

THE PRESENTATION OF SELF IN EVERYDAY LIFE—Erving Goffman, A174

PSYCHE AND SYMBOL—C. G. Jung, A136

Psychology (continued)

PSYCHOANALYSIS AND SOCIAL RESEARCH: The Psychoanalytic Study of the Non-Patient—Herbert Hendin, Willard Gaylin and Arthur Carr, A530
THE QUESTION OF LAY ANALYSIS—Sigmund Freud; James Strachey, trans., A424
SUICIDE AND SCANDINAVIA—Herbert Hendin, A457
WHY MAN TAKES CHANCES: Studies in Stress Seeking—Samuel Z. Klausner, ed., A623

p. 70
   72
   87
   99
   110
   112
   134
   138 - Universal symbols
   144 -
   281
   288
   300
   311 - 315 - 332
   333 - hun = cloud-demon
   339 - Detachment
   342 - Acceptance